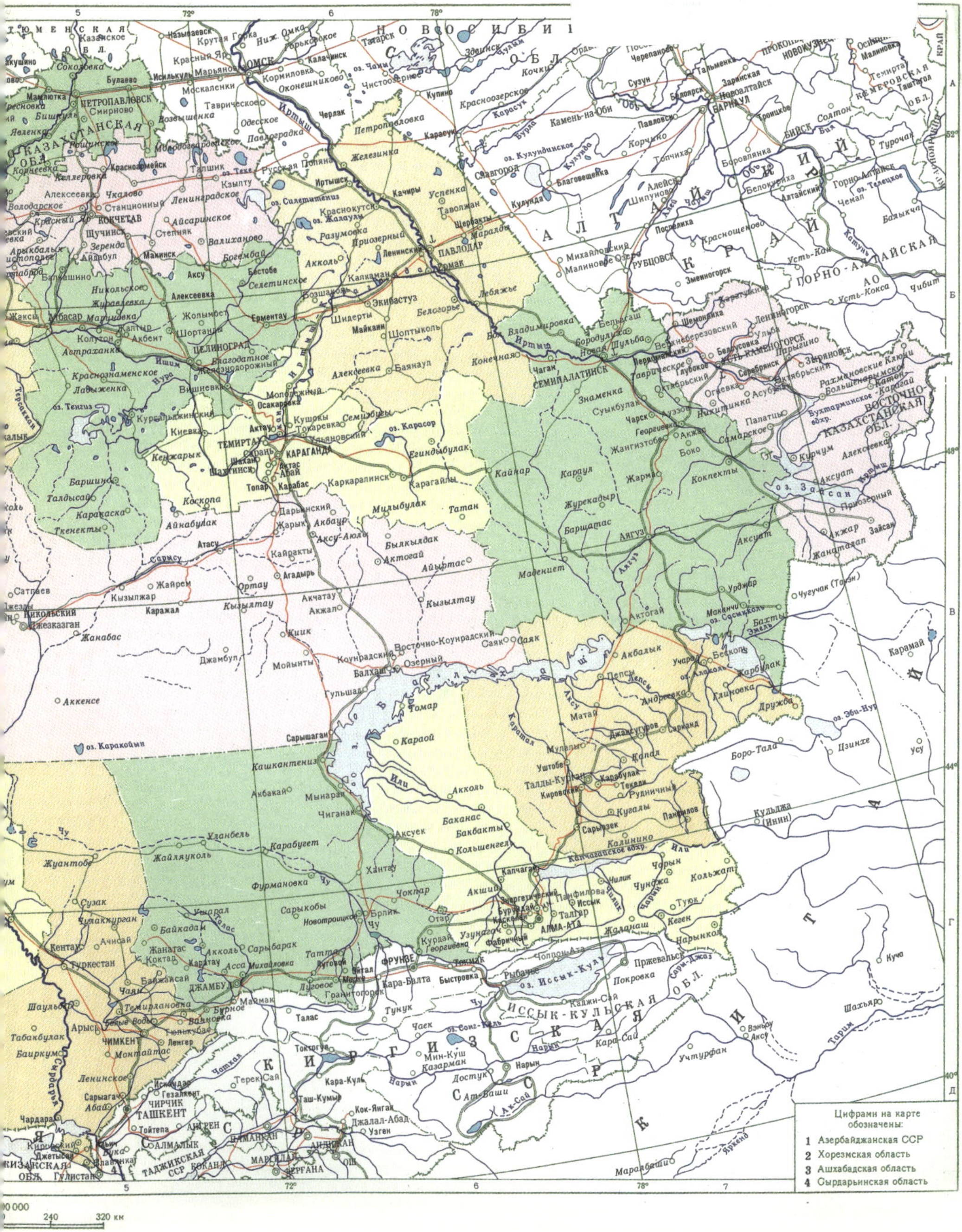
Цифрами на карте обозначены:
1 Азербайджанская ССР
2 Хорезмская область
3 Ашхабадская область
4 Сырдарьинская область
240
320 км
ОМСК
ПЕТРОПАВЛОВСК
КОКЧЕТАВ
ЦЕЛИНОГРАД
ПАВЛОДАР
СЕМИПАЛАТИНСК
УСТЬ-КАМЕНОГОРСК
КАРАГАНДА
ТЕМИРТАУ
БАРНАУЛ
БИЙСК
РУБЦОВСК
АЛМА-АТА
ФРУНЗЕ
ДЖАМБУЛ
ЧИМКЕНТ
ТАШКЕНТ
НАМАНГАН
АНДИЖАН
Талды-Курган
Пржевальск
Нарын
оз. Иссык-Куль
оз. Балхаш
оз. Зайсан
оз. Тенгиз
Иртыш
Или
Чу
КАЗАХСТАНСКАЯ ОБЛ.
ВОСТОЧНО-КАЗАХСТАНСКАЯ ОБЛ.
ИССЫК-КУЛЬСКАЯ ОБЛ.
ГОРНО-АЛТАЙСКАЯ АО
АЛТАЙСКИЙ КРАЙ
КИРГИЗСКАЯ ССР
ТАДЖИКСКАЯ ССР
НОВОСИБИРСКАЯ ОБЛ.
ТЮМЕНСКАЯ ОБЛ.

ROBERT WIGHT

VANISHED KHANS
AND
EMPTY STEPPES

A HISTORY OF KAZAKHSTAN
From Pre-History to Post-Independence

London, 2014

Published in United Kindom
Hertforfshire Press Ltd © 2014

9 Cherry Bank, Chapel Street
Hemel Hempstead, Herts.
HP2 5DE, UK

e-mail: publisher@hertfordshirepress.com
www.hertfordshirepress.com

VANISHED KHANS AND EMPTY STEPPES
A HISTORY OF KAZAKHSTAN
From Pre-History to Post-Independence
by Robert Wight

First edition

Proof editor Carole Mitchell
Typeset Aleksandra Vlasova & Allwel Solutions

*British Library Catalogue in Publication Data
A catalogue record for this book is available from the British Library
Library of Congress in Publication Data
A catalogue record for this book has been requested*

ISBN 978-0-9930444-0-3

For Jonathan and Nicholas

Contents

Appendices

CHAPTER ONE: PROLOGUE

Almaty - Zailisky - Verny - Alma-Ata - Almaty

When Major Mikhail Peremyshelsky, leading a detachment of imperial Russian troops and scouts, reached the northern foothills of the Tien Shan Mountains, and established a camp in a green and wooded valley at the foot of the Zailisky Alatau Ridge, his arrival was to mark a turning point in the history of Kazakhstan, and in the Russian colonisation of Central Asia. Throughout previous centuries, Russian territorial expansion had been towards Lithuania and Poland to the west, over the land oceans of prairie grassland and treeless steppe to the south, and across the infinite expanse of Siberian forest and tundra to the east. Now further progress in a south-easterly direction was emphatically blocked by the near-impenetrable chain of mountains ahead, a formidable barrier towering up from the empty plains. From now on, Russia was to concentrate on settlement and consolidation in this vast region, and incorporation of the new lands into its growing empire, until eventual independence for Kazakhstan nearly 140 years later.

The date was 8 August 1853, and in the fierce heat of that summer, after a month-long trek on horseback across the arid deserts of eastern Kazakhstan, the weary Russian soldiers could at last rest and relax in the cool, fresh air, high above the stifling atmosphere of the dusty plains below. Tall firs, pines, and silver birch trees gave welcome shade for the camp, a great relief after constant exposure to the blazing sun, while icy streams and rivulets, fed by melting snow and ice from the mountains and glaciers above, provided an endless supply of the clearest, coldest water. For days during their journey, the soldiers had observed how the majestic, snow-covered mountain summits on the horizon ahead appeared to float in the sky like clouds, a hazy, ever-receding mirage; in another trick of the light in the crystal-clear mountain air, pristine snow fields and distant glaciers, glinting in the dazzling sunshine, now seemed almost near enough to touch.

The Russians soon began to make clearings in the forest where they could build wooden cabins and stables. Acrid wood smoke from camp fires drifted slowly in the still mountain air, since although the days were hot under the blazing sun, in the evenings the temperature fell sharply, and the nights under the cloudless black sky, lit with millions of bright stars, were already intensely cold. In a few weeks the first snows of winter would be falling. But it was not only the approaching winter that was a cause for concern. Defensive stockades were also necessary to protect the encampment against the threat of attack from hostile local tribes, since the site was in the territory of the 'Great Horde', one of the three Hordes (broad groups of local khanates, nomadic tribes, and family clans) which made up the indigenous population of Kazakhstan. The Great Horde occupied the eastern and southern parts of Kazakhstan, from the region around Lake Zaisan in the north to Lake Balkhash and the foothills of the Tien Shan Mountains in the south. Four years earlier, in 1849 the tsarist government had signed a treaty with the khans of the Great Horde, formally incorporating their territory into the Russian empire. In the previous century, the territories of the Little Horde in the west around the Caspian Sea, and the Middle Horde, in the centre and the north of Kazakhstan, had already been absorbed by Russia. But in this new country, far from Russia itself and despite the 1849 treaty, which was readily ignored by local tribesmen, there was still deep hostility and resentment at Russian encroachment on Kazakh lands.

As they settled into their new surroundings, the Russians contemplated their situation. Not far to the south, beyond the first mountain range, lay the deep warm-water lake of Issyk Kul, a remote and mysterious inland sea rumoured to be the site of an ancient civilisation destroyed in an earthquake many centuries before. The ruins of houses and palaces, formal gardens and elaborate squares, according to legend, now lay deep below the surface. These legends turned out to have a basis in reality one hundred years later when underwater excavations in the 1950s revealed the remnants of buildings and settlements including Christian monasteries and Islamic minarets and mausoleums. The high mountain passes between the lake and the plains to the north were still known, even after six hundred years, as the routes taken by invading Mongol armies in the thirteenth century. Beyond Issyk Kul the rudimentary Russian maps, which mostly consisted of blank and empty spaces, showed a vast, mountainous wilderness, stretching for enormous distances towards China and the Himalayas. This hostile terrain of high peaks and inaccessible valleys, and unimaginable cold and desolation, was the home of wild animals, ravens and eagles, wolves and tigers, and the elusive and near-mythical snow leopard, a prominent subject in the art and decoration among the nomadic tribes on the plains below. This was also a region of ferocious blizzards and snowstorms, and violent tremors and earthquakes which occasionally sent thousands of tons of boulders and devastating mud slides crashing down into the valleys below. But all was silent now, as the white peaks of the mountains stood out with brilliant clarity against the enamel blue of the sky, massive sentinels guarding the entrance to another world.

In the other direction to the north, the plains and empty scrubland which the Russians had just crossed offered some means of life to the indigenous nomadic communities, but were uninviting to any form of permanent habitation or settlement. By contrast, between the mountains and the plains, the broad and verdant country of untouched forests, quiet valleys, and fertile pastures where the Russians now found themselves provided a source of food, water, and everything necessary for life, all of which enhanced the site of the encampment and the surrounding countryside as a viable place for a permanent settlement. Among the Russian troops was a contingent of locally-recruited Kazakh horsemen who confirmed the attractions of the region. Thus Major Peremyshelsky was able to report back to St Petersburg: 'Given its favourable position in the Semirechie (Seven Rivers) region, and with plentiful supplies of wood, and wide expanses of fertile arable land and crops far superior to those of neighbouring areas of Issyk and Talgar, we propose that (this area) should be a place for future settlement'. In sending this message, Mikhail Peremyshelsky in effect became the founder of the modern city of Almaty.

The Semirechie region (*Zhetisu* in Kazakh) lies in south-eastern Kazakhstan between the Tien Shan Mountains (the Mountains of Heaven) and the shallow and semi-arid Lake Balkhash. The region has occupied a unique place in Kazakh history, as the centre of ancient empires and with gathering places for early tribes. Most of the land consists of dry, sandy plains and sparsely-populated desert. To the east lies the Dzungarski Alatau Ridge, a range of high mountains beyond which lie the western-most regions of China. In reality the Semirechie contains several hundred short, fast-flowing rivers descending from the Dzungarski Alatau Mountains, but six of the most prominent seven rivers which give the region its name – the Naryn, Karatal, Aksu, Lepsi, Saribulak, and Shalikti – manage, at least in the spring, to reach the shores of Lake Balkhash. The seventh river, and the longest and most significant, is the Ili, a majestic but deceptively fast-flowing current which flows in a westerly direction, south of the Dzungarski Alatau Ridge, from its source high in the mountains of western China. Carrying enormous volumes of melting snow and ice, it descends into Lake Kapchagai at the foot of the Tien Shan Mountains; from there it turns to the north-west and continues for a further three hundred kilometres across the steppe, before ending its journey in a broad, marshy area at the southern end of Lake Balkhash. In common with the other rivers of the region, in the blazing heat of summer the Ili loses vast amounts of its water to evaporation and absorption in the parched sands along its route, and as a result Lake Balkhash remains poorly supplied with fresh water. The river gives its name to the Ili Gap, a wide, sandy valley stretching for hundreds of miles between the Dzungarski Alatau Ridge and the

Tien Shan Mountains. In earlier centuries this had been a major corridor for Mongol and other invaders from the east. To the north lies the Dzungarski Gate, another invasion route in the narrow gap between the eastern end of the Dzungarski Alatau Ridge in Kazakhstan and the Tarbagatai Mountains in western China. The whole of the Dzungarski region, a borderland between Kazakhstan and China, has been marked by unrest and conflict; historically invasions have always come from the east, and the region has remained remote and sparsely populated.

Further north, the steppes of southern Russia had also been subject to incursions and raids by tribes of Kazakhs, Kalmyks, and Dzungarians, and as a defence Tsar Peter the Great had ordered the construction in the early eighteenth century of a chain of military forts and look-out posts, known as the Orenburg Line, along the border between Russia and Kazakhstan. It was from one of these forts, at Semipalatinsk on the Irtysh River in north-east Kazakhstan, where in early July 1853 the Russians had embarked on their journey. Having loaded teams of packhorses with tents, axes, spades, water, rations, and other supplies and equipment for the uncertain conditions ahead, they set off south across the steppe, traversing the Karakum (Black Sands) desert and skirting the eastern shore of Lake Balkhash, passing through the tiny caravanserai of Lepsi. Their route then headed south-west around the Dzungarski Alatau Ridge, before continuing further across the empty steppe and crossing the Ili at a point near Lake Kapchagai. Climbing the foothills of the mountains ahead, they soon found a suitable stopping place at the site of a ruined medieval settlement, which from earliest times had been known as Almaty (or *Almatu* in the original Turkic name meaning 'Land of Apples' as this region was believed to be the birth-place of the wild apple plant.) The later Russian name of Almaty is derived from the Turkic name, although initially the Russians called their settlement Zailisky ('beyond the Ili'). Almatu was one of a line of small oasis communities and caravanserais along the northern slopes of the Tien Shan Mountains, and formed part of the network of trade routes collectively making up the Silk Road, linking China and Mongolia in the east with Byzantium and Europe in the west. These settlements had been destroyed by waves of Mongol invaders under Genghis Khan coming through the Ili Gap in the early thirteenth century, although the burnt and charred ruins were still clearly visible when the Russians arrived over six hundred years later.

Three thousand, six hundred kilometres away in St Petersburg, the tsarist government of Nicholas I responded favourably to the findings of the Peremyshelsky mission. Russia was in need of a demonstration of strength and security, and tangible evidence of further expansion of the empire would meet this requirement. Nicholas had been emperor for twenty-eight years, at the head of a reactionary and repressive regime that depended on widespread censorship, thousands of informers, and a vast bureaucracy of civil servants for its survival. In Europe, Nicholas still enjoyed considerable prestige; on a visit to England in 1844, he presented his friend and admirer the Duke of Devonshire with a writing table made of heavy green malachite transported at great cost from the Ural Mountains, and a lake and fountain were created in his honour at Chatsworth House in Derbyshire. But his meeting with Queen Victoria at Windsor Castle was less successful; heavily pregnant at the time, she was not well disposed to visitors and was greatly concerned that Nicholas might be assassinated by Polish exiles while he was in England. Victoria later described Nicholas as 'a sinister tyrant with wild eyes', and was said to have been profoundly relieved when he left for home.

Within Russia Nicholas' position was fragile and insecure. His reign had started badly with the ruthless suppression of the Decembrist Uprising, when in December 1825 a group of army officers, inspired by European ideals of liberty and constitutional government, staged a demonstration in the centre of St Petersburg to demand a National Assembly and a formal constitution. The demonstration was put down by troops loyal to the tsar; 60 people were killed and several hundreds injured, and many surviving army officers were exiled to Siberia, accompanied by their wives and families. The episode cast a dark shadow over the country and the government; the 'Decembrists' had gained much public sympathy and admiration, with a corresponding loss of loyalty to the tsar, and over the following years and decades the regime became increasingly suspicious and insecure. Abroad, the situation facing Russia was equally disturbing. Relations with Turkey were deteriorating rapidly, and in July 1853 Nicholas ordered a vast army of 80,000 troops into Romania, part of the Ottoman Empire but where the Orthodox Christian population in the provinces of Moldavia and Wallachia was nominally under Russian protection. Simultaneously war in the Crimea, which would severely expose Russian military weakness, was approaching. In Central Asia, beyond the vast and empty steppes of Kazakhstan, China was seen as a potential enemy to the east, while in the south there was a perceived threat of encroachment from the British Empire in India and Afghanistan. The conflict between Britain and Russia in this remote part of the world became known in Russia as the Tournament of Shadows.

Unlike other European imperial powers, Russia was continually involved with often hostile tribal populations in its adjacent territories, and the need to ensure stability along the southern borders of the empire had become a matter of vital concern. In support of its strategic and security objectives, and in preparation for further expansion southwards, the government ordered the construction of two new lines of fortresses, to the south of Peter the Great's Orenburg Line. Thus in the 1830s a chain of forts was built from Kokchetav in central Kazakhstan, to Akmolinsk (later Astana), and Karkaralinsk, 300 kilometres east of Akmolinsk. Each of these locations was already a caravanserai and stopping point on the ancient caravan routes from Bukhara and Tashkent to Russia, but the construction of a fort in 1832 at Akmolinsk may be taken as the date of the foundation of the future state capital. This line of forts was followed by construction of the 'Syr Darya Line' along the Syr Darya River (the Oxus of historical times) in the south of the country, from Aralsk at the north-eastern tip of the Aral Sea (1847), to Kazalinsk east of the Aral Sea (1850), and Perovsk, at a strategic location further upstream on the Syr Darya (1853). A fourth and more substantial fortress and settlement, in the little-known but strategically-important territory of Semirechie further east, would serve notice to the population of Russia and Kazakhstan, and to foreign governments, especially those of China and Britain, that Russia's presence in the region was intended to be permanent.

Over the coming months the new encampment expanded and the number of wooden enclosures increased steadily, as more troops arrived from Russia to secure the region, and to prepare for an influx of settlers. In February 1854 the settlement was renamed Verny ('loyal'), to demonstrate that despite its remote location in the far south-eastern corner of the empire, it was loyal to the tsar in St Petersburg. Major Peremyshelsky returned to Russia and the original wooden palisades were soon demolished and replaced with a more substantial stone fortress. However the wooden barracks and stables remained intact and some still exist today, just to the east of present-day Almaty; now overgrown and neglected, they stand as a poignant reminder of the origins of Russia's empire in Central Asia. In the following years, growing numbers of civilian immigrants and settlers arrived from southern and western Russia, their numbers increased by the emancipation of serfs in 1861 which led to a further influx of Slav settlers. Many of the new arrivals settled in northern Kazakhstan, where they caused deep resentment among the indigenous nomadic population whose grazing lands were taken and whose seasonal migrations were severely disrupted. The ancient routes of these migrations were regarded virtually as the property of individual family groups and tribes, and other groups of nomads were not permitted to travel on the same paths. Thus the influx of Russians, intent on making permanent homes on Kazakh land without regard to the local population, was doubly resented. But the Russian incomers, seeking to escape from their own poverty and taking advantage of their new freedom, cared little for these concerns, and with the encouragement of the tsarist authorities they established communities wherever they wished. As well as settling in the north of the country, large numbers travelled further across the steppe to the fertile lands in the south, where they established farms and built new villages near the growing town of Verny.

Initially the construction of houses and other buildings, almost all of which were wood, proceeded at random, until a plan drawn up by the local authorities in 1868 laid down that the town was henceforth to be built in a systematic manner. The principal architects and planners were Paul Gurde from France, a Russian horticulturalist named Edward Baum, and the renowned architect Andrei Zenkov, whose father had been the first mayor of Verny and who later designed the Cathedral of the Holy Ascension. Zenkov and Gurde determined that the main thoroughfares of the town should be aligned from north to south, and minor streets from east to west. The streets were to be straight and wide, lined with irrigation channels carrying water down from the mountains, with rows of trees, and interspersed with squares, parks, and gardens to provide shade and cool air in the hot summer months. The parks and gardens were largely the work of Edward Baum and Medeu Pursumanov, a Russian businessman and shopkeeper, after whom was named the ice-skating rink built in the mountains above the city in the following century. The first governor of the Semirechie region, Gerasim Kolpakovsky, and his successor Konstantin von Kaufman, both actively promoted the planting of birch, oak, and other types of trees. New settlers in the town were required to plant trees in their gardens or neighbourhoods; one of the most popular trees planted at this time was the white willow, producing a soft fluffy down known as *pookh* which drifts in the breeze and fills the streets and parks in summer.

The north-south alignment of the major thoroughfares meant that they benefited from the warmth of the spring sunshine as early as possible, whereas houses and pavements along the smaller east-west streets had to suffer much longer under the effects of the severe winters. Even today the longer duration of ice and snow on the north-facing side of the streets causes more damage to pavements, and demands more care from pedestrians, than on the other side of the road, and icicles hang dangerously like swords from roofs and gutters before plunging to the street below. In spring, after a brief period of mud and melting snow, the ice and snow-drifts disappeared and Verny was transformed into a verdant town of trees, flowers, and gardens. In 1885 the Russian geographer and explorer

Pyotr Semenov described how from 'a bare hillside on the banks of the Almatinka River where previously there stood a few wooden huts and yurts, there now stands a fine town, overflowing with greenery…...Verny is unarguably the most pleasant and most colourful town in Central Asia, the best adornments of which are the beautiful gardens planted around the town by Russian settlers'. In the surrounding countryside, much of it still remote and unexplored, a wide range of animals and plants, many unknown to science, had been preserved in an untouched state, and Verny began to attract the attention of scientists and explorers. The most notable was Chokan Valikhanov, a Kazakh from Kustanai in the north of the country, and on his premature death in 1865, at the age of 29, one of the new streets in the town was named *ulitsa Valikhanova*. Like many streets in the new city, Valikhanova was a quiet, tree-lined avenue, gently sloping from the higher southern suburbs to one of the many quiet parks (later named Panfilov Park), before continuing to the lower, northern suburbs. Many other prominent botanists, naturalists, and zoologists from St Petersburg, Moscow, and western Europe, also came to Verny to explore and study the region.

In addition to its parks and gardens, and its attractions as base for scientific research and exploration of the surrounding country, Verny in the second half of the nineteenth century was becoming increasingly important both as a base for army operations, and as an industrial centre. From here the tsarist army launched punitive raids to subdue uprisings and rebellions among the native population. It also mounted campaigns against territories to the south, intended to incorporate the neighbouring khanates of Central Asia into the Russian empire. Simultaneously, the local economy of Verny and of the Semirechie was expanding steadily. Production was often in the hands of immigrants from Russia who set up hundreds of small workshops for processing cotton, wool, leather, and silk, for markets in Russia, China, and other parts of Kazakhstan. Industry was concentrated in the lower, northern suburbs of the town, where the land was flat and open, and room for expansion northwards to the steppe was virtually unlimited. This area became exceptionally hot and polluted in summer, and was the poorer, more densely-populated part of the town. To the south, where the land began to climb to the foothills of the mountains, the air was cooler, and here, roughly 1,000 feet higher than the northern suburbs, Russian industrialists, financiers, and entrepreneurs built large wooden houses and villas where they could reproduce as closely as possible the conditions of their native but distant country. Set amid the open countryside and with views over the plains, these houses were decorated in the traditional style of the Russian *dacha,* with ornately-carved and brightly-painted shutters on the windows and wooden Chekhovian-style verandas, with steps leading down to spacious gardens and extensive apple orchards.

On two occasions, in 1887 and 1911, Verny was severely damaged by earthquakes; the 1887 earthquake, the aftershocks of which continued for several months, destroyed all the stone buildings in the town and killed 332 people. Only wooden houses and yurts survived. Another minor earthquake two years later gave rise to the science of earthquake engineering in Kazakhstan under the leadership of Andrei Zenkov. Thanks to his efforts the town was better prepared for the next seismic upheaval, in January 1911, which although stronger than the 1887 earthquake claimed the lives of only fifty people. In addition to earthquakes, Verny suffered from devastating flash floods and mudslides, notably in July 1921 when widespread damage and loss of life were caused by boulders and debris brought down from the Alatau Mountains and crashing into the town.

The beautiful and elaborate Russian Orthodox Cathedral of the Holy Ascension, built in 1904-1905 to a design by Andrei Zenkov and constructed entirely from wood, survived the 1911 earthquake with only minor damage. It was soon restored, and except for a period during Soviet times when it became a museum of atheism, it has remained in use as a cathedral ever since. By 1897 the population of Verny had reached nearly 23,000 and was the third largest city in Kazakhstan after Uralsk (36,000) and Semipalatinsk (26,000). The influx of workers from Russia, combined with more families leaving the land in the surrounding countryside to seek work in the city, meant that by 1921 the population had more than doubled to nearly 50,000. By then much of the surrounding forests, and the early colonial settlements had long since disappeared, although the original wooden barracks remained in use until the 1980s. In 1921, four years after the Russian Revolution, as the name Verny was no longer applicable, the town was renamed Alma-Ata (an artificial name retaining the reference to apples but inspired more by the political need to abandon the link to tsarist times; the choice may have pleased Russians in the city but it alienated many Kazakhs). Many street names were changed in honour of leading Bolsheviks; *ulitsa Valikhanova* became *ulitsa Krasina* named after Lev Krasin, a prominent figure in the Bolshevik party and Commissar for Foreign Trade in the Soviet government. Krasin spent many months in London in 1920 negotiating a trade agreement between Russia and Britain, but he was of no significance to the majority of ordinary Kazakhs and citizens of Alma-Ata, who increasingly resented the growing Russianisation of their country. By contrast streets named after famous Russian writers, notably Gogol, Pushkin, and Dostoyevsky, who were widely admired in Kazakhstan, retained their original names up to and after Kazakh independence in 1991.

But changes of street names were trivial irritations compared to subsequent developments. From 1923, Soviet control of Kazakhstan was greatly strengthened by the arrival, first in Kyzyl-Orda and later in Alma-Ata, of two particularly unwelcome officials from Moscow, who most represented the dark and brutal side of the Russian Revolution. Filipp Goloshchekin, who had organised and overseen the execution in 1918 in Ekaterinburg of Tsar Nicholas II and the Romanov family, was appointed by Stalin in April 1923 as First Secretary of the Kazakhstan Communist Party, and became the key figure in the disastrous collectivisation of agriculture in the country. With him was Nikolai Yezhov, later head of the NKVD, precursor of the KGB, who implemented a regime of fear throughout Kazakhstan, during which vast numbers of innocent citizens were subject to arrest, imprisonment, deportation, and execution.

In the nineteenth century Kazakhstan had been seen by the tsarist government in St Petersburg as a useful country of exile for writers, artists, and revolutionaries, and this tradition was continued in 1928 when Alma-Ata received a prominent political outcast from Russia in the form of Leon Trotsky, an ally of Lenin and one of the founders of the Soviet state. After the death of Lenin, Trotsky had fallen out of favour with Stalin and the Soviet leadership, and he was banished from Moscow and deported to Alma-Ata where it was thought he could do no harm. He lived with his family in a large wooden house on the site of the present Otrar Hotel, until he was forced into exile abroad in January 1929.

Later in 1929 Alma-Ata was made the capital of what had become the Kazakh Autonomous Socialist Republic, taking over from Kyzil-Orda, the former fortress of Perovsk on the Syr Darya River. In the following year the first scheduled air service between Alma-Ata and Moscow came into operation. At the same time Alma-Ata was connected to the 'TurkSib' (Turkestan–Siberia) railway, linking Central Asia to Moscow and Leningrad in the west and to Siberia in the east, and enabling the export of cotton and agricultural commodities and the import of industrial and agricultural equipment. Southern and central Kazakhstan had long been connected to Russia by railways constructed in the nineteenth century; these railways had promoted economic development and facilitated Russian control, but the more difficult and mountainous terrain in eastern Kazakhstan had delayed similar contact with the Semirechie region and connection to the Trans-Siberian railway until after the Revolution. By improving transport connections between Alma-Ata and Russia, the railway enabled the government in Kazakhstan to deport thousands of political prisoners arrested in the mass purges of the 1920s and 1930s to labour camps in Siberia. It also ensured that following the German invasion of Russia in 1941, and despite the enormous distance from the front, Alma-Ata and the whole of eastern Kazakhstan were fully engaged in the war effort. The sacrifices of this period are commemorated in the Panfilov Park opposite the Otrar Hotel on Gorky Street.

After the war, Alma-Ata continued to develop and expand in relative prosperity as the political and economic centre of Kazakhstan. In the mid-1950s a hydro-electric power station was built at the western end of Lake Kapchagai and the conversion of the lake into a reservoir provided the residents of Alma-Ata with an attractive resort for swimming and sailing, although the lack of trees and any vegetation meant that there was no shade in the hot summer months. Politically it was also difficult to relax as the city, and the whole of Kazakhstan, remained under the tight control of the Soviet government in Moscow. In 1954, as if to emphasise this subordinate relationship, a monumental granite statue of Lenin, one of the tallest in the Soviet Union, was erected in one of the city's many parks, where it remained until it was removed in August 1996.

Alma-Ata occupied an attractive location with fertile countryside to the east and west, but the city was under continual threat from tremors, earthquakes, and damage from storms and floods in the Alatau Mountains only a short distance to the south. No major damage had been recorded since the mudslide of 1921, but in the early summer of 1973, after weeks of intense heat during which glaciers had melted and water levels in the mountain streams and rivers had risen alarmingly, a violent storm and a series of earth tremors caused a torrent of thousands of tons of water, mud, rocks, and boulders to plunge down the Malaya Almatinka valley towards the city, carving a wide gash in the countryside and causing devastation to houses and villages along its route. The avalanche and mudslide were mostly spent before reaching Alma-Ata, although several massive boulders were deposited in the southern outskirts of the city. Shortly afterwards a vast concrete dam was built in the valley to protect the city against further storm and flood damage from the mountains above.

Over a period of seventy six years, Alma-Ata evolved from the simple wooden fortress built by Russian troops in 1853 to become the capital of Kazakhstan in 1929. In 1993, two years after the country became independent, the city adopted its ancient historical name of Almaty, and many streets discarded their Soviet names and reverted to the earlier, more popular, names of national figures. *Krasina* once again became *Valikhanova*, although it was to take years for all the new street names to be adopted by the public. In 1997 Akmola (later renamed Astana), One thousand two hundred kilometres to the north-west, became the political and administrative capital, although Almaty has retained its position as the commercial and financial centre of the country.

CHAPTER TWO

The Land of Kazakhstan

In the empty heartland of Central Asia, Kazakhstan occupies the emptiest and widest space. The largest land-locked country in the world, its area of over one million square miles far exceeds the combined territory of its southern, also land-locked, neighbours of Turkmenistan, Uzbekistan, Kyrgyzstan, and Tajikistan. It is a land of extremes, of arid deserts and fertile plains, of high mountain ranges and endless expanses of immense, open steppe. It is also a country of leafy oases and shaded chaikhanas, and ancient caravanserais along the old Silk Road between China and Europe. The half-forgotten medieval cities of Otrar, Shavgar, and Sayram have their modern counterparts in the industrial wastelands of abandoned and derelict Soviet-era factories.

For hundreds of years throughout its history, Kazakhstan was considered to be part of Russia rather than Asia, and it was not until the 1920s, after the Russian Revolution, that Kazakhstan began to be regarded as a distinct nation, although still very much part of the new Soviet Union. Its people were not even known by their own name, but instead were referred to as *Kyrghyz,* the name of the neighbouring tribes to the south. But geographically Kazakhstan is the dominant country in Central Asia. From the mouth of the Volga River in the west to the Altai Mountains near the border with Mongolia in the east, it extends for nearly 3,000 kilometres (1,800 miles), and from the Russian steppes in the north for roughly 1,700 kilometres (1,060 miles) to the deserts of Uzbekistan in the south. In the westernmost part of the country around the Volga Delta lies the Caspian Depression, a desolate, low-lying and windswept region of salt marshes and treeless, sandy desert. The terrain is flat, much of it below sea level, and nowhere does the land rise to more than a few tens of metres. Little vegetation can survive in this hostile environment, and human settlement is mostly confined to a few towns and villages along the banks of the Volga and Ural Rivers. Like the Ural Mountains to the north, the Volga River is geographically the unmistakable frontier between Europe and Asia in the south. But the border between Russia and Kazakhstan lies a few kilometres to the east of the river; from the Volga delta on the Caspian Sea, it runs broadly parallel to the river for about two hundred kilometres before it turns in an easterly direction and follows the course of the Ural River for a short distance between the towns of Uralsk and Orenburg. The Ural River is the only non-seasonal river in western Kazakhstan, flowing constantly throughout the year from its source far to the north in the Ural Mountains, and into the Caspian Sea. Further east is the Emba River, which rises in the Mugodzhary Hills, a ridge of low hills between the Russian border and the Aral Sea, and which flows in a south-westerly direction towards the Caspian. But like many rivers in Kazakhstan, the Emba is in full spate during winter and spring, swollen by heavy rainfall in the hills, only to disappear in the sands and desert in its lower reaches in the summer, when it evaporates before it can reach the Caspian shore.

Between the Caspian and Aral Seas lie the vast plateau lands of Ustyurt and Mangyshlak; the Ustyurt is a flat, featureless plain extending for hundreds of square kilometres into Uzbekistan and Turkmenistan. Mangyshlak consists of more varied and hilly terrain, and from where two peninsulas, the Buzachi and the Tyub-Karagan, project out into the Caspian Sea. Between the two peninsulas are the Mangyshlak Gulf, and the Tyulen archipelago of dozens of tiny low-lying islands, home to hundreds of seals. The coastline of Kazakhstan along the Caspian weaves and curves through a series of wide bays, gulfs, and inlets for a distance of 2,300 kilometres, in contrast to the much straighter coastline on the opposite shore in Russia and Azerbaijan. The surface of the Caspian Sea lies about thirty metres below world sea level, although it occasionally rises and falls several metres, a phenomenon thought to be due to changing volumes of water flowing into the sea from the Volga River, as well as to cyclical factors related to the rotation of the earth. When the sea level is high there is considerable flooding along the shore, causing widespread damage to roads, villages and buildings. The northern part of the sea and the broad gulf extending into Kazakhstan are shallow; further south the sea becomes deeper in the Derbent Hollow off the Russian coast, then rises to a ridge between Baku in Azerbaijan and Turkmenbashi in Turkmenistan, before falling away again to much greater depths in the southern part between Azerbaijan and Iran.

East of the Mugodzhary Hills the land of Kazakhstan descends to the flat, dry, and treeless expanse of the Turan Depression, another low-lying area through which flows the Syr Darya River, before rising again to the Golodnaya (Hungry) Steppe, a vast and sparsely-inhabited desert stretching as far as Lake Balkhash. The topography of this region is unlike that of anywhere in Europe. The empty landscape of enormous distances and gently undulating or flat, featureless countryside extending in every direction, contains no landmarks, no trees or shade from the blazing sun, no fields or hedgerows, and no buildings, farms or villages. Occasionally a dusty track may stretch aimlessly to an unknown point in the distance, and a dried-up river bed, strewn with rocks and stones bleached white in the summer sun, winds its way among the low hills. Sometimes on the distant horizon a few tiny specks of a group of Kazakh yurts, known as an *aul,* or a thin wisp of smoke rising from an open camp fire, may just be visible, but otherwise the land is empty and devoid of any sign of human life. But despite present appearances, historically this was not a sterile area, and archaeological excavations have revealed extensive evidence of diverse Stone Age and Bronze Age settlements. Over the millennia many parts of the land came to be regarded as sacred, and about two thousand years after the end of the Bronze Age when Jochi, the eldest son of Genghiz Khan died in 1227, his body was buried in a grave at the foot of the Ulytau Mountains near the Aral Sea, in a place which had long been revered and worshipped by the early people of the region.

To the north of the Golodnaya Steppe is the more fertile region of the Western Siberian Plain, where the vast and empty countryside of northern Kazakhstan merges imperceptibly into the even more extensive lands and endless forests of southern Russia. It was this area which in 1860 the Russian writer Fyodor Dostoyevsky described in *The House of the Dead,* the account of his years spent in prison in Omsk, on the Irtysh River just north of the border between Kazakhstan and Russia:

'In winter, especially if the day was gloomy and overcast, the view across the river to the opposite bank in the far distance was a melancholy one. There was something dreary and heart-searing about this wild, empty landscape. But it was perhaps even more painful when the sun shone on the endless white sheet of the snow; if only one could have flown away somewhere into those steppes, which began on the opposite bank and spread out to the south in a single unbroken expanse for some fifteen hundred versts* to the south'.

But later as he neared the end of his prison term, Dostoyevsky's feelings towards his surroundings in the steppe became more mellow:

'On the river bank one could forget oneself: one would look at that immense, vacant landscape in the way a prisoner looks out at freedom from the window of his cell. Everything here was beloved and enchanting: the brilliant, hot sun in the bottomless, blue sky, and the distant singing of a Kyrghyz peasant floating across from the Kyrghyz side of the river. One would scrutinise the distance for a long time and at last make out

---

* A verst is 3,500 feet, two-thirds of a mile.

the poor, smoke-stained yurt of some nomad; one would see a wisp of smoke above the yurt, a Kyrghyz woman fussing over her two rams. The whole scene would be one of poverty and a primitive wilderness. One would catch a glimpse of a bird in the blue, transparent air and follow its flight for a long time, attentively: now it would skim the water, now disappear into the blue, then appear again, a barely decipherable moving point. . . . '

Beyond Lake Balkhash to the east is the Semirechie region from where the land rises again, this time steeply to the more rugged, mountainous regions of the Altai. In the south-east lies the Zhungarsky Alatau Ridge, rising to nearly 4,000 metres above sea level, and further south still is the Zailisky Alatau Ridge, where the Russians first established a camp and whose summits rise to over 5,000 metres above sea level. Both these mountain ranges, dramatic in their own right and in sharp contrast to the undulating landscape of most of Kazakhstan, are merely the foothills of the high peaks of the Tien Shan and Pamir Mountains of China. In the extreme south-east corner of the country lies the majestic 6,995-metre peak of Khan-Tengri, at a point where the frontiers of Kazakhstan, Kyrgyzstan, and China meet.

Far from the moderating influences of any ocean, Kazakhstan has an extreme continental climate; on the steppes the harsh winters of heavy snow and sub-zero temperatures are followed by a short spring season and then by long summers of blistering heat with temperatures ranging from over 40 degrees by day and often falling to below freezing at night. Annual rainfall in central Kazakhstan is low thanks to an almost permanent area of high pressure producing cloud-free skies throughout much of the year. Periodically severe winter storms, known as *zhuts,* descend in a disastrous combination of blizzards, ice and snow, and prevent the herds of cattle, sheep, and horses being able to feed on the grass below the ice, causing widespread starvation to the animals and heavy losses to the nomadic herdsmen. In spring the countryside, watered by melting ice and snow, is briefly covered in vivid carpets of wild flowers and tall grasses, swaying gently in soft breezes, but before long the earth turns dry and brown under the relentless summer heat and dry *sukhovy* winds. Eastern and northern parts of Kazakhstan are relatively well supplied with water, principally from the Irtysh River which has its source in Lake Zaisan in the foothills of the Altai Mountains, which in turn is supplied by the 'Black Irtysh' flowing from the Altai and by numerous other mountain rivers and streams. But much of Lake Balkhash is now dry throughout the summer, the result of less water reaching it from the rivers of the Semirechie. A similar but more serious phenomenon has affected the Aral

Sea in the west of the country. Here and in the south of Kazakhstan the land consists mainly of arid desert; the only major rivers are the Syr Darya and the Chu. Both rise in Kyrgyzstan in the Tien Shan Mountains, and whereas the Syr Darya flows into the northern part of the Aral Sea, the Chu disappears into the desert between Lake Balkhash and the Aral. Further south the Amu Darya flows broadly parallel to the Syr Darya into a wide and now arid delta in the southern part of the Aral Sea; the desert region between the Syr Darya and the Amu Darya is the ancient land of Transoxiana.

***

The land occupied by present-day Kazakhstan has been inhabited for around 40,000 years, but evidence of primitive pre-human forms of life goes far back to much earlier times. After the cataclysmic geological upheaval which brought the Tien Shan Mountains into existence, the climate and terrain in that part of Central Asia, especially in the northern foothills of the mountains, were largely conducive to the emergence of human life. The valleys and pastures were fertile, water from mountain streams was plentiful, and the hills gave protection against the harsh arid winds from the plains. But despite these favourable conditions, the land had to wait many hundreds of thousands of years, unseen and untouched, before the arrival of the first forms of homo sapiens. In the early Palaeolithic period, around 500,000 years ago, groups of primitive hunters and fishermen first emerged and began scavenging a basic existence of hunting and foraging for edible plants and grasses. From around 150,000 BC in the middle Palaeolithic era, Neanderthal groups became widespread throughout the region, developing simple stone implements and primitive tools, and constructing monuments to mark their presence. Modern humans (homo sapiens) did not appear until the later Palaeolithic period in about 40,000 BC, by which time the use of more advanced implements such as knives, spears, and axes for hunting, as well as decorated cups and vessels and ornately-carved sculptures, had become more widespread and sophisticated. By the Neolithic age, from around 5,000 – 3,000 BC, permanent settlements and communities had evolved, and visible remains of hundreds of these settlements survive throughout Kazakhstan, especially in the south. Some had simple forms of workshops for making spears and arrowheads, and many *kurgans* (burial chambers) for prominent figures were built throughout the countryside in which there were also buried weapons, knives, and other items of daily use. In the Neolithic period tribes occasionally gathered in the desert and undertook a division of labour for the communal benefit in which some would undertake hunting and cattle raising, and others farming and hunting. Evidence of these communities has been found throughout the country especially around the shores of Lake Balkhash, along the Irtysh River, and around other lakes and rivers. These activities involved some movement from one place to another but the communities were mostly static.

By the time of the early Bronze Age around 2,000 BC, many tribes were extending northwards from the foothills of the Tien Shan Mountains to the more open spaces around Lake Balkhash and to the Aral and Caspian Seas to the west. Bronze was becoming widely used, as deposits of copper and tin to form the basic alloy were plentiful in southern and eastern Kazakhstan, and weapons began to be produced not only for hunting animals, but also for fighting other tribes. The constituents of bronze implements and weapons could be varied with different proportions of lead and other minerals depending on the use to which they would be put. Bronze had considerable advantages over the flint and copper used in earlier times since it was stronger, more adaptable, and had a golden lustre which appealed to the primitive artistic instincts of the early tribesmen. It became the basic material in the production of implements for domestic, hunting, and warlike purposes. Similar developments were taking place at the same time in Europe, not only in the use of bronze in ornaments and tools but also in the structure of society, with the emergence of a ruling class and the construction of elaborate burial mounds and barrows to commemorate tribal leaders.

It was during the Bronze Age between around 2,000 and 1,000 BC, when cattle raising and farming became more developed and more extensive tribal groups began to emerge and coalesce, that the beginnings of a nomadic form of agriculture started to appear. Although some parts of Kazakhstan offered relatively favourable conditions for agriculture, permanent settlement was not to be a feature of its development. The unlimited open spaces of this part of Central Asia provided the setting not for the growth of towns and cities, but instead for the evolution of itinerant communities and simple forms of farming and agriculture. Of the various key phases in the history of Kazakhstan, including, in a much later century, the first contacts between indigenous tribesmen in northern Kazakhstan and primitive herdsmen of southern Russia, one of the most critical could be said to be the development of nomadic agriculture, which later came to characterise the country. This process took place over a long period of gradual climate change lasting several hundreds of years, during which warmer, drier weather led to more arid conditions throughout the territory now occupied by Kazakhstan; this in turn caused a fall in the level of lakes and rivers, and a thinner covering of desiccated, less fertile soil throughout the land. The need to let the soil recover necessitated the regular movement to new pastures and grazing lands. By around 1,000 BC the majority of the population had abandoned any form of settled agriculture and converted to a way of life in which people were on the move for much of the year. Strictly-observed systems of migration routes and land use developed, which other tribes and family groups were not permitted to use or interfere with. The country was remote and isolated by vast distances from outside influences, and there was no impetus for the growth of towns or even villages. The nomadic tribes came to regard living in settled communities as unworthy for outdoor people such as themselves, who lived in close and permanent contact with their natural surroundings. Even walking was considered undignified by people who from the earliest age learnt to ride. This attitude was similar to but more pronounced than the European preference for travel on horseback, which was indicated by the contrast between words such as 'chevalier' and 'pedestrian'. Settled communities were always vulnerable to attack from hostile tribes and even armies from further afield, and living in them was best avoided. Constant movement in accordance with the demands of the seasons and the land became the basis of life on the steppes.

The pattern of the nomadic year in Kazakhstan evolved over centuries, but in essence was dictated by the grazing needs of the herds of livestock. In different parts of the country different migration routes and distances were set according to climatic, water, and soil conditions. In the south and south-west, in the arid steppes between the Caspian and Aral Seas, and in the plains of central Kazakhstan, summer migration to the fertile, grass-covered pastures in the northern regions near Russia entailed journeys of hundreds of miles every year; whereas in the mountainous areas of the east, distances between different pastures were often much shorter. Each move to the next grazing land was a festive occasion. Family possessions were loaded onto horses and camels in a well-rehearsed procedure that had evolved over centuries. Apart from their animals, the main item owned by each family was the *yurt*, the circular tent with a dome-shaped roof which has become almost synonymous with Kazakhstan and the countries of Central Asia. In its original meaning a yurt indicated an area of pasture and grazing land which would be sufficient to support the small group of people living there. Each yurt consisted of groups of *gers*, which was the original word for the collapsible and transportable dome-shaped tents, and which is still used in Mongolia and other parts of the region. The ger, or yurt, consists of a wooden frame of long poles made from branches of flexible wood, usually willow, birch, or poplar, covered over with animal hides and felt, made from the fur from animal skins, interwoven and compressed until it becomes hard but flexible. Its basic design has remained unchanged for hundreds of years, although the size and style of individual yurts vary considerably, in accordance with the owners' status and family position. Inside the yurt, rugs, mats, and carpets, decorated with intricate embroidery and patterns representing natural scenes and animal life, line the floors and the sides; sometimes more affluent families decorated the exterior of their yurts as well. During transportation all these rugs and mats were rolled up and loaded onto the camels. Entrance to a yurt was through a pair of wooden doors, usually with no particular adornment but sometimes decorated with elaborate carpentry and carvings, while elsewhere in the walls, rolled-up sections, secured with leather cords, allowed for ventilation in the hot summer months. Separate sections were set apart for men, women, children, and guests, with other parts for working and cooking. An open fire in the centre provided warmth in winter and heat for cooking, with a circular opening in the roof to allow smoke to escape. Known as the *shanyrak,* this was often the most precious, even revered, part of the yurt; consisting of a latticework of flexible wooden sticks attached to the top of the yurt, it provided ventilation and light. Unremarkable in itself, the shanyrak was often handed down from one generation to the next as a family heirloom, even while other parts of the yurt fell into disuse. The nomadic family had few other possessions or furniture, except for wooden beds, some chests and boxes for storing items, and a *dastarkhan,* a low wooden table around which everyone sat for meals in winter. In summer meals were taken sitting on a mat on the floor. For Kazakhs and other native peoples of the region, historically the yurt has had a significance much deeper than simply somewhere to live. It embodies the traditions of ancient times, and has direct associations with the wide open spaces of the steppe and the mountains. Nowadays at times of weddings, funerals, other family occasions, or local festivals, town-living Kazakhs may erect a yurt in the courtyard of their block of flats in the centre of the city, in which they can welcome guests, provide hospitality, and preserve the family memory.

At each departure in the migration calendar, everyone in the aul, or large family group, dressed in their best clothes and set off in a colourful procession of horses, camels, cattle, and sheep. At the head of the caravan rode the women of the aul, in order of the seniority within the family or clan, and wearing their most exotic and colourful gowns and robes. Seated on equally ornate saddles and rugs, they rode on the best horses of the herd. Following the women were the men herding the animals, some with a falcon, the size of a young boy, perched on their arm. Alongside the caravan children played, sang, and raced one another on horses; no one travelled on foot, since walking was regarded as demeaning and everyone, from the youngest child to the oldest grandparents, rode on horses or camels. Movement between one pasture and the next took place in spring, summer, and autumn, in strict accordance with the seasons, since travel in winter was difficult or impossible. The first move was in early spring when the caravan left its winter camp; by early summer, when new-born lambs were strong enough to travel and the heat dictated a further move, the caravan set off again to the cooler pastures and grassy plains in the north of the country. By mid-summer most families had reached their destinations, where they stayed until autumn, when the caravan was again loaded up for the journey back towards the winter camp, usually arriving after the first snowfalls. The final move was always made as late in the year as possible, so as to conserve the pastures for grazing during the harsh winter months. Although the yurts provided shelter and warmth in winter, the winter camps often consisted of more substantial brick or log houses. These simple abodes had a flat roof and consisted of two or three rooms, or one big room for all the members of the family. In the one-room houses people would spend the night in different corners, separated by curtains. The families remained in their winter homes until early spring, when the nomadic cycle would start again. Centuries later, the arrival of Russian settlers in Kazakhstan disrupted this ancient way of life by obstructing historic migration routes and forcing the Kazakh nomads away from the most fertile pastures. Later still, in the overcrowded Soviet apartment blocks of Alma-Ata and other cities, lack of space forced Kazakh families to arrange their living accommodation in a style similar to that of the yurt, as old and young slept in different corners of the same room. Other traditions followed Kazakh families to their new lives in city apartments, where instead of wallpaper, colourful rugs were hung on the walls, reminiscent of the yurt and of a lost way of life on the steppe; centuries of hospitality meant that if guests arrived unexpectedly, all other arrangements were abandoned so as to welcome and accommodate the new arrivals; and many families brought with them a few hens or goats from the countryside, which provided a rural feel to the quiet urban courtyards.

CHAPTER THREE

The Golden Man and the Scythians

The countryside east of Almaty is flat and generally featureless, although the permanently snow-covered foothills of the Tien Shan Mountains to the south provide a spectacular background to the wooden houses, farms, and *posyolki* (settlements) that line the main road. In places the ground suddenly becomes uneven and undulating, the result of earthquakes and massive mudslides from the hills above. This is a fertile agricultural region of green fields and extensive orchards, where apples, cherries, peaches, tomatoes, figs, potatoes, carrots, onions, small yellow honeydew melons and heavy, dark-green water melons, are grown for the thriving markets and street-corner stalls of Almaty and other towns and cities. Nowadays the main road running out of Almaty is constantly busy with heavy lorries, buses and cars. But in the 1960s there was little traffic to disturb the tranquility of the countryside, and the tiny farming settlement of Issyk, 50 kilometres east of Almaty, was a lonely spot, rarely visited except by historians and archaeologists. The ancient burial ground here was already well known; it stood on a site slightly higher than the surrounding fields, and some of the many kurgans had already been partly excavated. In spring the ground is a sea of bright red poppies and other wild flowers, but for the rest of the year the kurgans are covered in dull brown grass, and the whole area was regarded as hallowed ground separate from the nearby orchards and farms. It was here in the peaceful summer of 1969 that a team of Soviet archaeologists, excavating one of the kurgans, made a dramatic discovery – a discovery which opened a new window on the vanished world of the warriors and nomads of the steppes.

For many Kazakhs and Russians, prehistoric burial grounds with their tumuli, barrows and kurgans, hold an aura of mystery and of the unknown, a link with the remote and forgotten past of distant ancestors. A kurgan must always be treated with respect and not interfered with, except for excavations which must be conducted with proper reverence, and only for serious scientific purposes. To walk on a kurgan is to disturb the spirit of those who lie inside, and is a serious transgression which must be atoned for by a prayer said at the foot of the kurgan. Failure to do so, many believe, results in endless feelings of restlessness and negativity. To point to a kurgan, even at a photograph of one, is also something which should never be done. Tumuli and burial mounds have often featured in Russian literature, and in his 1932 novel *Virgin Soil Upturned,* the Soviet writer Mikhail Sholokhov described a kurgan in southern Russia:

'At the side of the road stands a burial mound. On its windswept summit the bare twigs of last year's wormwood rustle mournfully…Over its slopes, from its foot to its summit, clumps of yellow grass, faded with the sun and the wind, stretch over the ancient, weather-beaten ground. Even in spring-time, amid the exuberant flowering of the myriad grasses, the mound looks agedly despondent, out-lived. Only towards autumn does it gleam, flooded with a proud, frosty white. And only in autumn does it seem as though, clothed in a scaly silver chain-mail, the grandly dignified mound is on guard over the steppe. In the sunset glow of summer evenings a steppe eagle flies from beneath the clouds of the summit. Its wings whistling, it drops to the mound, clumsily hops a couple of steps, and stops, using its hooked beak to clean the brown fan of its outstretched wing…. Looking like a native stone, the immobile, yellow-brown eagle rests before its evening hunt. Then it lightly breaks from the earth and flies away. Before sunset the grey shadow of its regal wings will be flung again and again over the steppe. In the winter, the burial mound is clad in an ermine mantle of snow, and through the pearly-grey shadows of the early morning an old, crafty fox makes his way to the summit. Only his moist, agate nose is alive in the mighty world of mingled scents, avidly inhaling the damp, all-enveloping odour of the snow and the undying bitterness of the frost-nipped wormwood. The arid eastern winds corrode the dry, crumbling soil of the mound, the midday sun bakes it, the heavy rains wash it, the winter frosts rend it. But the mound still reigns inviolably over the steppe as it did half a thousand years ago, when it arose over the remains of the slain Polovtsian prince who was buried here with martial honours, and over whom it was heaped up by the swarthy, braceleted hands of his wives and the hands of his warriors, kinsmen and slaves'.

The kurgan at Issyk dated from a much earlier period of about 500 BC, during the time of the Scythians, an ancient nomadic civilisation which dominated the steppes of southern Russia and Kazakhstan from around 700 to 300 BC. Unlike most tribes and people of the central Asian steppe, who came mainly from the Turkic lands of central Siberia, the Scythians were of Indo-Aryan origin and were closely related to the Persians, who referred to them as Saka, although the Persians were to become their most dangerous enemies. Between 750 and 700 BC, Scythian tribes migrated westwards from central Asia and western Siberia, in the process dispossessing the Cimmerians, an earlier tribe which inhabited the steppes of southern Russia.

Ultimately the Scythian empire extended from the steppes of Central Asia to the regions to the north and west of the Caspian Sea, as far as the forests of southern Russia and the shores of the Black Sea. But the spiritual heartland of the Scythian universe was the Semirechie region of Kazakhstan where, far from other human contact, the mountains and deserts, lakes and rivers, were seen as the centre of the natural world. Although almost the entire territory of Kazakhstan is dotted with prehistoric tumuli and barrows, it was to the Semirechie, and in particular to Issyk and Boraldai, another ancient cemetery not far to the west, that Scythian khans and princes, warriors and priests, came to bid farewell to fellow warriors and tribesmen. The burial ground at Issyk contains a total of twenty-seven mounds, and a further forty-seven mounds were constructed at Boraldai. Both locations, in open countryside on the banks of a river (many centuries later named the Bolshaya Almatinka) flowing down from the high mountain summits a short distance to the south, were chosen in the belief that the dead would travel back along the river to the mountains and on to the next world. Without written sources, and with only a few monuments and artefacts which have been found, the scene depends on conjecture and imagination. But nonetheless it is perhaps possible, peering into the darkness of prehistory, to make out the shadowy forms of chieftains, priests and warriors, who had travelled vast distances through deserts, steppes and forests, to gather in this remote but familiar spot, where they had been coming for hundreds of years. Rough shelters were built, camp fires were lit, acquaintances renewed and alliances made. Not only funerals were conducted here, but a complete calendar of ceremonies, rites and rituals, acts of worship and sacrifices, was devised and enacted, in a system in harmony with the seasons of the year and the movements of the sun and the moon, all of which was part of the same natural world as the heavens and the constellations, the mountains and the plains, in which the Scythians lived.

In death the Scythian khans and princes sought to immortalise their wealth and social position in the size and structure of the kurgans in which they were buried. Three types of burial chambers have been identified throughout the Semirechie and in other parts of the Scythian territories. The most substantial and imposing were for the graves of khans and princes; more modest barrows and tumuli were built for tribal leaders, while the smallest constructions were for the graves of ordinary tribesmen. In each case, a circular earthen embankment, supported by logs and stone columns, was built over a shallow grave. The kurgans were not especially tall, about six metres in height, but the sides were steep and at the summit was a circular flat area where ceremonies for the departed were held. Inside the hollow chambers was space for the array of riches, weapons, ornaments, and utensils, which were placed there to accompany the deceased on the final journey to the afterlife. After millennia of erosion by wind and rain the original structures have lost their dramatic appearance and are now simple and unremarkable grass-covered earth mounds. But the locations of the burial grounds at Issyk, Boraldai, and elsewhere still retain their sense of ancient mystery, and of belonging to an ancient time.

The Scythians were a hierarchical society of khans, priests and warrior kings who ruled with absolute power over the lives of the nomads of the steppe. According to portraits painted on vases found in Russia, Kazakhstan, and as far afield as Greece, Scythian men were bearded and wore pointed caps to protect the ears against the bitter winds of the plains, and baggy tunics and trousers suitable for unending days spent on horseback. They lived in a world of warrior horsemen who gave rise to the myth of centaur, and who are credited with the invention of the stirrup, which gave them a great advantage over horsemen of more sedentary tribes. In Europe the stirrup was not used by either the ancient Greeks or the Romans, and is thought to have come into common use only in the sixth century AD among the Avar tribes of Hungary. Scythian horsemen were renowned as great archers, famous for unleashing arrows at enemies directly behind them in what became known as a 'Parthian shot', a reference to the Parthians, a related tribe of steppe horsemen, and supposedly the origin of the term 'parting shot'.

The Scythian tribes were war-like and itinerant in their way of life, with no permanent settlements or communities. But their migrations were more than simple journeys to new grazing lands; instead they were more like travelling cities consisting of great convoys of cattle-drawn wagon trains. These contained not only their families (although children tended to ride with the men) but all their property of tents, carpets, gold, weapons, domestic utensils, and herds of animals, which were rounded up to be transported to different locations throughout the year. This became the practice which persisted over the following centuries, albeit on a smaller scale, in Kazakhstan and Mongolia. The tents were substantial and elaborately-decorated dwellings, and usually loaded fully assembled on to sturdy four-wheeled wooden carts hauled by teams of up to twenty oxen. The generally flat terrain and the absence of rocks and boulders in the gently-undulating countryside meant that the carts could be built with a low chassis, facilitating the transportation of bulky tents and possessions. Later these tents were to evolve into the smaller yurts characteristic of the nomads of Central Asia, the easily-dismantled and portable dome-shaped structures made from wooden struts and felt, and ideally suited to the nomadic way of life.

By rejecting the construction of any form of permanent settlement, and not engaging in agriculture, instead depending on their cattle for food, and living wherever they happened to be, the Scythians successfully avoided attempts by hostile neighbours to contain them. No enemy was able to attack, let alone defeat them, a factor which helped ensure their survival over hundreds of years. Invading armies were lured into the steppe only to be attacked by Scythian forces when the invaders were at their weakest. This reality was discovered to its cost in about 529 BC by a Persian army in a campaign against the Massagetae, a Scythian tribe in the region south of the Aral Sea. The Persians came up against the young queen Tomyris, the most famous Scythian leader, and an exception to the male-dominated rulers, whose ruthlessness in defending Scythian territory was on a par with that of Boudicca, who over five centuries later led the Iceni tribes of southern England in revolt against the Romans. Ancient Kazakh legends relate how Tomyris defeated the superior Persian forces, and how she personally beheaded their arrogant king Cyrus. According to the Greek historian Herodotus:

'The Scythians have managed their own preservation better than anyone else on earth. Such is their manner of life that no one who invades their country can escape destruction, and if they wish to avoid engaging with an enemy, that enemy cannot by any possibility come to grips with them. A people without fortified towns, living as the Scythians do, in wagons which they take with them wherever they go, accustomed one and all, to fight on horseback with bows and arrows, and dependent for their food not on agriculture but upon their cattle: how can such a people fail to defeat the attempt of an invader not only to subdue them but even to make contact with them?'

This account relates to an equally unsuccessful attempt by the later Persian king Darius to lead an army into Scythian territory around the Black Sea in about 514 BC. Darius abandoned efforts to defeat the Scythians, who as a result escaped Persian influence and remained in possession of southern Russia and the steppes of Kazakhstan for a further two hundred years. Instead it was the Scythians themselves who presented a greater threat to outsiders, and who developed their own form of mobile steppe warfare to an exceptionally high degree, using only horses and chariots, and swords and bows and arrows to attack and destroy other cities or even other civilisations further afield. Vast areas of the Caucasus and Armenia, Turkey and Asia Minor, fell to invasions by the Scythians, who over the centuries gained a terrifying reputation for barbarity and ruthless and bloodthirsty treatment of enemies or anyone else who stood in their way.

The excavation at Issyk caused great excitement not only among archaeologists and historians, but throughout the whole of Kazakhstan. Within the tomb was found the skeleton of a young man dressed in an elaborate and well-preserved ceremonial costume, together with a vast array of weapons and ornate jewellery, bracelets, necklaces, earrings, and pendants. The headdress consisted of a metal crown decorated with carvings of a horse, birds, snow leopards and wild goats on mountain tops, a gold statuette of a wild ram, feathers of eagles, and four golden upward-pointing arrows. Around the waist was a belt with large gold buckles, with a sword and dagger, each with engravings of a horse and an elk on the blades. Alongside the body, in accordance with Scythian ritual, was placed a whip with a gold handle, plus thirty one ceramic vessels, three metal cups, one of which was silver with an inscription of twenty six symbols. In total over 4,000 separate gold items, many in the form of tigers, eagles and other birds and wild animals, were discovered in the burial mound. The figure, subsequently known as the Golden Man, was an unknown Scythian prince or warrior, but someone who had clearly held a position of great status and esteem. Some of the nearby kurgans had been vandalised and robbed in earlier centuries, but the remains of the Golden Man with his costume and jewellery had lain undisturbed in their dark and silent tomb for about 2,500 years.

As with many archaeological finds which throw new light on previously-familiar subjects, the discovery of the Golden Man was of great significance to the understanding of the early history of Kazakhstan at the time of the Scythians, since it showed a different side to Scythian civilisation from the familiar one of violence and destruction. The Scythian art of the steppe was already known to consist of representations of simple hunting scenes and fighting animals engraved on bronze axes and daggers. But the costume in which the Golden Man was dressed demonstrated a degree of craftsmanship and artistry of an order of magnitude unsurpassed in the earlier history of the region, and which had clearly evolved over a considerable period of time. Despite the apparent splendour of the golden costume and weaponry, the animal sculptures were made of bronze and wood, and overlaid with the thinnest layers of gold leaf. But the overall effect produced by the Golden Man is one of great artistic skill, illustrating the spiritual relationship which the Scythians believed they held with the natural world of the sun, moon, and sky, and in which they saw themselves as being as one with the animal life of the mountains, forests, and steppes. Apart from swords, arrows, and other weaponry used by warriors on horseback, there was no representation of any form of human activity or type of settlement.

In about 330 BC Scythian tribes achieved their last major victories when the north-easterly progression of the armies of Alexander the Great was brought to a standstill in the vast region between the Syr Darya River and Lake Balkhash. But Scythian dominance of the steppe finally came to an end in around 300 BC, when the Sarmatians, a related tribe of nomadic horsemen and archers originating in the northern plains near the Ural Mountains, confined the Scythians to a small area around the Black Sea. After several hundred years, Scythian supremacy was superseded by the similar tactics and the even greater skill as warriors of the Sarmatians, although the latter were themselves eventually defeated by Roman armies in the western steppe in the second century of the present millennium. In later centuries, the steppes and plains of Kazakhstan provided the setting for the campaigns and empires of three powerful warlords: Attila the Hun, Genghis Khan, and Tamerlane. All three left their individual mark on the history of the region, but their empires and achievements differed considerably; but the common features to all were acquisition of territory by conquest and destruction, and the creation of empires which, except in the case of Genghis Khan, did not survive their death.

By around 350 AD, the powerful state of the Huns, which incorporated the Sarmatians and various other local tribes, had already emerged on the steppes north of the Aral Sea, and before long they crossed the Volga River and continued into Europe. Like the Scythians, the Huns were nomadic and warlike. They carried all their possessions with them on wooden carts drawn by teams of cattle, and the rhythm of their existence was regulated by their flocks of sheep, and herds of horses, cattle, and camels, as they travelled with their livestock in search of water and pasture. But this was far from an idyllic, pastoral way of life, as they are chiefly remembered for their skill in mobile warfare, and for the violence and destruction which they caused wherever they went. The Huns posed a serious threat to the Romans, as the two empires were now adjacent to each other. The Romans debated whether they were in fact human, since their appearance was so different to that of the Europeans, North Africans, or of any other national group in their empire. According to the Roman historian Ammianus Marcellinus:

'The Huns exceed anything that can be imagined in ferocity and barbarism. Their huge arms, stocky body, and disproportionately large head, give them a monstrous appearance. . . They live like beasts. They neither cook nor season their food; they live on wild roots and on meat pounded tender under the saddle. They are ignorant of the use of the plough and of fixed habitations, whether in houses or huts. Being perpetually nomadic, they are inured from childhood to cold, hunger, and thirst. Their herds follow them on their migrations, with some of the animals being used to draw the covered wagons in which their families live. If you enquire of these men where they come from or where they were born, they cannot tell you. Their dress consists of a dark linen tunic and a coat of rat skins sewn together. The tunic is worn until it rots away from their bodies. They never change it until it drops off. A helmet or cap pushed back on their heads and goatskins rolled about their hairy legs complete their attire. Their shoes, cut without shape or measure, do not allow them to walk properly thus they are quite unsuited to fight as infantry. Yet when mounted they seem riveted to their ugly little horses, which are tireless and swift as lightning. They spend their lives on horseback, drinking and eating, even sleeping, lying on the neck of their mounts. In battle they swoop upon the enemy, uttering terrifying yells. When opposed they disburse, only to return with the same speed, smashing and overturning everything in their path. They have no notion of how to take a fortified position or an entrenched camp. Yet there is nothing to equal the skill with which, from prodigious distances, they fire their arrows, which are tipped with sharpened bone as hard and murderous as iron'. Another Roman account warns: 'Armed with a huge bow and long arrows, the Hun never misses his mark. Woe betide him at whom he aims, for his arrows bring death! . . . The Huns have high cheek bones and eyes sunk in their sockets as in a cavern, yet their piercing gaze commands the farthest expanses… They have the eagle eyes of the nomad, accustomed to scanning vast areas and discerning herds of deer or wild horses on the far horizon of the steppe'.*

The Huns were united from different groups and tribes into a single national entity by their most famous leader Attila, who reigned from 443 to 453 AD, and whose name, and the vast army under his command, inspired such terror that he was known as the 'Scourge of God'. Although he is renowned primarily for skill in warfare and ruthlessness towards enemies, both domestic and foreign, Attila is also said to have been a fair and just leader, someone who was content to lead a simple life amid the excessive luxury of the court. He supposedly preferred to eat off plain wooden plates rather than the more normal gold and silver dishes used by courtiers, and wore a simple costume without elaborate adornment (although he was prone to drunkenness, as well as being deeply superstitious with a primitive belief in shamanic rituals). Attila was known for his extensive diplomatic and negotiating skills, which had been essential for subduing and uniting the disparate tribes of the kingdom, and in dealing with foreign

*Quoted by Rene Grousset: *The Empire of the Steppes* (1939)

enemies, although in the case of the latter such diplomacy was usually a prelude to attack and conquest. But after an inconclusive battle against a Roman army and their Gothic and German allies near Chalons-sur-Marne in 451, Attila was forced to retreat to the Hungarian plains, on the western edge of the empire, before launching another campaign of violence and destruction in northern Italy the following year. A year later, in 453, he married a German woman called Ildiko, but died during his wedding celebrations, possibly due to excessive alcohol consumption or the rupture of an artery, although it was rumoured that Ildiko may have poisoned him. After his death the Hun kingdom of Central Asia dissolved as a cohesive state, no longer posing a significant threat to outsiders.

The Hun campaigns in the west against the Romans in Gaul and in Italy are well known, but less is known about how they lived on their original home territory of the plains of southern Russia and Central Asia. Like all nomads the Huns left no written records of their lives, and there have been no equivalent discoveries similar to that of the Scythian Golden Man. Although some examples of decorative and artistic work have been found, their creative energies were devoted primarily to the design and manufacture of spears, swords, arrows, bows, and shields. After the death of Attila, various smaller clans survived and continued to lead a nomadic existence on the steppes north of the Black Sea and around the Sea of Azov. But the empire which had inspired terror and had dominated the vast region between Gaul and the border with China, after only one hundred years was coming to an end. The remaining clans, weakened by fratricidal wars and lack of leadership, survived until around the middle of the sixth century AD. For a short period of no more than a few years, the Huns were followed by a little-known race of Mongolian tribesmen known as the Ephthalites, sometimes known as the White Huns, who dominated the Semirechie region and the whole of southern Kazakhstan from Lake Balkhash to the Aral Sea, before they in turn were driven out by other invading hordes and tribes from the east. The Ephthalites were overwhelmed and disappeared in around 565 AD, although a group of Ephthalite nomads who had been pasturing around the Aral Sea, were able to flee to the west, and are thought to have founded a new Mongol khanate in Hungary.

From the end of the sixth century the region from the Altai Mountains as far west as the Aral Sea fell under the khanate of Tu-Chueh, the western part of a vast empire of Turkic tribes of southern Siberia. During the seventh and eighth centuries Arab armies from the south encroached into Central Asia, and captured the cities of Bukhara in 709, Samarkand (712), and Tashkent (713). But they failed to establish effective control and the period was marked by a succession of rebellions by the local population, compounded by numerous incursions by Turkic armies from the east which added to the chaos in the region. The subsequent collapse of the Turkic khanate, weakened by its own internecine wars and strife, attracted the attention of China, which now came into conflict with the growing Muslim presence in the region. In 751 a crucial battle took place between Chinese and Arab armies at Talas on the Talas River, the present-day city of Taraz in southern Kazakhstan. Militarily the battle was inconclusive; the Chinese armies were forced to retreat to the east but the Arab armies were unable to progress beyond the area they already controlled. But the conflict was one of the most important events in the history of the region. From now on China ceased to exert a significant influence, and the southern part of Central Asia became firmly linked to the economy and the religion of the Arab world.

For the region of what is now southern Kazakhstan, this became a time of cultural and economic development, when the traditional nomadic economy began to evolve towards a more settled urban, oasis culture and one which was developing strong trade and handicraft traditions. South of a line roughly from Lake Balkhash to the Aral Sea, the Islamic empire was increasingly influential, although as was to happen in later centuries and empires, including the tsarist and the Soviet empires, local families and clans were relied upon for government and administration in their own areas. The Samanids, the principal dynasty from 875 to 999, extended their control from their capital in Bukhara; mostly this was to the south and west, but in 893 they captured the cities of Otrar on the Syr Darya River and Talas on the Talas River, two neighbouring cities to the north-east, converting them both into important military outposts of their empire and major centres of Islamic culture and learning. Commercial and artistic life flourished in Otrar, as well as in Samarkand, and Bukhara, and everywhere new ideas in philosophy, music, and art began to take root. The most prominent exponent of the new era of intellectual growth and creativity was Al-Farabi, born in Otrar in 870, and renowned as a philosopher, astronomer, musician, mathematician, botanist, and doctor. Al-Farabi was known to his students as 'the second teacher', meaning second only to Aristotle, and his reputation extended far beyond the deserts of southern Kazakhstan. The Samanid empire reached its peak in the first half of the tenth century by which time it extended from the Caspian Sea in the west to the shores of Lake Balkhash in the east. This was a period of significant developments in art and architecture, and in the building of mosques, palaces, caravanserais, and elaborate monuments and lavish mausoleums dedicated to writers and poets. All this was in sharp contrast to the simple lives of nomadic communities, whose traditional practice had been not to leave any trace of their presence, and whose history was kept alive through oral traditions. Political stability under the Samanids brought economic growth and prosperity, stimulating the expansion of trade, both locally and further afield, and the mining and trading of valuable minerals, especially silver, gold, and jade from the Ferghana Valley in present-day Kyrgyzstan. The most enduring feature of the Samanid dynasty was the spread of Islam, which due to the work of missionaries became widely accepted amongst the Turkic population not only in the south but also in northern regions of the steppes beyond the realms of the Samanid empire.

But it was religion which presented the most serious threat to the survival of the Samanid dynasty, when in the middle of the tenth century the political stability and cohesion of the regime was undermined by theological schisms dividing the different sects of Islam. Religious disputes were compounded by yet more internecine strife and military conflicts within the dynasty. Local rulers who had earlier been entrusted with a significant degree of autonomy now used the power bases which they had built up over the years to pursue their own interests, often in opposition to the ruling family. By the end of the tenth century another empire under the Karakhanid tribe was emerging in the Semirechie region to the east. In 999 the Karakhanids advanced westwards and captured Bukhara, the Samanid capital, and overthrew the Samanid dynasty. After little more than a hundred years the Samanids ceased to exist as a political entity, although they left a rich legacy in southern Kazakhstan and Central Asia, not only in religion but in many fields of human endeavour and achievement unrelated to war and conquest.

The empire of the Karakhanids was more a grouping of individual khans and clans than a stable political state, and as such it contained the roots of its own demise. Centred in the Semirechie, it extended as far west as Talas until 1040, when a member of the ruling family, Ibrahim bin Nasr, declared himself to be the supreme ruler and set up his capital still further west in Samarkand. This action effectively divided the empire into two parts: the Eastern Karakhanids who remained in Semirechie, and the Western Karakhanids, who under bin Nasr turned their attention back to the east, where they launched a series of campaigns designed to establish full control over the entire empire. Tashkent, Talas, and the Ferghana Valley were all subdued by bin Nasr, but these victories proved temporary, and feuding continued between western and eastern khanates. Ultimately the Karakhanids failed to establish any enduring stability or permanence. In the east the nomadic khans had no fixed base and were vulnerable to attacks from Mongol tribes sweeping through the Ili Gap, while in the west the Seljuk sultanate emanating from Turkey established control over a vast territory around the Aral Sea. A degree of stability and cohesion was brought to southern Kazakhstan when Akhmed Yasavi, a philosopher, teacher, and poet, became the leading exponent of Sufism, a mystical form of early Islam which in the twelfth century was spreading throughout Central Asia. In the ancient city of Turkestan* (formerly known as Shavgar) on the Syr Darya River, Akhmed Yasavi established himself as a spiritual leader unifying the disparate tribes and khanates, and creating a harmony from the different religious beliefs swirling through the region at the time. He was widely revered by ordinary people, writing and speaking in the local Turkic language and able to convey profound philosophical ideas in simple words understandable by everyone. After his death in 1166, a majestic mausoleum was constructed to house his tomb, alongside a richly-decorated *khanaka,* or meeting place, where people could gather for collective prayer and meditation. The azure blue dome of the khanaka in Turkestan, eighteen metres in diameter, is the largest in Central Asia, and the khanaka and mausoleum have become places of pilgrimage for thousands of people throughout the region and from around the world. The enduring legacy of Akhmed Yasavi is that Islam is still a force throughout much of present-day Kazakhstan, and has survived many vicissitudes over the centuries, not least the decades of oppression during the Soviet era of the twentieth century.

Despite the stabilising influence and growing spiritual unity brought about by Akhmed Yasavi, by the middle of the twelfth century the Seljuk Empire in Central Asia was collapsing and was succeeded by the small and prosperous principality of Khwarezm, a region to the south of the Aral Sea. The rulers of Khwarezm extended their control over much of south-western Kazakhstan, and in 1216 its khan Mohammad II conquered the city of Jend, near the present-day Kazalinsk, on the Syr Darya River, and invaded the lands of the steppe tribes to the north. These actions brought him into fatal contact with invading Mongol armies from the east, in what was to become the next phase in the history of Central Asia.

By contrast in the north of the country, the pastoral way of life of the nomadic people meanwhile continued on the Eurasian steppe, largely untouched and undisturbed by the ebb and flow of transient empires and feuding khanates in the south. The tribes of

---

*The city of Turkestan later lost its importance as a regional centre but gave its name to the vast region of Turkestan extending from the Aral Sea to the Tien Shan Mountains.

the northern region united into the early feudal states of the Kipchaks in the west and the Kimaks in the north and east, but there was little of the violent conflict between rival armies and khans, or of the artistic and cultural achievements under the Samanid dynasty, that characterised the history of the south during this time. The nomadic tribes and remote communities in the north of the country had little, if any, awareness of life beyond their migration routes, and what they may have heard of developments in the cities probably had little attraction for them, having little relevance to their own itinerant and pastoral traditions. They were even further removed from awareness of the outside world which may have come through the Silk Road, the great trading and commercial network which brought at least parts of southern Kazakhstan into contact with Europe and with China.

The establishment of the Turkic khanate in the eighth century, and later of the Islamic empire in Central Asia, served to revitalise trade along the Silk Road. The Silk Road already had an ancient history; according to the Greek geographer Ptolemy, the original Silk Road started in the first century AD at Antioch on the Mediterranean coast, and extended through Iraq and Persia, south of the Caspian Sea to Kashgar in western China. Other historians assert that the Silk Road emerged even earlier, in the second century BC, when Chinese traders attempted to reach the Mediterranean Sea by means of the long overland route through Central Asia. Traders travelling from west to east, before the Silk Road reached Kashgar, could either take a southern route at Samarkand, to continue through Osh in present-day Kyrgyzstan, and from there further south of the Tien Shan Mountains and the Taklamakan Desert and into China; alternatively a northern route from Samarkand ran through Talas (which became known as the City of Merchants), Bishkek, Almaty, along the northern foothills of the Tien Shan Mountains, and through the Ili Gap into China. Caravanserais were established at intervals along the route, providing shade and lodgings, stables, and stores, and it was the charred ruins of one such resting place that was found by Russian soldiers when they arrived in the area in 1853. By the eleventh century a new route had emerged connecting the Volga River in Russia, through western Kazakhstan, to Otrar on the Syr Darya River, opening up a market in the east for Russian furs and sable, and providing an outlet through eastern Europe for goods from China and Central Asia in the west. Between the sixth and ninth centuries, relative political stability and rising living standards in the towns and cities promoted a growing two-way trade in the vast territory between China and the Mediterranean. From the east came silk and textiles, as well as jade, precious stones and jewels, porcelain, paper, weapons, and salt; in the other direction went manufactured items and leather goods, glass, gold, silver, horses, raisins, nuts, honey, spices, and all types of exotic foodstuffs, as well as slaves and concubines. An extensive network of regional trade routes and intermediary markets developed, where goods were bought and sold before being despatched to their eventual buyers, and where sophisticated trading, banking, and credit systems were introduced and developed, alongside the bazaars and chaikhanas of Samarkand, Bukhara, and Tashkent.

The Silk Road not only encouraged the growth of trade and commerce but also allowed an inflow of new ideas in science and art. This had special significance in Central Asia, cut off by immense distances and geographical barriers from other contact with the outside world. New movements in religion, philosophy, music, and art, flowed in and flourished, and had a profound effect on the social and intellectual development of the region. As well as trade in goods and ideas, the Silk Road provided a conduit for the exchange of diplomatic messages and documents between east and west, and a means of conducting political, economic, and military surveys for the enlightenment of rulers and governments in Europe and China. But for much of the territory of Kazakhstan, the Silk Road had little significance. Its influence was confined to a narrow strip in the extreme south and east of the country, mostly in the Semirechie region, and the impact on the rest of the country of trade and commerce and of new ideas in art and music, was very limited. The present-day cities of Almaty and Bishkek publicise the tourist attraction of the route of the Silk Road on which they stand. But as had happened with the empires of the Samanids and Khamanids, the vast distances of steppe and desert separated the Kazakh herdsmen and nomads, whose traditional migration routes did not extend this far south, from the markets and bazaars, the caravansaries and meeting places of the Silk Road. Life on the steppe retained its ancient and tranquil pace, largely oblivious to the outside world. Elsewhere the Silk Road retained its essential characteristics and functions up to the sixteenth century, before it went into inevitable and irreversible decline. The discovery of the sea route between Europe and south-east Asia removed the need to travel long distances over land, while political strife and conflict between warring khans along its route added to the dangers for travellers, and destroyed many of the bazaars and caravanserais.

CHAPTER FOUR

Otrar: Siege and Destruction under Genghis Khan

By the early thirteenth century, the period of artistic creativity and development, and the expansion of trade and commerce along the Silk Road, came under a new threat from the east in the form of the Mongol empire under its warrior leader Genghis Khan. For Kazakhstan, the most traumatic episode of this period involved the siege and annihilation of the ancient Silk Road city of Otrar, and the massacre of its inhabitants, by the armies of Genghis Khan in 1219. This devastating event is now commemorated in Kazakhstan by monuments, exhibitions, and in the names of public buildings and hotels, as an act of war and terror against an innocent population. But most accounts of the period relate that what took place was not without provocation on the part of the local sultan Mohammad II of the Khwarezm empire, who led his army into a futile battle against the forces of Genghis Khan, leading to the destruction of Otrar and culminating in the end of the Khwarezm empire.

In 1218 the Mongol armies of Genghis Khan descended through the Ili Gap and overwhelmed the khanates of the Semirechie region which mostly surrendered without resistance. From there Genghis continued to sweep westwards and annexed the whole of eastern Turkestan, including the Ili, Issyk Kul, Chu, and Talas regions to the Mongol empire. Further west Mohammad II had greatly extended the empire of Khwarezm from its original territory around the Aral Sea, westwards to the Caspian Sea and southern Russia, and east to the cities of Samarkand, Bukhara, and Otrar on the Syr Darya River, which had become the easternmost point of the empire. Khwarezm was now an immediate neighbour of the Mongol empire of Genghis Khan.

Apart from the religious differences – Khwarezm was Islamic, the eastern part of the Muslim world, while the Mongols, to the extent that they practised any religion, were Buddhist or shamanist – the two rulers were also in complete contrast to each other. Genghis Khan was a ruthless military leader, but was also prudent, tenacious, and methodical; Mohammad was vain and disorganised, and his leadership was divisive and erratic. After years of campaigns and conquests in northern China and having established a vast and unchallenged empire stretching from Mongolia to Europe, Genghis Khan was now said to be reluctant to engage in further warfare. Unwilling to over-extend his resources he preferred to pursue more peaceful activities and relations with neighbouring states. Mohammad had rejected earlier approaches to build up commercial links, but in 1218 Genghis made another attempt to strengthen relations and sent a caravan of about one hundred traders and merchants to Otrar. As a diplomatic gesture the caravan consisted entirely of Muslims. But in an act of foolishness the governor of Otrar, a provocative man named Inalchik, with the complicity of Mohammad, had all the traders put to death, supposedly on the grounds that they were spies. This may have had some basis in reality but the execution of Genkhis Khan's emissaries was bound to have severe consequences. The action prompted Genghis to send another team of three envoys to Mohammad with a demand that he should disclaim what had been done and hand over Inalchik to face Mongol justice. Mohammad refused to comply; instead he murdered two of the envoys and sent the third back to Genghis Khan with his beard shaven, another severe provocation and fatal misjudgement which was to lead to disastrous conflict with Genghis Khan and eventually to the end of the Khwarezm empire.

In the autumn of 1219 Genghis Khan gathered a vast army of between 100,000 and 150,000 men on the desert plains of Semirechie east of Lake Balkhash and around the Ili River, where he attracted additional troops from the khanates in the region which had been conquered the previous year. Despite its size the Mongol army was greatly outnumbered by the even more numerous Khwarezm forces, but the Mongolian soldiers were better disciplined and better motivated. The Khwarezm army included large numbers of mercenaries recruited from a wide range of recalcitrant tribes on the remote steppes who had no special loyalty to Mohammad, and many of whom wanted to change sides and join the army of Genghis Khan. The leadership and tactics employed by the Mongol forces were far superior to those of Khwarezm, where the advantage of greater numbers was outweighed by lack of cohesion, discipline, and motivation. Mohammad divided and scattered his troops so that despite their numerical superiority they were outnumbered at individual points along the frontier, where they were subject to attack and breakthrough by the Mongol army. One such breakthrough occurred near the city of Otrar. Genghis delegated the task of taking the city to two of his sons, Jagatai and Occodai. The defence of the city was led by Inalchik, whose earlier actions had provoked the original conflict. The inhabitants of Otrar held out against a prolonged siege lasting five months, during which time the armies of Jagatai and Occodai used the new siege technology of scaling ladders, battering rams, and four-wheeled mobile shields developed in earlier Mongol campaigns in China. In the end the city was destroyed and its inhabitants were either killed or taken for transportation to Mongolia. Inalchik was captured and according to contemporary accounts, was killed by molten silver poured into his eyes and ears. The Mongol armies moved on and the ruins of Otrar eventually disappeared in the sands of the desert, but the story of the city survives in contemporary legend as a symbol of heroic resistance to a merciless invader. The siege of Otrar also had historical significance beyond its immediate impact. By demonstrating that, unlike the Huns and other empires of the steppe, they could successfully take any city by means of siege warfare and the military skills perfected in earlier conflicts, the Mongols showed they were even more dangerous to towns and cities, and ensured that the nomadic tribes of northern Kazakhstan had even less desire to seek any form of permanent settlement.

After taking Otrar, Genghis Khan and his sons proceeded to capture and raze to the ground other major cities of the Khwarezm empire, notably Bukhara, Samarkand, and Urgench. Urgench was formerly the Khwarezm capital, but which was destroyed by flooding in 1221 when Mongol soldiers broke the dams on the Amu Darya River on which the city had stood. By far the worst loss of life was suffered in Merv, another ancient city which more than six centuries later was to experience another devastation during the Russian colonization of Central Asia. In every case the local inhabitants were either massacred or, if they had a useful trade or skill, deported to Mongolia. Mohammad escaped from the death and destruction which he had helped to bring about, and fled to an island on the Caspian Sea where he is said to have died alone and unlamented. Years later, after the death of Genghis Khan, Otrar slowly recovered from the devastation of 1219, and eventually became an important economic and political centre once again. Commerce expanded and the town minted its own coins with which to promote the growth of trade and business. Over the coming centuries Otrar continued to flourish and became part of Tamerlane's empire in the fourteenth century, and was where Tamerlane died in 1405. But it never fully regained its earlier prominence or prosperity, and by the middle of the eighteenth century, together with other towns along the Syr Darya River, it had fallen into decline. Marauding raids by Dzungarian tribes from the east in the 1720s, combined with continuous internal strife between local khans which prevented any effective defence, ensured that Otrar was eventually doomed. By the early nineteenth century what had once been a world-famous seat of learning and centre of art and commerce had become a deserted ruin.

Genghis Khan died in 1227 near Pingliang in western China, and his body was transported to Mongolia where it was buried near what was believed to be a sacred mountain at the source of the Kerulen River. Mongol law required that the youngest son, Tolui, should become responsible for guardianship of the ancestral homelands on the death of his father, and should act as regent until the election of a new grand khan. Tolui received all the tented palaces which constituted the Mongol court, and the vast majority, over 100,000 men, of Genghis Khan's army. The rest of the army was divided between his father's other sons and brothers. It was not until nearly two years after the death of Genghis Khan, in the spring of 1229, that an assembly of Mongolian princes met on the banks of the Kerulen River, in an empty land of forests, mountains, and rivers, to appoint a successor. In the event, this had already been decided by Genghis Khan himself, who had chosen his third son Occodai to succeed him, and the meeting of the gathered princes did little more than to confirm this decision.

Since his death Genghis Khan has been regarded as the personification of destruction and terror, which under him had become a system of government. He rejected all forms of agricultural and urban economy in favour of the austere life of the plains. He was dismayed at the prospect that his descendants would adopt a more peaceful and settled way of life, more concerned with the best food, the most glamorous costumes, and the fastest horses, than with the rigorous Mongol traditions of hunting and destroying settled communities in towns and cities which did not immediately surrender to him. The siege of Otrar and the massacre of its population were devastating and traumatic events, as was to a lesser extent the destruction of the caravanserais and trading settlements along the northern foothills of the Tien Shan Mountains. But apart from Otrar, there were no significant towns or communities of any size elsewhere in the territory of what became Kazakhstan, which could have offered resistance. Moreover the nomadic way of life of the Kazakh population was more in keeping with Genghis Khan's own outlook on the world, and most accounts of the period show little impact of the Mongol empire on the life of pastoral communities on the steppe. Despite being absorbed by the Mongol empire and ruled over by the sons and descendants of Genghis Khan, Kazakhstan avoided the deep-rooted fear of the Mongols, which later became a profound psychological feature over many centuries in Russia and other vanquished territories.

On his death the empire of Genghis Khan was divided between his four sons: Jochi, Jagatai, Occodai, and Tolui. During Genghis' lifetime each of his sons had been allocated an *ulus,* or group of tribes and family communities, together with a yurt, originally meaning an area of pasture and grazing land sufficient to support the people living there.

Each yurt consisted of groups of *gers,* in each of which lived a family of about five to eight people. Communities of gers gathered together to divide labour and form a camp, or yurt, although the word yurt (except in Mongolia) came to replace ger as meaning the tents in which people lived. This became the universal form of dwelling among the nomadic communities of Mongolia and Kazakhstan, and its practicality has been demonstrated by its unchanging design over succeeding centuries to the present day. The Mongolian camps were generally much larger than those elsewhere in Central Asia and contained many more tribes and families. The most palatial tent, in which lived the ruler of the tribe, was known in Mongolian as an *ordon,* which became the origin of the Mongolian, and subsequently Kazakh 'hordes'. Originally applied to mean a whole community, in a further change of meaning, the word later came to signify marauding tribes and armies.

The eldest son, Jochi, had died six months before Genghis Khan, and the relationship between Genghis and Jochi had long been strained since it was not certain that Genghis Khan was in fact their father. When Jochi died, in early 1227 in western Kazakhstan near the Aral Sea, Genghis, far from any feeling of paternal bereavement, was thought to be relieved that a potential conspirator no longer presented a threat to his leadership. Jagatai, the second son, was regarded as an effective soldier and administrator, but he was unimaginative and lacked the leadership qualities needed to ensure the stability and continuation of the empire. Occodai, by contrast, was held to be a sensible and wise choice as a successor, unlikely to be challenged by others, and he supervised the distribution of territory under the empire on his accession. The regions of what is now northern and western Kazakhstan were to have been given to Jochi; Mongol tradition held that the land bequeathed to the eldest son should be the furthest away from the centre of the empire, which was located in Siberia between the Onon and Kerulen Rivers. Thus the land acquired by Jochi was a vast swathe of territory west of the River Irtysh in Siberia, and including the areas around Semipalatinsk, Akmola, and extending westwards to Aktyubinsk on the Caspian Sea and as far south to Khiva in Uzbekistan. In the event, control of this territory went to Jochi's son Batu, who established his own capital at Sarai, north of the Caspian Sea. His armies became known as the Golden Horde, believed to be because of the colour of their tents. Batu subsequently assigned part of his territory to the north and east of the Aral Sea to his brother Orda, whose armies were known as the White Horde. In Mongolian accounts Batu is described as a 'wise and gentle prince, and a good khan', although later he became known in Russia as a ruthless conqueror, instrumental in the destruction in 1235 of Moscow and of other

Russian cities and principalities. But given the doubt surrounding the legitimacy of his father, Batu did not achieve any great prominence in the Mongol empire; instead the predominant role was held for many years by his more statesmanlike uncle Occodai. Jagatai, the second son, was given control of an even greater land area, stretching from western China into southern Kazakhstan and the Ili region, as well as the mountains around Lake Issyk-Kul, and further west to Bokhara and Samarkand. Occodai himself had control of eastern Kazakhstan, to the east of Lake Balkhash, and much of present-day Mongolia. The fourth son Tolui, was given land much further east in Siberia, in the vast forested regions around Lake Baikal. This was also in accordance with Mongol custom which held that the youngest son was to be heir to the ancestral lands of the Mongol empire. Tolui is said to have been an able and ambitious soldier, but he died a premature death in 1232 at the age of forty due to excessive alcohol consumption. His wife, a princess from a local tribe, assumed control of the region from Tolui after his death and ensured some stability and security in the region.

After this division of the lands of Genghis Khan, his successors paid little attention to settlement or domestic life in Kazakhstan, or any of the inherited territories. Instead their outlook turned once again to campaigning and warfare, now mainly directed against Russian towns and principalities to the west. Moscow was burnt to the ground in 1235, and Suzdal, Vladimir, Kiev, and other cities suffered a similar violent fate in the following years. By 1241, the Mongols under Genghis Khan's grandson Batu had advanced westwards and had established camps in the woods around Vienna; having left a trail of devastation and destruction in Ukraine, Poland, and Hungary, they were now poised to invade western Europe. At this point news of the death of his uncle Occodai reached Batu, having taken about six weeks to arrive from Karakorum in western Mongolia where Occodai had made his capital. The Mongolian armies abandoned their positions, ostensibly so as to be present at the election of a successor, and this development is seen as almost certainly having saved Europe from a fate similar to that which had befallen every other territory threatened with invasion by the successors of Genghis Khan. But there were already divisions forming between the sons of Genghis Khan, now without the steadying influence of Occodai, and Batu was concerned that to be absent from crucial developments following the death of his uncle would not have been strategically wise. The khan chosen to succeed Occodai was his brother Mangu; although Mangu no longer pursued hostilities against Europe, he was unable to prevent the eventual dissolution of the Mongol empire into a number of autonomous khanates or principalities.

The existing khanates, in particular the khanate under Jagatai in southern and eastern Kazakhstan, had shown little sign of stability, and the population had no concept of living in a settled state or of the development of urban life. The Jagatai khanate was the most traditional and least independent of the territories which had been allocated amongst the sons of Genghis Khan, partly because of its proximity to the Mongol capital in Karakorum in the west of present-day Mongolia. The other more distant khanates pursued their own paths, although in practice development was virtually static and all shared the same essential characteristics. In none of the individual khanates was there any historical background to allow for the evolution of laws and other social structures, nor was there any desire or motivation to seek a different or more settled way of life. Instead the various populations continued to practice simple nomadic and pastoral traditions, although in the Jagatai territory these were by no means entirely peaceful and included more war-like tendencies of attacking the cities of Samarkand and Bokhara, even though these were within the Jagatai khanate itself. The result was that the development of a more stable society and a more durable economy was severely impeded. A similar situation prevailed in the west of the country in the region around the Caspian Sea which had been ceded to Batu. As had happened in earlier centuries, almost the whole of Kazakhstan was again effectively isolated from the stabilising influences of the more progressive social and economic developments taking place in China to the east and Europe to the west. By the time of the birth of Tamerlane in 1336, the Jagatai khanate in eastern Kazakhstan had split into two territories, of Mogholistan in the north around Lake Balkhash, and consisting mainly of steppe and mountains, and Transoxiana in the south, consisting of deserts and plains to the west of the Oxus River, corresponding roughly to present-day Uzbekistan.

Tamerlane (Timur Lenk, or Timur the Lame) was born in Kesh, near Samarkand, and throughout his adult life he suffered a limp as a result of arrow wounds received at an early age. These handicaps did not impede his rise to power, an ascent which resulted from his ability to lead armies and to engage in campaigns and warfare against opposing khans. In the short term his methods were successful in building an empire based on terror and destruction; but in the longer term these methods contained the seeds of insecurity and instability, and led to the eventual collapse of the empire which did not endure after his death. At the age of 20 Tamerlane married a young girl named Sultanat, the daughter of a local emir, but rather than stay at home he joined with Sultanat's brother Mir Husain to campaign as a mercenary in Persia and Transoxiana. It was during these adventures that Tamerlane received two arrow wounds, in the shoulder and in the thigh, which gave him the name by which he has been known throughout history. In 1363, in a campaign conducted with Mir Husain, Tamerlane freed his homeland of Transoxiana from the Mongol-Jagatai khanate, forcing the Mongol rulers to retreat to the Ili region in the east of the country. Local tradition dictated that Tamerlane, as previous conquerors before him, needed a local figurehead from among the Mongol-Jagatai khans so as to legitimise and lend authority to his rule. The individual chosen on this occasion was a minor official named Kabil-Shah, a reclusive relation of a local lord; he was appointed as the new khan of Transoxiana and given a throne and the outward appearances of power, and then subsequently ignored (and later murdered) by Tamerlane. This procedure was a relatively straightforward takeover of control from the individual khanates under the Mongol empire of Genghis Khan, which by then was in decline from its earlier all-pervading supremacy. However the success in liberating their own country was overshadowed by a deepening feud between Tamerlane and Husain. Conflict had existed between the two already, as Husain was thought to be secretly in league with the Mongols; now they disputed who should be the supreme ruler of Transoxiana. The rift became complete on the premature death of Sultanat, Husain's sister, in 1370, after which Tamerlane turned his forces on Husain. Husain was forced to surrender and to relinquish his power, and subsequently embarked on a pilgrimage to Mecca. En route he was murdered, supposedly without the knowledge of Tamerlane, although it seems likely that this was the final step in Tamerlane achieving complete control over Transoxiana. Tamerlane had disposed of Kabil-Shah, the puppet figure appointed in accordance with Mongol tradition, and now installed his own khan to govern the territory on his behalf.

Although marred by the murder of his former ally, the successful outcome of the Transoxiana campaign was the exception rather than the rule under Tamerlane. He tried to emulate Genghis Khan but his campaigning was haphazard and erratic, and lacked the clear strategy and cohesion of his Mongol predecessor. In 1371 Tamerlane embarked on two simultaneous campaigns which exemplified his method of empire-building. First he launched an unsuccessful attack against the Mongol khan of Mogholistan to the east, intended to bring the territory under his control, but this failed when his opponent used the well-tried Mongol tactic of withdrawing and disappearing into the depths of the steppe. Tamerlane then turned his attention in the opposite direction to the neighbouring empire of Khwarezm, which he intended to consolidate with Transoxiana. He besieged the capital city of Urgench, which was eventually captured and the population massacred; Khwarezm thus became part of the Tamerlane empire, but not before Tamerlane had returned to Lake Balkhash in a further unsuccessful attempt to annex Mogholistan.

In 1376, a Mongol khan named Toktamish, from the White Horde north of the Aral Sea and a descendant of the Jochi branch of the khanate of Genghis Khan, emerged as a challenger to Tamerlane, despite Tamerlane having earlier helped him gain the throne of the White Horde. Toktamish was not regarded as a great military leader, but he now sought to extend his authority and gain control of the Golden Horde - the Mongol empire of southern Russia. In a major battle near the Sea of Azov, he succeeded in uniting the Golden and White Hordes, accounting for almost the whole of the early Jochi domain. By seizing control of this vast region, Toktamish had emerged as one of the most powerful Mongol khans of the time. Initially he turned his attention to renewed expeditions against the Christian principalities of Russia, and destroyed Moscow, Vladimir, and other cities in 1382-83, cities which were still recovering from the devastation under Genghis Khan in the previous century. But thereafter his main objective was to achieve supremacy over Tamerlane, who he saw as lacking in any authentic claim or title to Mongol lands, compared to his own direct lineage from Genghis Khan. Moreover he resented the fact that Tamerlane had in 1386 annexed Azerbaijan to his empire, since this was historically regarded as part of the rightful territory of the Mongol khans.

In 1387 while Tamerlane was in Armenia, Toktamish led a small army through the Derbent Pass on the western shore of the Caspian Sea, and launched a sudden attack on his former benefactor. Toktamish had gravely misjudged the strength of Tamerlane's armies, and after a brief battle was driven back to the steppe. But instead of following Toktamish and ensuring he could no longer mount any further attacks, Tamerlane – who was concentrating on other ventures in Armenia and Persia – let him escape unharmed. Such an action would never have occurred under Genghis Khan. Eventually Tamerlane defeated Toktamish in a major battle in western Kazakhstan on the Ural River near the Aral Sea. By achieving this victory Tamerlane virtually destroyed the Golden Horde of Toktamish, but he neglected to consolidate his gains, and instead simply divided the conquered territory among various Mongol princes whom he erroneously imagined would be loyal to him. This error of judgement allowed Toktamish to resume his campaigns, and led Tamerlane to mount a further expedition against him in 1395, leading an army northwards from Azerbaijan, rather than across the plains of northern Kazakhstan. During this campaign Tamerlane demolished the cities of Astrakhan and

Sarai, the capital of the Golden Horde near the mouth of the Volga River. Eventually Toktamish was deprived of all his earlier power and status, and was obliged to seek refuge in Lithuania, before ultimately fleeing to Siberia. Tamerlane had succeeded in neutralizing any further challenge from Toktamish, who no longer presented any threat to his supremacy.

Similar tactics, of ad hoc response to specific developments rather than as part of a planned strategy, characterised much of Tamerlane's activities. His campaigns in Russia, the Caucasus, and elsewhere in Central Asia, were marked by the absence of clear and coherent planning, which was a prominent feature under Genghis Khan. Often there was no arrangement made for the control of conquered territories, and on several occasions Tamerlane had to re-conquer land already gained. The result was that the empire he built up suffered from deep-seated weaknesses and inherent instability. In 1389, a more decisive campaign was waged against Mongol domination of the Ili region south of Lake Balkhash. This time Tamerlane was more successful and Mongol princes and nomads were driven from the region. Tamerlane thereby became the supreme ruler of Central Asia, and sought to present himself as the rightful successor to Genghis Khan. But the Mongol empire of Genghis Khan, although built on ruthless territorial conquests and destruction of cities, was underpinned by an ethnic and social framework of nomadism; this was all the more stable for being simple and based on established traditions. Tamerlane had no such basis to support him or his attempts to extend his empire, and much of his efforts were directed in opposition to the traditions of nomadism and Mongol beliefs. Instead he spent much of his time speeding back and forth across his territories to deal with numerous crises and uprisings, rather than imposing complete control at the outset.

Tamerlane died in Otrar in 1405 at the age of seventy one, while preparing an invasion of China. On his death not only did the invasion not take place, but the prospect of new conquests evaporated, and earlier victories, and the empire which he had built up, began to unravel. Conflicts and wars broke out among the various component territories, ultimately leading to the dissolution of the empire, as had happened after the death of Attila nearly one thousand years earlier. Tamerlane is remembered mainly for the vast scale on which he operated on the steppes in warfare and conquest, in campaigning against neighbouring territories, but with no interest in consolidation of gains or strategy for the future. Under Tamerlane, destruction for its own sake acquired a form of quasi-religious zeal, combining Mongol barbarity with Muslim fanaticism.

Consequently Tamerlane is regarded more as an extreme form of warrior of the steppes rather than a successful empire-builder. In the end his enduring achievements were few, and by destroying the main trading cities of the Golden Horde, Tamerlane had dealt a paralysing blow to trade between Europe and Central Asia, further reinforcing the isolation of Kazakhstan, and retarding its commercial and social development.

CHAPTER FIVE

Abul Khair, Kasim Khan, and the Birth of the Kazakh State

The structure of the Mongol empire - such was the enduring legacy of Genghis Khan - was still in evidence at the time of the death of Tamerlane. Mongol power and influence did not disappear for many years, and although many of the original families and descendants of Genghis Khan had died out, other Mongol tribes and princes - who may have been overlooked in the two centuries since the death of Genghis Khan but who still inhabited the northern steppes - emerged to take their place. The most prominent was Abul Khair, a young warlord who claimed descent from Jochi, the eldest son of Genghis Khan. In 1428, at the age of seventeen, Abul Khair was proclaimed khan of his horde in southern Siberia, and soon afterwards seized control of extensive territories from neighbouring khanates and princes. By around the 1450s he had achieved sufficient status and influence to put an end to the tribal conflicts and power struggles between rival clans which had been prevalent throughout the region, especially in the south of the country, and had re-established an empire of tribes and hordes known as Ozbegs. This became known as the Uzbek khanate and extended over much of the territory between the Caspian Sea and Lake Balkhash, territory which later became Kazakhstan. But the khanate was not sufficiently strong or stable to survive, and although Abul Khair attempted to unite the various tribes and nomadic clans, and establish a semi-sedentary empire based at Signakhi, on the Syr Darya River not far from the ancient city of Otrar, he was unable to repel the onslaught of successive attacks from other more ruthless tribes, less wedded to the idea of a sedentary life.

Abul Khair himself had seized lands from other princes who claimed descent from Genghis Khan, and he himself was proud of his own Mongol ancestry. But he was now subject to attack from Mongol invaders from the east, and lost considerable territory and authority as a consequence. In addition, in the west the Golden Horde, which had been severely weakened by Tamerlane, still roamed the grasslands and prairies of southern Russia and around the Caspian Sea, but was effectively disintegrating into separate khanates, each with its own leader and identity. However Abul Khair was undermined mainly by the defection of some of his own tribes, and historically the most significant development occurred between about 1465-66, when large numbers of nomad clans broke away from the Uzbek khanate, rejecting the more settled way of life which Abul Khair had sought to impose, and seeking greater independence and freedom of movement for themselves and their herds. After their separation from Abul Khair and his khanate, these nomads became known as Qazaqs, or Kazakhs. *Kazakh* is variously translated as 'adventurer', 'rebel', 'free', or 'independent', and has the same root as *Cossack*, the nomadic hunter and horseman who roamed the plains of southern Russia and who had much in common with the Mongol Hordes. This included coping with the harsh and dangerous life of the steppe, and a disdain for any form of settled agriculture which was regarded as unworthy of their status as independent steppe dwellers. The secession of the Kazakhs was of considerable historic importance: not only from the point of view of the land which they occupied, which incorporated much of the territory of present-day Kazakhstan, but also from their designation for the first time as Kazakhs, or *Kirghiz-Kazakhs* as they were originally known. Abul Khair did not allow the Kazakhs to secede from his khanate without a struggle, but he was killed in battle in 1468 while trying to bring them back under his control. What remained of the Uzbek khanate dissolved a few years later.

It is from this time, in the period after the death of Abul Khair and between the late 1400s and early 1500s that the first indications of an identifiable Kazakh state began to emerge. A process of consolidation among the nomadic Kazakh tribes, evolving from a shared way of life and common view of the world, and encouraged by the failure of Abul Khair to incorporate them in the Uzbek khanate, had already begun. The Kirghiz-Kazakhs attempted to form a purely nomadic state in around 1471, and the first use of the name of Kazakhstan, for a khanate in the western part of the Semirechie region between the Chu and Talas Rivers, appears in about 1480. During the reign of Kasim Khan, from 1503 to 1518, the main Kazakh tribes of the region - the Kipchaks, Naimans, Usuns, and Dulats - were brought together for the first time, and it is Kasim who is usually regarded as the founder of a unified Kazakh khanate. He claimed descent, as Abul Khair and others before him had done, from Genghis Khan's son Jochi, and under his leadership the khanate established itself as a strong and independent entity. It gradually extended its authority from Semirechie westwards, to incorporate the southern regions of Otrar and Turkestan south of the Aral Sea, while consolidating its influence and power in its home territory in the Semirechie region. In the summer months Kasim established his headquarters in the ancient city of Turkestan on the Syr Darya River, while in winter he stayed in what was his original home in the Karatal valley, one of the 'seven rivers', just south of Lake Balkhash.

During this period the consolidation of the Kazakh tribes, and the evolution of a distinct Kazakh identity, began to take hold. The process was encouraged by the emergence of folklore and traditional epics and other forms of literature, which were now being spread throughout the region by itinerant bards and story tellers, using dialects which were intelligible to wider groups of people. But while the disparate tribes were coming together as a recognisable ethnic group, Kasim was trying to dismantle the feudal structure of nomadic life and society, and impose his own leadership and authority. In this he was not entirely successful, and paradoxically achieved greater success in strengthening the military capability, and with it the sense of independence, of each of the tribes. But the main source of weakness in the emerging Kazakh khanate was the lack of any physical base or permanent foundation. Neither the summer capital at Turkestan, nor the winter settlement at Karatal, was regarded as a viable centre of an expanding empire, and in reality Kasim was more of a nomad himself than a leader or nation builder. His reign was a time of great geographical expansion of the territory of the Kirghiz-Kazakh tribes, but a contemporary account reports him as saying: 'We are the men of the steppe; all our wealth consists of horses; their flesh is our favourite food, mare's milk is our favourite drink. Houses we have none. Our chief diversion is to inspect our flocks and our herds of horses.'* This view reflected the traditional values of the pastoral and itinerant communities, in which the need to establish the basis for a secure and independent state was a low priority. Kasim was to discover, as Abul Khair had before him, the impossibility of reconciling traditional nomadism with the demands of a stable and static, or partially static, empire. His admission that 'houses we have none' fatally undermined any serious attempt to ensure a lasting presence, and highlighted another paradox of life on the steppe. Whereas the Scythians and other earlier empires had endured for centuries precisely because they had no permanent settlement, and thus avoided subjugation by hostile tribes from other lands, the absence of a strong focal point was now proving to be a weakness rather than a strength. Three hundred years before Kasim, Genghis Khan had created a vast and mighty empire in Central Asia, but over the following centuries the more usual experience was that any attempt to impose a permanent structure among the nomadic people of Kazakhstan was doomed to fail.

Kasim Khan died in 1518, by which time such unity as he had managed to achieve was disintegrating, as the various family groups resisted further unification and broke away from any form of central control. It was during the years soon after Kasim's death that

---

*Quoted by Rene Grousset, *The Empire of the Steppes*.

the three Kazakh 'hordes'- the broad groups of clans and tribes that were to characterize Kazakh society for the next three hundred years - began to emerge. Each horde was ruled by its own khan, although other leaders and sultans often competed for supremacy. When not engaged in internal struggles, the tribes of each horde came together on a voluntary basis, unlike the earlier unsuccessful attempts by Abul Khair and Kasim Khan to achieve unity through force; and whereas earlier clan groups had coalesced around individual leaders, the new hordes were based on loosely-defined but separate geographical regions of the country. In the west the Little Horde *(Kishi Zhuz)* occupied a vast area around the Aral and Caspian Seas, while the Middle Horde *(Orta Zhuz)* emerged in an equally wide region of central Kazakhstan, between the Ural River in the north-west and the Irtysh River in the north-east. The area to the south and east of Lake Balkhash was held by the Dzungar tribes. The boundaries were imprecise and in many areas overlapped, but territorial disputes between the different hordes were generally avoided.

The names of each horde do not reflect the extent of the territory which they occupied, and indeed the Little Horde possibly extended over the largest land area, whereas the Great Horde occupied a relatively small area; the Russian designations (Youngest, Middle, and Oldest) reflect the stages in which each horde came into recognisable existence. This division of the hordes was originally thought to have come down from earlier tribal leaders including Abul Khair, but a more probable explanation was the practical need of each nomadic tribe to secure its own winter and summer pastures, and its own migration routes, without conflict with each other. Many of the original tribes and clans retained their separate identities within their horde, and were very aware of their own descent and lineage, their place in society, and their rights to grazing land. Over the following two hundred years, between the 1520s up to the early 1720s, the tribes of each horde converged every autumn in the hills above Sairam, near the present-day city of Chimkent, in a colourful gathering of caravans, tents, and yurts. Now a small town on the Sairamsu River, Sairam was the historic site for this annual assembly at which the khans and tribal leaders met to deliberate and decide such matters as migration routes for the coming year, access to water and pastures, defence of their territories against outsiders, and other areas of mutual interest. This tradition fostered a sense of national identity and unity of purpose in relations with the outside world. But as pressure on land and pastures increased, disputes arose and over time these meetings became less frequent, until about 1720 when they eventually ceased to take place altogether. The relationship between each horde, and between various tribes within each horde, fragmented and disagreements and conflicts began to appear, notably as to what sort of relationship there should be with Russia, which was increasingly extending its presence and influence into Kazakh territory. The final separation of the three hordes came in 1723 when Dzungar tribes from western China invaded and seized the town of Sairam, as well as Tashkent and Turkestan. But the broad structure and organisation of the various tribes and hordes remained essentially intact for another hundred years, until the hordes were officially abolished by the tsarist government in the early part of the nineteenth century.

From about 1540, the unified khanate which was established but then lost under Kasim, regained some of its earlier political strength and stability under the leadership of two little-known khans: Khak-Nazar, the son of Kasim and who ruled from 1538 to 1580, and Tevekel (1582-98). Khak-Nazar achieved considerable success in strengthening the khanate and bringing together many nomadic clans, and he defended its territory against Mongol tribes from the east, who in the 1540s and 1550s were launching attacks against the Semirechie and settlements in the Ili region, from the mountains to the south of Lake Issyk-Kul. Internally, greater stability during this period enabled the development of agriculture and simple domestic economic activity, as well as closer trading links with Russia and with the oasis communities in central Asia. But these connections were at best tenuous, and more viable and durable contacts with the outside world would be necessary if the khanate was to develop more fully. Its remote location, whose isolation was accentuated to the south and east by high mountains and vast deserts, and repeated attacks from Mongul khans, meant that trade routes to the west through central Asia assumed growing importance. To this end Khak-Nazar concluded a treaty with the sultan of Bukhara, allowing greater trade and contact with western regions, although this treaty was violated in 1583 by Khak-Nazar's successor Tevekel, who seized a number of towns on the Syr Darya River so as to protect these trade routes and ensure completely unrestricted access to western regions. This strategy led to more unrest and fifteen years later, in 1598, in an attempt to capture Bukhara itself, Tevekel was fatally wounded during the siege of the city. In the same year Tevekel's successor Esim concluded a second treaty with the sultan of Bukhara, under which Tashkent and a number of towns on the Syr Darya River became part of the Kazakh khanate. Yet this also failed to prevent further conflict between the khanates of Kazakhstan and Bukhara, which retarded the economic and social development of both.

***

The sixteenth century was a time of instability and invasion in the east and the south of Kazakhstan, but other events were unfolding to the north-west of the country, which would have a far more profound and lasting impact, and which would lay the basis of future relations between Kazakhstan and Russia. The years in which the Kazakh nomads and tribes in the northern steppe first came into contact with herdsmen and farmers in central Russia and southern Siberia, are lost in the mist of ancient history. But it was around the middle of the sixteenth century when Kazakhstan and Russia became aware of each other's existence on a more formal basis. In 1536 Tsar Vasilii III of Russia died and was succeeded by his son Ivan IV, later known as Ivan the Terrible, who at the time was only three years old. Ivan's mother was the principal figure in the regency government, but her death five years later, allegedly due to poisoning, was followed by a period of turmoil as successive regents were removed from power and either banished or executed by groups of scheming boyars. Ivan grew up in an atmosphere of terror and cruelty, a factor which had a profound effect on his personality and his behaviour towards other people. In 1549, at the age of sixteen, he had himself crowned and one month later married a girl named Anastasia. He quickly established his authority by putting an end to the instability and factionalism which had prevailed in the medieval principality of Muscovy since the death of his father. He introduced and enforced new laws, strengthened the system of government, and worked closely with religious and military advisers, while trusting no one except himself and Anastasia. Like Peter the Great a century and a half later, Ivan developed a keen interest in western ideas and progress, especially in science and technology, and more particularly in how these ideas could be applied to military purposes.

The Muscovy of which Ivan became tsar was fragile and fragmented. Most of its territory lay in northern Russia, extending to the Arctic Ocean, from where there was little threat, but its land borders everywhere were insecure and vulnerable to invasion. Before there could be a Russian empire there had to be a stable and unified Russian state, and Ivan was instrumental in creating such a state, by consolidating the existing territory of Muscovy and clearly defining, and then extending, its borders. He was also keen to experiment with the new artillery which had been developed with the assistance of European experts. In 1552 he launched a campaign against the khanate of Kazan, which occupied a strategic site on the River Volga just beyond the southern frontier of Muscovy. The khanate of Kazan had emerged from the disintegration at the end of the fourteenth century of the Golden Horde, the name given to the territory and armies established by Batu, grandson of Genghis Khan, and which had long been a source of potential trouble and instability to the emerging Russian state. The city of Kazan could offer no defence to the serried battalions and the guns and cannons of Ivan's armies, and in October 1552 after a siege lasting four months, its walls were breached and the city surrendered. A large part of the male population was massacred, women and children were taken into slavery, and mosques and other signs of the city's Islamic origins were demolished. Thereafter Kazan became a province of Russia, extending Russian territory to the south and south-east almost as far as the steppes of Kazakhstan. As was to happen with later acquisitions, Russian peasants and farmers from the north of the country were soon being encouraged to leave their native lands and to settle in the conquered territories.

Russia's eastern border was now more secure, but the vast country to the south, around the estuary of the River Volga and the steppes around the Caspian Sea, was a land without clear authority or government, and posed a potential threat to stability. This was the khanate of Astrakhan, centred on the city of the same name near the mouth of the Volga, and which like Kazan had emerged from the end of the Golden Horde. It was inhabited mainly by a tribe of Kazakh nomads known as the Nogai, who had developed some trade with Russia, selling horses from the steppes, silk from China, and precious stones from India. The Nogai were not opposed to Russia taking control of their land if this would protect their business in Russia itself. Ivan however was intent on the certainty of military conquest and in 1554, after warning the inhabitants of Astrakhan against resistance by reminding the inhabitants of what had happened in Kazan, he sent an army of 30,000 soldiers to take the city. Ivan's forces met with no resistance and he appointed a compliant khan named Dervish as governor. In 1555, Dervish attempted to lead a rebellion against the same Russian authorities which had installed him, but he was put to flight in the following spring of 1556, when the Russian army reappeared in much greater strength and completed the annexation of the whole of the territory of Astrakhan.

Ivan now had control of the strategically-important steppe-land around the Volga delta, which gave access to the Caucasus Mountains and Azerbaijan, to the northern part of the Caspian Sea, and to the plains of Kazakhstan in the east. This gave Russia stability and relative safety in its border regions, where previously there had been a political and military vacuum. But if Ivan had a more secure frontier to the south and east, he had no interest in the deserts and steppes of Central Asia, and it would be almost two hundred years before Russia established any closer relationship with the khans of Kazakhstan. Instead of looking eastwards, Ivan was more keen to develop diplomatic and commercial relations with Europe, and in 1584 the port of Archangel was established on the White

Sea, the northernmost settlement of the Russian empire, to promote the growth of trade with England and with Europe. Access to Western Europe, from where military equipment and other modern goods could be obtained, was far preferable to anything that Asia had to offer, and the nomads and tribes of the steppe remained virtually undisturbed by Russia for at least another hundred years.

In 1564, Ivan devised a plan which he believed was essential to enable him to ensure that Russia could fulfil its potential as an imperial power. Despite its territorial gains in the east and south, Russia came under attack that year from Lithuania in the west, and from the khanate of Crimea (the third khanate with Kazan and Astrakhan to emerge from the Golden Horde) on the Black Sea. These attacks were successfully repelled, but nonetheless they demonstrated Russia's continuing vulnerability to invasions from its enemies. At the same time, the Russian church had tried to restrain Ivan from the excessive severity with which he carried out the murder of opponents. Ivan's mind was greatly disturbed by the death in 1560 of his wife Anastasia, who like his mother was believed to have been poisoned in a plot by the boyars. Tormented by conspiracies, real or imagined, and confronted with external and internal obstacles to his rule, in December 1564 Ivan abandoned the Kremlin and retreated to a nearby monastery at Kolomenskoe, before moving away completely to Alexandrova, a village outside Moscow. Here he withdrew from all responsibility of government, refusing to see anyone who came to seek decisions or instructions. If he was return to Moscow, Ivan demanded that the boyars and the clergy must give him the right to govern as he alone saw fit, without their interference or restraint; he also demanded the right to set up his own army of bodyguards, informants, and officials known as the *oprichnina,* which would carry out his orders and be responsible to him alone. According to popular mythology, as related in Sergei Eisenstein's classic 1944 film *Ivan the Terrible,* large crowds of ordinary Muscovites, priests, boyars and counsellors, fearing the anarchy and chaos which would result without his leadership, set out on foot to Alexandrova and implored Ivan to return to the Kremlin and to govern the country as he wished. The tactic was successful and gave Ivan a free hand to eliminate any opposition in the pursuit of his domestic and imperial ambitions. His strategy thereafter was to subjugate the boyars and the aristocracy to his will, set up the oprichnina, and establish a rudimentary civil service; in doing so he laid the basis of the country's imperial power, and ensured that Russia would be able to govern and administer an empire eventually extending far beyond its existing borders. (A similar episode in Russian history occurred in June 1941, when shortly after the German invasion Stalin retreated to his dacha until he too was persuaded to return to Moscow and given complete authority to conduct the war as he wished. The parallels are not exact, as Stalin was said to have suffered a mental breakdown and feared that he might be arrested by the other Soviet leaders. But he is also widely thought to have deliberately emulated Ivan the Terrible in demonstrating his indispensability to the country in a time of acute need, and in removing all opposition to his rule.)

Ivan IV was the founder of the Russian empire, and he adopted the double-headed eagle as its emblem which lasted until the overthrow of the Romanov dynasty in 1917. His achievements lay in the annexation of Kazan and Astrakhan and in the consolidation of Russia as a unified state, and in the establishment of the political and administrative foundations in Moscow which would be needed for future territorial expansion. These were the fundamental cornerstones in the building of an empire which was to culminate in the foundation of the USSR in 1922, three hundred and seventy years after the conquest of Kazan. Not until 1991 did the colonising process which had been started by Ivan go into reverse, with the collapse of the Soviet Union and the emergence of independent states, although Kazan and Astrakhan have both remained within Russia. The reign of Ivan the Terrible is chiefly remembered for plots, conspiracies, the murder of opponents in the name of securing the throne from challenge from illegitimate claimants, and a campaign of terror conducted by Ivan against his own people. Despite this he is also still revered by many Russians, as Stalin was later to be revered, as a strong and unifying leader of the type which Russia has always needed throughout its history. When Ivan died in 1584, the country was plunged into a further period of crisis and turmoil, feuds and invasions, known as the Time of Troubles, a period which continued until the establishment of the Romanov dynasty and the accession of Michael Feodorovich, the first Romanov tsar, in 1613.

CHAPTER SIX

The Years of Great Calamity

Kazakhstan was soon to have its own Time of Troubles, which became known as the Years of Great Calamity. Throughout the 1600s the nascent Kazakh state was able to maintain a basic form of identity and territorial integrity, despite continuing conflict with the Uzbek khanates in the south, and the emergence of the three individual hordes within its own territory. The process was consolidated under Tauke, a khan from the Middle Horde who ruled from 1680 to 1718, and who emerged as the most powerful khan among the three hordes. Tauke strengthened the role of the khan, and extended his own authority over the individual tribes of each of the different hordes, by appointing a representative in each to ensure that his wishes were carried out. Under his leadership a basic legal system was established, setting out fundamental principles governing the relationship between different tribal and family groups, while reflecting the norms and traditions of the nomadic way of life. The existing tribal law, known as *adat,* did not attach importance to the protection of property since nomadic tribesmen had no interest in land ownership, but were more concerned with access to pastures and unrestricted migrations. These were matters which had evolved over centuries but for which there was no legal basis, but instead were largely decided at annual gatherings in the hills near Sairam. The only property owned by tribesmen consisted of livestock, which was more vulnerable to natural conditions than to theft, although after a severe *zhut* tribes used to mount raids on each other's territory with the aim of restoring lost herds. The legal reforms under Tauke sought to prohibit such activities, with a strict code of penalties for specific offences. Tauke also attempted to limit the importance of family feuds and 'blood revenge' which had been features of nomadic society.

Islam had already been widely adopted in the south of the country, especially among more prosperous clans and families, but any Islamic influence on the new legal code was superficial. Nor did it extend to the north, where the nomadic tribes remained in near total isolation with little contact with Islam or exposure to any other foreign influences. Even in later centuries, Islam did not make a deep impression among the itinerant northern tribes. Throughout the country a number of mosques were built, especially later during the nineteenth century, but orthodox Islam was combined with local Kazakh traditions deriving from centuries-old beliefs and practices. The Arabic alphabet and educational system were now being merged with indigenous musical and cultural traditions of nomadic songs, and oral epics and poetry, which expressed the history and philosophy of the people. The influence of the *akyn* (writer or poet) and *bi* (sage) had become well established, and played a prominent role in the development of the Kazakh national identity, as had happened under Kasim Khan in the early 1500s. Poets and writers such as Tole-bi, Aiteke-bi, Kazybek-bi and others, now commemorated in street names in Almaty and other towns and cities throughout Kazakhstan, promoted the spread of a cultural and ethnic unity through their writings, while the *batyr*, or military leader, remained a powerful figure among many tribes and clans. The *batyr* was a severe and imposing figure, traditionally dressed in a heavy ankle-length leather costume and a conical helmet, armed with a short sword and with a fierce expression exuding authority and leadership. But the underlying political structure of the country which was now emerging remained fragile and precarious. The rigidity of the established social and tribal hierarchy, and cultural traditions dating back to ancient times, instead of providing a basis for stable growth, became deep-rooted obstacles to progress. Similarly the education system was rudimentary and based on traditional beliefs and values, and completely unsuitable if the society was to change and develop. The majority of the population remained nomadic, and the absence of any alternative economic development made it difficult for stability or permanent settlement to take root. In addition to all these problems a new threat was emerging in the east, in the form of the Dzungar empire, in the territory between eastern Kazakhstan and western China, and which was becoming a more powerful and dangerous enemy.

The Dzungars were a warlike tribe of Mongolian origin and Buddhist beliefs, and had begun moving into Central Asia in the late seventeenth century, when they launched a series of raids against the tribes of the Great Horde. In the Ili area south-east of Lake Balkhash, Dzungar horsemen had clashed with local Kazakh tribes, and Tauke, the leader of the Kazakh hordes, was anxious to assert his authority and avenge these attacks. Tauke is remembered chiefly as a reformer and legislator, but he was ruthless in his determination to protect what he had achieved in uniting the hordes against external threats. At the time Russia was also threatened by incursions by Dzungar raiders into its own territory along the Irtysh River, and in 1694 Russia sent its first diplomatic mission to the region, to discuss common action against the Dzungars. But Tauke believed he was sufficiently strong to act without external support. In 1699, at a time when Dzungar tribes were themselves in conflict with China, he had a number of Dzungar envoys, who had come to him as part of an official delegation, put to death, together with five hundred men of their escort, in what a contemporary account described as 'particularly odious circumstances'. This massacre, in a remote field south of Lake Balkhash between the Ili and the Syr Darya Rivers, was little known at the time, but later acquired great historical significance. Far from being merely another battle between rival tribes and hordes, it came to symbolise an ancient ethnic and religious conflict, between Kazakhs and Mongols, Muslims and Buddhists, as to who should have control of the Kazakh steppes. In the short term, it was the Mongols who gained the upper hand, and in the following years the Dzungar tribes continued to mount raids and incursions from the east, partly in revenge for the murder of their fellow tribesmen at the hands of Tauke, and partly to continue their efforts to drive out the Kazakhs from the Semirechie and the land to the north, lands which the Dzungars wished to colonise. But in the longer term the threat from the Dzungars provided a common cause between Russia and the country which was to become Kazakhstan, a cause which was to have enduring consequences in bringing the two countries together over the following centuries.

The legal reforms introduced under Tauke were positive achievements, but the Kazakh hordes were still deeply divided, and the authority of subsequent khans often failed to extend to their own populations, let alone to neighbouring tribes and clans. At home, feuds between rival khans, and externally, disputes concerning ill-defined borders, and conflicts for access to the best land, all had a detrimental effect on stability, especially in the eastern regions bordering China. After his death in 1718, Tauke was succeeded by another khan of the Middle Horde named Semeke, a self-important but ultimately weak ruler, who was unable to put an end to the persistent feuding between rival clans, or to reverse the fragmentation which had been taking place under Tauke. The continuing attempts to attain superiority over each other, rather than unite and face the common Dzungar enemy, eventually led the three hordes to abandon any attempts to try to live together. In a series of battles between 1718 and 1730 the Kazakh tribes suffered devastating losses inflicted by the stronger and better organised Dzungar invaders. The town of Sairam was destroyed in 1723, finally putting an end to the annual gathering of tribes and clans which had been held in the nearby hills since the 1520s. Tashkent and Turkestan suffered a similar fate, and thousands of men were killed and women and children were taken as hostages or into slavery. None of the three hordes escaped from the violence and destruction inflicted by the Dzungar tribes, who in the manner of the earlier Mongol invasions spread terror as far west as the Aral Sea. The Middle and the Great Hordes were the most exposed to the Dzungar onslaught, but further west the Little Horde was also subjected to repeated attacks, and many Kazakh tribes and families were forced to flee to the west, to the region around the Caspian Sea and into Russia. Ultimately the strains of defeat became unsustainable and the hordes effectively separated from each other; some of the chiefs of the Great and Middle Hordes formally submitted to the Dzungars, and once again the Kazakh khanate broke up and ceased to exist as a unified state, in a repetition of the experience under Kasim nearly two hundred years earlier.

The 1720s, subsequently known in Kazakh history as the Years of Great Calamity, echoed the Time of Troubles in the late sixteenth and early seventeenth centuries in Russia when the principality of Muscovy was nearly destroyed by feuds among the boyars, and by invasions from Lithuania and Sweden. Now the Dzungars were presenting a threat not only to the tribes of Kazakhstan, but were mounting incursions deep into Russian territory, in the southern provinces of Kazan and other regions further east. Seen from St. Petersburg, this vast region of Central Asia was dangerous and unstable. Action needed to be taken not only to protect the border regions, but to provide a basis for Russia's own ambitions of further expansion towards Persia and China. With this in mind, in 1716 the Russian tsar Peter the Great ordered the construction of a line of military forts, later known as the Orenburg Line, to be established along the ill-defined borderlands between Russia and Kazakhstan. The first of these forts was built at Omsk in 1716, followed by Semipalatinsk (1718), Ust-Kamenogorsk (1720), Orenburg (1734), and Petropavlovsk (1752). Initially the forts consisted of simple barracks and depots of military equipment, with the purpose of protecting Russian territory against the threat of raids by Dzungars as well as by Kazakhs. Between each fort, separate wooden redoubts maintained a watch over the surrounding country and beacons were lit to signal the approach of hostile tribes. There was little agriculture or any other activity in the neighbouring regions, although Semipalatinsk was so named to reflect the number (seven, or *semi*) of rough tents (*palatki*) which grew up around the fort, and where local inhabitants sold food and milk to the soldiers. Over time the forts expanded into centres from where the movement of the people and tribes of the steppe could be observed and from where the tsarist authorities could gain a better knowledge of life and conditions in the little-known border regions. Thus in addition to their military purpose the forts became centres for studies of the local terrain, soil, geology and raw materials, none of which had been systematically investigated before. As farming and some basic trade developed between Russia and Kazakhstan, the forts soon grew into towns and administrative centres. In the following century, some of these towns became places of exile for writers and political opponents of the tsarist government, the most notable of whom was the writer and philosopher Fyodor Dostoyevsky who was banished from St. Petersburg to Semipalatinsk from 1854 to 1859. But in the early 1700s the forts represented the first permanent points of contact between Russia and Kazakhstan, and their main functions were to provide a forward base for further expansion to the south and east, to repel attacks from the Dzungars, and to secure the submission of the Kazakh hordes to the tsarist empire.

***

Towards the end of the 1720s some degree of unity among the Kazakh hordes was once again re-established and more effective resistance was mounted against the Dzungars, culminating in significant, albeit temporary defeats of the invaders in 1728 and 1729. But the threat of further incursions remained, presenting a continuing danger to the Kazakh tribes. The Little Horde in the west of Kazakhstan was the least exposed to this threat, but by the 1740s Dzungar raids were extending as far west as the Mugodzhary Hills and the steppes to the north of the Aral Sea. Abul Khair, leader of the Little Horde and a descendant of the fifteenth-century khan of the same name, emerged as the most powerful Kazakh leader and attempted to rally the khans and clans of the various hordes. But there was considerable disagreement as to how to respond to the Dzungar threat. The annual tribal gatherings at Sairam, which for two hundred years between the 1520s and 1720s had provided an opportunity to agree on migration routes and pastures, were now a thing of the past, and there was no longer an agreed meeting place at which the hordes could assemble. Even if the meetings at Sairam were still being held, it is unlikely that any significant agreement could have been achieved. The scale of the threat was now much greater than anything the tribes and their khans had had to confront in the past, and the scope for division was equally great. The Kazakh hordes had potentially natural allies in the Russians to the north, but they were wary of seeking an alliance with one foreign power as a means of defence against another. Abul Khair's attempts to reunite the hordes and to present a united front to both the Russians and the Dzungars met substantial opposition from other khans and batyrs.

In the early 1730s the Little Horde had its main settlement at a remote point on the steppe near the confluence of two rivers, the Irgiz and the Turgai, in the plains of western Kazakhstan. The Irgiz is a short, fast-flowing mountain river, one of many in Kazakhstan which rise and disappear inland without reaching the sea. It originates on the eastern side of the watershed in the Mugodzhary Hills at a point near the present border with Russia, from where it flows south towards the Aral Sea. On its journey it receives more waters from a series of shorter rivers and streams running down from the hills – the Baksais, Karabutak, Sholak-Kairakti, Taldyk, and Karasai - before turning in an easterly direction towards the open steppe. From here, in the blazing heat of the summer months, the waters of the Irgiz evaporate and the river vanishes, leaving a wide, shallow, and dry river bed littered with branches, rocks, and boulders bleached white in the sun. In winter the Irgiz rapidly fills again and flows on further to join up with the Turgai, a more substantial river flowing down from hills further east, before it too disappears in the parched sands of the desert. It was here at a point north of where the two rivers converge that Abul Khair had established a camp on the banks of the Irgiz, and in October 1731, he and a group of local batyrs and khans from the Middle Horde, notably Bugenbai Batyr and Khudai-Nazar, were awaiting the arrival of a mission from the tsarist government in St Petersburg. It was a tranquil scene in the autumn sunshine, with women cooking over open fires outside the yurts, colourful flags and banners fluttering in the breeze, and children playing by the river. Horses and cattle grazed peacefully in the surrounding pastures. When the Russian delegation arrived they would be welcomed with the best food and drink that could be provided. But despite the outward appearances of harmony and unity, between Abul Khair and the other batyrs there were deep fears and divisions as to how they could resist further attacks from the Dzungars, and what sort of relationship – submission, resistance, or uniting against a common enemy – they should have with Russia.

Six years earlier, in the spring of 1725, Abul Khair had himself sent a delegation to St Petersburg, seeking an alliance with Russia and protection against the Dzungars, but the mission had returned empty-handed. If Abul Khair had been more aware of what was happening in Russia at the time he would have realised that it was not a propitious moment for diplomacy. Tsar Peter the Great had only recently died, an event of great significance in Russia, and for several years there was no-one in St Petersburg who could fill the enormous void left by his death. Since he became tsar in 1696, Peter had taken gigantic strides to modernise Russia, a country which had been backward and introspective, and oblivious of advances taking place in almost every aspect of society, especially science, medicine, and technology, in the outside world. In March 1697 Peter embarked on a 'Grand Embassy' of Europe, the first tsar to leave Russia, and in Holland and England he studied engineering, shipbuilding, botany and printing, areas in which Russia was particularly deficient. In 1703, at the age of 32, Peter ordered the construction of the city of St Petersburg, on a desolate, marshy site on the banks of the River Neva at the eastern end of the Gulf of Finland. He named the city after his own patron saint, and in 1712 it became the new capital of Russia. In many respects the location was highly unsuitable, in a harsh environment and damp climate, and subject to frequent flooding. But the city had access to the sea, and Peter intended that St Petersburg would be a window to the West and would open up the country in a way which could never be achieved from the byzantine and eastward-looking city of Moscow. When Peter died in February 1725, no one knew what would happen to the country. The previous year Peter himself had conducted the coronation of his second wife Catherine as tsarina. The ceremony was performed in the Dormition Cathedral in Moscow, after which Peter declared that Catherine would succeed him on the throne when he died, a decision which had caused great consternation and controversy in the royal household and in the country at large. Under the established laws of succession the rightful heir, after Peter's son Alexis had been murdered (allegedly on Peter's instructions), was his grandson, not Catherine. But his grandson, also called Peter, was a child at the time and in any event Peter wanted to reward Catherine for her loyalty and support for him during the earlier war with Sweden. However the whole of Russia was deeply alarmed; never before had a woman succeeded to the throne, and Peter's decision was seen as an affront to the convention of the time.

Notwithstanding the turmoil resulting from the death of Peter, Catherine duly took her place as tsarina and empress, and was to remain in these roles until her death two years later. But the early months of 1725 were a period of great confusion and uncertainty in St Petersburg, and the mission from Kazakhstan, whiling away its time in the icy streets and draughty halls of the new capital, was ignored. When they could turn their attention away from what was happening at court, government ministers agreed that there would have been no point in receiving the delegation from Abul Khair. It was too soon for Catherine to negotiate with the Kazakhs; moreover the government was fearful of provoking more clashes with the Dzungar empire, and believed there was no advantage to be had from any agreement with the Kazakh tribes.

However, the threats to its own borders continued, and as time went by Russia increasingly saw potential benefits of a treaty with Abul Khair. Abul Khair also saw an advantage arising from the Dzungar threat to Russia, and claiming to act on behalf of both the Little Horde and the Middle Horde, whose territory extended much further to the north, he once again sought an alliance with Russia against a common enemy.

This time the tsarist government was more responsive. By now both Catherine, widow of Peter the Great, and Peter's son Peter II, had died after each ruling Russia for little more than two years, and were succeeded by Anna, the daughter of the retarded tsar Ivan V who had nominally shared the throne with Peter I until Ivan's death in 1696. Anna became Empress in 1730, and was an unpopular ruler who did little to advance the cause of Russia or to improve conditions for its citizens. She had no serious interest in an unknown part of the country in the steppe, thousands of miles from St Petersburg. Her reign is traditionally known in Russia as a time of government by foreigners, as typified by the Foreign Minister Count Andrei Ostermann, who like several other ministers, was of German descent and largely disliked by most Russians. Despite Anna's lack of involvement, the tsarist government was now keen to promote Russia's imperial expansion, and Ostermann and other ministers saw that the territory of northern Kazakhstan could be both a defensive region for Russia's southern border, and a base for further territorial extension. Colonising this region would provide greater security for trade caravans, with the possibility of exploring new trade routes to India and Persia. For his part Abul Khair assumed that a treaty with Russia meant that he could rely on Russian protection against the Dzungars, and also support in strengthening his own position against rival batyrs and other khans within the Little Horde. He further believed that he could increase trade with Russia, and would have access to pasture and grazing lands between the Ural and Volga rivers north of the Caspian Sea, new lands further west than the traditional territory of the Little Horde.

After renewed approaches from Abul Khair, a Russian mission led by Alexander Tevkelev, a senior official from the Foreign Ministry in St Petersburg, was sent to Kazakhstan, with instructions to deliver to Abul Khair in Irgiz an official treaty document and formally to accept the submission of the Kazakhs to the Russian state. The tsarist government believed that the desire to submit to Russia was shared by all the tribal chiefs and batyrs of the Little Horde, a notion that was partly due to what it had been led to believe by Abul Khair. This was the mission which arrived at Irgiz on 5 October 1731. But it soon became clear that not everyone was of this opinion, and in his report back to the government in St Petersburg Tevkelev described a scene which was far from harmonious. It was apparent that beneath the effusive welcome from the batyrs and khans there was sharp conflict between them as to the desirability of any form of association with Russia. Many of the rival leaders were strongly opposed to Abul Khair's attempts to secure unanimity towards Russia, fearing for their own position, and rejecting Russian nationality, which they saw as being more in Russia's colonial interests than as a form of protection for them against Dzungar incursions. They also rejected what they saw as a power struggle by Abul Khair for control over the Little Horde. The fact that they would be submitting to an empress in the form of Anna, and not an emperor, was also difficult to accept in the male-dominated Kazakh society.

Nonetheless, Abul Khair had managed to gather on his side a tenuous majority of khans and batyrs within the Little Horde. On 10 October 1731, in a huge ceremonial yurt in Irgiz, collectively and with varying degrees of enthusiasm, the assembled group took an oath of allegiance to Russia, in an act which marked the beginning of the long process of formal unification of Russia and Kazakhstan. It took two more years of negotiations, conducted first in the border town of Ufa and later in St Petersburg, between Tevkelev and Abul Khair and other khans, before all the terms of a comprehensive treaty were concluded. Under the treaty Abul Khair and the tribes of the Little Horde would submit to Russian sovereignty and to the incorporation of their lands into the Russian empire. In return Russia would provide protection against attacks and incursions from Dzungarian raiders, while the Little Horde under Abul Khair would similarly ensure that Russian caravans and traders travelling through western Kazakhstan would be protected. Abul Khair would also prevent raids by Kazakh tribes against Russian territories in the Volga and Orenburg regions. On 4 January 1734, in a historic ceremony in St Petersburg, the treaty formalising the act of allegiance in 1731 and establishing the basis of the subsequent relationship between Russia and Kazakhstan, was signed.

In justification of Russia's early colonial expansion in Kazakhstan, which two centuries later the USSR was to consolidate and strengthen rather than attempt to dismantle, Soviet versions of the history of this period dwelt on what was always referred to as the voluntary nature of the 1734 treaty, in which the khans willingly sought Russian nationality and protection. Soviet historians dismissed the conflicts which had been deeply divisive within Kazakhstan before the treaty was signed, and which continued for many years afterwards. Abul Khair was portrayed by both tsarist and Soviet governments as a wise and far-sighted statesman who did much to bring Kazakhstan and Russia together, despite the fact that in reality he had limited control or authority within the Little Horde, and could not be said to be truly representative of his own people of the Little Horde, let alone the people of the Middle and Great Hordes. He may have acted in good faith in pursuing what he thought was best for his territories in Kazakhstan, but there were many who opposed his actions. Some tribal leaders felt insulted by his submission to Russia and refused to guarantee the safety of Russian caravans, as provided for under the treaty, and such caravans remained in danger of attack both from Dzungarian tribes and from recalcitrant Kazakhs on the steppe. Soviet histories of this period also emphasised the desire of ordinary tribesmen and nomads to escape from the oppression suffered under the arbitrary rule of feudal khans, and asserted that most Kazakh tribes and communities sought the stability and security offered by association with Russia. Everyone was weary of the interminable internecine conflicts within the various hordes, while Kazakh incursions into Russia had brought retaliation from tsarist troops resulting in more death and destruction. There remained a strong desire for an end to the continuing and devastating Dzungar raids, and this became a powerful motive for seeking a closer, defensive relationship with Russia.

But despite the 1731 and 1734 treaties, neither Russia nor the majority of the Kazakh khans were in favour of a very close relationship. The Russian government had no real interest in the well-being of the Kazakh tribes, and it would protect the Kazakh territories only to the extent that such protection secured the Russian border against attacks from Dzungarian tribes. The khans remained irreconcilably divided about the treaty with Russia. The fact that many khans in the Little Horde were weak and lacked authority over their own people and clans, supposedly because they were from the so-called 'white bones' or nobility, rather than from the 'black bones' of the common people, further diminished their legitimacy in the eyes of many Kazakhs. Powerful leaders such as Tauke Khan and later Syrym Batyr, a tribal chief from the 'black bones', and Ablai Khan were rare, and Abul Khair himself had struggled for years to achieve and maintain unity within the Little Horde. These conflicts strengthened the hand of Ostermann and other ministers in the tsarist government, which exploited the divisions among the khanates in its quest for control of the steppe.

In post-Soviet times a less flattering picture of Abul Khair has emerged, as someone who was too ready to accept friendship with Russia, and who sought to suppress any form of Kazakh nationalism. Allegedly he also pursued secret negotiations with the Dzungars, and sent emissaries with a proposal of marriage of his daughter to a Dzungar prince, in an attempt to strengthen his bargaining position with Russia. In the end Abul Khair pleased neither the Russians nor his own people in Kazakhstan. Such was the opposition to the treaty which he had signed, and the sense of betrayal engendered by his abandonment of resistance to the Dzungars, that eventually he was deposed as leader of the Little Horde. He was later allegedly murdered by a khan from the Middle Horde, who was said to be acting either on behalf of the many Kazakhs opposed to the treaty, or as an agent of the Russians who had discovered his attempts to forge an alliance with the Dzungars. At a time when the tribes of the Middle and Great Hordes were still actively fighting the Dzungars, Abul Khair was seen as a traitor to his people, and none of his descendants could aspire to become khan. Many in the Little Horde no longer wished to be associated with his name and joined the ranks of Ablai Khan, khan of the Great Horde, in the eastern part of Kazakhstan, who was ultimately responsible for eventually defeating and expelling the Dzungars from Kazakhstan. According to post-Soviet histories, if Abul Khair had not submitted to Russia in 1731, the tribes of northern and eastern Kazakhstan would have mounted a stronger and more sustained defence against the Dzungars, and would have preserved Kazakh independence for much longer; but by accepting Russian nationality and protection, Abul Khair was said to have significantly accelerated the Russian colonisation of Kazakhstan.

Divisions within the Little Horde were matched by similar disagreements and conflicts among the tribes of the neighbouring Middle Horde, whose lands extended further to the east, between the Syr Darya and Irtysh Rivers. Semeke, the principal khan of the Middle Horde, was annoyed by Abul Khair's claims to act on behalf of both the Little and Middle Hordes, and did his best to frustrate the negotiations between Abul Khair and Tevkelev, the Russian representative. Abul Khair had an ally among the more influential khans in the Middle Horde in the form of Bugenbai Batyr, and they tried to engage Semeke in presenting a united front to Russia and joining their attempts to seek Russian nationality. Semeke eventually agreed to this approach, albeit with the stipulation that this was of his own desire and not as a result of the advice of Abul Khair. In the event he was unable to implement his own decision; the tribal leaders supposedly under his authority had no desire to show allegiance to the tsarist government, and continued to carry out raids into southern Russia, in retaliation for Russian encroachment on their lands. These raids in turn merely provoked harsh and punitive retaliation by Russian troops. At the same time raids continued from the Dzungars in the east, and the khans of the Middle Horde, weakened by internal divisions and poor organisation and leadership, and facing a militarily superior enemy, were generally incapable of providing any effective resistance. Semeke and other recalcitrant khans of the Middle Horde came to realise that Russia would eventually gain control over the whole of their territory and that an agreed settlement would be preferable to one imposed on them by violence and force. But it was not until 1740, in a separate treaty six years after that between Russia and Abul Khair and the Little Horde, that Semeke and the khans of the Middle Horde finally signed their own treaty and submitted to Russian sovereignty.

After the 1740 treaty, further attacks from the Dzungars in the east diminished in their severity, and those that were made were swiftly and effectively repulsed. According to Soviet history, this was due to armed intervention by Russian forces, and to incorporation of the Middle Horde, whose lands had been dangerously exposed to Dzungar incursions, into the tsarist empire; this had effectively saved the Middle Horde from complete annihilation. Post-Soviet Kazakh versions by contrast claim that it was Ablai Khan, the principal khan of the Great Horde, who had saved Kazakhstan from further attack. In any event the Dzungar empire ultimately collapsed in 1758, as it was itself under constant attack from China. But although this development removed a danger from the east, there was now a new and more pernicious threat to the traditional Kazakh way of life, from the new imperial power to the north.

The treaties of 1734 and 1740 marked the beginning of a new era in the Russian colonisation of Central Asia. Russia now controlled roughly two-thirds of the territory of Kazakhstan, since the vast lands of western and central Kazakhstan had become part of the tsarist empire. Only the country of the Great Horde, from Lake Zaisan to the Semirechie in the most remote and distant part of Kazakhstan, as seen from St Petersburg, remained outside Russian control, and were to remain so for another 109 years, until these territories were also formally incorporated into the empire in 1849. Throughout this period Russia slowly extended and strengthened its control over its new acquisitions. As part of the colonisation of its new territories, the government in St Petersburg embarked on a policy of large-scale transportation of whole farming communities and villages from within Russia to the Kazakh steppe. Fertile pastures were forcibly expropriated from indigenous tribes and allocated to the new settlers; while seasonal migration routes, which for centuries had been followed by Kazakh nomads taking herds of horses, cattle, and other livestock to new grazing lands, were now suddenly and irreversibly disrupted, causing a severe loss of livelihood for many of the tribes and clans. The local khans and leaders were generally powerless to resist this process and many families were forced to turn to a more settled way of life in permanent farming communities, for which they were by nature ill-suited and ill-prepared.

Meanwhile the 1734 treaty with the Little Horde enabled Russia to resume work on the line of army forts and outposts which had been initiated under Peter the Great. After the signing of the treaty Orenburg was chosen as the next fortress to be built, on a site commanding a strategic position on the Ural River in Bashkiria, to the north of the westernmost corner of Kazakhstan. The existing forts at Omsk, Semipalatinsk, and Ust-Kamenogorsk were too far to the east to be of use to Russia in dealing with its new priorities. Foremost among these was a war it was waging with Turkey in the Crimea and the northern shores of the Black Sea, and simultaneously a need to put down the growing unrest among the peasantry in Bashkiria, a vast, open region north of the Caspian Sea between the Volga and Ural Rivers. This was followed by a more serious uprising in the Volga region led by a Cossack from the Don region of southern Russia named Emilyan Pugachev, when Russian peasants of the region, and nomads from the Little and Middle Hordes of western Kazakhstan, joined forces against the tsarist regime. The uprising in Bashkiria, and the later rebellion led by Pugachev, were early instances of turmoil in Russia spilling over into Kazakhstan, and of Kazakhstan becoming caught up in social and political upheavals in a distant country which were not of its own making. In later centuries other historic events, notably the emancipation of the serfs, the Bolshevik Revolution and the Russian civil war, the foundation and subsequent collapse of the USSR, were all essentially Russian in origin, but all had profound consequences for Kazakhstan, and for other parts of the Russian empire.

Bashkiria had long been a thorn in the side of the Russian empire as Russia expanded southwards, and would continue to be so after the 1917 Revolution, when a nationalist rebellion was ruthlessly suppressed by the Red Army in 1920. In the eighteenth century, the dire conditions of the peasants and serfs, and the unwelcome and increasing intrusion into their lives by the tsarist government, meant that the whole region was liable to erupt in rebellion. The construction of the fort at Orenburg was frequently disrupted by anti-Russian uprisings in Bashkiria and by raids on columns bringing labourers, building materials and supplies from Russia. Such raids were harshly suppressed by tsarist forces, although fighting continued for the next five years, at great cost to both Russian and Bashkir communities, in what was in effect the first colonial war in the region. For the next few decades after completion of the Orenburg fortress, Russia continued to build and strengthen similar fortresses along the Orenburg Line further east. New forts were built at more points along the border between Russia and Kazakhstan, including Presnogorkovsk and Petropavlovsk on the Ishym River and at Koriakovski (later Pavlodar) between Omsk and Semipalatinsk on the Irtysh River. As well as providing a base for sorties against hostile Kazakh and Dzungar tribes, in more peaceful times these forts became gathering points for local trade and commerce, where nomadic Kazakh communities met and traded in horses and other livestock amongst themselves and with Russian soldiers and civilians living nearby. There developed a growing trade in leather goods, rugs, and carpets especially among Russian buyers who came from Moscow and St Petersburg, where there was a strong demand for exotic and colourful items from the east.

This type of commerce, although useful to local communities in the northern border areas of Kazakhstan, was of little benefit to the growing numbers of impoverished peasants and nomadic tribes in the west, especially in the deserts and hills between the Emba and Ural Rivers. The tsarist government under Catherine II, who had acceded to the Russian throne in 1762, prohibited nomadic camps to be set up in this region as more settlers from Russia were encouraged to move here, and complaints by Kazakh tribesmen to the Russian authorities concerning the loss of their land and disruption to migration routes had been in vain. Catherine suppressed still further what meagre rights the local serfs and peasants managed to retain, and forbade any further petitions to be presented to her, thereby ending a centuries-old tradition of ordinary people having direct access to the monarch. Once again the scene was set for unrest and rebellion, and news and rumours of an uprising led by Pugachev, in the Volga region of southern Russia, spread rapidly among the Kazakh tribes. In Russia the Pugachev rebellion was the last and most serious in a long series of uprisings in its border lands, and represented a violent conflict between free-spirited Cossack horsemen and peasants, and the harsh authority of the tsarist government, increasingly assertive in the new regions of its empire.

Pugachev is usually described as a charismatic and colourful leader, and he clearly had strong appeal to the mass of impoverished and illiterate Russian peasantry, and to dispossessed Kazakh nomads. He claimed to be Tsar Peter III, the grandson of Peter the Great, who had recently been deposed from the Russian throne. Peter was in fact murdered in July 1762, allegedly on the orders of Count Orlov, the lover of Peter's wife Catherine, and Catherine succeeded Peter as the Empress Catherine II (and later became known as Catherine the Great). Peter had become tsar in January 1762, and in his short reign until July of that year, he had introduced reforms designed to improve the conditions of the peasants, and had prohibited some of the trading in serfs that had been taking place between the owners of the new factories springing up in Russia. He expropriated lands belonging to the church, thereby converting the ecclesiastical and monastic serfs living there to the more favourable status of state peasants, and he alleviated the persecution of Old Believers, the devoutly traditional religious sect that had broken away from the Orthodox Church in the previous century. This was a deep-rooted schism which had divided the church in Russia since before the founding of the Romanov dynasty in 1613, but its repercussions were not confined to the Church. The Old Believers opposed all attempts at liturgical reform and in effect became a form of opposition against the Russian state. The measures introduced on their behalf by Peter III gave rise to hopes among the ordinary and deeply religious peasantry that the tsarist government would pursue a more sympathetic policy towards their own material condition and their spiritual beliefs. Similar hopes extended into Kazakhstan, where although people were unaffected by the religious divisions in Russia, life among the vast majority of the indigenous population had worsened since the arrival of Russian troops and the seizure of Kazakh land by Russian settlers. But any expectations of an improvement in the conditions of the peasantry or of the nomadic tribes were abruptly ended when Peter III mysteriously disappeared from the scene. According to Catherine and her acolytes he had died of a short illness, a story which no-one believed. In any event his sudden removal from the throne caused alarm and suspicion in southern Russia and western Kazakhstan, where the Pugachev uprising was gathering strength among the independently-minded Cossacks, and little persuasion was needed for whole tribes and communities in Kazakhstan to join the revolt.

When Catherine succeeded to the Russian throne on the death of Peter in 1762, she was determined to follow in the footsteps of Peter's grandfather Peter the Great, who had died in 1725, particularly in the government of the empire. As a fervent admirer of her illustrious predecessor, who had done so much to strengthen and modernize Russia, Catherine commissioned and dedicated to him the famous Bronze Horseman statue which still stands on the banks of the River Neva in St Petersburg. Designed by the French sculptor Etienne Falconet and immortalized in the equally famous poem by Alexander Pushkin, the statue has since come to represent all that Peter the Great achieved in the Russian empire. As well as sharing Peter's admiration for western ideas and progress in almost every field of activity, Catherine was equally determined to suppress any challenge to the authority of the monarchy, as became apparent in her ruthless suppression of the Pugachev uprising.

The insurrection had started fourteen years earlier among the Yaik Cossacks in the southern Ural region, after the government decreed in 1748 that they should provide men for a new army which would serve in the forts along the Orenburg Line. The same year marked the death of Abul Khair, the divisive leader of the Little Horde, who had done much to bring about a closer relationship, for better or for worse, with Russia. He was succeeded as khan of the Little Horde by his son Nurali, who favoured an even closer relationship with the tsarist government, and which caused further disunity and conflict among his own people. As for the Yaik Cossacks, they and other cossacks historically had only a loose association with Russia, but like the Kazakhs they had become increasingly resentful at ever more intrusive intervention in their lands, and the latest decree aroused further strong hostility. They responded eagerly to Pugachev's appeal to his campaign against the Russian government and aristocracy. Simultaneously Pugachev appealed to Russian peasants and serfs by demanding the abolition of serfdom and the distribution of land away from the nobility. These demands were enthusiastically taken up by the many Bashkiris and Kazakhs who had also suffered badly under Russian rule and who hoped for a return of their lands. According to the Soviet version of this episode, the Kazakh khan Nurali sided with the tsarist government and rejected Pugachev's call to join his cause, whereupon Pugachev went over his head and appealed directly to the Kazakh peasants and nomads, who enthusiastically joined his crusade in great numbers. In a letter to the commander of the Russian garrison at Yaitsky (now the town of Uralsk in north-west Kazakhstan), Nurali complained 'the Kazakhs no longer listen to me, thanks to the villain calling himself Peter III'.

By the early 1770s Pugachev had gathered a large but ill-disciplined army, which wrought havoc among the country houses of Russian aristocrats in the Volga and Caspian regions. Marauding gangs and mobs roamed the countryside, committing atrocities, burning down estates, and forcing landowners to flee to Moscow. In October 1773 Pugachev reached Orenburg where with an army of 5,000 Russians and Kazakhs he laid siege to the Russian fortress in the city. In January 1774 their numbers were swelled by the arrival of more tribesmen from the Middle Horde from central Kazakhstan, who joined the siege as well as supplying the Pugachev forces with food and livestock. In March the tsarist government went over to the offensive and dispatched reinforcements to relieve Orenburg and take the attack to the rebels. Pugachev was forced to flee into the hills of Bashkiria while many of the rebels were captured and executed. Nurali began openly to cooperate with the tsarist authorities, although in the summer of 1774 tribesmen of the Little Horde continued to mount attacks against Russian forces. In July Russia achieved a major victory in the war it had been waging against Turkey, as a result of which Russia gained control of territory previously held by the Ottoman empire in the northern Caucasus, the Black Sea coast from Georgia to the Sea of Azov, and the Crimean peninsula. Abroad this was seen as a great diplomatic success for Catherine II, while at home the military implications were equally significant, since it enabled the Russian army to divert its full resources to dealing with Pugachev revolt. In August 1774 Pugachev was betrayed by some of his own commanders, who secretly negotiated with

Catherine in return for a pardon. He was handed over to the tsarist forces near Yaitsky, from where he was transported in a cage to Moscow where he was executed on Red Square outside the Kremlin in January 1775.

Violent unrest in the Ural region of southern Russia and in western and northern Kazakhstan, and what was in effect a civil war between the local inhabitants and Russian imperial forces, continued until the end of 1775. As had happened so often in the past, the Kazakh tribes were disunited and poorly organised, and after the death of Pugachev they no longer had a strong leader around whom they could rally. Nurali and other local khans attempted to form an alliance with Russia, but Catherine rejected these approaches; Nurali was left without any power or influence and finally sought and eventually was given refuge in Russia. The continuing insurrection in the strategically-important corner of western Kazakhstan between the Ural and Emba Rivers, and elsewhere in the north of the country, was ultimately doomed to defeat, given the growing strength of Russian forces and the severity of punitive raids on Kazakh villages and *auls*. Throughout 1775 raids were launched from Orenburg and from the new fortresses at Iletskaya and Tanalytskaya, covering long distances as far south as the Emba, and against which the Kazakh tribes of the Little and Middle Hordes were largely defenceless.

What became known as the Peasant War of 1773-1775 had far-reaching implications for Kazakhstan and its relations with Russia. The 1734 treaty between Russia and the Little Horde, and the subsequent treaty in 1740 between Russia and the khans of the Middle Horde, had marked the formal beginning of the process of unification between the two countries on an inter-state level. But the Pugachev uprising, and the continuing conflict after the death of Pugachev, were the first occasions when Russian and Kazakh peasants and tribesmen came together to fight against the common enemy of tsarist Russia. The earlier treaties had little practical significance for most Russians, but those Kazakhs who were affected by the treaties had been deeply opposed to the ensuing Russian intrusion in their lands. The Peasant War brought ordinary people of the two countries together in a way that had never happened before, when the restless and temperamental Cossacks found common cause with the more placid Kazakh herdsmen. According to Soviet histories, this prepared the ground for closer unity, based on the shared interests of the common people rather than the concerns of their imperial and aristocratic rulers. This may have been more of a political notion than a practical reality, but the episode gave a more enduring basis for future relations between Russia and Kazakhstan than had been provided by the treaties between tsars and khans.

CHAPTER SEVEN

Unrest on the Steppe: Russia Takes Control

The suppression of the Pugachev uprising restored some stability in southern Russia. The Peasant War had been disastrous for much of the country, and the desire for further resistance was virtually extinguished. Catherine ordered that scaffolds should be erected in the main square of every village, and that all those who had taken a leading part in the revolt should either be executed or returned to the most menial form of serfdom. But in the neighbouring regions of western and northern Kazakhstan, after a few years of relative but resentful peace, the rebellion was to resume and to continue for another two decades.

Further to the east, the nomadic people of the Great Horde had been largely unaffected by the uprisings against the Russians, and continued to roam largely unhindered in the vast and remote territories of eastern and southern Kazakhstan. Contact with Russia had been more limited, although tsarist troops mounted occasional raids from the new forts along the Irtysh River, but in peaceful times there was a growing amount of small-scale trading with Russian military and civilian personnel. Disruption of migration routes by Russian settlers in these regions had hardly begun, although the nomads of the Great Horde were aware of what was happening in the north and west of the country. They were also more exposed to incursions by the Dzungars, who had terrorised much of Kazakhstan from the 1720s until the collapse of the Dzungar empire in 1758. The most prominent khan of the Great Horde in the mid-eighteenth century was Ablai Khan, who later emerged to become leader of the Little and Middle Hordes as well. To counter the danger from the Dzungars in the east, and the later threat from the Russians in the west and north during the Peasant War, Ablai Khan made a new attempt to unite all the tribes and clans of Kazakhstan. He did not seek confrontation with Russia, but was more concerned to keep alive the Kazakh national identity and its ancient traditions, which he saw were in danger of being lost. Ablai Khan was admired by Catherine the Great, who welcomed his efforts to bring stability to a volatile region on Russia's borders. But there was no formal relationship or treaty between the Great Horde and Russia during the lifetime of either. After his death in 1781, however, any renascent Kazakh unity quickly disintegrated, to be followed by more internal conflicts and growing rebelliousness against Russian domination. Relations with Russia once again erupted into violence as a new campaign was fought under a new Kazakh hero, named Syrym Batyr.

Syrym Batyr was a military leader of the Little Horde who came to prominence following his rejection of the 1734 treaty between Abul Khair and Russia. Nowadays he is regarded in Kazakhstan as a heroic figure similar to Shamil, the nineteenth century leader of the mountain rebels in the Caucasus, but unlike Shamil he was never captured, and unlike other tribal leaders in Kazakhstan he never made any concessions to or deals with Russia. Syrym Batyr did not regard Abul Khair, the earlier leader of the Little Horde, as the main enemy, since Abul Khair was now widely discredited among the tribes of the Little and Middle Hordes, and no longer had many followers. Nor was Abul Khair's son Nurali a serious opponent. In the winter of 1785, most of the tribal leaders of the Little Horde in the west of Kazakhstan, encouraged by Syrym Batyr, convened an assembly to express their opposition to Nurali and disclaimed him as their khan. There were two main reasons for their disillusionment with Nurali: the Yaik and Ural Cossacks, who until recently had been their allies in the Pugachev rebellion, were now making periodic raids on Kazakh territories, causing widespread casualties, the destruction of homes and auls, and the loss of livestock. Also, due to a shortage of pasture land, the Kazakh tribes and nomads needed access to the abundant grasslands to the west of the Ural River, access to which was granted only to the followers of the khan. In neither instance did Nurali take a strong lead in defence of his fellow Kazakhs. Opposition to Nurali increased when he tried to impose taxes after harsh winters had caused further severe loss of livestock and had impoverished many herdsmen. By the time of his death in 1786, Nurali had suffered the same fate as his father Abul Khair, of losing credibility and the following of the tribes in his khanate, and while he was alive he presented no threat to Syrym Batyr. For Syrym Batyr the main enemy was Russia, and it was the Russians who now had to be expelled from Kazakh lands.

Resentment at continuing incursions and seizures of grazing lands in western and northern Kazakhstan, which had been home to Kazakh nomads for centuries, deepened and extended further throughout the country after the suppression of the Pugachev rebellion in 1775. Hostility increased in 1782 when a decree issued by the tsarist government prohibited nomadic tribes from crossing the Ural River into Russia. Other movement restrictions added to the discontent and anger felt by the nomadic herdsmen, and the weak response of Nurali and other local khans, who were keen not to antagonise the Russians, compounded the offence in the eyes of many

Kazakhs. Throughout the 1780s Syrym Batyr was able to gather large bands of landless tribesmen, armed and seeking restitution of their lands, and to lead a series of violent attacks against tsarist forces. His tactics were to avoid direct engagement with the better armed and better organised Russian army, but instead to mount raids against Russian settlements and the forts at Tanalytskaya and elsewhere along the western Orenburg Line, from where Russian troops had launched raids against the Kazakhs in 1773-1775. After wreaking as much havoc and devastation as possible he would retreat, like his Scythian and Mongol predecessors, into the vastness of the Kazakh steppe. His campaign gained in strength when many more thousands from the Middle Horde openly joined his campaign. For much of the 1780s, this new conflict, in effect a new colonial war rather than an internal civil war within Russia, raged in the region between the Ural and the Emba Rivers. After defeat in several battles, which had been forced on him by Russian troops from the new forts on the Ural River, and from which he could not disengage his forces, Syrym Batyr was compelled to retreat to the south, beyond the Emba. Thereafter the struggle continued from the relative safety of the enormous desert regions between the Caspian and Aral Seas, and further east in central Kazakhstan along the Syr Darya River. Punitive raids by superior Russian forces from the fortress at Orskaya, the easternmost of the new Russian outposts, ultimately penetrated far into the desert and forced Syrym Batyr to flee to Khiva, south of the Aral Sea, where he died in 1802.

In Russian and Soviet history Abul Khair, khan of the Little Horde, was elevated to the status of a great leader, responsible for bringing the people of Russia and Kazakhstan together under the treaty of 1734, while Syrym Batyr was condemned as a rebel and rabble-rouser, acting to further his own power. In later Kazakh versions the roles are reversed; Abul Khair is reviled as a traitor who put the interests of Russia above those of his own people, and Syrym Batyr became a hero in the struggle for the freedom of Kazakhstan. But the true picture was more confused. The Kazakhs were always weaker and militarily inferior to the forces of tsarist Russia, and not only Abul Khair and Nurali but other khans and sultans had often colluded with the tsarist authorities so as to strengthen their own positions. In reality this had the opposite effect of alienating them from their own people and from other tribal leaders, who refused to recognise their authority or have anything to do with Russia. Often this resulted in mutual antagonism and hostility between tribes and clans, and different alliances springing up to compete for summer pastures and winter quarters. Over the years the ability of different tribes to join together and sustain their own way of life was severely weakened by Russian domination, a factor which had enduring and far-reaching consequences for the future of Kazakhstan.

An exception to the difficulty of establishing a relationship between Russians and Kazakhs that was acceptable to both sides, occurred under the leadership of Bukey, khan of the Little Horde and grandson of Abul Khair. At the end of the eighteenth century, the status of western Kazakhstan, the land between the Volga and the Ural Rivers where the western extremity of the Little Horde adjoined the Russian province of Astrakhan, was still uncertain. Technically this had been part of the Russian empire since Ivan the Terrible conquered and annexed the khanate of Astrakhan in 1556, and the Ural River formed a clear border between Russian and Kazakh territory. But the region was now inhabited both by tribes of Kalmyks, who had fled from their homeland of Kalmykia further to the west during the Pugachev uprising, and by Kazakhs, who had descended from or been allied to Abul Khair, and who had been expelled by the khans of the Little Horde east of the Ural River. The more 'genuine' Kazakhs who lived east of the Ural wanted to remove all trace of Abul Khair and his supposed treachery in his dealings with Russia, and they evicted the followers of Abul Khair and his son Nurali from their traditional homelands. After the defeat of Syrym Batyr, the new khan Bukey attempted to establish a more stable relationship with Russia under which the Kazakhs living in the region could continue to live there unmolested and in peace, unthreatened by either Russians in the west or other Kazakhs in the east. The land consisted mainly of a vast, arid, and sandy tract north of the Caspian Depression known as the Rynpeski Desert, and was suitable for habitation only by nomadic people. In 1799 Bukey petitioned the tsarist authorities that this territory should formally be given over to the indigenous inhabitants who, as Bukey explained to the governor of Astrakhan, the Russian General Korring, simply wished to roam freely and pursue their itinerant way of life undisturbed. Korring realised this would be beneficial for both sides, implying stability for Russia and for Kazakhstan in a sensitive border region, and with a recommendation of acceptance he forwarded the petition to St Petersburg.

Bukey was fortunate in the timing of his request. Three years earlier Tsar Paul I had acceded to the throne after the death of his mother Catherine the Great in 1796. There would have been no possibility of Catherine agreeing to a request to concede Russian land to non-Russians, whatever the possible benefits to Russia might have been. Her life had been spent furthering the cause of Russia, in its cultural and economic development and especially in extending and securing its borders. Paul, who had grown up very much in the shadow of his mother, came to the throne with a completely different and independent outlook, and with a history of mental instability. But whatever his state of mind, he rejected all the advice of his counsellors and ministers, and seemed determined to reverse everything Catherine had done. This included prohibiting foreign travel and imposing severe restrictions on anything imported from abroad, in direct contrast to Catherine's policy of opening up Russia to foreign influences and ideas. In foreign policy Paul made an alliance with Turkey, a traditional enemy which had been defeated by Russia in 1774, greatly to the alarm of the army and the diplomatic service. Eventually Paul was murdered in a palace conspiracy and was succeeded by his son, Alexander I, in December 1801. Alexander introduced a more stable regime, abandoning the contrary policies of his father, dispensing with the superfluous formality and elaborate state occasions which Paul had favoured, and repealing some of the excessive security measures and restrictions on foreign travel and imports of foreign books. But Alexander was indecisive and hesitant in government, and his attention was soon fully taken up by relations with France, in the years leading up to the 1812 invasion of Russia. He would not have known what to make of a request from a remote tribe of nomadic Kazakhs, and would have postponed indefinitely having to make a decision. But in the short period of time between the reigns of Catherine and Alexander, Paul considered the request from Bukey for land to be allocated to Kazakh tribes, and in March 1801 gave his formal approval. In support of his decision he had the recommendation of the local governor General Korring, and a perverse desire to go against the advice of ministers and counsellors, as well as the wishes of his late mother, who would have strongly opposed the request. As a result a wide area of land between the Volga and Ural Rivers, extending from the shore of the Caspian Sea to a point on the Ural just east of the town of Uralsk, was formally transferred to Bukey. The Volga itself would have made an unmistakable border, but given the existence of a few Russian settlements along the eastern banks of the river, and a need to provide an extra security zone, the frontier was drawn some kilometres to the east, before turning to the north and east above the town of Yaitsky on the Ural River. In Kazakhstan the territory became known as the Bukey khanate, while in Russia it was referred to as the Inner Horde, reflecting its ambiguous position as a semi-independent state on the borders of the empire.

Under the terms of the agreement with Russia, Bukey was expected to maintain peace and stability, and to collect on behalf of the tsarist empire an annual tax based on the number of yurts in the khanate. In return he obtained exclusive pasture rights, and Russian farmers and Ural Cossacks were not permitted to move into the area. The arrangement provided much greater security for the nomadic population; it consolidated Kazakh territory in the extreme west of the country, and the border delineated under the agreement with Russia has endured to the present day. The land may have been barren and inhospitable, unsuitable for permanent human settlement, but for Kazakhs it was regarded as part of their natural inheritance, and for Kazakh poets it became a source of inspiration and wonder. But the peace of the region did not last for long, and renewed unrest and Russian intervention were to follow within a few years.

Bukey, a minor sultan of the Little Horde, succeeded in regaining land and ensuring stability for his people in a small but strategic part of western Kazakhstan. But elsewhere in the country, in the vast expanses to the east, more problems were building up, and the territory bequeathed by Ablai Khan, the leader of the Great Horde who had done much to unite the different tribes and khanates before his death in 1781, was under threat. At the beginning of the 1800s, much of the south of Kazakhstan was controlled by the khanate of Kokand from its capital just east of present-day Tashkent, while further west the khanates of Bukhara and Khiva extended into what had traditionally been Kazakh lands in Transoxiana and on the Ustyurt Plateau between the Aral and Caspian Seas. In the north, tsarist troops, Cossacks and Russian settlers, civil servants and other officials, all acting with encouragement from the tsarist government, extended their reach further into the depths of the Kazakh steppe. The tsarist empire by now effectively extended from the northern shores of the Caspian Sea in the west, across the whole of the northern steppes, to Ust-Kamenogorsk on the Irtysh River in the east. The unity among Kazakhs which had been achieved by Ablai Khan was now rapidly dissolving, as rival clans and khans struggled for supremacy and for territory. Where there had once been unlimited expanses for pasture and grazing, Russian incomers were now taking land and disrupting migration routes, causing severe hardship and loss of livelihoods to the local population. But instead of uniting the Kazakhs against a common enemy, the gradual Russian annexation of territory brought about more conflict and turmoil amongst the indigenous people, which in turn prompted more Russian intervention. Concerned about the growing unrest in the new parts of the empire, and determined to bring about greater stability, the tsarist government, as its predecessors had done, began to strengthen its position and assert Russian control more decisively. The man chosen to implement this policy was Mikhail Speransky, appointed as governor-general of Siberia and Kazakhstan and formerly a close adviser and personal confidant of Tsar Alexander I. However the choice of Speransky was as much due to the desire to remove him from

St Petersburg as it was to the need for new policies in Kazakhstan and other parts of the empire.

Speransky came from an ordinary background in provincial Russia, the son of an impoverished priest, and had none of the connections to the aristocracy or the army normally required for career progression in government service. Despite this handicap, by 1808 after an education at the leading ecclesiastical academy in St Petersburg, he had joined the civil service and soon became one of the key figures as a State Counsellor in the government, enjoying the confidence of senior ministers and eventually of Alexander himself. Such was the trust that Alexander had in him that he chose Speransky as an aide in his negotiations with Napoleon in the years before the French invasion. However it was in domestic affairs that Speransky acquired most prominence, at a time when the need for change and reform was increasingly apparent. It was evident to everyone that Russia was not being well governed, and Alexander had been attempting to introduce constitutional reforms since he succeeded to the throne in 1801. Unbeknown to his other advisers, Alexander discussed plans with Speransky for the fundamental reform of Russian society and government, including the emancipation of the serfs, and the introduction of elected assemblies throughout the country. On a more immediate practical level, it was clear that the government could not cope with the day-to-day administrative demands being placed upon it, and that a much larger and more professional bureaucracy would have to be created if Russia and its empire were to develop in an effective way.

Speransky introduced radical reforms into the Russian administration and bureaucracy, including a requirement for officials to pass examinations before they could be promoted to higher grades, which were generally intended to raise the level of professionalism in the civil service. As an admirer of much of what had been achieved under the post-revolutionary government in France, many of his proposed reforms were taken from the French system. In 1809 he recommended to Alexander that a Council of Ministers should be set up, similar to the State Council in France, which would draft laws and would provide a forum for discussion and coordination of government policy. Lack of coordination between ministers and departments was a perennial problem in Russia, but the idea of a Council or cabinet, and many of Speransky's other proposals, were considered to be too radical, and were only partly implemented. Alexander himself, like his ultimate successor Tsar Nicholas II a century later, preferred to deal with each of his ministers individually, rather than having to sit through cabinet meetings at which he would be expected to take decisions which he was temperamentally unsuited to do. In the case of Nicholas II this character deficiency contributed to disaster and the overthrow of the Romanov dynasty, whereas in the case of Alexander it merely perpetuated inefficiency and confusion in the government. But it was a clear and early indication of the widening gulf which existed between the way the monarchy functioned, and the reality of having to govern the country. In management of the economy, Speransky proposed reforms to regulate government spending, to control the printing and supply of money, and to sell land and state monopolies, for example in forestry, to private entrepreneurs who would operate them more efficiently. By transferring ownership of some state land to peasants, agriculture, trade, and local economic activity would be encouraged, and by generating more tax revenues the government's budget deficit would be reduced.

However, this was not an auspicious time to introduce far-reaching reforms, or especially to seek to emulate the French experience, and throughout the early 1800s Alexander and the Russian government were increasingly concerned at the worsening relations with France. Speransky's reforms and proposals came up against intense opposition from the aristocracy and from within the government, where many officials were suspicious of his professed admiration for some of the features of the French political system. His main opponent was Nikolai Karamzin, an influential figure at the court, who had no political office but who like many others at the time was devoted to the preservation of Russian culture and values, and to the protection of their ancient Slav roots from foreign influences. Speransky's ideas, such as the need for a Council of Ministers and a more open style of government, were rejected by Karamzin as unsuitable, even dangerous, for Russia, which unlike France was of an immense size and diversity, and which needed a strong and unquestioned central authority, an opinion widely held in the present day.

In the febrile political atmosphere of the time, the criticisms from Karamzin and others fearful of what was happening in France carried more weight with Alexander than Speransky and his reforms. In March 1812 Alexander dismissed Speransky as his adviser and from his position as a State Counsellor, and banished him from St Petersburg to Omsk, where he was appointed as governor-general of Siberia and Kazakhstan. Alexander may have had many regrets at losing a close friend and confidant, but his mind was now fully taken up with the imminent threat of war, and he had little time for personal considerations. For his part Speransky was now free from the intrigues and conspiracies of the court in St Petersburg, and with his wide experience of government and law, he could concentrate on the task of bringing what he saw as Russian civilisation to Siberia and to Kazakhstan, and incorporating the new lands more fully into the empire. The removal of Speransky from the centre of power meant that Russia's loss in St Petersburg and in Europe was to be its gain in Kazakhstan and Asia.

In its management of its expanding empire, the tsarist government faced the enormous dilemma as to whether and how far it should devolve power to the distant regions and territories, or whether it should retain and centralise control in St Petersburg. This became an enduring problem throughout Russian history, never more so than nearly two hundred years later when in the 1990s the government of Boris Yeltsin encouraged the regions of Russia to take as much sovereignty as they could, and become responsible for their own affairs. But at the beginning of the nineteenth century this dilemma was only just beginning to crystallise, and it was unclear whether local governors should be given the freedom to act as circumstances in their provinces demanded, which would go against stronger control from the central government, or whether different parts of the empire should all comply with what the government in St Petersburg dictated, irrespective of local conditions and customs. A system of government that was suitable for Russia's territories in the Baltic, and for Russia itself, was clearly not ideal for the nomadic herdsmen of Kazakhstan and elsewhere in Central Asia and Siberia. It was against this background that Speransky was to play his most significant role, in effectively extending Russian authority in the territories for which he was now responsible, but it would be another ten years before any substantial or practical measures could be introduced.

In June 1812 the 350,000 men of the French Grande Armee crossed the River Niemen at the start of Napoleon's ill-fated advance on Moscow. From October to December 1812 the same army, having reached and then being forced to abandon Moscow, and now greatly reduced in strength and numbers, was making a desperate and chaotic retreat through the snows and blizzards of Russia. The diplomatic and political implications of the war were to occupy Alexander and the government in St Petersburg for much of the next decade, and relatively little attention could be devoted to the government of the colonial territories in the east. The Napoleonic invasion and the occupation and subsequent burning down of Moscow by vindictive French troops before they embarked on their disastrous retreat, were deeply traumatising events for the people of Russia. But the eventual victory over Napoleon marked a further decisive stage in the evolution of Russia as a European power, and one with an expanding empire in the east. This was to have far-reaching consequences for Kazakhstan and other territories in Central

Asia. The war in the West had had little direct impact on life on the steppes, except to reduce the Russian military presence and activity in the region, as most of the troops were drafted to fight against the French, which had the effect of alleviating some of the harassment of the native population. But many of the new Russian settlers arriving in Kazakhstan after the war increasingly felt themselves under threat from hostile Kazakh tribes and this factor, combined with worsening economic conditions within Kazakhstan and continued unrest among the Kazakhs themselves, called for a new strategy for the country.

With this in mind, over the next ten years Speransky devised the creation of two vast administrative regions, or military districts. The first, established in 1822, covered the whole of north-eastern Kazakhstan, extending from Kustanai in the north as far as the border with China in the east. This region was inhabited by the people of the Middle Horde, and was designated by Russia as 'the land of the Siberian Kazakhs'. The second district, established in 1824, extended from the Ural River in the west to a line roughly in the centre of Kazakhstan and included the tribes of the Little Horde; this was known as 'the land of the Orenburg Kazakhs'. In the middle of this district, near the confluence of the Irgiz and Turgai Rivers, was Irgiz, the remote site of the original treaty in 1731 between Russia and the Little Horde, and which by now had grown into a small town. The administrative centres for both districts – Omsk and Orenburg – were both located in Russian territory, reflecting Speransky's intention to maintain control from Russia and eventually to absorb these regions into Russia itself. Subsequently a third, smaller district was created and squeezed in between the Ural River and the Bukey khanate, inhabited by the 'Ural Kazakhs'.

The new military districts were to be governed according to sets of 'Rules', the name itself reflecting the colonial attitude of the imperial authorities. These Rules differed considerably in what they contained and how they were applied in each district, but a common factor in all three districts was to have radical and far-reaching implications for the future of Kazakhstan. As part of his overall strategy, Speransky formally abolished the position of khan in both the Siberian and Orenburg districts. This measure was later extended to other regions as they fell under Russian control so that the khan, who fulfilled an ancient role and who had been part of Kazakh life for centuries, was now replaced by a local Russian or Russian-appointed governor. In a further decisive break with Kazakh tradition and history, in 1824 the concept of the horde was also abolished. The Little and Middle hordes had been the dominant features of the country since they emerged as distinct entities in western and central Kazakhstan three hundred years before in the early 1500s; as a result of the new edicts, the Kazakh communities in these regions were now effectively leaderless, deprived not only of their familiar social structure of khanates and hordes, but even more fundamentally of their sense of identity and their place in the world. These actions effectively removed any possibility of Kazakhstan gaining independence or self-government under tsarist rule. In the south and east of the country, the vast territories of the Great Horde were not affected by these measures and for the time being remained intact, but within a few decades they also would come under Russian control.

Under the 'Rules for the Siberian Kazakhs', Speransky divided the region into administrative units of diminishing size, from the county authority known as the *okrug,* down to the smallest *aul,* or village. Local officials were to be appointed by Russian administrators rather than through the hereditary system of khans. As he had tried to do in St Petersburg, Speransky established a forum in each county known as a *prikaz,* which was responsible for discussing local issues and balancing opposing interests and groups, as well as maintaining law and order, preventing raids between different clans, and collecting a tax levied on all livestock. Exempt from this Rule were camels, which were seen as unproductive and thus used only for transport. The prikaz acted as a court to which cases of resistance to state authority, as well as of theft or other crimes, had to be submitted. Membership of the prikaz consisted of tsarist officials and local leaders, but the ultimate authority lay with the Russian officials who were appointed by Speransky from his headquarters in Omsk. Speransky's objective was to pacify the steppe by establishing a settled form of agriculture and bringing about an end to the nomadic way of life, thus unauthorised crossing of okrug borders was prohibited. Land was given to those Kazakhs who agreed to accept these provisions, and schools, hospitals and other administrative buildings were built in the okrug centres. By these means Speransky hoped to prevent uncontrolled migrations and reduce disorder on the steppe, but for Kazakhs this all amounted to more unwanted intrusion in their own affairs, and would not bring the stability which Russia had hoped for. The 'Rules for the Orenburg Kazakhs' to the west likewise divided the district into smaller, more easily governable areas. These areas usually remained under local tribal leaders, who abandoned their previous roles in the tribe or clan and became quasi-tsarist officials, receiving salaries and taking responsibility for collecting an annual yurt tax, as well as carrying out other civil functions on behalf of the tsarist authorities. It cannot have been an enviable position, similar to that of other Russian-appointed officials in earlier times, and in many cases detachments of Cossacks, now reconciled to Russian command, were sent to Kazakh villages and auls to enforce compliance with the new government rules.

Speransky did not apply the ruthless cruelty or the authoritarian excesses which Josef Stalin was to exhibit in the 1930s, but some of his policies were to have a detrimental effect on traditional Kazakh society almost as profound as those of Stalin. Notwithstanding his own modest origins, Speransky had a superior, even disdainful, attitude towards the native populations of Kazakhstan and Siberia, believing that the people of these vast areas could not be treated like Russians, given their primitive and itinerant way of life and their rudimentary systems of law and government. To a certain extent he pursued an enlightened policy, trying to establish a balance of power between tribal leaders on the one hand and the Russian authorities on the other. But his underlying motivation was to incorporate Kazakhstan into Russia, and to ensure that the indigenous population should become Russified as soon as possible, as had happened under Ivan the Terrible in Kazan and Astrakhan in the sixteenth century. To a large degree these objectives were achieved, but by obstructing centuries-old Kazakh nomadic traditions, and dismantling the social structures of khans and hordes, Speransky also gained an enduring legacy of resentment towards Russia and its empire in Kazakhstan.

In the Bukey khanate the position of khan was not immediately abolished. When Bukey died in 1823, a new khan by the name of Jangir took control of the khanate and strengthened his own position, contrary to the abolition of the role of the khan which was taking place elsewhere. This suited Speransky, who did not wish to destabilise the region by upsetting the 1801 agreement approved by Tsar Paul I. Jangir effectively occupied two positions, as a tsarist official with the military rank of major-general, while also retaining the role of khan. He was not from a nomadic background, having been brought up more as a Russian than as a Kazakh, in the house of the Russian governor of Astrakhan. Thus he was more comfortable in establishing his headquarters in a permanent location at Saralzhin, a remote settlement in the north of the Rynpeski Desert. From here he encouraged the settlement of the nomadic tribesmen by promoting other types of farming and forestation, while at the same time looking after the interests of Kazakh tribes, encouraging trade and Islamic (and not Russian Orthodox) education, and representing Kazakhs in disputes with the Russian authorities. Once again the timing of these developments in the khanate, and in the new districts of Omsk and Orenburg, was fortunate, as they took place before the next major upheaval in St Petersburg: the Decembrist Uprising of 1825, and the accession of Nicholas I to the throne. Thereafter it is unlikely that Speransky would have been able to act as he did, and a completely different policy, more harsh and severe than what had gone before, was soon to be enacted on the steppe. The relatively harmonious situation in the Bukey khanate would not last for long, and eventually the khanate was abolished in 1845 and absorbed into the Orenburg military district. Meanwhile on the steppes of Kazakhstan, Russian hopes of introducing its version of civilisation were not to be fulfilled as planned.

CHAPTER EIGHT

Russia Expands Eastwards, and the Great Horde Joins the Empire

Towards the end of 1825 the court in St Petersburg, and thus the Russian imperial administration throughout the empire, were once again plunged into confusion and uncertainty. In November of that year, while staying at Taganrog on the Sea of Azov where his wife the Empress Elizabeth was recovering from a mild illness, Tsar Alexander I himself unexpectedly fell ill and died. The succession should have fallen to the eldest of his three brothers, the Grand Duke Constantine, who was at the time living in Warsaw where he was serving as Viceroy of Poland. Constantine had long made it plain, however, that he had no wish to take over the throne of Russia from his brother, and that the succession would have to pass to Alexander's younger brother Nicholas. Initially Nicholas also refused to accept the succession, and only agreed to do so when it was clear that Constantine would not change his mind. Nicholas also wanted to be certain that the regiments of the Imperial Guards, who had served under Constantine during the Napoleonic campaigns and who strongly preferred Constantine for the role of tsar, would in fact be willing to serve under him. After a second refusal from Constantine, and unable to put off a decision any longer, Nicholas realised he had no choice and reluctantly agreed to accept the succession.

This prevarication and hesitancy undermined Nicholas' credibility as a tsar and emperor even before he had succeeded to the throne. Matters became worse the following month, when what had been a near-farcical situation of neither brother wanting to become tsar, turned into a much more serious threat to Nicholas and to the institution of the monarchy itself. For months the same officers from the regiment of Guards, from whom Nicholas had been waiting for a pledge of loyalty, had been conspiring against him. Many were attracted to the type of political freedom which they had seen in France after the defeat of Napoleon, and were determined to achieve a form of government in Russia which was more representative of the people. They now sought to challenge the legitimacy of Nicholas as the new tsar, demanding that Constantine, despite his refusal, should accept the role, and that in addition a National Assembly should be established which would govern Russia according to a proper constitution. However, the conspirators neglected to organise any substantial support, either among the ordinary people who they claimed to represent, or among their own numbers in the army. In the freezing dawn of 14 December 1825, a small group of officers gathered on Senate Square in St Petersburg, near the Bronze Horseman statue of Peter the Great, and made their demands for a National Assembly and formal constitution. More soldiers and simple spectators joined the crowds during the day. The uprising failed when Nicholas gave the order for the Artillery and troops of the Preobrazhensky regiment, which remained loyal to him, to fire on the demonstrators and disperse the crowd. Scores of people were killed and many more were injured in a stampede to escape from the gunfire. Nearly three hundred of the conspirators were subsequently sentenced to exile in Siberia, a journey which they were compelled to make on foot. Many were accompanied by their wives and families.

The Decembrist Uprising became another of the many deeply unsettling episodes in Russian history which not only determined the subsequent nature of the government in St Petersburg, but also had a decisive impact on the evolution of the empire. After the shock of the failed attempt to overthrow him, Nicholas was quick to revert to the strict regime of censorship and pervasive security and controls which had been introduced by his father Paul, but which had been relaxed by his brother Alexander. Unlike Alexander, Nicholas was decisive and clear about what he wanted for Russia, which above all was that there should be no further conspiracies against him, or threats to the monarchy or to the empire. He sought to revive a sense of national confidence in the Russian state and its people, harking back to the 1812 victory over Napoleon, which had demonstrated how Russia had prevailed against foreign invaders, and how Russia would rise again in the future against any who challenged or conspired against the empire. Nicholas devoted much of his time to military matters, but he was also keen to strengthen the rule of law, as a means by which the monarchy could reinforce its authority. To this end he recalled Mikhail Speransky from his post in Omsk. No doubt Nicholas remembered how effective Speransky had been when working with his brother Alexander before Alexander appointed him as governor of Siberia and Kazakhstan. Nicholas now assigned to Speransky the task of codifying all the legislation which had been enacted in Russia since the earliest years of the Romanov dynasty but which had not necessarily extended to all parts of the empire. The result was the publication in 1833 of a 'Complete Collection of Laws of the Russian Empire', which consolidated all the various laws, decrees and edicts introduced over the centuries and which were now to apply to every corner of the empire. Within Russia itself, Nicholas' harsh methods of government meant that political and social stability was generally preserved, although the chasm between the wealth of the nobility and the impoverishment of the ordinary people and the peasantry continued to widen. In remote non-Russian parts of the empire, unrest was never far below the surface, and in Kazakhstan in the 1830s, without the stabilising influence of Speransky, discontent was once again about to erupt into violent conflict with the tsarist government.

During his term as governor-general of Siberia and Kazakhstan, Speransky had introduced Russian administration into all the regions for which he was responsible, and in effect incorporated those territories, principally northern and western Kazakhstan, into the Russian empire. His institutional reforms, including the setting up of local councils, and appointing Kazakh leaders to positions of authority to act on behalf of the tsarist government, were less successful. Nomads and herdsmen increasingly realised the bitter truth that they could no longer depend on their own local khans for protection of their way of life, or even for their survival, but that their future now lay on individual relations with tsarist officials, either Russians or Russian-appointed Kazakhs. The widening social divisions between the aristocracy and peasantry in Russia were matched by a deepening rift between tsarist officials and the local population in Kazakhstan, a development which gave rise to considerable resentment, directed at Russians and at those Kazakhs who conformed to the new regime.

The most significant policy attempted by Speransky was to encourage nomadic tribes to adopt a settled form of agriculture along Russian lines of landowner and farm worker. This was doomed to failure, or to a form of success which could only be imposed by military force. Two completely different social orders now came into conflict: a tsarist-imposed system of self-contained and static agriculture within the newly-established territorial areas, and the ancient Kazakh tribal order, which could not exist on a local scale due to long migration routes between winter pastures on the southern steppe and summer pastures in the northern steppe. Economic pressures on Kazakh tribes and communities were also increasing due to incursions in the south from the khanates of Kokand, Bukhara, and Khiva, and the conquest by local khans of the whole of the Syr Darya region, which in turn considerably added to the demands imposed on the northern steppe. The extent of the northern lands may have been vast but the soil was dry and friable, and the grasses were of limited nutritional value for grazing, thus enormous areas were needed to sustain even modest herds, and constant movement of cattle and horses was essential. Different tribal groups competed for influence and for better access to grazing land and pastures, and in the tsarist-administered areas the authority of clan chiefs and tribal leaders increasingly depended on their relations with local tsarist officials. The policy of promoting the settlement of nomadic tribes, either by persuasion or by force, was also having religious consequences. Kazakh khans and herdsmen had no inclination towards the Russian Orthodox Church as practised by Russian settlers around them, but instead they were increasingly driven towards Islam, not least as a means of establishing an identity separate from Russia.

All of this was leading to intense hostility against Russia and the officials of the tsarist empire, partly because of the iniquity of land allocation and the administrative system, but also because of the friction and unrest which it was causing between local tribes. The Russian administration in Omsk and Orenburg could not fail to notice these developments, but rather than seeking to modify its policies, the response was to persist with the aim of pacifying what the government saw as uncooperative and hostile nomadic herdsmen, and effectively destroying the old tribal political order of Kazakhstan. In theory this was a relatively easy task given Russian military superiority, the weak pastoral economy of Kazakhstan, and persistent divisions between local clans and tribes. But in practice it was to take many more years of conflict and suppression before the steppes and the native people could be fully subjugated and brought under Russian control.

After a period of relative stability in the early years of Nicholas' reign, the peace of the steppe was again upturned by rebellions and uprisings. Unrest started in the Bukey khanate in the far west of Kazkhstan, where the supposedly independent status of the khanate, and the freedom granted to the nomadic tribes, were coming under great strain. The authority of Jangir Khan was rapidly declining as he personally was doubly tainted in the eyes of the local Kazakh population: he was a tsarist official appointed by the Russian authorities in Astrakhan, and he was not a true Kazakh tribesman by background, having been brought up and educated within the Russian community in Astrakhan. He did not conform to the Speransky model of Kazakh leader appointed to a tsarist position, and while he tried to mediate between Kazakhs and Russians, his connections with the local people were tenuous. Discontent among ordinary herdsmen spread when the allocation of pastures and land favoured the owners of large herds and wealthy families close to Jangir and his relations, and movement restrictions imposed on nomadic clans were a further source of resentment and unrest.

By the mid-1830s opposition to Jangir had turned into open revolt. The notion of the Bukey khanate as a separate region free from Russian control had by now ceased to exist; Jangir could no longer maintain his twin roles of Kazakh leader and Russian-appointed mediator, and became instead the focus of Kazakh discontent. In an uprising which was as violent and as destructive as the earlier rebellions of Pugachev and Syrym Batyr, the steppes of north-western Kazakhstan were again engulfed in turmoil and conflict. Leading the rebellion were two tribal leaders, Isatay Taiman and Makhambeta Utemisov, who in the summer of 1836 in the desert region along the eastern coast of the Caspian Sea organised groups of rebel fighters to campaign against Jangir and against Russian control. From there the conflict spread northwards and before long the whole of the khanate and the Ural region was in flames. In October 1836, detachments of tsarist troops were sent from the forts at Orenburg to the east and from Astrakhan in the west, and struggled to subdue the uprising in a campaign which lasted for two years. Isatay Taiman was forced to flee eastwards across the Ural River and into the steppe as far as Emba, but in a repeat of the campaign against Syrym Batyr fifty years earlier, he was constantly pursued by Russian troops and forced back towards the Ural. Eventually Isatay Taiman was captured and killed at Sakharnaya, a small settlement on the Ural River, in July 1838. Utemisov met a similar fate in the desert near the Emba River.

The suppression of the revolt of the 'Orenburg Kazakhs' brought a temporary lull to anti-Russian activity in western parts of the country, but more unrest was developing further east, among the Siberian Kazakhs of northern Kazakhstan. By early 1838 a new rebellion was spreading in a large area around the Turgai River near its confluence with the Irgiz and the site of the treaty between the Little Horde under Abul Khair and Russia in 1731. The principal leader of the Kazakhs now was Kenesary Khan, a khan of the Middle Horde, who initially tried to negotiate an agreement with Russia to limit its further expansion. When the tsarist authorities refused to conduct any discussions with him, Kenesary turned south to seek an alliance with the khanate of Kokand. Unfortunately for Kenesary, at the time the khans of Kokand were oblivious to the dangers of Russian encroachment towards their borders, and refused to negotiate with him. Having failed to achieve his aims through diplomatic means, Kenesary led a series of campaigns in the early 1840s against Russian settlements and military positions. A particularly violent battle was fought at the new Russian fort at Akmolinsk in 1843, triggering punitive raids by Russian forces from the forts at Petropavlovsk and Omsk. From 1844 to 1845 a vast area extending over the whole of north-eastern Kazakhstan was caught up in conflict between Kazakh tribes and Russian forces. The uprising was ultimately futile and Kenesary was killed on the battlefield at Uzunagach, a remote spot not far to the west of present-day Almaty, in 1847. Alongside Syrym Batyr, Isatay

Taiman, and Makhambeta Utemisov, Kenesary is nowadays remembered in Kazakh history as a patriot who led Kazakhs in their campaigns against tsarist forces, although another member of the same family - Chokan Valikhanov - is also revered for his attempts to bring Kazakhstan closer to Russia. But Kenesary's main historical significance is that as a result of the Speransky reforms, he was the last khan of the Middle Horde; after his death the role ceased to exist throughout the Little and Middle Hordes, and within a few years the same would apply in the vast region of the Great Horde.

By the middle of the nineteenth century the whole of south-eastern Kazakhstan, including the extensive lands between Lake Zaisan, Lake Balkhash, and the Tien Shan Mountains, was still independent of Russia. Nomadic communities and local khans still freely roamed the steppes, and the Great Horde itself still existed as a vital concept among the indigenous Kazakhs, even if it was not recognised by Russia after the Speransky reforms. Early attempts had been made by some of the khans of the Great Horde to seek a treaty with Russia, notably by Tole bi, the principal khan of the 1730s, at the time when Abul Khair, khan of the Little Horde, was also seeking a treaty and a defensive arrangement with Russia. In 1734 Tole bi, aware of the treaty that had been signed in January that year between Abul Khair and the tsarist government, approached the Empress Anna requesting protection against the Dzungars, and a draft treaty was eventually drawn up by Russia in 1739. Nothing came of this initiative, due to the same divisions among the different clans and khans within the Great Horde that affected the other hordes, and which despite the unifying efforts of Tole bi, remained acute and intractable. After the failure of the draft 1739 treaty, the khans continued to resist the threat from the Dzungars, until the collapse of the Dzungar empire in the 1750s, without Russian protection. The conflict with the Dzungars and the loss of much of the territory of the Great Horde, effectively prevented the emergence of a united approach to Russia, and when Tole bi died in 1756 the problems facing the Great Horde were still unresolved. Matters were made no easier by the accession to the throne in St. Petersburg six years later by Catherine II. The arrival of Catherine meant that from the time of the death of Peter the Great in 1725 to when Catherine died in 1796 (apart from the seven-month reign of Peter III from January to July 1762, and of the infant Ivan IV in 1740), the imperial throne in St Petersburg was occupied by a tsarina. For most of the austere and feudal khans of the Great Horde, in their remote mountain fastness of eastern Kazakhstan, submission to a female ruler would be demeaning and impossible. The colonisation of Central Asia by Russia would have been very different if this had not been the case. Continuing oppression by Russian imperial forces against the Little and Middle Hordes throughout the second half of the eighteenth and the first half of the nineteenth centuries, made the prospect of a new treaty even less likely.

By 1848 almost a century had passed since the death of Tole bi, and Russia had now been governed by male emperors, initially Paul I and Alexander I and since 1825 by Nicholas I, for over fifty years. The time had come to seek a new relationship with Russia, and in July 1848 the Kazakh khans of the Great Horde came together and once again approached the tsarist authorities, in the form of the Russian governor of western Siberia, with according to Soviet history an unequivocal request for Russian nationality and protection. Russia and the Great Horde now shared a common desire for stability and security in the region. The threat from the Dzungars had ceased, but to the south the lack of clear frontiers was leading to frequent skirmishes between Russian forces and the tribes of the Great Horde on one hand, and the Central Asian khanates of Khiva, Kokand, and Bukhara, on the other. Russia and the remaining part of Kazakhstan outside its empire were now allies facing a series of common enemies. Within the Great Horde, incessant conflict between different warring groups had reversed many of the achievements of Ablai Khan and Tole bi in the previous century in bringing the various tribes together, and had brought virtual ruin to large areas of the local economy. The Horde had escaped the radical reforms of Mikhail Speransky in the 1820s, but it was weak and deeply divided, and unable to defend itself against incursions and attacks from the southern khanates. According to the same Soviet version of this period, the mass of the Kazakh people now leaned towards closer ties with Russia, with which there was already close contact and substantial volumes of trade. Speransky had long since returned to St Petersburg, but Nicholas I was anxious to build on his achievements and extend Russian control beyond the 'Land of the Siberian Kazakhs' north of the Irtysh River which had been established by Speransky in 1822.

The Kazakh request was duly granted on 18 January 1849 when the khans of the Great Horde formally submitted to Russian sovereignty, and Russia accepted the territory and people of the Great Horde into its empire. This historic development was marked by the creation of a new 'Land of the Semirechie Kazakhs', and completed the formal Russian annexation of Kazakhstan. But as had happened earlier with other territories, it was fiercely opposed by many of the local khans and clans, who rejected the loss of sovereignty and submission to a foreign power, and continued to make sporadic attacks on Russian troops and settlers. In the end effective resistance was slight, and over the following years Russia proceeded to incorporate its new territory into the empire through the same administrative and economic measures which Speransky had introduced in Orenburg and Omsk in the 1820s. Foremost among the policies of the tsarist government was to be the further large-scale resettlement of farming communities from Russia; this had already been widely implemented in the northern and western parts of Kazakhstan, and was now to be extended to the south and east of the country. As yet there was no administrative centre for the new territory, and for the next four years the government was conducted from Semipalatinsk in the region of the 'Siberian Kazakhs', several hundred kilometres to the north of Semirechie. But in a far-reaching strategic decision determining the future not only of the Semirechie region but the whole of Kazakhstan, a new military fort and administrative centre was established at Verny in 1854.

Construction of a new chain of forts south of the original Orenburg Line had already begun in the 1830s, to counter the uprisings led by Jangir in the Bukey khanate, Isatay Taimanov in western Kazakhstan, and Kenesary in the north. The new forts extended from the caravanserais at Kokchetav in central Kazakhstan, to Akmolinsk in the centre of the country, and Karkaralinsk, 300 kilometres to the east. Karkaralinsk was a particularly isolated and unviable location, and unlike the other two settlements it did not develop into a major city. In preparation for further expansion to the south, the tsarist government now saw a need for a new line of fortresses, to be known as the Syr Darya Line, the first of which was established in 1847 at Aralsk on the north-eastern tip of the Aral Sea. Three years later the next fort was built at Kazalinsk, 120 kilometres to the south on the Syr Darya River; this was followed in 1853 by the capture by tsarist forces of Ak-Mechet ('White Mosque'), a fortified town in the khanate of Bukhara 300 kilometres upstream. Ak-Mechet was renamed Perovsk after the Russian general responsible for its capture, and later briefly became the capital of Kazakhstan, renamed as Kyzyl-Orda, in the 1920s. The last and the most substantial in this line of fortresses was Verny.

The death of Kenesary in 1847, followed by the 1849 treaty with the Great Horde, marked the end of most of the uprisings and violence which had dominated much of the territory of Kazakhstan in the first half of the nineteenth century. Russian control could now be asserted both from the forts in the north of the country and from the new Syr Darya Line in the south. The land was not completely pacified, and unrest in the Emba region brought punitive raids from Uralsk and Orenburg in 1854 and 1855, which in turn led to another mass rebellion in 1856 under the leadership of a minor Kazakh khan named Eset Kotibarov. Ultimately the whole of the Kotibarov aul was displaced by

Russian troops and forcibly resettled in the Ustyurt Plateau. Elsewhere the steppes were quiet; the native population may not have been happy to be under Russian control, but they had been forced to the conclusion that this was to be their way of life from now on. From the Russian point of view, as had been anticipated by the tsarist government, the attention of troops stationed in the forts at Aralsk, Kazalinsk, and Perovsk was now directed to a new source of unrest: the khanates of Khiva, Bukhara, and Kokand, south of the Syr Darya River. This was to develop into large-scale conflict and conquests in the 1860s and 1870s, when Russian strategy became much more aggressive in its drive to incorporate these territories into the tsarist empire. But for the moment the medieval and backward khanates represented an irritation along the new southern frontier of the empire, and in another historic development, joint Russian and Kazakh military action was taken for the first time.

For the Kazakhs who had already been forced off their lands in the north of Kazakhstan and had attempted to establish grazing lands in the Syr Darya, armed attacks from Khiva and Bukhara were far more than irritations. The khanates for their part were incensed at Kazakh settlements in what they saw as their territories along the river. In 1856 a new Kazakh uprising led by Zhankhozha Nurmukhamedov took place around Kazalinsk and Perovsk, and this time the violence was directed not at the Russians but against the khans from the south. The following year Kazakh tribes joined forces with tsarist troops in military action against the khans and sultans of Khiva. Further upstream on the Syr Darya around the present-day towns of Chimkent and Tashkent, Kazakhs were also in conflict with the khanate of Kokand. These small-scale but violent campaigns were to continue over the next two decades, when Russia extended its control further into the desert khanates of Central Asia, and brought it into conflict with Britain in the Tournament of Shadows.

The extent to which the accession of the Kazakh territories to the Russian empire was 'voluntary' may be disputed, and it is easy to dismiss Soviet versions which stressed the Kazakh requests for Russian protection and citizenship as propaganda. Russian control of Kazakhstan put an end to many of the interminable internecine conflicts which had gravely weakened many Kazakh tribes and families, and was a development widely and genuinely welcomed by much of the indigenous population. In addition, the Speransky reforms of the 1820s introduced a more effective legal system and a greater degree of justice and equal treatment for the mass of the population. The abolition of khans and hordes was still resented, and many nomadic tribes, especially in the north and west of the country which were most exposed to Russia, suffered greatly, but communities in other parts of the country stood to gain from a more stable economic relationship with the colonial power. Farms and orchards began to produce more and more food for the Russian market, and small artisanal workshops and nascent industries were beginning to spring up in the growing towns and cities. 'Despite the burden of tsarist colonial oppression, the unification of Kazakhstan and Russia gave a sharp stimulus to the development of Kazakhstan, and the local economy was drawn into the whirl of the wider Russian market', was how one official Soviet history summarised the essential aspects of the new relationship with Russia. But the economic benefits were less certain, as the traditional nomadic communities had little need of external markets or trade with Russia. The influx of many thousands of incomers resulted in Kazakh lands being seized and allocated to Russian settlers and farmers, and in irreparable disruption being caused to seasonal migration routes, which had been used by Kazakh nomads for centuries. All of this caused great hardship, loss of livelihoods, and deep resentment. Violent rebellions and campaigns against Russia continued into the 1850s and 1860s in the west of Kazakhstan in the region between the Caspian and Aral Seas, which had been part of the tsarist empire since the treaties of 1731 and 1734. These uprisings were forcibly put down by punitive military expeditions from the fortresses at Orenburg and Uralsk. Kazakh cultural traditions of ancient oral epics told by itinerant bards were also under threat from Russian interference and domination.

But if Kazakhstan was to evolve from a traditional and conservative nomadic society of feuding clans and khans, the relationship with Russia was probably the best, if not the only, way of achieving progress. In addition, the threat from the Dzungars in the east had disappeared in the previous century, but new dangers were emerging from the khanates in the south, and here Russia and Kazakhstan now shared a common interest. Without Russian support, many Kazakhs would have suffered even more from attacks from the khanates of Khiva and Bukhara, and the incidence of joint military action against a common enemy marked a new stage in the relationship.

Meanwhile major political and economic developments were taking place in Russia in the second half of the nineteenth century. After nearly thirty years as tsar and emperor, on 18 February 1855 Nicholas I died from pneumonia and was succeeded by his son Alexander. Unlike his father, Alexander II was more inclined towards progress and reform rather than political repression, and was concerned to resolve some of the deep social and economic problems facing the country. Foremost among these were the weakness and disorganisation of the army which were exposed by the calamitous losses suffered by Russia in the Crimean War, and the urgent need to improve the disastrous state of the country's roads and the transport network as a whole. But the most deep-rooted problem was the growing burden of serfdom which was having a debilitating effect on the economy and on the country as a whole. The eventual emancipation of the serfs in 1861 was to have profound consequences not only for Russia but also for Kazakhstan and the empire.

The serfs were in a dire position in Russia in the mid-nineteenth century; they were supposedly the mainstay of the Russian empire and on them lay the responsibility for providing food for the population, recruits for the army, and taxes to the government. But in return the government accepted no responsibility for the serfs; instead the serfs, as well as providing for the needs of the state, had to fend for themselves. The peasant was bound to a landowner who had full powers of ownership over him, and could be bought and sold at markets, sometimes separately from their families. Serfs had to pay dues to the landowner either in the form of labour known as *barschina,* or in money or goods which they produced, in a system known as *obrok.* As well as these onerous levies, serfs were also liable to taxation in their own name, and to conscription in the army for a term of twenty-five years. Some peasants managed to buy small areas of land of their own in addition to the communal allotments on which they worked for the benefit of the landowner, but overall the system served to accentuate the differences between the peasants and the rest of society, and highlighted the widening gulf between the peasantry and the nobility. The peasants were parochial and lived according to an egalitarian system of communal government, whereas the aristocracy was cosmopolitan, hierarchical, and complacent. Few landowners had any knowledge of agriculture or management of the land. The end result was poverty and instability throughout the countryside, a situation which threatened not only the land-owning classes but also the government, which could not rely on the system to meet its needs for revenue, or to provide a credible army with which to defend the country.

By the 1850s it was apparent that serfdom was severely restraining the development of Russia, which was now lagging far behind Western Europe where serfdom was in decline or had disappeared altogether. It was also a permanent source of potential unrest in the Russian countryside, where although the vast majority of peasants were generally acquiescent, uprisings and attacks on the farms and mansions of landowners and aristocrats were not uncommon. But it was the poor condition and illiteracy of serfs who made up the country's armed forces, and the inability of the serf economy to sustain the country at war, as had been exposed by the disaster of the Crimean War, which made the need for reform unavoidable. Much of the blame for Russia's backwardness was laid at the door of Nicholas I, who had wilfully ignored the corruption and incompetence in the army and navy, which had both proved unequal to the task of defending the country on its home territory in the Crimea against an invasion launched from over a thousand miles away by Britain and France. The poor state of the roads, the lack of railways, but more profoundly the whole structure of the country and its autocratic system of government, all contributed to Russia's defeat and to the inescapable realisation that there must be change. Increasingly it was understood that Russia could not survive and function normally in the modern world unless the serf economy was abolished. This was something which united all sections of Russian society, including Westerners and Slavophiles. The schism between the Westerners and Slavophiles was one of the main features of life in nineteenth-century Russia; the Westerners looked to Europe for ideas and inspiration, in government, politics, art, and literature, while the Slavophiles believed in the primacy of Russia's own history and traditions, and rejected what they saw as the superficial and seductive culture of the West. But the two opposing camps agreed that the single problem undermining Russia's strength and position in the world was serfdom. 'Serfdom is a shackle which we drag around with us, and which holds us back just when other countries are racing ahead unimpeded. Without the abolition of serfdom none of our problems, political, administrative, or social, can be solved', was the view of the Westerner and writer Boris Chicherin, who later became mayor of Moscow. Slavophiles viewed serfdom as a moral and legal divide running through the middle of Russian society, in which millions of serfs paid tax to the state but were effectively outside the law and outside any direct relationship with the government.

The mood in the country became more favourable to the possibility of change on the death of Nicholas I in 1855. This was a year before the end of the Crimean War but it was this event which encouraged Leo Tolstoy, who had already established a reputation as a writer and had served in an artillery brigade in the Crimea, to put forward proposals for reforms in the army. Initially his plans were for the modernisation of the country's entire military forces, based on his experience as a serving officer. But the time he spent living in close quarters with ordinary soldiers, who until recently had been serfs on the land, had awakened him to the simple virtues of the peasantry and an awareness of the injustices of serfdom. Tolstoy's ideas and those of many others advocating reform met with a positive response from the new tsar Alexander II. Alexander believed it was better to abolish serfdom from above than for it to be abolished from below, and called upon the generally hostile aristocracy to accept emancipation of the serfs as an essential measure to prevent revolution. In 1858 Alexander appointed a commission to draw up proposals as to how the system should be dismantled, but the commission was soon faced with intense opposition from reactionary landowners, who presented innumerable seemingly intractable administrative problems of surveying, assessing, and allocating millions of acres of land. Emancipation without giving land to serfs on which they could support themselves would cause widespread poverty and further alienate the peasantry; this had been the experience in the Baltic region at the beginning of the century. Emancipation with land, on the other hand, without compensation for landowners, would similarly cause uproar among the aristocracy. Two years of intense controversy and dispute between landowners on one side and almost everyone else on the other side, followed before Alexander signed a Statute of Emancipation on 19 February 1861.

The Statute provided for land to be allocated to the peasants, but which they would have to pay for by means of payments known as redemption dues. These payments were largely calculated according to the landowners' own valuations of the land to be allocated, and would be made to the government over a period of forty-nine years, while the government compensated the landowners for their loss of land straightaway. In practice much of the money paid to landowners was used to settle the enormous debts which they had incurred with the government and with banks, and relatively little was left over to compensate them for the loss of land or serfs. For their part the serfs had expected to be given land without payment, and the new arrangement left them in not much of a better position than before. But the serfs also now had freedom if they wished to leave the landowners to whom they had been bound for many generations, and to move to other parts of the country in search of work. Many took advantage of their new liberty, seeking work in the expanding towns and factories, and on the railways and rivers. The greater ability to travel, and improvements in education and literacy which were introduced following emancipation, served to broaden the horizons of many peasant families; combined with the disappointment at not being granted ownership or control over the land which they cultivated, many were now prepared to look further afield for employment and a new life. In this search they received active encouragement from the government.

The result was a mass movement of individuals, families and whole communities, not only between different regions within Russia, but beyond its borders to the new territories of Central Asia and especially Kazakhstan. Here they were given land by the government without having to pay redemption dues, since the Russian government did not pay compensation to the local Kazakh population. To do this it would have had to identify the owners of the land, which in Kazakhstan was difficult, if not impossible. Among the indigenous nomadic communities, the notion of land ownership was entirely different to that in Russia; in Russia, ownership rights were fixed in relation to individual estates and properties, whereas in Kazakhstan, land ownership involved the transient use of the land according to the seasons, soil conditions, weather, and other natural phenomena. The compensation scheme for landowners was not entirely successful in Russia, where redemption dues became increasingly difficult to collect from the emancipated serfs, and the government had no wish to introduce it in Kazakhstan.

The departure of large sections of the population after emancipation was expedient for the tsarist government in several ways. Most significantly, whereas previously the migration of serfs from Russia to new territories in Kazakhstan had been piecemeal and limited in its extent, now the way was open for a much more significant demographic movement; by removing the historic and formerly-unbreakable tie between the serf and the landowner, emancipation enabled a large increase in the Russian population in Kazakhstan, and advanced the strategic objective of colonising the new country and absorbing it into the empire, or rather into Russia itself as no distinction was made at this stage between Russia and its new territories in Central Asia. It also avoided the need to pay compensation to landowners in Russia for the serfs who previously worked on their land, since those serfs would not now be taking ownership of that land; and it alleviated the potential for unrest and rebellion among disaffected peasants, disillusioned with emancipation, in the Russian countryside. But it was not without risks; many landowners were angry that although they may have retained their land, they lost their labour force without receiving compensation, with the result that much of the land could no longer be cultivated. This was to have severe consequences for food production, and for the banks which could not recover the substantial loans they had made to impoverished landowners. But it also stored up deep resentment among Kazakhs, as thousands of newly-liberated agricultural workers and settlers arrived from Russia, taking over grazing land and pastures, obstructing migration routes, and generally causing great hardship to local communities in Kazakhstan.

The tsarist government was impervious to criticism and complaint, and now began to impose its own direct rule in Kazakhstan. It had abolished the position of khan and dismantled the leadership structures within the Kazakh hordes in 1824. Control was now to be implemented through the various administrative centres and fortresses along the original Orenburg Line and the more recent regional settlements such as Akmolinsk in the centre of the country, and the expanding town of Verny in the south. In this respect Russia adopted a system of colonial administration closer to the French model, in which its new territories were regarded as part of the mother country, in contrast to the British system of establishing local governments in its colonial possessions. Just as Algeria was regarded as part of France, so Kazakhstan was part of Russia, until it became one of the nominally-independent republics of the Soviet Union after the Russian Revolution. Kazakhs as well as Russians had responsibility for agriculture, taxation, and other matters of local government, within the confines of Russian policy for the region.

Notwithstanding their official status, Kazakhstan and other colonial possessions were regarded by much of the Russian public with aloofness and disdain, an attitude which persists among some Russians to the present day. Russian perceptions of these territories and their inhabitants in the mid-nineteenth century had much in common with contemporary attitudes in Victorian England towards the British Empire. The Russian historian Vasili Grigorev referred to 'these rude children of the forests and deserts' and Russia's civilising mission to 'protect these peoples from the destructive influence of Nature, hunger, cold, and sickness'. Many Kazakhs may have taken offence at such opinions, but others were willing to recognise the benefits of Russian science, medicine, education, and literature that opened up in Kazakhstan. There was now the possibility to explore new ideas and opportunities of a comparatively more developed European society; and whereas it was mostly families of farmers and emancipated serfs who were coming from Russia to settle in Kazakhstan, it was mainly students seeking education and opportunity who travelled in the opposite direction, from the towns and villages of Kazakhstan to the universities of Moscow, St Petersburg, and Kazan. Ambitious parents sent their children to Russian schools either in Kazakhstan, or preferably in Russia itself.

The traditional nomadic way of life was now more under threat than at any time since the Speransky reforms of the 1820s. But at the same time the ancient legends and oral epics, through which the history and philosophy of the people were expressed, were now receiving a new lease of life. Major poets and writers, notably Abai Kunanbaev and Ibrai Altysarin, played an active role in the development of Kazakh literature and language, at a time when Russian was becoming more prominent, and might have overwhelmed the indigenous culture. Paradoxically the influx of Russians in the second half of the nineteenth century acted as a stimulus to Kazakh writers and artists, anxious to revive and protect their own identity and traditions, while at the same time there was a breaking down of the barriers between the two countries and cultures. Abai Kunanbaev, known in Kazakhstan simply as Abai, was born in 1854 in the Chingiz Mountains between Semipalatinsk and Lake Balkhash, to a wealthy and aristocratic family. His early education was in a local madrasah, but in common with many children from his social background, he was sent to a Russian school in Semipalatinsk, where he became immersed in Russian literature and culture, and began translating the works of Pushkin, Lermontov, and other authors into his native Kazakh. More significantly he began to write his own poems and stories in Kazakh, which had a wide appeal throughout the country, especially among the young. But his writings were not universally popular, and his work was strongly opposed by some of his more conservative and anti-Russian countrymen. Nonetheless he did more than any other public figure to encourage the development of Kazakh literature, away from its age-old traditions of ancient epics and legends, and backward-looking to an imaginary better era in the past. Abai incorporated the best of Russian and European characteristics, and is now regarded as the founder of modern Kazakh literature, and the most prominent cultural figure of his time in Kazakhstan. He died in 1904, and is commemorated by a huge statue on the Prospect Dostyk in Almaty and in street names in towns and cities throughout the country. But possibly his most abiding legacy is the popularity of the name Abai for boys in modern-day Kazakhstan.

Ibrai Altynsarin was a contemporary of Abai, born in 1841 and educated in a Russian school in Orenburg. On leaving school he returned to Kazakhstan where he developed a new system of education which included setting up joint Russian and Kazakh boarding schools in each district for children of nomadic families. Like Abai, Altynsarin was anxious to see Kazakhstan progress from the backwardness and religious obscurantism that characterised much of the educational system, and he drew inspiration from Russia, especially from the democratic and humanist principles of Leo Tolstoy and the children's writer Ivan Krylov. But whereas Abai stressed the development of Kazakh literature while incorporating the best from Russia and Europe, it was Altynsarin who was largely responsible for bringing Russian language and literature to Kazakhstan. He did this through children's stories, fables and textbooks including the *Elementary Guide to Teaching the Russian Language to the Kazakhs,* published in 1879. The contribution made by Abai and Altynsarin to the spread and acceptance of Russian ideals and the Russian way of life was enormous, at a time when by no means the whole of Kazakhstan was reconciled to the inevitability of becoming part of Russia. They both sought to bring the two countries together in a spiritual sense, in contrast to the forcible imposition of Russian government through military conquest and the seizure of Kazakh lands. But the most central figure in the process of integration between Kazakhstan and Russia in this period was Chokan Valikhanov.

CHAPTER NINE

Kazakh – Russian Integration in Person: Chokan Valikhanov

One of the most attractive parts of central Almaty is *ploshchad Valikhanova* (Valikhanov Square) and the surrounding streets and gardens, an area known locally as 'Chokanka'. Only a stone's throw from the noise and traffic on the busy Prospect Dostyk (formerly Lenina), this is a peaceful, residential area of blocks of flats, little cafes, academic institutions, and squares, fountains, and gardens. The main square is at the southern end of Valikhanova, a wide, quiet street like many in Almaty, built specifically for pedestrians and lined with tall firs and pine trees, and with well-tended flowerbeds in the centre. The far-sightedness of the original town planners in excluding horse-drawn carts and later motorised traffic from parts of the city between the major thoroughfares, has now paid great dividends in terms of peace and quiet, air quality, and safety for residents especially children. Extending across the whole of the south side of the square stands the prestigious and imposing Kazakhstan Academy of Sciences. Designed by Alexey Shchusov, one of the most prominent architects of the Soviet Union, the Academy was built between 1948 and 1957 in the grandiose style of the post-war Stalinist period. Shchusov was also responsible for the Lenin Mausoleum in Moscow, the National Theatre building in Tashkent, and many other famous buildings throughout the USSR. His work combined the architectural traditions of tsarist Russia with the neoclassical and monumental style favoured by Stalin. Although completely dominating its surroundings, the building does not have the cold formality of much of Soviet architecture, but instead its honey-coloured stone gives it a warmer and more graceful aspect than many other buildings of the same period. On the opposite side of the square, in a quiet corner shaded by larch and pine trees, is the Institute of Chemical Science and Industry, and further down Valikhanova is the Institute of Geological Sciences, in another substantial building but one built in complete harmony with its surroundings. In common with almost every public body, all three Institutes experienced serious financial difficulties in the immediate post-independence years, and were forced to devote space to art galleries, dance classes, and other commercial concessions. As economic conditions improved, such extraneous and what were seen as demeaning money-making activities were no longer needed, and the Institutes have reverted to their original purposes. Adjacent to the Academy of Sciences is an 'Oriental Calendar' Fountain of bronze statues of a dragon, horse, dog, snake, and other symbols of the Chinese calendar. This is a favourite area for young children on roller skates and mothers with young babies in push-chairs. On the other side of the road is another array of fountains, and a bronze statue of the figure after whom the square and the street are named: Chokan Valikhanov.

Chokan Valikhanov was the most renowned individual to emerge from, and contribute to, the fusion of Russian and Kazakh cultures in the nineteenth century. In many ways the Valikhanov family encapsulated the divisions and dilemmas which confronted the whole of Kazakhstan in the face of Russian colonial expansion: should the relentless tide of new influences, in education, religion, economics, and society, coming from the north and all so alien to traditional Kazakh beliefs and customs, be welcomed and adopted, in the interests of national progress and development? Or should these influences be resisted and opposed, so that Kazakhstan could remain free and independent, and hold on to its old ways of life? Chokan Valikhanov demonstrated that it was possible to have the best of both worlds, by accepting the best that Russia had to offer while at the same time reviving and preserving Kazakhstan's own ancient culture, history, and legends. But his views were far from universally shared, and his early life in particular was a period of violent rebellion and uprisings throughout Kazakhstan against Russia, which caused deep divisions within his own family and in the country as a whole.

Chokan Valikhanov was born in 1835 at Kushmurun, near Kustanai in northern Kazakhstan, and was the great-grandson of Ablai Khan, the eighteenth-century leader of the Great Horde. Ablai Khan had achieved a legendary status as a warrior against Dzungar invaders, and as a national figure in the Great Horde. He was highly regarded by the Russian Empress Catherine II for his efforts in maintaining peace and stability throughout Kazakhstan, without which the territory of southern Russia would have been in danger from raids and incursions by Kazakh and Dzungar tribes. Despite Russia's imperial intentions, Ablai Khan was not overtly hostile to Russia but was more concerned to preserve Kazakh unity and national identity in his own region of eastern Kazakhstan, as well as in the areas of the Little and Middle Hordes which had been ceded to Russia in the treaties of 1734 and 1740. On his death in 1781 Ablai Khan was succeeded by his son Vali Khan, who had to confront not only the never-ending encroachment of Russian power in western and central Kazakhstan, but also the deep conflicts in his own family as to how they and the native people of Kazakhstan should respond to the Russian advance. Thanks to the good relations which had been achieved between Ablai Khan and the Russian Empress Catherine, the Vali Khan side of the family remained loyal to Russia and was rewarded with various appointments and positions in the local administration in northern Kazakhstan, even as Russia dismantled the traditional khan structure and extended its control over the Kazakh territories. Vali married a scholarly and ambitious Kazakh woman called Aiganym, who despite her ancestry was strongly supportive of Russian influence in Kazakhstan; Aiganym saw her own country as primitive and backward, and believed that much-needed development and progress could only come from outside. She and Vali had seven sons, but it was the eldest, named Chingis, to whom she devoted most of her love and care. At the age of fifteen Chingis was entered into the Russian army at Omsk, at the time the principal military and administrative centre of the region. Omsk was some considerable distance from Kustanai, just north of the border between Russia and Kazakhstan, but Aiganym was determined that Chingis should have the best training and education.

But Chingis had cousins in another branch of the family which did not feel any loyalty to or support for Russia. Two more grandsons of Ablai Khan, Sarzhan Kasimov and his half-brother Kenesary Kasimov, grew up in an atmosphere of hostility to Russia and to the administrative changes which it was making, which they considered to be unjust and illegitimate. Between them Sarzhan and Kenesary controlled wide areas of the country, stretching south from Kokchetav, and around the Turgai River in central Kazakhstan. From here between 1836 and 1844, leading thousands of armed but badly-organised tribesmen, they mounted attacks on Russian detachments and on Kazakhs who supported the changes which were being made under the Russians. Sarzhan was defeated in battle and escaped south to Kokand. Kenesary continued to oppose the new order, in particular demanding the restoration of the rule of the khan, and in 1841 he was himself elected khan at an assembly of tribal and clan leaders. Ultimately he also was defeated by tsarist troops and was killed in a battle in 1847. Similar sharp divisions and conflicts arose within many families in other parts of the Russian empire. In 1859 Imam Shamil, the leader of mountain tribes fighting against the Russians in their attempts to take control of the Caucasus, was captured by the tsarist army and deported to Russia. He avoided execution only by virtue of the fact that his courage and resistance to Russian forces in the mountains and forests of his native land, which had been popularised in the short stories of Leo Tolstoy, were admired by many people in Russia. Given the ruthlessness with which the tsarist army campaigned against the native people of the region, it might have been assumed that Shamil's own family would have been united in their determination to rid the Caucasus of the Russian invaders. But although two of his sons fought on the side of Turkey against Russia in 1877-78, two other sons became officers in the Russian army.

Meanwhile Chingis Valikhanov was progressing through the ranks of the Russian army. He took part in some of the actions against the rebellions led by his cousins Sarzhan and Kenesary, and it was partly on the strength of these campaigns that he was promoted to senior commands. In addition to his successful military career, Chingis was also appointed to important posts in the Russian civilian administration. No other Kazakh had achieved such a status, and by now this side of the Ablai Khan family was increasingly prevailing over the other, Kasimov, side who were opposed to Russian expansion. Chingis had six sons, the most famous of which was Chokan. Originally named Mukhammad-Khanafia, Chokan soon adopted the conventional Russian style of given name, patronymic, and family name, and became known as Chokan Chingisovich Valikhanov. In his childhood Chokan studied Kazakh folklore, hunting, music, foreign languages and art; while studying painting and drawing he developed a skill for the pen-and-ink sketches and drawings of landscapes and native people, which were to become a major feature in his later studies and travels. Close proximity to Russia meant that the area around the family *aul* in Kushmurun was increasingly affected by Russian incomers and settlers, often to the detriment of local inhabitants. But the Valikhanov family was less dependent on the land for their livelihood, and experienced less disruption from the incomers; Chokan's grandmother Aiganym, who had become an influential figure in the region, was more concerned that Chokan should take advantage of the educational and career opportunities which were available in Russia to promising Kazakh students, rather than that he should defend the interests of fellow Kazakhs who had been displaced by Russian settlers.

Possibly because of the frequent absences of Chokan's father in the army, Aiganym decided that it would be better for Chokan to leave Kushmurun and live with her at her estate in Syrymbet, further east near Kokchetav. Here she continued to promote his career as actively as she had done for that of his father. At the age of eleven, even younger than Chingis had been, Chokan followed in his father's footsteps and was enrolled in the Russian army at Omsk, initially in the Cadet Corps, regarded as the best educational establishment in Siberia, before later being assigned to a cavalry regiment. This prestigious appointment marked the young Valikhanov's growing involvement with Russia, an involvement which later extended to acquaintanceship with prominent Russia scientists, writers, and explorers. At the same time he was increasingly being recognised within Kazakhstan for his own activities in research, exploration, and ethnography.

Nowadays Valikhanov is principally known for his scientific writings, sketches, and drawings, the result of a series of expeditions undertaken between 1855 and 1859 exploring the little-known regions of eastern Kazakhstan, Kyrgyzstan, and Kashgar in western China. On these expeditions he examined every aspect of local history, geography, nature, and ethnography, and recorded many ancient poems, stories and legends which until then had existed only in oral form. In the first expedition, in the summer of 1855, he travelled from Omsk upstream along the Irtysh River to Semipalatinsk, then south across the steppe to the new Russian settlement at Verny, following the route taken two years earlier by the Peremyshelsky mission. From here he made exhaustive studies of the nature, terrain, and people of the Semirechie region and the Dzungarski Alatau Mountains, before travelling west over a vast distance to Kokchetav where he visited his grandmother Aiganym, before finally returning to Omsk. In 1856, his next expedition took him south from Verny, to the region of Issyk Kul where he made the first written record of *Manas,* an ancient oral epic poem of Kyrgyzstan, as well as conducting detailed investigations into the life and customs of the local people. None of these findings had been recorded before. The following year he undertook a further mission on behalf of the Russian government to Kuldja in Chinese Turkestan, where he spent three months discussing economic relations with Chinese officials. During this time he also studied the language and traditions of the Uighurs, a centuries-old Muslim community which had settled in western China. On his return he travelled to St Petersburg to report on his findings to the government and to the scientific community; appreciating the value of these reports, in 1858 the government commissioned Valikhanov to lead an expedition to the town of Kashgar, not far across the border in China, ostensibly for purposes of research into the local geography, customs, and languages of the region. But a widespread belief that he was engaged in spying on behalf of the tsarist government led to his expulsion from China. He returned to Verny in April 1859 and to St Petersburg the following year, where in a rare distinction for a non-Russian, he was appointed to a senior position in the Foreign Affairs Ministry.

Valikhanov's career and his life, already full of achievement, were about to be cut short: in 1861 he became seriously ill with tuberculosis and had to resign on health grounds from his new position in the Foreign Ministry. Returning to Verny where he hoped to recover, he undertook a major investigation into the Kazakh legal system on behalf of the Russian government, and attempted to pursue a new career in the local administration in Kazakhstan, although he had to abandon this due to persistent ill health. During this period he befriended the writer and philosopher Fyodor Dostoyevsky. Dostoyevsky had been exiled to Semipalatinsk in 1850 by Tsar Nicholas I for his part in the Petrashevsky group, a dissident political and literary circle in

St Petersburg. The group, led by Mikhail Petrashevsky, a junior official in the Foreign Ministry and consisting of a small number of writers and intellectuals, was critical of many aspects of Russian society, including serfdom, censorship, the church, and private property, and although few in numbers the group was nonetheless seen as a threat to the regime. In 1849 all its members were arrested on charges of sedition, and after a mass trial were sentenced to death, although this was to be a mock execution planned by Nicholas I as part of the punishment. At the final moment before the firing squad the sentences were commuted to imprisonment; Petrashevsky as the leader was given a life sentence, and Dostoyevsky was sentenced to four years hard labour in Omsk, to be followed by four years military service as a private in the army in Semipalatinsk. It was while he was in Semipalatinsk that Dostoyevsky met and befriended some leading figures in the region, notably Chokan Valikhanov; this became an unlikely and paradoxical friendship between Valikhanov, a non-Russian admirer of contemporary Russia, which Valikhanov saw as more progressive and a model in some respects for the more backward Kazakhstan, and Dostoyevsky, a reactionary Russian whose conservative and anti-state opinions of how life in Russia should be organised, were in sharp conflict with those of the tsarist government, and had nearly cost him his life. In their meetings and correspondence, Valikhanov and Dostoyevsky explored profound theological questions of religion and philosophy, but they also discussed practical matters concerning relations between indigenous people and an imperial power, and how the two groups could most effectively exist alongside each other. Such discussions had special relevance against the background of the emancipation of the serfs in Russia in 1861, and the influx of thousands of settlers into northern Kazakhstan. Valikhanov may have been less affected personally than many of the nomadic Kazakh communities in the region, but he had seen how this had become a deeply divisive and contentious issue, and it was one that was to influence Kazakh-Russian relations over the next century.

His close friendship with Dostoyevsky was not the only paradoxical relationship in Valikhanov's life. In April 1864, on the basis of his deep knowledge of the topography of the local steppe, Valikhanov was detailed to assist in the movement of troops from Verny under General Mikhail Cherniaev at the launch of the Russian campaign against the neighbouring khanate of Kokand. Cherniaev was a veteran of the Crimean War in which he had fought with distinction at the battles of Inkerman and Sebastopol. After the war he played a leading role in the Russian annexation of Turkestan and Central Asia, and through his aggressive tactics against hostile local tribesmen (whose ability to resist Russian forces was considerably weaker than Britain or France had been in the Crimea), he came to be regarded as a national hero in Russia. The first objective of the Kokand campaign was to capture the ancient town of Aulie-Ata (later named Dzhambul), 500 kilometres west of Verny. Valikhanov's pleas for negotiations with the local inhabitants were ignored by Cherniaev, and the town was besieged and taken, after a battle with great loss of life, by Cherniaev's forces. Despite his own military education and background, this violent episode was contrary to Valikhanov's ideals and beliefs; because of this, and because of his deteriorating health, he declined to remain with Cherniaev after the siege of Aulie-Ata and returned to Verny. The Russian army continued its march westward to take the cities of Chimkent and Tashkent, but Valikhanov and Cherniaev remained close friends. Cherniaev greatly valued Valikhanov's local knowledge and expertise and recommended him for further promotion in the army; Valikhanov, however, did not have much longer to live.

Now seriously ill, Valikhanov moved from Verny to a small village across the Ili River in the Semirechie region, where he married a local woman named Aisary. In the last few months of his life, between November 1864 and February 1865, he corresponded with General Andrei Kolpakovsky, the Russian military governor of the Semipalatinsk region, who sought his views on the Muslim revolts and rebel activity then taking place in the nearby Chinese province of Kuldja, where Valikhanov had led an expedition in 1858. Kolpakovsky also had a high opinion of Valikhanov and offered him a position in his administration once his health was restored. But this was not to happen, and Valikhanov died on 10 April 1865, at the age of twenty nine. He was buried at the tiny settlement of Kochen-Togan, in the foothills of the Dzungarski Alatau Mountains, where a tall granite statue of him now stares out over the empty steppe.

Conflicts and battles between Russian forces and Kazakh tribes were to continue for many years, especially in the south of the country and in the west around the Caspian Sea. In 1869 and 1870, anti-Russian uprisings in the Ural and Turgaiski regions, around the Irgyz River, where Abul Khair, khan of the Little Horde in the previous century had his encampment, were suppressed by punitive raids by Russian forces from Orenburg. Coming from one of the tribes of the Middle Horde in the north of Kazakhstan, Valikhanov was less well known in western parts of the country, and in those regions where he was known and where anti-colonial feelings remained strong, his Russian sympathies had little appeal. Any influence which Valikhanov may have had after his death in these conflicts in the west of the country was minimal or non-existent. He had never travelled in these regions, and local people had little knowledge of or interest in his investigations into life in the distant regions of eastern Kazakhstan. Similarly, the local army officers, concerned only with the military objective of securing the region for Russia, and despite the high opinion of Valikhanov expressed by Generals Cherniaev and Kolpakovsky, had no use for his knowledge or experience of an entirely different part of the country. But in a wider historical perspective, there is little doubt that through his writings and his understanding of Kazakhstan and of Russia, Valikhanov made a significant contribution to the life of both countries. He made the region more accessible and better understood not only by its own people but also by Russia and by Russian incomers, and in a sense eased the way for the absorption of Kazakhstan into the Russian empire. If he had lived for longer, Valikhanov would no doubt have achieved further distinction in many aspects of local science and ethnography, and in recording, preserving, and reviving the history and culture of eastern Kazakhstan.

Notwithstanding the efforts of Valikhanov, for most Russians in the mid-nineteenth century Central Asia remained unknown territory, and it was the exploration and research of Pyotr Semyonov, a contemporary of Valikhanov, who arguably did more to bring the region into the Russian national consciousness. Born in central Russia in 1827, Semyonov was the son of a veteran of the 1812 war with Napoleon, and the older Semyonov inspired in his son a love and fascination for the local forests and countryside. Pyotr Semyonov studied at St. Petersburg University where he became a member of the Petrashevsky Circle and where he also met Dostoevsky. But his interests lay more in geography and geology than politics, and after studying in Berlin in the 1850s under Alexander Humboldt and other prominent scholars, in the summer of 1856 Semyonov embarked on the first of his own expeditions to Issyk-Kul and the Tien Shan Mountains. Here he discovered new species of flora and fauna, and established that eighty rivers flowed into Lake Issyk-Kul but none flowed out, disproving earlier theories that Issyk-Kul was the source of the River Chu, a major Kazakh river and a tributary of the Syr Darya. He spent the winter in Verny, recording his findings and preparing for his next expedition further east, where in the summer of 1857 he became the first European to see the Tengri Tag mountain chain and the 7,000 metre peak of Khan Tengri. Semyonov described this experience: 'I was almost blinded by this magnificent sight; the chain consisted of more than thirty mountains covered by a huge blanket of eternal snow, and in which Khan Tengri seemed to me to be twice as high as the others'. The two-year expedition resulted in a complete and systematic account of the geography, vegetation and wildlife of the Tien Shan, published in 1859 and the first of its kind undertaken by a Russian scientist. On his return to Russia he worked at the Russian Geographical Society in St. Petersburg, of which he became the chairman in 1874, and supported expeditions by other explorers, notably Nikolai Przhevalsky, in the Russian Far East and in Central Asia. Przhevalsky gave his name to a breed of wild horses he discovered in Mongolia, and for a time was rumoured to be the father of Josef Stalin, although these rumours were later shown to have been unfounded. Pyotr Semyonov died in 1914, having been given the title 'Tien Shansky' by Tsar Nicholas II in 1910 in honour of his work in what was previously a little-known region of Central Asia. But the more prominent role in bringing Central Asia to the attention of the Russian public was played by the army as Russia extended its presence in the region in the 'Tournament of Shadows'.

CHAPTER TEN

Tournament of Shadows: Russia Conquers the Khanates

In parallel with the administrative and social measures which it was implementing in its colonisation of Kazakhstan, in the 1860s and 1870s Russia embarked on a new military strategy in the south of the region. In what became known in Britain as the Great Game, and in Russia as the Tournament of Shadows, this strategy was intended to extend Russia's borders and influence beyond Kazakhstan to the territories to the south, and to secure the region against a perceived threat from Britain and its empire in India and Afghanistan. The policy also marked a new departure for the Russian army. The army had engaged in the suppression of uprisings and rebellions, but Russia's acquisition of virtually the whole of Kazakhstan had largely been achieved without heavy losses. The weak and perpetually divided nature of the Kazakh tribes had ensured that until now no unified Kazakh force or army had emerged to pose a serious military challenge to Russia throughout the period of colonisation. This was now due to change as Russia undertook a more organised and assertive strategy against different enemies in the south, considerably further from its home territory. The strategy was also partly designed to revive morale in the army and in the country as a whole after the calamity of the defeat in the Crimean War. A key figure in the restructuring of the army, and in the new policy in Central Asia, was General Konstantin von Kaufman.

The humiliating experience of the war gave rise to a national urge within Russia to draw on the country's own cultural and religious strengths and identity, and for it to stand firm against the European powers which had colluded to bring about its defeat in the Crimea. In practical terms this meant that Russia now saw its future to lie in the east and in Central Asia rather than in the West and in Europe. This in turn meant abandoning any attempts to improve relations with Britain and France after the war, and the consequent loss of any technological or military progress that may be gained from closer ties with its former enemies. But such was the depth of resentment against Europe in general, and suspicion of Britain in particular, that no other course at the time was possible. In 1864 the Russian Foreign Minister Prince Alexander Gorchakov declared that Russian territorial expansion in the east was inevitable; other imperial powers such as France and Britain had expanded their empires far beyond their native territories, and Russia intended to do the same.

There was a difference in Russia's case in that its expansion derived not only from imperial motives but from the more immediate need to stabilise its borders and bring what it saw as civilisation to its neighbours in Central Asia. Unlike the European powers, Russia was continually involved with often hostile and tribal populations in its adjacent territories, and the need to pacify these regions was essential for its security. In Kazakhstan this had a self-perpetuating effect in the eighteenth century, in that initial contact with nomadic tribes led to control and subjugation, as had happened with Abul Khair and the Little Horde in western Kazakhstan, and Semeke and the khans of the Middle Horde in northern Kazakhstan. This was followed by unrest and rebellion beyond these boundaries, as tribes and khans attacked the areas which had been stabilised and absorbed into Russia in the early part of the nineteenth century. Now further expansion was needed to bring peace and stability to the khanates of Central Asia which lay still further beyond the Russian empire. In this policy Tsar Alexander II had widespread popular support, much of which came from artists and writers, poets and playwrights, whose works conveyed a sense of national pride in Russia's territorial ambitions and achievements. The government's official view was stated in November 1864 by Gorchakov in a message sent to Russian embassies abroad: 'The position of Russia in Central Asia is that of all civilised states which are brought into contact with half-savage, nomad populations, possessing no fixed organisation . . . border security and trade relations impel the civilised state to exert a certain authority, notably over Asiatics who respect only visible and palpable force'.*

Tsar Alexander, Prince Gorchakov, and the rest of the tsarist government were also deeply concerned about British policies which were seen as threatening Russian interests in three particular areas: in Persia and the Caspian Sea, where a growing British presence would prove a danger to Russian trade and influence in the region, and which may also threaten Russia itself; in southern Russia and on the Black Sea, where Britain was believed to be supplying weapons to Shamil and the mountain guerrillas of the Caucasus; but mostly in Central Asia, where it was feared that Britain might launch an invasion from its territories in India to the south. In reality the likelihood of such a threat was low and was dismissed in a report by the Russian War Ministry, but Alexander held to the belief that Russia needed to strengthen its presence in what was still a largely unknown and unsettled territory, and in this respect the recently established military fort at Verny now acquired greater importance. In a propaganda campaign to generate support for military

---

*Quoted by by Karl Meyer and Shareen Brysac in 'Tournament of Shadows', 2001

action in Transoxiana, the region beyond the Syr Darya River, rumours of Russian slaves being sold in bazaars in Central Asia were fostered by the government and readily gained credence among a largely uninformed Russian public. But more important was the need to bring stability to a volatile and strategically important region along the border with Russia's new territories in Kazakhstan, and in pursuing this strategy the settlements and the line of forts in the south of the country were to play a major role.

To the south of Kazakhstan lay a series of minor khanates and tribal regions. In the west, along the shore of the Caspian Sea and extending inland as far as the Amu Darya River, was the region of the Turkomans, a disparate group of independent tribes who were united only in their hostility to Russia. Between the Turkomans and the Aral Sea lay the khanate of Khiva; in the previous century an expedition of 2,000 cavalry troops, ordered by Tsar Peter the Great to explore this region and the Silk Road, had been led into a trap by the khan of Khiva and the entire force had been either killed or taken as slaves, an incident which earned for the khanate a lasting reputation for treachery and distrust. More recently, in 1840 the reputation of the region for danger was strengthened by the fate of an expeditionary army en route from Orenburg to Khiva, which was overwhelmed by severe blizzards and abnormally cold winter weather, in which nearly half the army was lost. Further to the east was the Emirate of Bukhara, which included the exotic and historical cities of Bukhara, Samarkand, and Tashkent. Samarkand had been known to the ancient Greeks at the time of Alexander the Great, and under Arabic rule in the seventh century had become one of the main centres of Islamic culture, where among many impressive architectural monuments was the mausoleum of Tamerlane. Further east still was the khanate of Kokand, centred on the ancient city of Osh, in present-day Kyrgyzstan, and the wide and fertile Ferghana Valley, surrounded on three sides by the dramatic foothills of the Tien Shan Mountains. Lastly, to the east of Kokand was the tribal region of the Kyrgyz around Lake Issyk Kul to the south of Verny, and the vast surrounding areas of high mountains and remote and inaccessible valleys. All of these territories were seen as politically and militarily unstable, and more particularly vulnerable to encroachment both from British colonial possessions in India and Afghanistan in the south, and from China not far to the east. Russia's strategic interests demanded that the whole region should be brought within the tsarist empire, and in a series of campaigns working from east to west, this was achieved between 1855 and 1881.

The first actions were taken in the Kyrgyz tribal areas in and around the Issyk Kul valley. Between 1855 and 1864, even while the new settlement and military outpost of Verny were still under construction, Russian troops ventured south into the Tien Shan Mountains and westwards to the nearby settlement of Bishkek. Later the capital of Kyrgyzstan, at the time Bishkek was no more than a simple village and rudimentary trading centre. Within a few years, and assisted by the detailed knowledge of the local population gained from the 1856 Valikhanov expedition, Russia brought the Kyrgyz areas under its control as a protectorate of the empire. Russia was also aided in this venture by the acquiescence or even positive reception from local tribes, resentful at their treatment under the neighbouring Khanate of Kokand, which had not long before subjugated much of the region. By taking control of the Kyrgyz region, Russia also contained the threat of Chinese expansion from the east. As the region became more secure, throughout the second half of the nineteenth century Russian settlers established new communities in Bishkek and in other parts of the surrounding country. For many new arrivals from Russia, the extreme remoteness of this region and the prospect of an undisturbed way of life, far from the hardships they had previously known under serfdom in Russia, were powerful attractions. In Karakol on the south-eastern shore of Lake Issyk Kul, a magnificent wooden Orthodox church, with five golden onion domes and silver crosses, was built by settlers in 1885-1890, and served as a religious centre for the growing Russian community.

Verny had not yet taken over from Semipalatinsk as the administrative centre for the Semirechie region, but it was increasingly important as a base for military expeditions against the khanate of Kokand. As well as attempting to dominate the Kyrgyz areas to the east, the khanate had also for many years been a source of trouble for native Kazakh tribes to the north. In the early part of the nineteenth century it had launched a series of raids and forays against the Kazakhs of the Middle Horde along the Syr Darya River, which in turn had led to conflict and fighting between Kazakhs and the khanate in the 1850s. From his palace in Osh, the ruler of the khanate, Khudoyar Khan, now became involved in clashes with the imperial Russian government and Russian troops when the Kyrgyz tribes became subjects of the Russian empire in the early 1860s. Switching his attention away from harassing the weaker Kazakh and Kyrgyz communities, and overestimating his own military strength, Khudoyar initiated what became a futile campaign against Russia. To deal with this threat, and to stabilize the whole region, Alexander appointed two of Russia's foremost military commanders, General Mikhail Cherniaev and General Konstantin von Kaufman, with the task of pacifying Kokand and bringing it and the other khanates of Central Asia into the Russian empire. Both generals were veterans of the Crimean War and von Kaufman had also fought in the Caucasus campaigns; he had also played a significant role in reorganising and strengthening the logistical capability of the army, greatly improving its ability to conduct campaigns at vast distances from St Petersburg and from Russia itself. Both generals enjoyed great prestige in the court at St Petersburg.

In joint action in 1864, Russian troops led by Cherniaev from Verny in the east (initially aided by Chokan Valikhanov) and by von Kaufman from Aralsk in the west, embarked on a series of expeditions against Kokand and against the Emirate of Bukhara. Cherniaev seized the small town of Uzunagach not far to the west of Verny, the site of the death of the rebel Kazakh leader Kenesary in 1847, before progressing on to take Aulie-Ata, Turkestan, and Chimkent. It was after the violent siege and loss of life in the capture of Aulie-Ata that Chokan Valikhanov left the service of Cherniaev and returned to Verny. Cherniaev continued his westward progression and in May 1865, with a force of less than 2,000 men, captured Tashkent, an achievement which Alexander called 'a glorious affair' and after which Cherniaev became known as 'the lion of Tashkent'. Weakened by repeated losses on the battlefield and mass desertions of his troops and followers, Khudoyar was eventually forced to sign a peace treaty with Russia in 1869, effectively ceding the khanate of Kokand to the Russian empire, although it retained a semi-independent status and control of some parts of the Ferghana Valley. Cherniaev was appointed as the first governor of Tashkent, although his over-bearing and aggressive attitude, which had made it impossible for Valikhanov to remain as part of his campaign, led to him being replaced by Alexander later the same year by Major-General Mikhail Romanovsky.

Tashkent – the largest and one of the oldest cities of Central Asia – had now become a Russian possession, marking another significant milestone in Russia's colonisation of the vast and mostly empty region on its southern borders. The city was roughly the same distance from St Petersburg as Verny, but it occupied a more central and strategic location, less exposed to China to the east and nearer to the Caspian Sea to the west. Thus it was designated to be the major Russian stronghold in the region, and the government steadily increased the strength of the army based in the city, reducing the need for support from troops from Verny, which was a considerable distance to the east. Military conquests in this remote and dangerous area of steppe and desert, loosely referred to as Turkestan, had seized the popular imagination in Russia, especially in St Petersburg, where the army had regained much of its prestige and status after the disasters of the Crimean War. The army's role in pursuing Russia's imperial aims in Central Asia was greatly admired, and failure to conform to the spirit of colonial expansion and adventure was regarded as dishonourable and shameful. In Tolstoy's novel *Anna Karenina,* Count Vronsky, the army officer in love with Anna, is offered a position in Tashkent, which initially he accepts 'without the slightest hesitation'. But on reflection he refuses to go so as to remain with Anna. Tolstoy summarised his dilemma: 'Once Vronsky would have thought it disgraceful and impossible to decline the flattering offer of a post at Tashkent, which was a dangerous one . . . but now he refused it, and observing disapproval in high quarters at this step, at once resigned his commission'.

Two years after the capture of Tashkent, in 1867 the government in St Petersburg decided that it should be the administrative centre of what was to be given the gogolesque name of Governor-Generalship of Turkestan. This was a vast area stretching from the Aral Sea as far as Verny, Issyk-Kul, and into the region south of the Ili River in the east, but not incorporating the Semirechie north of the Ili River; this area was to remain under Kazakh administration from Semipalatinsk as part of the 'Land of the Semirechie Kazakhs' established under Nicholas I in 1849, on the lines of the Speransky land reforms of the 1820s. General von Kaufman was appointed by Tsar Alexander as military governor of Turkestan, in succession to Romanovsky. The appointment of such a prominent figure as von Kaufman was seen as a further indication of the importance of the region and of Tashkent in particular.

In addition to its strategic military role, Tashkent became the political capital of the region, and despite the unfavourable living conditions in the city, of extreme summer heat, limited water resources, and the existence of a large and hostile Muslim population, it also soon became the main economic and commercial centre of Turkestan. Verny, by contrast, lost its status as the principal Russian town in Central Asia. But its favourable natural environment, the availability of fertile land between the mountains and the steppe, and the absence of an indigenous Muslim population who might resist incomers, all enhanced the attractiveness of Verny and the surrounding region as a place to live. Russian and other incomers from the Slav regions could settle here peacefully and practice Orthodox beliefs without fear of conflict with local communities. Verny remained an important army base in what was still a vital strategic area of southern Kazakhstan, but from now on it was overshadowed by the more significant political, commercial, and military centre at Tashkent.

Meanwhile Russia completed its conquest of the remaining khanates. In the Emirate of Bukhara, which before the arrival of the Russians covered an extensive area between

Khiva and Kokand, and included the cities of Tashkent and Chimkent, the Emir Muzzafar Khan found that his status and influence were now greatly reduced. Despite this, and like Khudoyar Khan in the Khanate of Kokand before him, Muzzafar underestimated Russia's colonial ambitions, and in a futile and provocative gesture demanded the return of Tashkent, although from his point of view this may have been merely an honourable attempt to restore national pride and dignity. Whatever the motivation of Muzzafar may have been, the response of General von Kaufman was to dismiss Muzzafar's demand, to strengthen the barracks at Tashkent, and from there to launch an attack against the ancient city of Samarkand. The Emir's army, untrained and equipped with obsolete cannons and muskets, was no match for the more experienced Russian troops, and Samarkand fell to von Kaufman's forces in May 1868. This was an event of special significance as it was from Samarkand that in 1382 the armies of Tamerlane had embarked on the invasion of Russia and the destruction of the ancient principalities of Muscovy and Vladimir. Although nearly five centuries had since passed, this traumatic episode had left an indelible imprint on the Russian psyche. Now Samarkand was safely incorporated in the Russian empire and von Kaufman's victories in the south gave assurance that Russia would be permanently safe from attack from this direction. After the loss of Samarkand, Muzzafar was forced to sign a treaty with Russia, although he was allowed to maintain autonomy for the internal affairs of the khanate of Bukhara and von Kaufman, realising the near-impossibility of imposing Russian laws in such an alien environment, agreed that the population should remain subject to its own legal system.

The Khiva khanate, occupying a relatively small area west of Bukhara and to the south of the Aral Sea, was the next to submit to Russia, but this could not be achieved before a violent rebellion of the Adaevsti tribes in the Mangyshlak Peninsula had been subdued. Jutting out into the Caspian Sea, the Mangyshlak Peninsula was of considerable importance to Russia; it was not far from its own ports of Guryev (later Atyrau) on the northern shore of the Caspian Sea, and Astrakhan at the mouth of the Volga River further west. It was also opposite the port of Baku in Azerbaijan, which was simultaneously falling into the Russian empire. By transporting troops from these ports, Russia could secure easier control of western Kazakhstan than was possible from Orenburg, which required a long and difficult trek across the steppe. The Mangyshlak Peninsula consists of two contrasting areas of land: the Buzachi, a marshy, low-lying and largely uninhabited area in the north, and the Tyub-Karagan Peninsula, a smaller but hillier stretch of land extending further into the Caspian Sea in the south. It was here in 1869 that the Russian government ordered the construction of a small port at Bautino in a sheltered bay at the western extremity of the Tyub-Karagan peninsula, so that troops arriving from Russia could be disembarked; and a short distance inland a small fortress was built and named Alexandrovsk, in honour of the tsar. Only a few months later, in April 1870 up to 10,000 tribesmen of the local Adaevtsi tribe who inhabited the Mangyshlak Peninsula joined an uprising against Russia, triggered by Russian encroachment on the shore, and by a clumsy attempt to raise revenue from people whose livelihoods had already been severely disrupted by interference with traditional migration routes. The Adaevtsi took control of the whole of the Tyub-Karagan Peninsula, and destroyed the landing stages, warehouses, and Russian cargo ships lying at anchor at Bautino, before briefly laying siege to the fortress at Alexandrovsk. The shock waves of this rebellion, which was in sharp contrast to the relatively easy conquests of the khanates to the east, quickly reached the tsarist government in St Petersburg, whose response was swift and equally violent. More troops were despatched to Bautino, and punitive raids were sent from the fort at Embinsky not far to the north; in two major battles, on the coast at Buzachi and in the desert east of Alexandrovsk, the uprising was ruthlessly suppressed. In December 1870 thousands of indigenous families were expelled across the steppe and over the Ustyurt Plateau to unknown lands in the khanate of Khiva. The port at Bautino was rebuilt and the fort at Alexandrovsk was reinforced and served as a major forward base for the conquest of Khiva.

The small and backward medieval khanate of Khiva might have been considered insignificant from Russia's point of view if it were not for the fact that it lay between the new possessions of Bukhara and Tashkent to the east, and Alexandrovsk on the Caspian Sea to the west. Until it could be incorporated into the tsarist empire it represented a gap in the strategic chain of khanates bordering Kazakhstan, and thus Russia itself, in the south. The expulsion of the Adaevsti from Mangyshlak, and the potential for further unrest in the region, added to importance of taking control of the khanate as soon as possible. Thanks to its distance from Russia itself and from the nearest fort at Orenburg, 1,500 kilometres to the north, Khiva had resisted all earlier attempts to bring it within the Russian orbit. Its remoteness acted as an effective defence against attack; Khiva was an oasis city surrounded by the blistering sands of the Karakum (Black Sands) Desert, nearly a thousand kilometres west of Tashkent, a similar distance from Alexandrovsk, and 800 kilometres from the new port of Krasnovodsk on the east coast of the Caspian. But its safety and immunity from attack were now about to change. After ensuring control of the Mangyshlak Peninsula in 1870, over the next three years tsarist forces made several expeditions from Alexandrovsk and Krasnovodsk, heading eastwards across the vast, empty Ustyurt Plateau and deep into the Karakum Desert, threatening the khanate from the west and from the south. General von Kaufman in Tashkent had been given the task of taking Khiva by Tsar Alexander, and in 1873 further expeditions were mounted from Tashkent and from the fortresses at Orenburg, Aralsk, and Kazalinsk to the north. After a series of minor battles in which the ruler of the khanate, Muhammad Rahim Khan, was badly beaten, General von Kaufman captured the city in June 1873. As a result Muhammad Rahim Khan was forced to capitulate but as had happened in Bukhara the khanate was permitted to maintain autonomy over its internal affairs, although in effect it was now under Russian control.

In the final stages of the strategy to secure the region south of Kazakhstan, the outposts established during the Khiva campaign now served as essential bases in what became a colonial war against the Adaevsti and Turkoman tribes of western Kazakhstan. Alexandrovsk had been at the centre of the suppression of the uprising in the Mangyshlak Peninsula in 1870, but subjugation of the whole of the Turkoman area was to prove far more difficult. A largely uninhabited region without easily definable natural borders, Turkoman was a vast territory extending from the Caspian Sea into the Karakum Desert as far as the Bukhara Emirate, and included the ancient city of Merv and surrounding desert areas in the south. The population had no significant khan or leader, but individual tribes from the region were hostile and well-organised, and united to defeat a Russian expeditionary force in 1879. Russian troops were anxious not only to avenge this defeat, but also to provide safety for the caravans and traders travelling between Persia and Russia which were frequently subjected to attack by marauding tribesmen, and above all to pacify what was still a politically sensitive region. It was not until two years later that this objective was finally achieved.

In 1881 Russian troops, led by General Mikhail Skobelev, finally overcame a force of Turkoman tribesmen in the desert fortress of Geok Tepe. Skobelev was known to Russians as the 'White General' for his habit of going into battle in a pristine white uniform, and to local tribesmen as 'Bloody Eyes'. He had served under von Kaufman in the campaigns in Khiva and Samarkand, where he had gained a reputation for ruthlessness and brutality, which he was to display in great measure in the destruction of Geok Tepe and the massacre of its population. Here, at a remote but strategic location deep in the Karakum Desert between the Caspian Sea and the town of Merv, the whole population of the oasis community of Akhal had taken refuge in the fortress of Geok

Tepe. In January 1881 Russian forces laid siege to the fort, and after demolishing part of the heavily defended walls, stormed in and killed thousands of the inhabitants. Skobelev had given orders that no prisoners were to be taken, with the result that many women and children were among the victims of the tsarist cavalry as they fled from the scene. News of the fall of Geok Tepe and the massacre of thousands of tribesmen as well as defenceless women and children, caused an outcry against Russia throughout Europe. In army and social circles in Moscow and St Petersburg, Skobelev was admired and widely praised, but to placate foreign criticism, and to remove his apparent delusions of grandeur and supposed political ambitions, Alexander relieved him of his command and transferred him to an administrative post in Minsk, far from any further adventures in Central Asia. Despite what public opinion in Europe may have thought, the defeat of Turkoman tribesmen at Geok Tepe was a further significant advance for Russia's colonial ambitions. For local people the episode had been a devastating experience, and there was no desire for further resistance as many clans and communities came to believe they had no choice but to submit to tsarist authority. As had been the experience in northern Kazakhstan at the time of the early treaties with Russia, there was widespread aversion to any submission to Russian authority, but in practice this opposition was of little consequence, and treaties signed in 1881 with various Turkoman leaders meant that the whole of Turkestan finally came under Russian control.

The defeat of Geok Tepe was the last major battle fought by Russia in Central Asia. The town of Merv, 300 kilometres to the east, was taken without a fight three years later when the local khans formally submitted to Russia in 1884. This marked the completion of Russia's acquisition of this volatile region of backward and unstable khanates. Not only could Russia ensure stability and security along the length of the southern border of Kazakhstan, but it now also had control of the whole of the eastern shore of the Caspian Sea. This was to be of vital importance in later campaigns in the Russian civil war and in the Second World War. But in the immediate future, and inland away from the Caspian Sea, the khanates of Bukhara and Khiva were now regarded more as self-governing colonies, under Russian control but not, as Kazakhstan and other territories had been, fully incorporated into the empire. Their inhabitants were known as *inorodtsy*, different people who were not Russian but of an alien and lower political and social status. By maintaining nominal autonomy for Bukhara and Khiva, the Russian authorities avoided interfering in religion, education, local administration, or the legal system. The Muslim influence in these territories was deep-rooted and in sharp contrast to Russian practices and Orthodox religious beliefs; thus not only would Russian attempts to impose its own ways have had little chance of success, but would have provoked strong resistance, which in turn would have been exploited by Britain as the rival colonial power in the region. The tsarist army was now spread thinly over a very wide area, and although the Turkoman campaign had ended successfully, it had also shown that Russia was not always stronger than local forces, and may not have been able to quell any sustained or widespread uprising. Given a hostile and unwelcoming background, and having achieved its aim of establishing its control over the length of the southern border of the empire, the imperial government in St Petersburg had little choice but to allow traditional local religious and social practices to continue. Individual khans were responsible for managing their own internal affairs and in particular, in view of the fact that the population was predominantly Muslim, they would not be required to provide men to fight alongside Orthodox Christians in the Russian imperial army. This exemption was to be tested during the First World War, with disastrous results for the future of the monarchy.

Meanwhile in Tashkent, General Konstantin von Kaufman set about consolidating Russia's position as the colonial power. Like Cherniaev, von Kaufman had little more than a slight knowledge of the region or its population. Cherniaev had benefited from Valikhanov's understanding of Semirechie and eastern Kazakhstan but Valikhanov had returned to Verny after the capture of Aulie-Ata, and in any case his knowledge was not particularly relevant in Turkestan. Von Kaufman had no similar intermediary with whom he could work with the local population. Unlike the situation in northern Kazakhstan, there had not been any significant immigration of Russian settlers into the less welcoming desert regions of Central Asia, nor were there any administrators with experience of the region who could implement Russian policies. The result was the need for greater use of military force by the overstretched tsarist army in subduing any resistance which might arise, than had been the case in Kazakhstan. In the northern steppes there had already been contact and integration between Russians and Kazakhs going back centuries, which had not always been harmonious but which had produced greater understanding and cooperation. In Tashkent, Verny, and towns throughout Turkestan, integration of the indigenous population into the tsarist state was officially an objective of colonial policy, which aimed at 'making both Orthodox and Muslims into useful citizens of Russia', according to an official report at the time. This policy was to be implemented in education, which as well as allowing local schools also allowed for the establishment of schools for both Russian and native children. The legal system would be adapted by 'preserving the native courts but with changes necessary for the good of the people and the lessening of their fanaticism, a process which would lead to the removal of barriers to their rapprochement to the Russians', according to the same report. The civil administration would be strengthened by the introduction of Russian-style local councils. Despite his reputation as a ruthless military commander, von Kaufman was sufficiently aware that such a far-reaching process could only be implemented slowly and carefully if latent resistance among the local population to the Russian colonisers was not to become violent. The Russians themselves did little to assist the process of integration, by living apart from the native population, refusing to learn the local languages, and not making any attempt to understand local customs. The widespread belief among Russians arriving from European Russia was that they were bringing a superior culture and civilisation to the people of Central Asia, an attitude which persisted until Soviet times and into the post-Soviet era. But in the late nineteenth century, many local people in the towns and countryside often opposed these alien influences, sometimes with violence, and anti-Russian riots in the khanate of Kokand and elsewhere were put down by military force. Under the terms of the 1869 treaty, Kokand was still semi-independent but the khan, who had earlier been shown to be weak as a military leader in resisting Russian expeditionary forces, was equally unable to ensure stability and effective government within the khanate. In 1876 the khanate was abolished completely by von Kaufman, and its territory divided between the new *oblasts* within Turkestan.

During his governorship in Tashkent, in addition to securing strategic and military control, von Kaufman established a pattern and style for urban development in Central Asia, which both reflected Russia's political dominance and its vision of how towns should be built in inhospitable desert environments. Von Kaufman ordered that a new city should be built in Tashkent adjacent to the walled, native town; the new city should consist of broad tree-lined streets, imposing public buildings, and numerous parks, squares, fountains and gardens to provide shade and cooling breezes in the summer heat. Tashkent became a model for other towns in Central Asia, most notably Verny which was rapidly expanding at the same time and in similar climatic conditions, although Verny had the benefit of a higher altitude and better access to water supplies from the nearby mountains. Unlike the experience of many densely-populated European cities where winding streets and the volume of traffic restricted the efficient transport of goods and people, the broad streets and avenues of Verny, Tashkent, and other towns throughout Central Asia and in Russia itself could easily accommodate the horse-drawn carts and wagons, and the heavily-laden camel trains which were characteristic of the native population. Later in Soviet times of austerity and limited motor traffic, these wide streets and thoroughfares were empty and under-utilised, but came into their own again in the age of mass car ownership in the twenty first century.

The acquisition of Central Asia, including the densely-populated khanates of Khiva and Bukhara, added a further five million subjects to the population of the empire. This represented a significant increase in Russia's domestic market, while Russia itself was now an enormous market for grain, cotton, fruit, leather, and exotic goods from Central Asia. The cost of maintaining army garrisons, of building roads and railways, schools and hospitals, became a heavy drain on the resources of the empire. But the strategic importance of Turkestan meant that this was a cost worth paying. In particular, the khanate of Bukhara, with a long border with Afghanistan, was now part of the empire, although this would represent a continuing source of friction with Britain for many years to come. In any event Russia would not relinquish its hold on the region until the end of the USSR in 1991.

CHAPTER ELEVEN

Kazakhstan Before the Russian Revolution

Now that the strategic position of Kazakhstan and its southern borders was secure, and Russia's military control of the country was established, the government in St Petersburg decided on a further round of administrative reforms in Central Asia. The Governor-Generalship of Turkestan, established in 1867, was no longer seen as suitable after the incorporation of the southern khanates into the empire, and a new administrative structure was called for. In the south, under a 'Statute for the Administration of the Turkestan Region' introduced in 1886, a series of five *oblasts,* or regions, was established, from the Zakaspian oblast in the west, to the Syr Darya, Bukhara, Samarkand, to Ferghana in the east. In the north of the country, a new Governor-Generalship of the Steppe was established in 1891, consisting of five oblasts - Ural, Turgai, Akmolinsk, Semipalatinsk, and Semirechie - and with its capital in Omsk. Tashkent had retained its status as the principal city for the whole of the Turkestan region, but Verny was now the capital of the Semirchie, which now included present-day Kyrgyzstan, Issyk-Kul, the Ili River, and the whole of the region to the south-east of Lake Balkhash. As a result of border changes between Russia and Kazakhstan, Omsk was incorporated within the Akmolinsk oblast, although the town of Akmolinsk itself became the capital of its own oblast. This new arrangement reinforced the existing division of Russian Central Asia between Turkestan in the south, and the Kazakh steppe in the north. Thanks to their closer proximity to Russia, the northern areas were destined to become more economically and socially advanced than the south. Local administration in towns and villages in both regions was traditionally in the hands of local native leaders, who like the Valikhanov family earlier were appointed by the Russian regional governors. In view of its greater distance from Russia, and its greater strategic importance, Turkestan was subject to much closer control from Russia than was the situation in the steppe region. This system lasted until the early 1900s when local leaders were required to receive some education and training, and to be elected on a competitive basis. This did little to improve the efficiency or development of the local administration, which soon acquired the negative aspects of the Russian government, notably its corruption, nepotism, poor management, and general level of incompetence. These factors acted to restrain economic development and provided a further source of grievances amongst local inhabitants.

Nonetheless, by the late-nineteenth century, the economy of Kazakhstan and of the southern part of Central Asia was developing rapidly, thanks largely to improving communications and contact with Russia. In 1879 Russian army engineers began the construction of a railway line, known as the Trans-Caspian, to Tashkent from Krasnovodsk on the eastern shore of the Caspian Sea, at a point opposite Baku in the recently-acquired territory of Azerbaijan and conveniently at the narrowest point of the Caspian Sea. Initially progress in building the line was slow; exploratory missions to survey the route were subject to attacks from Turkoman tribesmen until the defeat of the Turkoman army at Geok Teppe in 1881, and thereafter cranes and other heavy track-laying equipment, railway tracks, sleepers, and stones for ballast, locomotives and rolling stock, coal and water, and all other necessary supplies, could be shipped across the Caspian. Although railway lines had been built in European Russia, Russian experience of this type of major engineering project in difficult conditions in other parts of the empire was very limited. Work on the construction of the Trans-Siberian Railway did not begin until 1891, and the terrain through which the Krasnovodsk line had to run, across the inhospitable sands of the Karakum Desert, was barren and hostile. It was not until 1886 that the railway reached the oasis town of Merv, 900 kilometres from Krasnovodsk. Two years later it had been extended to Bukhara, Samarkand, and Tashkent which became the main terminus. Later two minor lines were built, one branch going north to Chimkent, the other to Kokand and Andijan. Completion of the Caspian railway was followed by the construction of a major line south from Orenburg, across the steppe of north-western Kazakhstan, to Aralsk and Kazalinsk on the Aral Sea, then along the course of the Syr Darya River to Perovsk, before reaching Tashkent in 1905. Now communication between Tashkent and St Petersburg was much improved, and Russia's control over almost the whole of Central Asia was correspondingly strengthened. The arrival of the railway in Tashkent coincided with growing civil disturbances in Russia after the Bloody Sunday massacre in St Petersburg of January 1905, and the railway became a vital means of containing the spread of unrest in Central Asia. Verny and Semirechie remained without a railway connection with Russia, but even here communication with the government in St Petersburg was greatly improved; troops, civilian administrators, and new settlers could now travel by train as far as Tashkent much more quickly, safely, and efficiently. From there it was still a long distance to Verny and Bishkek, but one that could be covered in a much shorter time than before, avoiding the slow and difficult journey across the steppe from Omsk and Semipalatinsk. The population of Tashkent grew rapidly, from about 120,000 in 1877 to 156,000 in 1897, mainly due to the influx of Russian settlers, and similar rapid growth took place in Bukhara, Samarkand, and Chimkent. Verny, meanwhile, remained a much smaller town, although even its population nearly doubled from 12,000 in 1877 to 23,000 by 1897.

The Trans-Caspian and the Orenburg-Tashkent railways reinforced the political and military importance of Tashkent, and by connecting the Turgai and Ural regions of north-west Kazakhstan through which it passed to Russia, the Orenburg line did much to draw Kazakhstan into Russia's economic orbit. Trade and industry in towns and villages along the line began to expand, and transactions for money increasingly replaced barter among Kazakh communities. Industrial goods, agricultural implements, and grain were imported from Russia, in exchange for exports of cotton, wool, leather and silk. Hundreds of small workshops sprang up throughout the region to process goods for export to Russia, and new types of equipment, and more advanced methods of cultivation, led to increasing numbers of families abandoning their old methods of subsistence agriculture and nomadic traditions and switching to growing commercial crops for sale in nearby towns or in Russia. Other social changes were also beginning to emerge, as many poor peasants left the land altogether in search of work in the new industries in the towns and cities. They were joined by a tide of immigrant workers arriving from Russia. Much of the economic growth was taking place in northern Kazakhstan, where coal mining and the extraction of minerals and raw materials were rapidly expanding to meet the growing demands of Russian industry. The railway from Orenburg, with a spur line to Kustanai in the Turgai oblast, gave further impetus to economic and social change among previously remote and isolated rural communities. In the eastern regions of Semipalatinsk and Semirechie, where transport links were still rudimentary, development was more localised, although the towns of Semipalatinsk, Ust-Kamenogorsk, and Verny were developing closer trade links with China.

In the regions of central Kazakhstan, the broad swathe of territory stretching from the vast Ustyurt Plateau between the Caspian and Aral Seas in the west, to Lake Balkhash in the east, was virtually untouched by the industrial and economic changes taking place in the Russia-oriented regions to the north. Except in areas close to the Tashkent-Orenburg railway, the economy of this region was static, as vast distances inhibited access to new markets; instead the impact of developments elsewhere was mainly negative, as old migration routes and pastures became more confined, and the itinerant way of life, which still managed to persist, was becoming increasingly unviable. In the south, the towns and cities in the old khanates were thriving, as the Russian influence and the economic impact brought by the two railway lines, from Krasnovodsk in the east and Orenburg in the north, became more pronounced. Nonetheless, Turkestan remained one of the most economically undeveloped parts of the Russian Empire. The khanates had been allowed to maintain their own internal government and many conservative social structures and religious practices, while the backward state of Russia itself provided no model or inspiration to the local populations to grow or evolve into more advanced societies. Contrary to developments in northern Kazakhstan, where social and economic forces were bringing the Russian and Kazakh populations closer together, there was no corresponding fusion in Turkestan, where Russians and the indigenous population generally kept apart. The region lagged behind the rest of the empire, especially compared to the Baltic States, Byelorussia, and Ukraine, all of which were far more exposed to modernizing influences from Europe, influences which failed to penetrate anywhere near as far as Central Asia.

The second half of the nineteenth century was a period of rapid political and economic change in Kazakhstan, as the country became more closely integrated into Russia. At the same time a growing closeness was taking place in other fields, in music, painting, and literature, where the two countries discovered that they had much in common. In music this closeness found expression notably in the works of the Russian composer Alexander Borodin, whose life from 1833 to 1887 coincided most closely with Kazakhstan becoming part of Russia. The son of a Georgian aristocrat, Borodin himself was not a 'true' Russian by descent, and was a chemist by training. But the inspiration for his music came from Russian history and legends, and from the relationship between Russians and the people of neighbouring countries. His 1880 composition *In the Steppes of Central Asia* combines Russian and Kazakh melodies in a vivid and poignant evocation of an oriental caravan making its way in a slow procession across the Central Asian plains. This produced a response in Russia which was completely different to the old colonial sense of superiority and aloofness widely felt, for example in the court in St Petersburg, towards what were seen as the primitive areas of Turkestan. Many ordinary Russians increasingly discovered an emotional contact with the nomadic Kazakhs, derived from a mutual yearning for a simple life and a shared heritage of the *prostor,* the vast and empty land of the steppe. A nomadic spirit also ran deep in Russia; this was often of a religious nature, particularly among the *stranniki* (wanderers), a sect of the Russian Orthodox Church who spent their lives walking in pilgrimage from one monastery to another, but was another intangible but no less real connection between Russians and Kazakhs.

This was also a period, before the chaos and turmoil of revolution and civil war of the early twentieth century, when Russian painting and literature were flourishing and were also finding a response in Kazakhstan. Landscape painters such as Isaac Levitan, Ilya Repin, and Arkhip Kuinji, drawing their inspiration from nature and the Russian countryside, composed tranquil scenes of endless steppes and distant villages, placid lakes and rivers, and vast open skies, while the paintings of Ivan Shishkin conveyed a sense of the timeless nature and impenetrable depths of Russia's ancient forests. These and other artists of the time evolved a distinctive Russian style and sought to express the poetic aspects of the Russian countryside, a countryside which extended far into the plains of northern Kazakhstan. In literature, the short stories and novels of Ivan Turgenev, notably *The Steppe, Bezhin Lea,* and *Forest and Steppe,* and the works of other contemporary writers contained lyrical descriptions of an idyllic way of life in the country. Although idealised and Slavophile in inspiration, such works of art and literature, and other writers and poets such as Pushkin, Gogol, Dostoyevsky, and Chekhov, became popular in Kazakhstan, not only among the Russian population but among Kazakhs as well, as Russian influence in all areas of life extended further into the Kazakh national consciousness.

A sense of the deepening relationship between Russians and Kazakhs was conveyed fifty years after this period by Pavel Nazarov, a Russian mining engineer and scientist living in Tashkent. In his book *Hunted through Central Asia* (1932) Nazarov wrote: 'Over an immense area in Asia where the wandering Kirgiz (Kazakhs) have scattered, their manner of life and their peculiar culture, developed through millennia of existence on the free open steppe, is the same (as in Russia), identical in space and time. These nomads were free to move about the plains at their own sweet will, as though upon an open sea, and there was nothing to prevent the Kazakhs of the Tien Shan from wandering away to the steppes of Siberia, or the Ural, or the Volga . . . . . . This freedom and the mobility of the nomads of the steppe have evolved from their own peculiar culture, character and manner of life, and have played a very important part in the history of Asia . . . Just as the Normans in their day made use of their mobility upon the seas to spread their influence and culture throughout the west, so these nomads of the steppes of Asia have done the same in the east. The broad belt of grassy plains across the old continent, which has given rise to the peculiar type of nomad and his inseparable comrade, the horse of the steppe, has had enormous influence on the destinies of the settled nations and of civilisation itself.'

But in practical terms a sense of common identity only went so far. Apart from following the exploits of the army, most people in Russia itself had little awareness of life in Kazakhstan or Central Asia. The aristocracy and landowners were far more concerned with affairs at court in St Petersburg and business on their estates in the countrside, and if they travelled anywhere it was to Paris and Rome, not Verny or Tashkent. Russians were less attracted to Kazakh writers and artists, partly for reasons of an imagined Russian cultural superiority, but also because Kazakh traditions of oral epics and legends had less appeal to the increasingly westernised Russian population.

Many Kazakhs also had their own feelings towards Russia which were often far from sympathetic. Bitterness and hatred were common sentiments towards the Russians who had disrupted their ancient migration routes, banished them from fertile pastures and grazing lands, and forced them away to infertile desert regions in the south. But as happened between other colonial and colonised nations, there was developing a relationship which was both hostile and mistrustful, and at the same time was close and enduring. The more positive aspects of the relationship were demonstrated by the Russian scientific and academic communities, and by the imperial Russian army, all of which welcomed Kazakhs to their numbers. For many Russians, Kazakhstan was not so much *part* of Russia, but *was* the same as Russia itself. Many Kazakh families, or at least those who had not suffered at the hands of the Russians such as the Valikhanovs, understood and accepted this situation, and took full advantage of the new opportunities opening up for them in Russia. Increasing numbers of Kazakhs went to study and live in Moscow and St Petersburg, while at the same time more Russians, encouraged by the Russian government, were settling in Kazakhstan, especially in Kokchetav, Akmolinsk, and other northern areas where the countryside and the climate were similar to those of Russia itself. More Russian-Kazakh schools were being established during this period, and reform of the educational system, incorporating Russian and Kazakh features, was taking place at a time when Kazakh writers and scholars such as Ibrai Altynsarin and Abai Kunanbayev were becoming more prominent and influential, particularly in the development of the Kazakh language. Notwithstanding the reforms of Abai Kunanbaev, Kazakh was still written in the Arabic script and did not adopt the Cyrillic alphabet until 1928. But Kunanbaev is widely regarded as the principal figure in Kazakh literature at this time, and it was because of the pioneering efforts of this generation of Kazakhs and Russians that by the turn of the century, the Kazakhs were better educated and more politically aware than the other peoples of Central Asia. Inter-marriage between Russians and Kazakhs became common, which made the violent upheavals and divisions in the years to come all the more painful and traumatic. For the tsarist government in St Petersburg, Kazakhstan was now firmly Russian; as such it was still a useful place of exile for those writers, political dissidents, and others who were less concerned with nature and the countryside and who were more critical of the tsarist regime.

Russia and Kazakhstan may have been growing closer together in many areas, but the political mood in Russia was deteriorating steadily, and threatening stability in both countries, and even the future of the Romanov dynasty. Alexander II had acceded to throne on the death of his father Nicholas I in 1855, and became known as the 'reformer tsar'. His reign saw the greatest social change in Russia in the nineteenth century in the form of the emancipation of the serfs, as well as a series of other far-reaching legal reforms, and the opening up of a more liberal atmosphere after the years of repression under Nicholas. Despite this, widespread dissent and violent opposition against the monarchy continued. One of the groups of political dissidents was a small organisation known as the People's Will, whose principal aim was the assassination of the emperor. The group, led by a murderous fanatic called Zhelyabov, consisted mainly of young people who claimed not to be nihilist, but whose outlook was similar to that of the nihilists who also had a growing following at the time: they had no real plan for the future except to destroy the existing structure of government so that the ensuing vacuum could be filled with a more representative system. Among the conspirators was Alexander Ulyanov, the elder brother of Vladimir Lenin. Some members of the group wanted to replace the monarchy with an ill-defined form of socialism, or to transform the whole of the empire into a 'Federation of Village Communes'. These vague notions may have had some tenuous appeal among uneducated country-dwellers in the villages of Russia and Kazakhstan, from where the group claimed to derive its support, but in practical terms they had no merit or substance. Instead the group focused its attention on its primary objective of assassinating the tsar, and made two unsuccessful attempts on the life of Alexander II, before finally succeeding on 13 March 1881. During a series of arrests after the earlier attempts, Zhelyabov had been detained by the police, but others of the group were still at large, one of whom managed to throw a bomb at the tsar's coach as he was passing near the Winter Palace. The explosion caused many deaths and injuries and Alexander himself died a short while later. He was widely mourned in Russia for his reforming achievements, and was described by a French diplomat Maurice

Paleologue in St Petersburg as having 'established Russian domination in the very heart of Asia'.

Alexander was succeeded by his son Alexander III, whose first official act was to reject a political manifesto which would have permitted a limited form of representative government. This had been a project which had had the support of Alexander II, but which was now consigned to oblivion, to be followed by a new period of repression and strict autocracy. More members of the People's Will were arrested and executed, including Zhelyabov and Alexander Ulyanov. The death of his revered elder brother was a traumatic loss for the teenage Lenin, and did much to inspire his own revolutionary ambitions. The new Tsar Alexander, on the recommendation of court officials, moved out of the Winter Palace in St. Petersburg to the village of Gatchina, sixty kilometres away where, surrounded by forests and lakes, he would be less at risk from assassination attempts. In so doing Alexander distanced himself physically and politically from the ordinary people of Russia, and any ideas of greater popular representation, or self-government in Kazakhstan and other parts of the empire, were now out of the question. Instead Alexander's thoughts turned inwards, away from European-inspired ideas of reform and progress, and towards Russia and its new territories. This was symbolized by the construction of the Church of the Saviour on Spilled Blood, begun in 1883 but not completed until 1907, on the spot in St Petersburg, not far from the Winter Palace, where Alexander II had been assassinated. The Church, whose many byzantine spires and colourful domes are in complete contrast to the elegant European-style architecture of the surrounding palaces and canals, was intentionally designed to resemble St Basil's Cathedral on Red Square in Moscow. St Basil's was built between 1555 and 1561 to commemorate the capture of Kazan by Ivan the Terrible in 1552; and the new Church in St Petersburg was said to represent a return to the ideals of Russia and Russian supremacy in its own lands, lands which now included the vast regions of Central Asia. Alexander III died from natural causes in 1894, although his death was accelerated by damage caused to his kidneys when the imperial train on which he was travelling crashed six years earlier. Popular opinion held to the belief that bombs had exploded on the track, but officially the disaster was attributed to one of the engines leaving the rails and pulling the carriages after it. Alexander was succeeded by his son, the twenty six year old Nicholas II, who like his great-grandfather Nicholas I in 1825, was unprepared and unwilling to accept the role.

By the turn of the century, the economic crisis in Russia was deepening, a development which was inevitably and increasingly being felt throughout the empire. Despite the deaths of Alexander II and III, and the tense political atmosphere throughout the country, the Russian economy had continued to expand during the 1880s, although few of the benefits were felt by the mass of the population. The economy started to fall into recession in 1899, exacerbating what were already appalling social conditions in Russian cities and widespread poverty in the countryside. It was not only European ideas of political reform that Alexander III had been anxious to suppress, but also the spread of revolutionary activities amongst industrial workers. Many workers were increasingly dissatisfied with deteriorating living standards and various revolutionary groups attempted to organize strikes and uprisings throughout Russia and in the major towns of Central Asia. In Kazakhstan, conditions for the mass of the population were no better. The old nomadic economy had by now almost ceased to exist, and was replaced by a combination of settled farming and semi-nomadic animal husbandry extending over much smaller areas than in the past. Only in isolated regions of the Turgai and Zakaspian oblasts, far from transport links to Russia or the rest of the country and without any alternative activities, was the traditional form of nomadic farming still practiced to any significant extent. In the northern regions, despite the unsuitable conditions of the soil in large parts of the country where it was mostly dry and friable, wheat and grain were becoming increasingly important, while in the south, new irrigation schemes from the Syr Darya, Talas, Chu, and Ili Rivers provided much-needed water for cotton, fruit, and vegetables to be grown for the Russian market and for the new industrial cities of Kazakhstan. Neither of these developments appealed to the indigenous population, who increasingly resented the negative impact of the Russian presence and interference in what had been their land.

On Sunday 9 January 1905 there took place in St Petersburg an event which marked another doleful turning point in Russian history, and one which was to have severe consequences not only for Russia but for Kazakhstan and the whole of the empire. In what became known as Bloody Sunday, a peaceful march by factory workers ended in a massacre of hundreds of demonstrators. A strike which had broken out earlier at the Putilov engineering works in the southern suburbs of St Petersburg spread rapidly to other factories, and was followed by a mass rally as thousands of workers, dressed as for a religious ceremony, marched to the Winter Palace. Here they sought to present a petition to the tsar in person, calling for better working conditions and protection against unscrupulous employers, as well as making a series of political demands including the establishment of a constituent assembly, freedom of speech and religion, and an amnesty for political prisoners. In his usual state of detachment and denial it did not occur to Nicholas to receive the petition himself, and responsibility for turning away the demonstrators fell to the army. As the vast crowd moved towards the Palace, carrying icons, religious banners, and portraits of the tsar, the troops opened fire, and hundreds, possibly thousands, were killed or wounded. The episode sent a shock-wave of anger throughout the country, and in a clear echo of the Decembrist Uprising seventy nine years earlier, which was mishandled with equally disastrous consequences by Nicholas I, the institution of the monarchy suffered another heavy blow, although on this occasion it was a blow from which it would not recover.

The impact of Bloody Sunday was such that strikes and protests quickly broke out in towns and industrial cities in Russia and throughout the empire. By October 1905, industrial unrest in Russia culminated in a general strike, but despite some concessions proposed by the government and reluctantly agreed to by Nicholas, social and political turmoil continued to spread. On 12 December an attempt by revolutionary groups to seize power in St Petersburg failed, after which martial law was declared, all political meetings were forbidden, and strict censorship was imposed. Despite these measures, in Moscow ten days later on 22 December 1905 other revolutionary groups decided to launch an armed uprising, despite considerable misgivings as to the possibility of success, and without the support of most of the city's population. The uprising was directed by the Council of Workers' Deputies, a group largely controlled by the Bolshevik Party, from a base in the Presnia textile district where most of the subsequent fighting took place. The revolutionaries managed to take control of a large section of the city, and held out against government forces for a further ten days. However they failed to take the vital Nikolaevsky railway station in the east of the city, and as soon as government troops received reinforcements by train they were able to advance to the city centre and suppress the revolt. Barricades set up by the revolutionaries were soon overwhelmed in fierce fighting, and the Council was forced to surrender. Similar ruthless repressions took place against revolutionary groups in the Baltic States and against peasant uprisings in the countryside. From the beginning of 1905, industrial workers had moved from being respectful petitioners seeking to put their requests to the tsar, to forming councils and soviets and launching armed and violent uprisings against the government at the end of the year. But they had not been able to create any viable or functioning representative institutions which could represent or advance their interests. Trade unions were given a semi-legal status but in practice they were weak and unable to enforce their rights. Nor were workers able to gain any support from the army, which had its own grievances but had no interest in supporting movements by workers or peasants. After 1905, a sense of national despair spread throughout the country, deepened by Russia's defeat in the war of 1904-1905 with Japan, which gave rise to more economic difficulties throughout the country and the empire, as trade and the supply of goods and raw materials were severely disrupted and living standards continued to fall.

In Kazakhstan and other non-Russian regions of the empire, 1905 was also a critical year, and as unrest spread from Russia it soon took on a nationalist as well as an economic character. In Kustanai, Petropavlovsk, and Pavlodar, a series of *mayovki* (illegal May Day protest meetings) was followed by more widespread disturbances among the northern cities. Many of the small independent artisan businesses which had grown up in the cities had been taken over or forced out of business by Russian companies, which in turn had been replaced by much larger factories. This development facilitated the growth of workers unions, while crowded tenements and squalid living conditions provided fertile grounds for the spread of radical political ideas. The downturn in the Russian economy was now being felt throughout the industries and farms in northern and eastern Kazakhstan which had become dependent on markets in Russia. Incomes in these areas, already low, fell even further. Relations between the Russian and Kazakh populations, which earlier had been relatively peaceful, began to worsen as resentment against exploitation by Russian factory-owners of local workers, and hostility towards corrupt Russian-appointed local officials, intensified. The 1905 general strike in Russia, and the ensuing strife and unrest throughout Russian cities, quickly spread to Kazakhstan especially in the north of the country and along the length of the Orenburg-Tashkent railway in the west, as well as in Krasnovodsk at the head of the Trans-Caspian line. Large-scale workers' uprisings took place in Semipalatinsk, Ust-Kamenogorsk, and Zaisan, and although not every city was affected by unrest, factories in Verny and as far afield as Tashkent experienced strikes, stoppages, and demonstrations. Even towns far from Russia and from the railways, notably Karaganda and Akmolinsk, became caught up in the turmoil which was now sweeping through the country. Between 1905 and 1907 a large number of revolutionary groups appeared throughout Kazakhstan and attempted to channel the growing industrial unrest into an organised political force. By 1907 all the major cities, from Uralsk in the north-west to Verny in the south-east, had their own 'social-democratic' organisations and groups, dedicated to challenging what was seen as a corrupt system of government, and improving the condition of industrial and agricultural workers. Rudimentary and illegal printing houses, publishing revolutionary propaganda were springing up throughout the country. The various political groups failed to coalesce into a national movement, but many clandestine and anti-Russian organisations continued to spread unrest, despite the increasingly desperate efforts of the tsarist government to suppress them,

A period of relative calm prevailed between 1907 and 1914, but the outbreak of the First World War, and the onerous consequences this had for Kazakhstan, gave rise to a new wave of disturbances and unrest. For Russia participation in the war was accompanied at home by renewed political turmoil, economic depression, and high inflation, and as had happened in 1905, all this unrest spilled over into Kazakhstan and to Turkestan in the south. In both regions the economic and political problems imported from Russia were compounded by a calamitous misjudgement on the part of the tsarist government, and one which was to convert latent hostility into open conflict. Under the treaties signed with the khans of Bukhara and Khiva in the previous century, the khanates retained political and religious autonomy within the Russian empire, and were not subject to Russian laws, particularly laws relating to compulsory military service. Much the same applied on a less formal basis throughout the rest of Turkestan, and even in Kazakhstan, service in the tsarist army was not obligatory. This situation changed dramatically in June 1916. The Russian army, in retreat from the German advance in the west, was in near-total disarray as mutiny and desertion became common occurrences. Army officers still loyal to the monarchy could no longer force defeated and demoralised troops to return to the battlefield. In response to the crisis threatening the regime and the country, Nicholas ordered that military conscription should now be extended to the male population of the whole of Kazakhstan and Turkestan; this meant that around 250,000 men were to be mobilised immediately to serve with the army. Given the exemption granted at the time of incorporation in the empire from serving in a combat capacity, the conscripts from Kazakhstan and Turkestan were to be assigned to ancillary functions in the rear, thereby releasing other forces for combat duty. But this concession did nothing to allay the deep resentment against the conscription edict and against the war. The conflict was taking place thousands of miles away in western Russia and had little significance in Central Asia, where the population had no desire to take part in a war which they knew was also widely opposed in Russia itself. In Turkestan the war caused particular resentment as it was also a war with Germany's ally Turkey, with which Turkestan and much of Central Asia had a long tradition of close relations. The people of Turkestan and Turkey had both descended many centuries earlier from the ancient Turkic tribes of western Siberia; historically and linguistically the two countries were closely linked, and neither had any desire for conflict between them.

Within Russia itself, Lenin declared that the war was between the imperialist powers and that Russia should have nothing to do with it. He was convinced that for Russia to withdraw from the conflict, albeit at the cost of surrendering large areas of land in western Russia, would bring about a collapse of the established social order, and thus a revolution more quickly. Developments in the country seemed to point in this direction. As the war progressed, opposition to the monarchy grew, to the point where the legitimacy of the tsarist regime was so weak that the sullen and resentful population no longer rallied in support of the government in its losing struggle against Germany. The defeatist mood of the country was in sharp contrast to the popular feelings of patriotism and the need to defend the motherland which had prevailed during the Napoleonic invasion of 1812. Lenin's views of the war and the possibility of imminent revolution found a ready response, not only among growing sections of the ordinary population in Russia, but also among the anti-colonial groups and revolutionary organisations which had sprung up in Kazakhstan and Turkestan. Here the majority of the population was far more concerned to improve working conditions and living standards than they were about what might happen in a distant and unpopular war. Some of the anti-colonial activists may have imagined with some justification that a revolution in Russia would lead to Russia renouncing its imperial possessions in Central Asia.

Coming after years of worsening living conditions and industrial unrest, the mobilisation decree in 1916 sparked off the most extensive anti-Russian uprising throughout the whole of the Russian territories in Central Asia. Violent attacks on government offices and army barracks became frequent occurrences, particularly in Tashkent and the surrounding areas of Samarkand and Kokand, and further east in the Ferghana Valley and the ancient city of Osh. In the north, armed conflicts took place around Akmolinsk and the industrial areas of Ust-Kamenogorsk, but violence was not confined to cities and towns. On the open steppe of the Turgai and Akmolinsk oblasts, decades of simmering resentment against loss of land to Russian settlers came to the surface when government forces tried to enforce the conscription edict, and Kazakh tribesmen once again fought in bitter clashes against the Russian army. In Semirechie, in Kyrgyzstan, and throughout southern Turkestan, many thousands of nomads and herdsmen fled across the border to safety in western China rather than comply with the edict. This was the second mass exodus of large sections of the native population, after the seizure of Kazakh lands by Russian settlers in the previous century. The towns of Bishkek and Tokmok near Lake Issyk Kul were the scenes of particularly violent clashes, as local farmers and workers fought with Russian troops sent from the garrison at Verny to restore order.

Despite the many more serious dangers threatening the survival of the Romanov dynasty, including invasion from Germany and popular unrest at home, Nicholas II was particularly alarmed by the uprising in Central Asia, and directed that overwhelming force should be used to suppress it. But it was not until the end of 1916 that stability was restored. Before then many thousands of people were arrested, shot, or forced from their land and homes. In present-day Kyrgyzstan, reminders of this uprising, in the form of memorials to those killed, and graffiti daubed in white paint on rocks and boulders by the roadside, can still be seen on the road from Bishkek to Lake Issyk Kul, and elsewhere around the country. For Russia the campaign to suppress the uprising was of limited benefit and even counter-productive, since the value to the army from the presence in its ranks of hostile and unwilling conscripts, even in non-combat roles, was outweighed by the cost of enforcing the conscription edict, particularly by the use of troops and resources which could otherwise have been sent to reinforce the military effort in the West. The longer-term cost lay in the deep and enduring resentment now being stored up against Russia throughout the region.

CHAPTER TWELVE

Revolution and Civil War

The political situation in Russia was descending ever-deeper into chaos. Since the disasters on the western front, the government could no longer rely on the army, and the hated 1916 campaign of repression in Central Asia meant that disaffection was spreading throughout the country. In the second half of 1916 and the early months of 1917 this became a critical factor in the downfall of the monarchy. At the outbreak of war in 1914 Peter the Great's European city of St Petersburg had been renamed Petrograd, but the more Russian-sounding name had done nothing to promote patriotic feelings, and by early 1917 almost all of the factories in the city were on strike, and the army was now more on the side of the workers than the government. The atmosphere was universally tense and the city seemed ready for dramatic upheaval, when on 27 February 1917 the first of two revolutions of that year took place. The Duma (the parliamentary assembly established under the limited political reforms of 1905) and a Soviet of Workers' Deputies, jointly established a Provisional Government and arrested most of the ministers of the former government. Nicholas II abdicated three days later, the end of 304 years of the Romanov dynasty. The Provisional Government was initially led by Prince Georgy Lvov, a member of the Constitutional Democrat Party, but in July 1917 he was replaced by Alexander Kerensky, a moderate socialist. Neither was able to stabilise the situation or bring about any improvement into everyday life. The new government introduced some limited political reforms, but it took no action on the vital question of land reform, which was of crucial importance to the peasantry and to agriculture in general. Nor did it seek to end Russia's involvement in the war against Germany; withdrawal from the war would have resulted in substantial loss of territory but would have eased the acute military and social crisis facing the country. After more months of confusion and near-paralysis, on 25 October 1917 (7 November according to the modern calendar) the Provisional Government was itself overthrown when the Bolshevik party stormed the Winter Palace and declared itself to be the only legitimate government in the country. At the same time it proclaimed the establishment of the Russian Soviet Federal Republic, so called after the soviets, or revolutionary committees, in Petrograd. Although it was officially designated to be a federation, incorporating several non-Russian republics including Kazakhstan, it was in fact to be a highly centralised government in Petrograd (and from 1918 in Moscow).

The upheavals in Petrograd were matched by equally dramatic struggles between various political forces in the empire, and especially in Tashkent and throughout Central Asia. The Provisional Government in Petrograd established some authority in the region in April 1917 by setting up a Turkestan Executive Committee based in Tashkent and which extended to Kazakhstan. But as with the recently-established Provisional Government in Russia, this was a 'dual-power' arrangement between the old Constitutional Democrat Party and the new Bolshevik Party, and as such had no basis for stability or durability. Over the following months the Bolsheviks and local supporters in the industrial towns and cities attempted to organise elections to workers' and soldiers' soviets, or local councils, to be managed under a central authority in Tashkent. By this means soviet power would more effectively be extended throughout the old tsarist empire. But the new authority in Tashkent, although in political terms closer to the government in Petrograd, was geographically and politically remote from Kazakhstan, where on the steppes and in the countryside large sections of the population had seen the revolution with alarm and fear. In some respects, Kazakh society had traditionally operated on the basis of the community, with common ownership of land and possessions, and it provided some grounds for the acceptance of the new socialist ideology coming from Russia. But at the same time the tribes and family clans of Kazakhstan had their own hierarchical structures, based on loyalty to a feudal khan. This structure had been formally abolished by the Speransky reforms in the 1820s, but there was still a strong adherence, especially in the more conservative parts of Kazakhstan and Central Asia, to old feudal practices, as well as to Islamic ideals and beliefs. In these areas the new atheist and socialist doctrines of the Bolsheviks were strongly rejected. Initially most of the population, including both indigenous communities and new Russian settlers, tried to remain uninvolved and to avoid further conflict. The memory of the recent devastation caused by the 1916 uprising was still far too painful for most people. But ultimately the Russian revolution was bringing about immense social and political changes, which made it difficult if not impossible for people to stand aside and remain apart from further conflict. In many areas most people were inclined to support their tribal or community leaders in resisting the revolutionary forces. But the revolution was providing new impetus to the growing anti-colonial movement and was strengthening the nationalist groups in Kazakhstan who were demanding independence from Russia. At the same time the large and now-entrenched Russian presence in the country, not only in the north but also in Verny and Aulie-Ata (originally a Kazakh fort and settlement captured by General Cherniaev in 1864 and now an expanding industrial town), were providing the Bolshevik forces with considerable political and military support. The Bolsheviks also established strongholds in other nearby towns where there were large numbers of Russian soldiers and workers, notably Bishkek and Samarkand.

The Russian Revolution unleashed a wide range of grievances and conflicts that had been gathering momentum within the empire for decades. Kazakhstan and Central Asia fell into chaos and turmoil, as power struggles and internecine disputes, reminiscent of the struggles between feuding warlords in earlier centuries, swept through the region. The countryside was torn between many opposing forces, some purely local in origin between rival tribes and clans which had lain dormant for many years, others reflecting the new political and social schisms which were opening up between tsarist and Bolshevik forces, and which were simultaneously engulfing Russia. Before the Civil War fully took hold, a series of important steps were taken in Russia in 1917–1918 which were to have special significance for Kazakhstan and other parts of the empire. In November 1917 Josef Stalin, recently appointed Commissar for Nationalities in the new Soviet government, published a 'Declaration of the Rights of the Peoples of Russia' which amongst other objectives asserted the right of non-Russian minorities to free self-determination, including the right to secession and the formation of independent states. This was amplified three months later in February 1918 by another declaration 'On the Rights of Oppressed Nationalities' which placed more emphasis on the class structure throughout the empire and aimed to create a supposedly free and voluntary union of the working classes of all the nationalities of Russia. As Kazakhstan was formally part of Russia it was preferable for propaganda purposes to refer to Russia rather than to the empire. How long the new Soviet government would be able to reconcile its anti-colonial ideals in Kazakhstan with its need for security in Central Asia remained to be seen, but for its immediate purposes the policy of giving support to nationalist movements had some success. The new regime in Petrograd urgently wanted to gain the backing of non-Russian nationalities in its struggle against the anti-Communist White forces, which were threatening to put an end to the revolution before it could fully take hold. The White armies were aided militarily by the governments of Britain, France, Japan, and the United States which, fearing that the Bolshevik Revolution might spread to their own countries, intervened in the Russian Civil War by sending armies in support of the tsarist forces. By offering the prospect of secession and independence to nationalist groups in Kazakhstan and elsewhere, the Bolshevik government hoped to secure their support in what was still a very dangerous situation for the Revolution.

A second critical development took place in March 1918 with the establishment of the Red Army under Leon Trotsky, who had recently been appointed as Commissar for Military Affairs. Trotsky had virtually no military experience but he had clearly emerged as one of the most effective orators and leaders of the Bolshevik Revolution, and was the key negotiator on the Russian side of the Brest-Litovsk Treaty. Under the treaty Russia ceded vast areas of territory to Germany but was finally able to withdraw from the First World War. After the defeats and desertions during the war, the tsarist army had almost ceased to exist as a fighting force, and the creation of a new army to defend the Revolution was vital. Initially the Red Army had no organisational structure or fighting capability, but Trotsky set about to remedy this by attracting experienced officers from the tsarist army who were willing to serve under the new government, and by attaching political commissars at every level of command, whose job would be to ensure loyalty and to spread propaganda. Trotsky is generally credited with establishing the Red Army, and in this monumental task he was aided by the availability, in the revolutionary climate of Russia, of many thousands of willing volunteers. By the summer of 1918 the Red Army was able to fight effectively for the aims and objectives of the Soviet government in Central Asia and elsewhere throughout the empire.

A third major development was the transfer in March 1918 of the Russian capital from Petrograd to Moscow. Originally intended as a temporary measure and precaution against the risk of a German advance on Petrograd, this soon came to be seen as a means of permanently turning the country away from its tsarist past based in St Petersburg, and towards a new socialist Russia, a Russia which would include the territories of the tsarist empire. From Moscow the government would be better placed to pursue the civil war more effectively, and thereafter to strengthen its control over the non-Russian parts of the empire, especially in Central Asia.

Meanwhile in Kazakhstan, by the end of 1917 a new semi-independent state had emerged out of the chaos and turmoil of the Revolution. The Alash Orda, established in December 1917, was a group of westernised but also nationalist writers and intellectuals led by a prominent local Kazakh named Alikhan Bukeykhanov. Encouraged by Stalin's declaration on minorities the previous month, it set up a government in an area broadly corresponding to the tsarist Steppe Governor-Generalship, extending across the whole of the north and centre of Kazakhstan from Uralsk in the west as far as Ust-Kamenogorsk in the east. The capital of this region was to be transferred from what had been the tsarist steppe capital of Omsk to Orenburg in the west. Alash Orda sought greater autonomy from Russia and a stronger system of law and order, but without attempting to achieve complete independence. It was not overtly hostile to the Bolsheviks, concentrating primarily on bringing stability and extending Kazakh culture and education across the wide area of steppes under its control. The Alash Orda had widespread popular support and for a time its efforts were successful. But in the longer term it was doomed, as there was no possibility that the Bolshevik government would allow the Alash Orda region to continue to exist as a semi-autonomous state, separate from the rest of Russia. Meanwhile in Turkestan in the south, a new Soviet government was established in Tashkent in November 1917. The Turkestan Executive Committee, which had been set up the previous April along the lines of the Provisional government in Petrograd, had been unable to assert its authority in the region, and the Bolshevik Party in Central Asia emerged as the only group with sufficient organisation and ruthlessness to fill the ensuing political vacuum. Using the same tactics of violence and terror adopted in Russia, the Bolsheviks forcibly removed the Constitutional Democrats from the Turkestan government and established their own power and authority throughout the region. This action was far from universally welcomed, and the bitterness and hatred generated against the Bolsheviks among 'tsarist' Russians and nationalist groups during this period were described by Pavel Nazarov, the Russian mining engineer, after he was arrested in 1918 by Bolshevik troops. In a vitriolic account in his book *Hunted through Central Asia,* Nazarov condemned 'these creatures, half-brutes, crammed with cheap Marxism…Not long previously (before his own arrest) ten members of the Constitutional Democratic Party had been arrested and barbarously done to death for the simple reason that they belonged to the 'bourgeois party'. They were taken out into the prison yard, undressed completely on a cold winter's night, and then the devils poured cold water over them. When frozen like statues, the drunken soldiers cut them to pieces with their swords.' In the prevailing climate of war and violence, many thousands of similar gruesome episodes took place under all the different groups and forces fighting in Kazakhstan at the time.

On 30 April 1918 the Turkestan Congress of Soviets, composed largely of Russian railway workers and soldiers in Tashkent, declared the establishment of the Turkestan Soviet Socialist Republic. The new republic incorporated much of the tsarist Turkestan Governor-Generalship, although its area now extended from Krasnovodsk on the Caspian Sea, to Verny and the Semirechie as far as the region around Lake Zaisan in the east. Despite its greater distance from Russia, this was the more Russian-dominated region, compared to the Alash Orda government in northern Kazakhstan. Since tsarist times under General von Kaufman, and especially since the completion of the railway line from Orenburg in 1905, Russia had maintained a strong and largely unchallenged presence in the south based in Tashkent. There was no similar centre of Russian authority in the north. Around the same time a number of smaller autonomous governments emerged in other parts of the region, although none lasted very long. In November 1917 groups of nationalist and Islamic leaders established an autonomous government in Kokand, the semi-independent khanate between Tashkent and Verny. But from the outset this was beset by divisions and clashes between local Bolsheviks, and other groups wishing to re-establish the old order under the khan. To the west in the old Turkoman region now incorporated in the Turkestan Soviet Socialist Republic, a 'Trans-Caspian Provincial Government' was set up in Askhabad with the support of British troops from across the border in Persia. But this also was doomed and was taken over by the Red Army at the beginning of 1920.

The new Turkestan Republic itself soon came under threat from local groups opposed to the Revolution, and by the middle of 1918 forces hostile to the Bolsheviks controlled between seventy and eighty percent of the territory of Central Asia. The area controlled by the Alash Orda and other anti-Bolshevik forces extended around to the west and south of the Aral Sea and eastwards through the old khanates of Khiva, Bukhara, and Kokand. The Turkestan Republic in Tashkent no longer had access to the Caspian Sea, from where it could receive supplies and reinforcements, and it was increasingly isolated from Russia. Over the following year until mid-1919, the Red Army was in retreat throughout the region, and the vital railway link between Russia and Tashkent was cut in the area held by the Alash Orda south of Orenburg, which further threatened the survival of the Turkestan Republic. The escalation of the Russian Civil War and the intensity of the fighting meant that neither Bolshevik nor anti-Bolshevik forces showed any mercy to their adversaries, and atrocities on both sides were frequent occurrences.

Bolshevik forces came under further attack as a result of a nationalist rebellion in Bashkiria in southern Russia on its border with Kazakhstan. In the eighteenth century there had been violent anti-tsarist uprisings and rebellions in Bashkiria, and the region was once again a source of unrest, this time directed against the new Bolshevik government. But as the Red Army extended its control in Russia it formed an alliance with local leaders who mistakenly believed that the new regime would give independence to Bashkiria and allow the expulsion of Russian settlers from land which had been seized over previous decades, especially since the emancipation of the serfs in 1861. A new Bashkiria Autonomous Republic was set up in March 1919. As with other similar attempts at self-government, this was short-lived and as soon as the Bolsheviks had gained complete control of the Urals region and southern Russia the Bashkiria Republic was abolished. Far from discouraging similar nationalist and independence movements, the experience did not prevent the emergence in 1920 of a separate Tartar Autonomous Republic in nearby Tatarstan. The leaders of this new republic consisted of Russian revolutionaries and local Muslim teachers and writers, who believed that a Communist government would abolish the country's feudal and tsarist government, and allow an independent Islamic nation to exist alongside a new Soviet government in Russia. The principal figure behind the Tartar Republic was a radical Muslim called Mirsaid Sultan-Galiev who joined the Bolsheviks in 1917, and later established an independent Muslim Communist Party. But as the Bolsheviks gained in strength the Tartar Republic met a similar fate as the Bashkiria Republic; it was dissolved in 1921 and Sultan-Galiev, lucky to escape with his life, was expelled from the Bolshevik Party.

The notion of Bolshevism and Islam working together as a progressive and modernising force, far from being naïve and unrealistic, gained credibility and momentum in what were soon to become the new Soviet republics of Central Asia. The Communist government in Moscow would later allocate substantial resources to the former tsarist colonies, especially to health, education and improving literacy rates in local languages. But as Sultan-Galiev had come to realise, the Russians and their Marxist beliefs were not going to provide the answers to the needs of the colonised people of Central Asia, since it would clearly not be in the interests of Russia to abolish the empire it had inherited. Instead another revolution would be needed, this time uniting native people on the basis of a common religion rather than on the basis of their class structure. Muslims in Central Asia and elsewhere in the Russian empire shared a common Islamic way of life, which according to Sultan-Galiev would provide the foundation for a new type of government; the industrial work force was too small to sustain a socialist revolution, but Islam and the Bolshevik movement could jointly be directed towards modernising the backward societies of the region. All attempts at any type of joint government however soon foundered on the deep incompatibility between the two beliefs, and on the superior strength and determination of the Bolshevik forces to impose socialism and to preserve Russian control in Central Asia.

Meanwhile, throughout the Alash Orda region in northern Kazakhstan, small and poorly-organised local groups fought in disparate armies under various tribal leaders, but their cause was gravely weakened by a lack of unity, discipline, and strong leadership, all of which were readily to be found in the new and highly motivated Red Army. Most of the local population was in favour of autonomy, and many fought alongside the White Army under the Russian Admiral Alexander Kolchak who proclaimed himself 'Supreme Ruler of All Russia', including Kazakhstan. Kolchak had been a distinguished officer in the tsarist navy and was a former commander of the Black Sea Fleet. He became a supporter of the Provisional Government under Alexander Kerensky, but was dismissed from the navy after the November 1917 Revolution and became leader of the White forces in Siberia and Central Asia fighting against the Red Army. But his abilities were as a naval rather than an army commander, and he was out-manoeuvred, captured, and eventually executed by the Bolsheviks in 1920. Among the followers of Kolchak was a particularly hostile anti-Bolshevik group consisting of Russian aristocrats and entrepreneurs, as represented by the Russian mining engineer Pavel Nazarov, who had settled in Turkestan and Kazakhstan, and who had their own deep-rooted animosity towards the Bolsheviks.

From the middle of 1919, the situation changed decisively as Bolshevik forces began to assert greater control throughout Central Asia. On a political level this included promises to bring about social and economic reforms, such as the redistribution of land and water resources, and the setting up of local district and provincial governments. Greater cultural and political autonomy was promised under the terms of Stalin's 1918 Declaration of Rights, including self-government for Bashkiria. But on the whole these promises had relatively little effect in bringing people round to the Bolshevik cause. Of greater consequence was a significant improvement in the military situation for the Red Army, which in June 1919 restored the vital railway link between Orenburg and Tashkent. Red Army troops also captured the port of Krasnovodsk, and from Baku in Azerbaijan on the opposite side of the Caspian Sea, substantial reinforcements of trained and motivated troops could now be sent to fight against anti-Bolshevik forces in Turkestan and Kazakhstan.

By the early months of 1920, the Soviet government in Moscow had reversed the gains which had been achieved by the anti-Russian forces in Kazakhstan. The Alash Orda government in Orenburg was overthrown in November 1919, ending what was the first and only national government in Kazakhstan which had not been imposed by external forces. In the spring of 1920 Bolshevik control had extended across central Kazakhstan as far as the Semirechie region in the south east. The Bolsheviks were to discover that this was a troublesome area and resistance was particularly strong amongst conservative Kazakh tribes on the steppes and in remote villages and settlements such as Lepsi on Lake Balkhash and Taldy Kurgan in the foothills of the Dzungarski Alatau Ridge. Resistance to the Bolshevik forces was strengthened by reaction to the policy, in those areas where Bolsheviks had gained control, of evicting local herdsmen from more fertile regions in favour of Russian farmers, and resettling native Kazakhs in less fertile areas. This was the practice from colonial times which not only had not been abolished but in some areas had been intensified since the 1917 Revolution. In parts of Semirechie, a form of Soviet slave labour was introduced in which indigenous workers were forced to work, on pain of death and without payment, on Russian-owned farms. The Bolshevik government in Tashkent, whose authority extended to Semirechie, did little or nothing to prevent this exploitation, and some Bolshevik officials expressed views of native Kazakhs which were based more on ideas of racial superiority than on comradeship and egalitarianism. Such attitudes played a major role in the persistence of anti-Russian sentiment in Kazakhstan throughout the Soviet era. In the towns and cities, the conflict was a more typical revolutionary struggle between capitalists and workers. In Verny, thousands of Russian factory labourers joined forces with the Bolshevik soldiers against factory owners and tsarist army officers, and by the summer of 1920, Verny had become a Soviet city.

The Bolshevik Revolution would almost certainly not have succeeded in Kazakhstan if it had not been imposed by force from Russia. The country had a large urban and industrial workforce in the north and in Verny in the south, which had been exposed to Marxism and other revolutionary influences from Russia, and the population in the towns was generally more politically aware, and conscious of the many social injustices, than people were in many other parts of Central Asia. But the industrial proletariat did not have any political or social base outside the towns, nor did it have any strong or distinctive leader who could unify the various disparate groups. If such a leader had emerged, he would have been removed by the Bolsheviks, who mistrusted local officials. Political groups were active and vocal in Kazakhstan, but were just as much riven by local disputes and feuding as those in Russia, with the added dimension of nationalism and the rejection of tsarist and now Bolshevik imperialism. Kazakhstan was still primarily a rural country with an agricultural economy, and as such it had many similarities with rural parts of Russia. But the population was deeply conservative and quasi-Muslim, and the centuries-old hierarchical and feudal structures and traditions of the nomadic tribes and families, far from providing fertile ground for revolution, meant that the population was deeply hostile to change, especially if that change was coming from

Russia. Tsarist Russia had provided education, better medical conditions, and other social benefits in the towns, but the forced removal of large numbers of Kazakhs from grazing lands and pastures had caused great anger and bitterness in the countryside. If Kazakhstan had not already been geographically and politically part of Russia before 1917, it is unlikely that revolutionary forces in the country would have taken root, let alone survived for over seventy years.

In the early years of the Revolution the Soviet government in Moscow consisted almost entirely of activists who came from the industrial towns of Russia and who, unlike the administrators under the tsarist regime, had relatively little awareness of life in the further parts of the empire. For Kazakhstan the implication was that, given the vast expanse of the country, and the enormous distance from Moscow, more effective control was required to ensure stability and compliance with the government's dictates. Some of the more unjust and extreme policies emanating from the government in Tashkent were modified and relaxed, since their effect was counter-productive to the Bolshevik cause. Some Kazakh lands illegally seized by Russian settlers were returned, and grain requisitioning was reduced and eventually ceased altogether. Local bazaars and mosques were allowed to function normally, and other religious practices which had been prohibited when the Turkestan Republic was set up in 1918, were once again made legal. These measures may have helped to calm local feelings, but simmering unrest among much of the population was always threatening to spill over into violence. As well as the removal of some unnecessary restrictions, closer management from the centre was needed if the region was to be properly brought under Soviet control. Thus in November 1920 the greater part of Kazakhstan was given a new administrative status within Russia. Having gone through various previous incarnations, as the tsarist Steppe Governor-Generalship, and the post-revolution Alash Orda region, the western and northern areas of the country were now reconstituted as the 'Kyrgyz Autonomous Republic' within the Russian Federation (until 1926 the people of Kazakhstan were known as 'Kyrgyz', while the people of Kyrgyzstan were known as 'Kara-Kyrgyz'). Much of the southern and eastern parts of the country, principally the Semirechie region and the area around Verny, where resistance to Bolshevik forces had been strongest, remained as part of Soviet Turkestan, since greater control could more effectively be exerted from Tashkent. Only later in 1925 were Semirechie and Verny re-incorporated into Kazakhstan.

The new Kyrgyz Autonomous Republic meant that for the first time Kazakhstan, although it did not yet have its own name, had a separate national identity, its own defined borders, and its own capital city, although this remained at Orenburg, as it had been under the Alash Orda; it was not until 1924 that the capital was transferred to Kyzyl Orda in central Kazakhstan. Constitutionally Kazakhstan was autonomous and self-governing, but in practice it was now more firmly under Soviet control. Geographically, the new national borders sought to delineate Kazakhstan's position on the map and to clarify a vague situation which had evolved over previous centuries and to which there was no clear answer: where did Russia end and where did Kazakhstan begin? For thousands of kilometres there was no natural frontier, no wide river or mountain range, between the two countries as they imperceptibly merged as two arbitrary names on the vast and indifferent landmass of Central Asia. In the west, the new border started on the eastern banks of the Volga delta on the Caspian Sea; the southern stretch of the River Volga itself, as it nears the end of its 3,690-kilometre journey through western Russia, might have been designated as an unmistakable and convenient frontier, but instead the actual border was drawn several kilometres to the east, to incorporate Russian villages and settlements on the eastern banks of the river, and roughly corresponded to the furthest extremes of the land occupied by the Little Horde in earlier times. From its starting point on the coast the border extended northwards, across the low-lying terrain of the Caspian Depression, where the highest point in thousands of square kilometres is the 150-metre hill of Bol Bogdo, 200 kilometres north of Astrakhan. Further north the border curved in a precise semi-circle to exclude the Russian Lake Elton, named after John Elton, an English trader and explorer who mapped large parts of this country in the early eighteenth century. Turning to the east the border then followed a sinuous path across the oceans of featureless plains and steppe, weaving around the most remote Russian villages and isolated Kazakh settlements, marking out the northernmost lands of the Middle Horde. Only in the east of the country did the border run in a straight line, parallel to and 130 kilometres east of the River Irtysh, as it crossed the uninhabited Kulundinskaya Plain. Just north of Semipalatinsk, the border turned back on itself before snaking high into the Altai Mountains, to the almost inaccessible Southern Altai Ridge on the frontier with China and fifty kilometres from the westernmost point of Mongolia. Thus the northern and north-eastern limits of the country were now defined, although subsequent modifications were made to exclude Orenburg, but in the south-east Verny and the Semirechie region remained within the Turkestan Soviet Socialist Republic (TSSR).

The TSSR, which had been established in Tashkent in 1918, continued to exist until 1924, when it was split into two new Soviet republics; the western region from the

Caspian Sea to the Amu Darya River became the Turkmen Soviet Socialist Republic with its capital at Askhabad; the eastern part, roughly between the Amu Darya and Syr Darya Rivers, and including Tajikistan as an autonomous Republic until 1929, became the Uzbek Soviet Socialist Republic. Tashkent temporarily lost its position as the principal city in Central Asia when Samarkand became the capital of the new Uzbek Republic. From here Soviet control of the volatile southern regions, where anti-Bolshevik resistance had persisted for longer than elsewhere, could be more easily enforced. By 1930 the situation had stabilised sufficiently for Tashkent to become the capital again. The anomaly of the Trans-Caspian Provincial Government in Askhabad, which had been set up as an enclave in the TSSR with the support of British troops from across the border in Persia, had already been overthrown by the Red Army at the beginning of 1920, and was now absorbed into the Turkmen Soviet Socialist Republic. Meanwhile the Kokand government to the east of Tashkent, which had been unable to set up any effective administration, was also overthrown after a short campaign and its leaders were forced to flee into the surrounding mountains and the nearby Ferghana Valley. Here there was still active opposition to the Soviet forces in the form of a local resistance movement called the *basmachi*. A guerrilla war against the Red Army continued in the mountains and the countryside until Soviet control was finally established in the late 1920s. Between Askhabad and Tashkent, the old emirates of Khiva and Bukhara, which had managed to retain their tsarist-era autonomy during the post-revolution turmoil in the region also finally succumbed to Soviet power in 1920.

The civil war ended in Russia in 1922, although in remote parts of Kazakhstan and in the mountains of Kyrgyzstan and Tajikistan, sporadic fighting continued until 1928. The war left the economy of Russia and the whole of Central Asia in ruins. Vast sections of industry and agriculture had been destroyed, and enormous numbers of the population had either been killed in the conflict or died of famine. The impact of the civil war in Russia between the White forces under Kolchak and the Red Army under Trotsky, was exacerbated in Kazakhstan by other more localised conflicts, between nationalist groups and Russian settlers, and between social and class divisions in the new industrial towns. The Bolshevik forces in Kazakhstan and Central Asia had been considerably more disciplined and effective than any of the local armed groups, and the Cheka, the 'Extraordinary Commission for Combating Counter-Revolution and Sabotage', established by Lenin in 1918, was particularly ruthless in seeking out opponents of the Soviet regime. Its army of agents and spies, spread throughout the country, were active in betraying and arresting anyone whose loyalty to the Bolshevik cause was open to the slightest question. In Kazakhstan as in Russia, Bolshevik forces in the form of the Cheka and the Red Army prevailed because of their better organisation and because of an ideology which was clearer and stronger than anything offered by their opponents. Despite their urban background, they quickly adapted to local conditions among the peasantry in the countryside and on the steppes. Against them were disparate bands of rival national groups, who lacked a coherent cause and a strong national leader, factors which contributed significantly to the defeat of anti-Bolshevik forces in Kazakhstan.

To add to the devastation caused by the civil war, Kazakhstan suffered another calamity when a catastrophic *zhut,* of severe blizzards and freezing weather lasting several weeks, struck the country in the winter of 1920-21. Almost half the total livestock perished, while production of grain, meat, milk and fodder after the storm dramatically declined, worsening the already severe famine resulting from the war. Many Kazakh tribes and families, having been forcibly resettled in the south, now had to cope with yet more difficult conditions, and Bolshevik promises of restoration of land had mostly come to nothing. Further damage to agriculture had been inflicted by the requisitionings of the civil war, when reserves of grain which had traditionally been built up against harvest failures in the past, were no longer held for fear that they would be seized by the Bolsheviks. By the spring of 1921, the area of famine extended from the Volga region of southern Russia and western Kazakhstan, through Bashkiria to the Ural Mountains and western Siberia. Ukraine was also severely affected, although the famine of ten years later would be even more devastating. Already weakened by hunger, hundreds of thousands of people were killed by typhus and cholera. In a reversal of the traditional migration of people driven by hunger from the cities to the countryside in search of food, many now flocked to the towns imagining that food would be more available there. The famine in Ukraine was exacerbated by the policy of the Soviet government of transporting large quantities of grain from Ukraine to alleviate conditions in the Volga region of Russia, as it sought to punish the Ukrainian peasantry for its opposition to the Bolshevik Revolution. In Kazakhstan, not only had the Bolshevik government done little to restore Kazakh lands to the indigenous population, but similar seizures of scarce food were also used as a weapon against the native population hostile to the revolution, and further aggravated the famine there. The country was now in desperate need of a long period of peace and stability.

But no such stability was forthcoming, and the end of armed conflict between the Red and White forces at the end of the civil war did not mean that a period of social harmony would follow. For millions of Russians and Kazakhs, conditions in the towns and in the countryside continued to worsen. In the chaotic months after the Revolution, when the productive economy in many regions virtually ceased to function, a primitive barter system had grown up between the towns and the villages. Throughout Russia, the more usual flow of people from the towns to the countryside reasserted itself, as thousands of people, known as 'bag-men', went in search of food and returned with sacks of flour, sugar, butter, meat, and any other foodstuffs that could be found. In exchange they offered cheap industrial and household goods, often stolen from factories and workplaces, as well as clothes, shoes, and fuel. Everywhere people scrambled for fuel and firewood to burn in makeshift stoves, risking severe penalties or even life in sawing up political notice boards and propaganda hoardings in the desperate search for firewood to provide warmth against the intense cold of winter. In Boris Pasternak's novel *Doctor Zhivago,* the plight of the Gromeko family is described as they struggle to survive in their Moscow bivouac, selling family possessions in exchange for firewood, in scenes which were to be found in households in towns and cities throughout Russia and Kazakhstan:

'One morning Tonya put on her shabby winter coat and went out 'hunting'. There were only two logs left. She wandered about the alleys in the neighbourhood where you could sometimes catch a peasant from one of the villages outside Moscow selling vegetables and potatoes. In the main streets, peasants with loads were liable to be arrested. Soon she found what she was looking for. A young man in a peasant's coat walked back with her, pulling a sledge which looked as light as a toy, and followed her cautiously into the yard. Covered up by sacking inside the sledge was a load of birch logs no thicker than the balusters of an old-fashioned country house in a nineteenth century photograph. Tonya knew their worth: birch only in name, the wood was of the poorest sort and too freshly cut to be suitable for burning. But as there was no choice, it was pointless to argue. The young man carried five or six armloads up to the living-room and took in exchange Tonya's small cupboard with looking-glass doors. He carried it down and packed it in his sledge to take away as a present for his wife. Hinting at a future deal in potatoes, he asked the price of the piano.'

The barter trade brought chaos to the transport system by clogging up the railways and preventing the movement of troops and the distribution of raw materials and agricultural supplies; it also caused enormous disruption to industry as essential deliveries seized up, and workers avoided shifts so as to search for food. In Kazakhstan, where access to the countryside was easier, the trade flourished even more than in Russia. But conditions outside the towns were desperate and the rural population was often unable to feed itself, let alone provide food for the towns. In the fertile countryside around Verny it was usually possible in the summer months to obtain basic fruit and vegetables, but in the Semirechie region the land was less productive, the treatment of native farmers and nomads by Bolshevik officials from Tashkent was harsh, and food production fell drastically.

Despite the chaos and inefficiencies of the barter trade, it nonetheless provided a rudimentary mechanism for the exchange of goods between the towns and the villages. In the absence of money which would hold its value and which could be converted into goods, basic rates of exchange evolved between different items, with flour the key reference point against which the values of other goods were set. But based as it was on supply and demand and the laws of the market, the system ran contrary to Soviet ideology and the aims of the revolution. A radically different approach was needed, which would bring the countryside firmly under the control of the government, and ensure the supply of food to the cities. As early as 1918 Lenin had in effect declared war against the peasantry, describing the kulaks as 'rabid foes of the Soviet government.... who had grown richer as the workers in the cities and factories starved'. The Bolshevik government attempted to eradicate the barter trade by prohibiting the bagmen from entering the towns with more than a minimal permitted allowance of items. Trains were stopped and searched and food, clothes and drink were confiscated. These efforts were not applied with the usual Bolshevik zeal, as the government realised it could not eliminate this trade altogether. Stopping and searching trains added to the already severe disruption to the railway system, and it was also evident that without this supply of food to the cities, starvation would spread and anti-government protests and unrest would increase. Instead the government sought to impose a monopoly over the production and supply of food, in what became known as 'War Communism'. This was to be the foundation of the planned economy, under which the government aimed to abolish the barter trade and all other private economic activity, to take complete control of distribution of goods and allocation of labour, and ultimately to enforce the collectivisation of agriculture.

However in those areas of Russia, and particularly of Kazakhstan, which were now under its control, the government in Moscow soon discovered that although it had established political and military dominance, it had very limited ability to achieve its aims for supplying the towns. War Communism may have made economic and strategic sense when viewed from Moscow, but the army of urban political activists and administrators sent out to impose the new system of state-determined production and distribution in distant regions of the country, had virtually no understanding of local conditions in the countryside or of nomadic life on the steppes. Many idealistic Bolsheviks were shocked to discover what life was like outside the towns. In many parts of the country, modern civilisation had scarcely penetrated at all, and an alien village culture of drunkenness and fighting, combined with archaic beliefs and pagan rituals and superstitions, was often the norm. This made the task of establishing War Communism all the more demanding.

In Kazakhstan, the actions taken by the new government in Moscow in the post-civil war period were to have far-reaching consequences for the old way of life on the steppe and for the inhabitants of the new towns and cities, more so even than for Russia itself, where there was a more settled form of agriculture without a nomadic population, and where heavy industry was more widely developed. Centuries of contact and familiarity between Russia and Kazakhstan counted for little as the ideologically-motivated and mostly young Bolshevik officials came up against the traditions of nomadic life, and the entrenched habits and beliefs of conservative and Muslim communities. Islam was not strictly or widely practised, but the feudal nature of many Muslim communities was accepted as a fact of life, and the new creed of socialism emanating from Russia found little response. Some villages and communities may have believed that the new regime would liberate them from the more oppressive aspects of feudalism of the past, and there was also a tradition in Kazakh society of communal ownership of land and property. These factors may have led some communities to be more receptive to a moderate version of the new Communist ideology. But no moderation was forthcoming under the Bolsheviks, and many in Kazakhstan became deeply opposed to what they saw as an alien ideology being forcibly imposed from outside. Earlier conflicts between Russian troops and Kazakh tribesmen in tsarist times had often been violent and one-sided, but the vast distances on the steppe meant that there was often a way of avoiding or ignoring the colonisers and their rules. The new Soviet government, however, was far more ruthless in imposing its will, and the opportunities for evading its control began to disappear.

Despite its victory in the civil war, and its zeal in taking socialism to the countryside, in reality the government's hold over large areas of Russia and Kazakhstan was still precarious. It had to contend everywhere with a predominantly hostile rural population, and without control of the countryside, it could not control the food supply for the cities, which in turn would severely impair its control of the economy and the country as a whole. The small farms had little incentive to produce anything beyond their own needs, since there was nothing they could buy in exchange from the towns, and any extra food production was taken by the state. Many farms and villages tried to turn their back on the outside world and revert to simple self-sufficiency, although this was a strategy that would not survive under the new regime. Having defeated the anti-Bolshevik forces in the civil war, the government was not going to let a recalcitrant and backward agricultural population obstruct its further plans for the country. The barter trade was now operating only spasmodically, and armed requisitioning brigades, consisting mostly of untrained and undisciplined industrial workers, were despatched to the countryside with orders to seize quantities of grain and other foodstuffs. The requisitioning brigades were fiercely resisted, and in the ensuing fighting and chaos not only grain and livestock were seized but also reserves of seed for future food production. Attempts to hide stocks of grain, flour, and seeds were countered by the brigades destroying farms and villages; armed resistance by peasants and farmers soon turned into open revolts and uprisings throughout the country. Hostility to the requisitioning brigades was intensified by their crude and violent tactics, including stealing the few personal possessions which peasants owned, by vandalising churches, and committing widespread murder and rape.

Matters were made worse by the setting up of 'Committees of the Rural Poor', which Lenin saw as a means of fomenting a socialist revolution in the countryside, and extending the class war from the cities to the villages. The new Committees were intended to create divisions where none existed before, by taking up the cause of the poorer peasants against those who were thought to be better off, and by radicalising the peasantry as a means of raising food production. The initiative was a failure, both in political and practical terms: by adopting the violent methods of the requisitioning brigades, the Committees stirred up the peasantry against the Bolsheviks themselves, and as a result of theft and destruction of grain and seed, food production fell even further. Many villages in Russia, and especially in Kazakhstan, already saw themselves as farming communes, functioning along egalitarian lines and sharing land, property, livestock, and implements. There was no need for hostile or artificial divisions between poor and rich peasants, since all thought of themselves as more or less equal. Fighting and armed rebellion against the requisitioning brigades, the Committees, and the Red Army spread rapidly, especially in the Tambov province of southern Russia, and throughout virtually the whole of northern Kazakhstan. Before long the Committees of the Rural Poor were recognised by the government in Moscow to have been acting against the interests of the peasants, and the attempt to divide rural communities for political purposes was abandoned. Disastrous harvests confirmed the extent of the damage which had been inflicted by the Bolsheviks on the countryside, and indicated that a more coherent and systematic approach was needed.

While the civil war between the forces of the Red and White Armies was still being fought out on the steppes of western Russia and the plains of Siberia industrial unrest, the causes of which were supposed to have been eliminated by the Revolution, was spreading through towns and cities of Russia. Throughout the country large sections of the peasant population also rose up in revolt in 1919 and 1920, and in vast areas of Russia, including the cities of Tyumen, Cheliabinsk, and Ekaterinburg and the surrounding regions, the new Soviet administration was under threat or completely paralysed by local peasant armies. The rebellion spread rapidly into Kazakhstan, where the regions around Orenburg and the Caspian Sea fell under the control of armed rebels who forcibly evicted the newly-installed Bolshevik officials from towns and villages. Red Army reinforcements from Moscow were unable to contain the situation as the rebels easily merged with the local population or disappeared into the surrounding hills and deserts. By March 1921 Soviet power in wide areas of Russia and Kazakhstan had virtually ceased to exist. Amidst the fighting and chaos, the food crisis in the cities grew worse as supplies from the countryside dwindled and rations became even more meagre.

A further damaging episode for the fledgling Bolshevik government took place in Petrograd, only a short distance from the site of the storming of the Winter Palace, in February 1921. The atmosphere of excitement and revolutionary change generated by the events of 1917 had soon dissipated and industrial workers protested against poor living standards and the iron discipline imposed in meeting production targets. The government found it could no longer rely on large sections of the Red Army, whose readiness to suppress labour unrest in the factories, or to enforce grain requisitioning from the countryside, was increasingly uncertain. In the navy the situation was also rapidly worsening, and matters came to a head early in 1921 when a mutiny broke out in the naval base at Kronstadt, the strategic fortress in the Gulf of Finland. Kronstadt was essential for the protection of Petrograd from the threat of western intervention by sea, and as such it occupied a vital position in defending the Revolution and the country. The sailors stationed there were initially regarded as unquestionably loyal to the Bolshevik cause, but conditions had been deteriorating and unrest had been growing since 1920. In February 1921 this unrest erupted into a mutiny, when the sailors turned in open revolt against the government which they had recently helped to install.

The mutiny was not entirely the result of poor conditions and much of the protest stemmed from nation-wide problems of grain requisitioning, poverty and disease throughout the country. Many of the sailors came from the countryside where their families and the farms on which they worked had been ruined by requisitioning and the ensuing destruction of crops and livestock. The mutineers also resented the fact that they were placed under the command of politically-appointed officers who had no naval experience, who lived in relatively luxurious conditions, and who refused to listen to their grievances. On a political level there was also strong opposition to the single party Bolshevik leadership, and the sailors made demands for freedom of speech and assembly, equal rations throughout the navy, an end to grain requisitioning in the countryside, and the right for peasants to manage the land without outside interference. In the fevered political atmosphere of the time it was to be expected that all types of workers seek to better their conditions. But for supposedly loyal naval personnel to take such action was a bad omen for the Revolution. The government maintained that the sailors should not be involved in political decisions, and it tried to portray the protesters as seeking a restoration of the tsarist regime. But in reality the sailors had been a militant revolutionary force, at the forefront of the events of 1917, and now wanted their voice to be heard. They formed a Revolutionary Committee of their own on the naval base, and arrested the political commissars and officials who had been sent from Petrograd to negotiate with them. Coming on top of the food riots and rebellions in the countryside, the mutiny was another severe blow for the regime. The Bolshevik government could make no concessions to the political demands of the protesters, for fear of prompting further unrest and rebellion against its own leadership, and the mutiny was ruthlessly suppressed, when hundreds of more reliable Red Army troops under the direction of Trotsky, the Commissar for Military Affairs, stormed across the ice from Petrograd to take control of the fortress. Many of the protesters were killed and many more arrested and sent to labour camps in Siberia.

The government's longer-term response to the economic demands of the Kronstadt rebels, and to the crisis in the countryside, was more considered, and the mutiny had consequences for even the most remote villages and farms in Russia and Kazakhstan. The uprising had made it plain that zeal and ideology were not enough to ensure control over the country. Violent suppression of the Kronstadt mutiny and of the Tambov rebellion and unrest throughout the country could only be temporary solutions to anti-Bolshevik resistance, and a profound change had to be made to agricultural and industrial policy if the Revolution was to survive, let alone lead to the establishment of a socialist state.

The change in direction was to be in the form of a New Economic Policy, introduced by Vladimir Lenin at a Bolshevik Party Congress in Moscow in March 1921, just one month after the violent suppression of the Kronstadt mutiny. This marked a significant turning point in the early history of the Soviet Revolution. The NEP was seen as a means of trying to introduce a controlled and limited measure of capitalism and a free market economy, while at the same time protecting some measure of socialism in what was still a backward peasant country, in which industry and agriculture remained in a highly undeveloped state. The industrial revolution in Russia was far from complete in 1917, and the basis for a transition from capitalism to socialism was correspondingly limited. What was applicable to Russia was even more relevant to Kazakhstan and other parts of the empire, where political and economic conditions were even further behind those in Russia. In practical terms, something had to be done to raise food production; the NEP was intended to be a temporary concession to market forces as a way of alleviating food shortages and other acute strains in the economy, and removing some of the sources of unrest and discontent, especially in the countryside. Moreover if the Red Army could be freed from grain requisitioning and suppressing unrest, it would be able to deal more effectively with eliminating residual opposition from White forces and other anti-Soviet groups which still posed a threat to the regime.

The New Economic Policy provided for a form of mixed economy in which traditional farming methods and small-scale private manufacturing were permitted, while the state retained control of heavy industry, finance, and foreign trade. It abolished compulsory grain requisitioning and introduced a form of taxation on farms, payable in grain and other foodstuffs and levied according to local conditions on the land. Surplus production could be traded on local markets. In industry, small privately-owned businesses were once again allowed to operate, with prices set according to supply and demand. As a result clothes, footwear, household goods, and other previously unobtainable items began to appear in shops and on market stalls throughout the country. In agriculture, this led to a boom in private trade and a sharp increase in the supply of bread, butter, cheese, meat, vegetables, and other basic foodstuffs. The earlier barter trade conducted between town and country by bagmen, which had been suppressed by requisitioning and War Communism, once again revived as more people travelled between the cities and the villages carrying goods of all description for sale. But for many in the cities even basic foodstuffs remained out of reach. The industrial economy had not yet reached the point of rapid growth, and in unemployment among industrial labourers was rising. At the same time money was being transferred out of the towns and to the countryside where more farmers and peasants were becoming prosperous from supplying food to the towns. In the early years of its operation, the NEP was largely successful and achieved its aims of increasing the national supply of goods and food. It stabilised the economy, which had been in danger of collapsing, and it brought other benefits, especially to distant parts of the country which had previously had little contact with the outside world. Under the policy the government relaxed its hold over the economy but it extended its reach in other areas, by providing electricity to remote villages, and building hospitals, schools, libraries, theatres and cinemas where none had existed before. Lenin's formula, that 'Communism equals Soviet power plus electrification of the whole country' was propagated everywhere.

Such state intervention that did take place in agriculture was more benign than it had been in the past, in the form of government grants for the acquisition of tractors and farm equipment, fertilisers, and improvements to irrigation schemes, with the result that output of food increased considerably. In industry, except for key sectors which remained under state control, businesses were allowed to invest and operate with the minimum of state direction, and production also increased accordingly. By the mid-1920s economic development was progressing and a greater degree of political and social stability had been achieved. In Kazakhstan the economic transformation under the NEP quickly gathered pace, as industry recovered to its pre-revolution levels of output, and trade with Russia across the border, and along the Orenburg to Tashkent railway, began to flourish. The many hundreds of small businesses and artisan workshops which had grown up in the industrial towns in the north began to recover from the devastation caused by the Civil War, and were free from government intervention to set their own prices and production targets.

The New Economic Policy was having a positive effect on agriculture and small-scale private industry Russia and in Kazakhstan, but financial policy and the allocation of capital remained firmly in state hands. In 1921 a State Bank was set up to manage the constantly-depreciating rouble, and to lay the foundations of a new banking system. The following year, in an attempt to stabilize the currency, the State Bank began to issue a new gold-backed rouble known as the *chernovets*, but financial control remained weak, beyond the experience of most personnel in the revolutionary government. In 1925 the Russian Bank for Industry and Construction, known by its Russian acronym as Promstroibank, emerged from the state take-over of the banking sector after the Revolution and became the largest bank in Russia. It soon extended its activities to the industrial areas of northern Kazakhstan and in the east and south, notably in Semipalatinsk, Ust-Kamenogorsk, Alma-Ata (which had recently abandoned its tsarist name of Verny), and Chimkent, where industry, construction, and mining, under the management of Russian industrialists taking advantage of the freedoms of the New Economic Policy, were beginning to play a major part in the economy. As was the practice with all banks after the Revolution, the new Promstroibank in Kazakhstan was intended to act as a channel for state finance to designated industries, rather than to provide loans to viable projects on a commercial basis and earn a return for the government. Over the following decades, the misallocation of credit became one of the major structural weaknesses in the Soviet economy, and seventy years later in the early post-Soviet era, Kazakhstan and those republics more distant from the economic changes which were then taking place in Russia, found it difficult to break away from the system of banking and credit which dated back to this period. Throughout the Soviet period, state control of the financial system, particularly in Kazakhstan and other less advanced regions, was regarded as an essential method of promoting industrial growth and economic development in accordance with the socialist ideals of the time.

Elsewhere in the rest of Kazakhstan, the western areas between the Caspian and the Aral Sea and the vast steppe lands in the centre of the country, were largely untouched by industrialisation, and the economy remained devoted to agriculture and herding. For the surviving nomadic herdsmen the benefits of the NEP, which had been of great significance in Russia, were of little importance. Nothing could offset the devastation caused by the combination of the *zhut* in the winter of 1920-1921, by War Communism, and by ill-fated early attempts at collectivisation, all of which were causing great hardship. But as industry and the urban population were growing, opportunities in the countryside around the towns for small-scale farming and trading were also expanding. The supply of grain, vegetables, and dairy products was still largely in the hands of individual families and farms, and in the northern regions of the country, the NEP was becoming increasingly important in supplying the needs of the towns in Kazakhstan and across the border in Russia. Many rural communities and villages achieved a level of if not prosperity, then at least of incomes higher than they had been since the Revolution.

In Moscow, the experiment with the New Economic Policy was losing its appeal. Vladimir Lenin, the leader of the Russian Revolution, and principal architect of the NEP, died in 1924, and the city of Petrograd, Peter the Great's St Petersburg, was renamed in his honour. Beneath the national sense of grief and loss, many ordinary factory workers and Bolshevik party officials, led by Josef Stalin, soon became disillusioned with the NEP, which they saw as a betrayal of the Revolution and not operating in the interests of the working class. The supply of basic goods may have improved but so had the numbers of rich people, and the gap between rich and poor was widening. A growing number of industrial workers believed that the policy was working against their interests as peasants and farmers became richer and they became poorer. In what was known as the 'scissors crisis', industrial prices were falling while agricultural prices were risisng, with the widening gap serving the interests of workers in the countryside at the expense of workers in the towns. In Kazakhstan, the dilemma for the government was particularly acute. The NEP had been successful, but when the government tried to impose its will in rebellious areas such as Semirechie, the result was hostility, unrest, and falling production. The new Bolshevik administration was weak and ineffective largely due to lack of knowledge of local conditions, and attempts to reform local government and administration on Soviet lines in rural areas often failed. Poor communications and transport difficulties, official incompetence and mismanagement, and apathy or open resistance in villages and communes, were all serious problems which propaganda and coercion had little effect in overcoming. Rural party meetings were often devoted to matters of no interest to villagers, such as government policy and international affairs, and attempts to raise awareness of such matters only further alienated the already hostile rural population.

By the late 1920s the days of the New Economic Policy were numbered and the economy was about to undergo another dramatic upheaval, in the form of central planning and the introduction of the Five Year Plan. The NEP had achieved a great deal in the industrial sector since it was introduced in 1921: by 1927 industrial production had regained pre-1914 levels, capital investment was rising, and the economy was growing rapidly. But industry under the NEP, especially in Kazakhstan, still largely consisted of small-scale and often family-owned businesses, each employing relatively small numbers of workers, most of whom were unskilled and often only recently arrived from the countryside. Heavy industry had yet to make any significant inroads into the Kazakh economy. Despite its success in stabilising the post-civil war economy, the NEP was now seen as incapable of enabling the complete transformation of industry which

Stalin believed to be essential for the country. Politically the policy had already become less defensible among Bolshevik officials and among the mass of industrial workers, as a reminder of the old order which was supposed to have been eliminated by the 1917 Revolution. A much faster pace of industrialisation was now needed, to build up the national economy and to provide a legitimate basis for the workers' state and the Soviet government. Now that Lenin had gone the NEP was no longer sacrosanct, and all these factors contributed to Stalin's decision in 1928 to abandon the policy, in favour of more direct control over all aspects of the economy.

A radical change in the country, from being a backward agricultural economy to an advanced and self-sufficient industrial power, was from now on to be the government's overriding objective, and Kazakhstan and the whole of the empire were to be fully incorporated in this process of nationwide economic transformation. By 1926 it had already been decided that every type of economic activity throughout the Soviet Union, from the industrial suburbs of Leningrad to the most remote farms of the Kazakh and Kyrgyz steppe, should be brought under the aegis of the government in Moscow. The State Planning Commission, known as Gosplan, was instructed to draw up regulations to enable government ministries to take control of industrial enterprises and hundreds of thousands of other businesses. Gosplan had been created in 1921 but its early life had been overshadowed by the NEP, when the economy expanded and flourished without state control; now it was to be given much greater power and significance. In 1927 it began work on preparing detailed directives and ambitious targets for the first Five-Year Plan for the entire USSR economy. The objectives of the Plan were decided and approved in 1928, and the Plan itself came into effect on 1 January 1929, to be fulfilled by December 1933. Half-way through the Plan, in a speech in February 1931 Stalin reminded the country of the dangers that Russia had experienced in the past due to its backward state and reiterated why the economy had to be transformed at what was to be a frenetic pace:

'The history of old Russia consisted, among other things, of her being ceaselessly beaten for her backwardness. She was beaten by the Mongol khans. She was beaten by the Swedish feudal rulers. She was beaten by the Polish-Lithuanian lords. She was beaten by the Anglo-French capitalists. Everyone gave her a beating for her backwardness. For military backwardness, for cultural backwardness, for state backwardness, for industrial backwardness, for agricultural backwardness. They beat her because it was profitable and could be done with impunity. . . . Russia has fallen fifty or a hundred years behind the advanced countries. We must make up for this backwardness in ten years. Either we do this or we shall be defeated. This is what our obligation before the workers and peasants of the USSR dictates to us'.*

Unlike later Soviet propaganda, Stalin was openly admitting the weaknesses of the new Soviet state, and exploiting these weaknesses to achieve his aims for the industrialisation of the country. The simplicity and clarity of the speech could not fail to have a profound impact, combining honest recognition of the true situation with an unstated but clear threat to anyone who did not comply with the demands of the Plan. Every sector of the economy of every republic was from now on subject to state control; to achieve this control, new ministries for each branch of industry were established to regulate production, issue output requirements, and to ensure compliance with the Plan. This marked the start of the planned economy which became the dominant feature of the Soviet Union until its collapse in 1991. Priority was given to the development of heavy industry, and complete new cities were constructed to meet the needs of the Plan. A new city of Magnitogorsk, named after a nearby mountain consisting of millions of tons of high-grade iron ore, was built for the express purpose of manufacturing iron and steel for factories throughout the USSR. Located just east of the southern end of the Ural Mountains and only a few miles from the border with Kazakhstan, Magnitogorsk attracted thousands of workers from the surrounding countryside to work in its foundries. Within Kazakhstan itself, industrial development was also assigned special importance. The Kazakh economy was particularly backward and largely agricultural, and did not conform to Soviet plans for its future as a modern workers' state; in addition the country had great strategic importance, far from any potential military threat from the west, while able to draw on the vast natural resources of Siberia to the east. As well as supplying labour for the new iron foundries and steel mills in Magnitogorsk and similar factories in other Russian cities, Kazakhstan was to become a major industrial economy in its own right. The small artisan workshops in the towns in the north and east of the country had to be swept away, and replaced with new factories, employing thousands of people, all working towards the needs of the central Plan. The main regions scheduled for heavy industrial development were in and around Karaganda to the north of Lake Balkhash, where a major iron and steel works was constructed to exploit huge deposits of coal and iron, and in the mountainous region in the east of the country around Ust-Kamenogorsk, where vast resources of non-ferrous metals including copper, tin,

---

*Quoted by Alexander Werth, *Russia at War 1941-1945*

zinc, and lead were to be extracted and refined before being loaded onto barges on the River Irtysh. From here the cargoes were transported downstream to Semipalatinsk where they were transferred onto the new 'TurkSib' (Turkestan-Siberian) railway line for transportation to western Russia and Siberia. The western regions of Kazakhstan were poor in mineral resources, but oil refineries were built during this period at Guriev, Fort Shevchenko, and Krasnovodsk on the Caspian Sea, to exploit the extensive deposits of oil which were beginning to be developed.

Targets for output and investment were set at extremely high levels, and although industrial production in Kazakhstan and other non-Russian republics was starting from a very low base, these requirements represented a heavy burden for a labour force and management with little experience of industry, construction, or any of the sectors designated for rapid expansion. More and more workers left the steppes and the countryside and arrived in Alma-Ata and other cities to work in extreme conditions in the new factories, building projects, and mines. According to government claims, the first Five-Year Plan for the USSR was fulfilled by December 1932, one year ahead of schedule. This had been achieved at a cost of enormous disruption and suffering, with millions of people uprooted from the land to work in oppressive and dangerous conditions in the towns. Famine was still widespread in large areas of Kazakhstan, as well as in Ukraine and southern Russia. But the economic achievements were real, and the transformation of Kazakhstan and the whole of the USSR into an industrial economy was now irreversible.

CHAPTER THIRTEEN

The Birth of the USSR

The New Economic Policy and the first Five-Year Plan were developments of major significance in the national economy, but of even greater political importance was the formal establishment, in December 1922, of the Union of Soviet Socialist Republics. The question of how the non-Russian parts of the tsarist empire should be governed had been a source of often bitter dispute in the Bolshevik Party since the Revolution. During the civil war the problem of nationalities and government of the non-Russian republics had been subordinated to the overriding need to achieve supremacy against the White forces. By 1922 the Red Army had taken control over the whole of what had been the tsarist empire in Central Asia and other non-Russian regions and imposed the same form of centralised authority as it had in Russia itself. A few of the revolutionary leaders had supported the notions of national self-determination and independence for the countries which had been colonised in the nineteenth century, notions which were theoretically in accordance with Bolshevik and socialist ideals. But in reality the main question centred on what form of constitutional structure for the border countries surrounding Russia would best serve the interests of the new Soviet state – a state which was still fragile and under attack from hostile forces at home and abroad. Under the first post-revolution constitution of 1918, the Russian Soviet Federated Socialist Republic (RSFSR) was formally established to incorporate the whole of Russia, Bashkiria, and much of Kazakhstan, except for the Semirechie region which was included in the Turkestan Soviet Socialist Republic, which had recently been set up in Tashkent in April the same year. The other newly-established Soviet republics of Ukraine, Belorussia, and the Transcaucasian Federation of Georgia, Armenia, and Azerbaijan, were effectively given a lower status to the RSFSR by means of a series of bilateral 'union' treaties which each had to have with Russia.

The countries to the south of the Caucasus Mountains had been incorporated into the tsarist empire during the time of Russian colonial expansion in the nineteenth century. As in the steppes of Central Asia, a similar outward movement impelled Russia to extend and stabilise its southern borders in the Caucasus. The northern side of the Caucasus had been declared to be a Russian province in 1785, and as had happened in Kazakhstan, a line of forts and Cossack outposts was established, stretching from the

Black Sea to the Caspian Sea along the River Kuban in the west and the River Terek in the east. The forts were intended to act as a defence against invasion and a base for expansion southwards, and as the Russians extended their control deeper into the Caucasus they established similar chains of forts on east-west parallels further south. Some of the peoples of this mountainous region, notably the Ossetians, accepted Russian rule without conflict, but others resisted fiercely, particularly the Circassians in the west and the Muslim Chechens and Lezgians in the north and east Caucasus, who fought against Russian domination until 1859. Unlike the flat and empty steppes of northern Kazakhstan, the mountainous terrain of the Caucasus greatly assisted the warlike and fiercely independent local tribes and made it extremely difficult for Russia to achieve military control. Deep valleys and dense forests gave ideal cover for raiding parties who continually harassed Russian forces, and who provided considerably stronger opposition than was given by the Kazakh tribes and hordes. In Kazakhstan, Russian troops had virtually complete freedom of movement on the open steppe, a freedom denied to them in the confines of steep and narrow valleys and fast-flowing rivers of the Caucasus. Confronted with a determined and hostile resistance, Russia pursued an aggressive policy of destruction and subjugation, especially under General Alexander Yermolov, the governor-general in the Caucasus from 1816 to 1826. In these circumstances there was no prospect of peaceful assimilation with Russia as there was in many parts of Kazakhstan. Tsarist policy eventually succeeded in achieving greater territorial control, but also had the effect of uniting the previously divided tribes of the indigenous population in opposition to Russia, the consequences of which are still being experienced today. South of the Caucasus Mountains, resistance to the Russian advance was generally less pronounced, and in the Christian areas of Georgia and Armenia, Russia was welcomed as liberating the population from the Ottoman Empire. Georgia was taken into the Russian empire in 1800, and in 1828 Russia took control of eastern Armenia and Azerbaijan, thereby preventing these territories being assimilated into Persia. Western Armenia remained under the control of the Ottoman empire until 1829.

As well as seeking to establish a clear and secure frontier between itself and Turkey and Persia, Russia had an additional strategic motive in extending its control further south: by obtaining control of the western shore of the Caspian Sea, it would facilitate access to its new territories in Kazakhstan and Turkestan. The harbour at Baku on the Aspheron Peninsula in Azerbaijan was only 300 kilometres from Krasnovodsk on the other side of the Caspian. A Russian presence here would not only provide a base for the empire in the southern Caucasus, but would also allow the more direct transport of troops and administrators to western Kazakhstan, avoiding the lengthy and dangerous trek across the desert from Orenburg. Later it would also facilitate the transport of engineers and equipment for the construction of the railway from Krasnovodsk to Tashkent, further strengthening Russian control in Turkestan.

The whole of the Transcaucasus region remained effectively part of Russia until the abdication of Nicholas II in March 1917. While the Provisional government in Petrograd was struggling to establish its authority in Russia the three Caucasian nations of Georgia, Azerbaijan, and Armenia united to declare their independence from Russia and to form a new Transcaucasian Federative Republic. This independence did not last long, and in May 1917, in the absence of any effective force from Russia, the whole region was taken over by Turkey. The Transcaucasian Federative Republic continued to exist in name only and remained under Turkish domination for another year, until May 1918 when the three countries again declared independence, this time as separate states. Individually each country was too small and politically weak to maintain its independence once the new Bolshevik government in Russia was in a position to reassert itself in the region. Russia was now anxious to regain what had been taken into the tsarist empire in the previous century and recently lost to Turkey, and Red Army troops marched down the western coast of the Caspian Sea to take control of Azerbaijan in May 1920, Armenia in December 1920, and Georgia in April 1921. Russia once again had relative stability in a volatile part of its southern borders; in addition it had control of the enormous oil resources of Azerbaijan, and easier access across the Caspian to Turkestan and Kazakhstan in the east.

With the military situation on the fringes of the empire more secure, the political battle in Moscow surrounding the future of the new Soviet republics resumed with greater intensity, and in the summer of 1922 a bitter and tempestuous dispute concerning the constitutional structure of the state came to a head. The main protagonists were Vladimir Lenin, leader of the Communist Party (which had changed its name from Bolshevik in 1918) and founder of the Soviet state, and Josef Stalin, Commissar for Nationalities in the new government. Lenin believed it was vital that the republics of the Russian Federation which included Kazakhstan, plus Ukraine, Byelorussia, Turkestan, and the Transcaucasus should co-exist on equal terms in a new federal state to be called the Union of Soviet Republics of Europe and Asia. This was an awkward title but avoided suggestion of Russian supremacy. In reality Russia would be the dominant partner, but this formula would discourage anti-Russian sentiment at a time when the need for unity within the new federation and against a hostile outside world was paramount. For Lenin and local Communist leaders in the different republics, this would be the best way to ensure Russian control; each republic would be permitted or even encouraged to use its own language and maintain its own national traditions, as part of a process of developing as new nations. Where Soviet power had been excessively harsh and badly administered, as in Semirechie in eastern Kazakhstan, this would now be moderated. But in every case, Russian political control would be enforced by local leaders who may be acceptable to the native population but whose ultimate loyalty was to the Soviet leadership in Moscow. Stalin, however, wanted the RSFSR to abandon the bilateral union treaties which had been forced on Ukraine, Byelorussia, Transcaucasus, and Turkestan, and formally absorb them all into Russia, as it had already done with Kazakhstan. These republics would have some notional regional autonomy, but an all-embracing RSFSR and undisguised control from Moscow was Stalin's preferred method of guaranteeing Soviet authority and preventing the spread of nationalism which might undermine the Soviet state.

After months of factional and hostile wrangling, it was Lenin's wishes which prevailed, although the reference to Europe and Asia in the new name for the country was dropped. The name chosen – the Union of Soviet Socialist Republics – deliberately avoided reference to any particular nationality so as to foster the misleading notion that present and future members of the Union would be equal parts of an egalitarian socialist entity. The decision to establish the USSR was agreed by the Communist Party on 31 December 1922, although the new constitution did not formally come into effect until January 1924. Thereafter the initials CCCP (*Soyuz Sovietskikh Sotsialisticheskikh Respublikh*) were eventually to proliferate to every corner of the new country.

January 1924 also marked the death of Vladimir Lenin, and Josef Stalin was now able to deal more freely with the problems of the different nationalities in the non-Russian parts of the Union. In Central Asia, some concessions were given to the aspirations of different national and ethnic groups, and various Kazakhs and other national figures who had taken an active part in the civil war alongside Russian Bolshevik leaders, became involved in developing a policy for the future of the country. But a rejection of the imperialism of tsarist times in favour of independence for Kazakhstan and the rest of Central Asia, which may have been more in keeping with socialist doctrine, was never considered. Instead the old traditions of imperial Russia, of control and subjugation, became the dominant themes of Soviet policy towards the non-Russian territories.

In the early years of the Revolution, official Soviet history portrayed the centuries before 1917 as an age of Russian oppression of non-Russian people and lands in the empire. The entire imperial system was seen as backward and repressive, just as other empires in the contemporary world were oppressing the native people. The tsars and generals of Russian history, even generals such as Mikhail Kutuzov who had defeated Napoleon, were either criticised, or erased from public consciousness. But from the mid-1930s, a new version of history began to emerge, in which prominent figures from Russia's past, notably Ivan the Terrible and Peter the Great, were now praised for bringing political stability and economic progress, while ignoring or at least overlooking the tyrannical and oppressive aspects of their reigns. The choice of these two figures for rehabilitation, and the comparison between them and Stalin, were not coincidental. The need for Russia to colonise the unruly regions of the Caucasus and the other unstable border regions in Kazakhstan and Turkestan, was now seen as a necessary historical development, albeit at the expense of the formerly heroic steppe warriors and mountain partisans who had fought against the tsarist armies. Now the overriding consideration was what form of political and geographical structure would allow Russia the best method of maintaining control over the disparate territories and peoples it had inherited from the tsarist empire. The Central Asian region in particular was of the same strategic importance to Russia that it had been in the nineteenth century, and the new government would do everything in its power to prevent any possibility of political unrest or foreign incursions taking place along its southern border. This included preventing any deviation from the policies laid down in Moscow.

Stalin's wish to take the whole of Central Asia under direct Russian administration and control within the RSFSR, would effectively have preserved the status quo of tsarist times. But other options for the region were now being considered. These included setting up a group of new nation states in accordance with existing, albeit ill-defined, ethnic lines, and the creation of a new single autonomous entity incorporating the whole of the Central Asian region, in effect a new federal republic, to exist alongside Russia itself. In the event the Soviet government implemented a series of political changes between 1922 and 1925 that culminated in the emergence of five separate Central Asian republics. All of the new nations were to be incorporated within the Soviet Union, but each with its own political and cultural autonomy. In 1924 Kazakhstan was redesignated as an autonomous Soviet

Socialist Republic, although it kept its Russian name of Kyrgyzia (the Kyrgyz ASSR), and constitutionally it remained part of Russia. A new capital was established at Kyzyl Orda, formerly the nineteenth century Russian fort of Perovsk, a strategic location in the centre of the country on the Syr Darya River and on the Orenburg to Tashkent railway. The national border which had been drawn up in 1920 was modified in the north-west of the country so that the former capital and predominantly Russian city of Orenburg was reincorporated within Russia. In other changes during the 1920s, Kazakhstan began to acquire some additional national characteristics of its own. In 1921 Verny discarded its tsarist-era name in favour of Alma-Ata, in recognition of its supposed ancient history as the original home of the wild apple plant, but falling short of renaming the city in honour of a revolutionary leader, as happened with many other towns and cities. In 1925, the Semirechie region from Lake Balkhash to the border with China, and to the Chu River in the south-west, and including Alma-Ata, all of which had been part of the Turkestan Soviet Socialist Republic, was formally transferred to Kazakhstan. This recognised the closer ethnic links between the Semirechie region and the rest of the Kazakh population, and by incorporating the vast areas of Semirechie it greatly increased the size of the republic. In 1926, Kazakhstan dropped its former name of Kyrgyzia in favour of the Kazakh Autonomous Soviet Socialist Republic. In 1929, after only five years as the capital, the heat, remoteness, and general unpleasant living conditions meant that Kyzyl Orda, despite its central location, had become unsuitable as a capital city, and everyone recognized that Alma-Ata was a more pleasant place in which to live; since Alma-Ata and the Semirechie had become part of Kazakhstan in 1925, the capital was now transferred to Alma-Ata. At a similar distance from Moscow, Alma-Ata was equally or more remote than Kyzyl-Orda, but the inauguration of the first scheduled air link to the Soviet capital in 1929, and the imminence of the completion of the TurkSib railway line to Semipalatinsk and to Russia, meant that communications between Alma-Ata and Moscow were much less difficult than in the past.

The final step in the development of the USSR was a new Soviet Constitution introduced in 1936. Known as the Stalin Constitution, given Stalin's overriding role in drawing up and dictating its provisions, it dealt mainly with domestic and social matters such as the supposed civic rights and freedoms enjoyed by Soviet citizens. Everyone was guaranteed food, education, shelter, and employment, and Soviet propaganda declared that no other constitution in the world provided so many benefits and privileges for its people. The Constitution defined the USSR as 'a socialist state of workers and peasants', but one in which despite individual rights and freedoms there would be no weakening of the Communist dictatorship. The social benefits of the Constitution were not widely recognized in Kazakhstan, where everyone was aware of the gulf between the fiction and the reality. But in one important respect the 1936 Constitution made a significant break with the past and provided a vital basis for the future: Kazakhstan was given the status of a Union republic in its own right, separate from Russia but within the USSR, and was renamed the Kazakh Soviet Socialist Republic. It already had its own borders and capital city, but for the first time since before the tsarist colonisation of the eighteenth and nineteenth centuries, Kazakhstan was no longer officially part of Russia. The 1936 Soviet Constitution unwittingly prepared the ground for eventual complete independence in 1991. Despite this historic development, many people in Kazakhstan, and even more in Russia, could not comprehend that Kazakhstan now had a legal existence and a separate identity of its own, so long had it been in one form or another part of Russia. Without the provisions of the 1936 Constitution, it is difficult to imagine what might have happened in Kazakhstan when the USSR collapsed fifty-five years later. The Russian Socialist Federal Soviet Republic (RSFSR), which had been established in 1918, itself had become a constituent republic of the USSR in 1924. It was clearly the dominant republic, but it shared its capital city with that of the USSR, and did not its own ministries or other national institutions, factors which would later give rise to resentment among many Russians at what they saw as their subordinate status and the supposedly preferential treatment given to the other republics.

Among Kazakhstan's neighbours in the south, the Turkestan Soviet Socialist Republic, which had also been established in 1918 in Tashkent, was abolished in 1924 and replaced by a series of newly-created republics and autonomous entities. The Turkmen Soviet Socialist Republic and the Uzbek Soviet Socialist Republic became Union republics within the USSR, twelve years before Kazakhstan. The Kara-Kyrgyz Oblast, which later became Kyrgyzstan, continued to be designated as part of Russia, and the Tajik Autonomous Oblast (later Tajikistan) was designated as part of the Uzbek Soviet Socialist Republic. The Karakalpak Autonomous Oblast, a desert region around the south of the Aral Sea, was established as part of Kazakhstan, although in 1930 it was detached from Kazakhstan and transferred to the Russian Federation. In the 1936 Soviet Constitution, the Kara-Kyrgyz and Tajik oblasts were separated from Russia and Uzbekistan respectively and became republics in their own right within the USSR, and the Karakalpak oblast was transferred from Russia to Uzbekistan. These changes recognised geographical and ethnic realities of the region, and formalised the constitutional structure of Kazakhstan and the other Central Asian republics of

Turkmenistan, Uzbekistan, Kyrgyzstan, and Tajikistan, a structure which remained intact until the eventual dissolution of the USSR in 1991.

Although genuine independence for the new republics was never a realistic prospect, the earlier Bolshevik emphasis on promoting national autonomy and greater freedom for ethnic groups had some basis in reality. The Soviet regime was ruthless in eliminating opposition and in imposing its will in the new USSR, but it also had a more constructive and progressive side in accommodating some of the ambitions of national groups, although this was to disappear in the Great Terror under Stalin in the 1930s. In its early years, in its efforts to gain public approval and support, the Bolshevik government pursued enlightened policies towards ethnic minorities and towards the role of women; it promoted the spread of education and literacy, including the use of national languages, and appointed capable and talented local officials to positions of leadership. Once formally taken under Soviet control, the new governments were permitted to set up their own ministries and institutions; in some cases such as local ministries for foreign affairs, these were purely facades, but the objective was to foster a sense of national awareness, and to this extent they were largely successful. Given that all economic and political policies were strictly coordinated in Russia, local officials were able to develop close personal connections with Communist Party officials and their own opposite numbers in Moscow. From the Russian point of view this had the dual benefit of encouraging loyalty to the new system, by conferring upon officials from distant republics the prestige of traveling to Moscow, while at the same time permitting close control from the centre.

By promoting local leaders and encouraging the spread of education and the use of national languages, the new Soviet state was preparing the way for its own ultimate demise. For the time being supreme political power was retained at the centre of government in Moscow, and many of the national policies of the 1920s were to be reversed in the 1930s. But the new republics now had the basic structures for their own governments in their own countries, and some form of nationalism, whether latent or overt, was to remain a feature throughout the Soviet era.

***

The political transformations of the 1920s and 1930s were accompanies by other major developments affecting the leading personalities of the time. In May 1922 Lenin suffered a stroke brought about by uninterrupted work since his return to Russia from

Switzerland in 1917. The crises of the Kronstadt rebellion and famine in the countryside, and the growing threat to his leadership from Stalin, all contributed to his worsening health. He recovered briefly in September 1922, but his condition deteriorated further the following year, culminating in a second major stroke in December 1923, and in his death on 4 January 1924 at the age of 53.

His death was followed by a period of deep national mourning throughout Russia and the new Soviet state. Streets and cities throughout the USSR were renamed in his honour, most notably Petrograd which in March 1924 was renamed Leningrad. In Alma-Ata, as in thousands of towns and villages across the length and breadth of Kazakhstan, the main thoroughfare of the city, a central street descending from the hills in the south of the city to the industrial suburbs in the north, was renamed Prospect Lenina. But in the more remote and rural parts of the Soviet Union, the impact of Lenin's death on the population was more muted. Even in Alma-Ata the main Lenin statue, one of the tallest in the Soviet Union, was not erected until 1954, where it stood on a massive granite plinth opposite the Parliament building until it was removed in 1996. In Moscow and throughout Russia, the display of extreme national mourning and hysteria, largely orchestrated by Stalin, would almost certainly not have met with Lenin's approval. In his will he had expressed the wish to be buried next to his mother's grave in Petrograd, but this was ignored by Stalin who insisted that Lenin's body should be preserved in a granite mausoleum to be constructed on Red Square. This idea was strenuously opposed by Lenin's family, and by Trotsky and other leading members of the government, who saw it as a throwback to primitive religious cults and practices. But this was probably Stalin's specific intention; he wished to preserve the cult of Leninism while at the same time linking it to ancient rites of the Russian Orthodox Church. In any event he saw this as a means of ensuring his own position as the primary guardian of Lenin's heritage. During the final years of Lenin's life Stalin, who had been the Commissar for Nationalities in the post-revolution government, greatly extended his power base and authority. He became general secretary of the Communist Party in 1922 and when Lenin died two years later Stalin emerged as his successor. Not everyone accepted his new role and Stalin was increasingly in sharp conflict with former Bolshevik friends and allies, until eventually all of Stalin's revolutionary comrades were removed from power.

One of Stalin's main opponents was Leon Trotsky, one of the central figures of the Revolution and a close ally of Lenin. Trotsky had been the principal negotiator of the Brest-Litovsk Treaty, and was appointed Commissar for Military Affairs in the

Bolshevik government, in which role he was the founder of the Red Army. Now he was opposed to Stalin's policies in several areas: he opposed the abandonment of the New Economic Policy in 1928, and believed that the Soviet economy would continue to need some degree of private enterprise at least until output had reached a stable and sustainable level. In agriculture he advocated the setting-up of voluntary co-operatives rather than the enforced and comprehensive collectivisation of production being pursued by the government. Trotsky's ideas may have had greater chance of success in Kazakhstan, where there was already a tradition of collective values, combined with resistance to edicts dictated from above. But the option of a more gradual and voluntary approach to increasing output on a shared and collective basis was in direct conflict with Stalin's wishes. In industrial policy, Trotsky was equally at odds with the government, by urging a more restrained pace of investment in production and especially in sectors owned by the state, while maintaining a role for private entrepreneurs and small-scale businesses. This also was in direct opposition to the ambitions of Stalin, whose impatience for achieving a rapid build-up of heavy industry and complete transformation of the economy meant that there would be no room for any private ownership.

In foreign policy, Trotsky fell foul of Stalin's policy of concentrating on the development of a socialist economy and society in Russia, known as 'Socialism in One Country'. Trotsky remained committed to international revolution, believing that popular uprisings would soon take place in Germany and elsewhere in Europe, and that the Soviet Union should do all it could to promote the spread of socialism abroad. For Stalin this was all a distraction from the imperative need first and foremost to strengthen the Soviet state, which was still weak and vulnerable to interference from hostile governments in the west. Trotsky increasingly believed that the Bolshevik Party, which thanks to the Red Army which he himself had founded and which had secured victory in the civil war, had lost its socialist and revolutionary integrity, and that under Stalin it had become little more than a party of bureaucratic administrators. The party, according to Trotsky, had become increasingly authoritarian, as the opportunity for expression of diverse opinions on policy and organisation was becoming highly restricted or eliminated altogether.

By 1927 Trotsky's persistent criticisms of Stalin and his policies made it inevitable that Stalin would have to remove him. This was still a time of great economic and political uncertainty in the USSR; industrial production was still at a low level, and food supplies from the countryside to the cities were precarious. Stability could not be taken for granted. Trotsky and his ideas were seen as increasingly irrelevant and a diversion from the path which the government had embarked upon, but which could still have an appeal to others who may be disillusioned with Stalin's policies. He was no longer a useful member of the government and he had to be got rid of. In the period before the show trials and mass purges which were to follow in the 1930s, Trotsky could not simply be arrested and executed, as would later happen to thousands of other Bolshevik leaders. Nor was quiet, enforced retirement in a Moscow suburb something that Trotsky would accept. He turned down a position in Astrakhan, on the Caspian and far from Moscow, stating that he preferred outright exile to what he regarded as the political hypocrisy of an artificial posting, in which he would ostensibly remain part of the government but in reality would be removed from any power or influence. Towards the end of 1927 Stalin decided that Trotsky should be sent to exile in Alma-Ata, where the vast distance from Moscow, the long, snow-bound winters, and poor communications with the outside world, would effectively eliminate him as a political force. Alma-Ata had not yet become the capital of Kazakhstan and was sufficiently remote to ensure that Trotsky would no longer be able to exert any influence on the government. It would also avoid unfavourable comparisons with Stalin's own experience of being exiled to Siberia under Nicholas II.

On 18 January 1928 Trotsky, his wife Natalya and son Leva, plus an aide by the name of Igor Poznanski, were put on a train which set off from the Kazan Station in Moscow for the long journey to Kazakhstan. The route took them via Samara, Orenburg, Kyzyl-Orda, and Tashkent, where they had to change on to the line to Bishkek; work on building a connection from the Trans-Siberian railway at Novosibirsk to Semipalatinsk and Alma-Ata had only recently started and would not be completed until 1930. From Bishkek the party travelled by a horse-drawn cart along rough and empty roads as far as the southern outskirts of Alma-Ata, from where a car was provided by the city council for the final stage of the journey. After a nine-day journey from Moscow, Trotsky and his family arrived in Alma-Ata, in the middle of the Central Asian winter, to find an alien and silent town under deep snow and cut off from the outside world. With nowhere to stay and far from the comforts and privileges of their earlier life, they embarked on a search for somewhere to live. After a few days in a cheap hotel, they found a large three-storey wooden house to rent, on the north side of Gogol Street not far from the Cathedral of the Holy Ascension, on the site of the present-day Otrar Hotel, and with a view to the snow-covered mountains of the Alatau towering above the town in the distance.

Trotsky spent the following year in almost total seclusion in Alma-Ata. He was permitted to correspond with former colleagues and fellow political exiles in other remote parts of the USSR, and wrote pamphlets on the programmes of the Communist international movement, and articles criticising the government's policies. The postal service was slow and unreliable and letters and parcels of newspapers and magazines took weeks or months to reach him. The enforced isolation must have been a period of profound emptiness for him after the years he had spent as one of the great orators and military leaders at the centre of the tumultuous events of the Revolution and the Civil War. He was shunned by the Red Army units in the nearby barracks, units of the Army which he had created after the Revolution but which now did not want to be associated with a notorious political figure who had incurred the disapproval of Stalin. Others in the Russian community similarly turned their backs on him as he wandered the quiet streets of Alma-Ata. He could write newspaper articles but he had no audience for speeches, and no committees to chair, meetings to organize, or campaigns to lead. When not writing, he spent much of his time reading in the Alma-Ata public library, and on hunting expeditions to the mountains or to the steppes, where he and Leva used to spend days or weeks on end sharing primitive accommodation with local Kyrgyz herdsmen. In the summer of 1928, following the example of nineteenth-century Russian industrialists and landowners in Kazakhstan, he left the town and rented a wooden house in the nearby hills, surrounded by apple orchards and from where he could organise hunting trips to the mountains. Trotsky may have been fortunate that Filipp Goloshchekin, Stalin's appointee as First Secretary of the Kazakhstan Communist Party, and Nikolai Yezhov, Soviet Commissar for Internal Affairs, were still in Kyzyl-Orda, but theirs was not the sort of company that he would have sought.

This restless and suffocating way of life could not continue at a time when the whole of the Soviet Union was in turmoil as a result of the mass collectivisation of agriculture and the start of rapid industrialisation of the economy. Trotsky was completely excluded from any active role in these developments which were to transform the country, but by now he was even more hostile in his views of Stalin, and believed that only he and other like-minded revolutionaries could preserve the socialist ideals which they had fought for. Even in exile he was seen as a threat to the government, and in December 1928 he rejected an ultimatum from the secret police that he should either end all his activities opposing the regime and accept his political defeat, or he would be sent to an even more isolated place of exile. He replied by stating that he would never surrender to the wishes of Stalin, to which Stalin's response was to issue a decree expelling him from the USSR. In January 1929, one year after his arrival, Trotsky was charged with having formed an anti-Soviet party, with being engaged in counter-revolutionary activity, and with organising violent opposition against the authorities. He and his family were given orders to leave the house in Alma-Ata and once again they were forcibly removed, this time in a bus which was to take them back across the mountains to Bishkek. Snowdrifts blocked their route and the family was obliged to transfer to sleighs. Eventually they travelled by car to Bishkek where they were put on a train which would take them to Odessa, from where they would board a ship for the journey across the Black Sea to Istanbul. The Soviet authorities had agreed with the Turkish government that Trotsky would be given asylum in Turkey.

Trotsky's period of exile in Kazakhstan, and his enforced departure from the Soviet Union, marked a major step in the elimination of all opposition to Stalin. If even Trotsky, as the founder of the Red Army and hero of the civil war, could be removed, there was no prospect for the survival of anyone else who might oppose Stalin as the supreme leader of the USSR. In 1932 Trotsky was compelled to leave Turkey and lived for a while in France, before moving to Norway where in 1936 he heard he had been sentenced to death in a show trial in Moscow. Eventually he travelled to Mexico, where he was assassinated by a Soviet agent in 1940.

CHAPTER FOURTEEN

Turksib: Kazakhstan Joins the Trans-Siberian Railway

The 1920s and 1930s in Kazakhstan, as elsewhere in the USSR, were years of rapid economic change, combined with political oppression, mass arrests, and deportations. Alma-Ata was over three thousand kilometres from the Stalinist terror and show trials in Moscow of the late 1930s, but the city and the whole country were already caught up in the same stranglehold of fear and suspicion. The major instrument of political control from Moscow was the local network of the NKVD, the forerunner of the KGB. In the economy, the most important development was the completion in 1931 of the 'TurkSib' (Turkestan-Siberian) railway connecting Alma-Ata and Tashkent with the Trans-Siberian railway, the route of which ran along the northern border between Russia and Kazakhstan. The two existing railway lines in Central Asia, from Krasnovodsk on the Caspian Sea to Tashkent completed in 1888, and from Orenburg in Russia to Tashkent, completed in 1905, had done much to extend Russian military and political control, and to encourage economic development in the western and southern regions of Kazakhstan. But communications with Alma-Ata, Semirechie, and the whole of eastern Kazakhstan were still rudimentary. In these areas the only transport links consisted of rough dirt tracks and unmade roads, with primitive facilities for supply and accommodation en route. Until this region could be brought within the rest of the Soviet transport system and connected to the rest of the country, it remained a potential source of dissent and unrest.

Construction of the Trans-Siberian railway, from Moscow 9,600 kilometres east to Vladivostock on the Pacific coast, had begun in 1891 in the reign of Alexander III. Many of the same strategic and economic motives which lay behind the earlier colonisation of Kazakhstan and Central Asia, namely access to new land for resettlement of serfs, fear of foreign encroachment on Russian territory, and an imperial desire to assert ownership and control, impelled Russian expansion to the furthest reaches of Siberia as far as the Pacific Ocean. In 1892 Alexander appointed the Finance Minister Sergei Witte to take charge of the construction of the line. Coming from a modest social background and having worked as a railway official in Ukraine Witte, like Mikhail Speransky eighty years before him, was not accepted in court circles in St Petersburg. But his efficient administration of the railways, and later his abilities in the government, first as Minister of Communications and later as Finance Minister, identified him to Alexander as possibly the only person in Russia capable of undertaking such a huge task of constructing a railway from one end of the country to the other. Witte not only had practical knowledge and experience of managing the existing railway network, but his position as the leading figure in the Finance Ministry enabled him to raise the necessary capital from western banks and governments, and gave investors the confidence to make substantial loans for what was the largest construction project Russia had undertaken. Numerous foreign railway engineers and other specialists were invited to help in the construction of the railway.

Apart from building railways in the relatively undemanding conditions of western Russia, and across the arid but predominantly flat terrain of Kazakhstan and Turkestan, Russia had no experience of major engineering projects on this scale. The new line had to traverse high mountain ranges, unexplored forests, wide, fast-flowing rivers, and vast tracts of country, which in summer consisted of swampy marshland and in winter of permafrost and frozen tundra. Construction of the Trans-Siberian railway reached Novosibirsk in central Siberia in 1896, crossing into and out of the northern parts of Kazakhstan. The final part of this stretch of the line traversed the broad River Irtysh over a bridge nearly one kilometre long at Omsk. Further progress now continued eastwards to Lake Baikal, a vast and exceptionally deep body of water effectively blocking the path of any communication between Russia and eastern Siberia. Here trains and passengers would have to be ferried across the lake by steamer, from Irkutsk and Port Baikal on the western shore to a new, specially-constructed harbour on the eastern shore, from where construction of the line continued to the small fur-trading settlement of Ulan-Ude in the Buryat region near the Mongolian border. The later circumnavigation around the southern end of the lake, the most tortuous section of the route, required the construction of scores of tunnels, bridges, viaducts, and precarious ledges carved into the sides of precipitous cliff faces, and was not completed until the rest of the line had already reached Ulan-Ude in 1904. An earlier line from Ulan-Ude, traversing Chinese territory in northern Manchuria, had already been built to Vladivostock in 1900, but for political or military reasons this was not viable and was soon abandoned. Work continued on the final section of the Trans-Siberian railway, avoiding Chinese territory and running to the north of the Amur River as far as Khabarovsk, before turning south and finally reaching Vladivostock in 1916. Now the whole of the railway was in Russia, and the railway was acclaimed as a triumph for the country. Alexander had died in 1894 while construction was underway, and had been succeeded by his son Nicholas II.

But Witte, who by then had become a senior diplomat and had been made a Count in recognition of his services to the government, had a difficult relationship with Nicholas and resigned from the government in 1905, although he remained in overall charge of construction of the Trans-Siberian until its completion. Completion of the line in 1916 was fortunate, since the consequences of the First World War, the 1917 Revolution, and the chaos and turmoil of the ensuing civil war would have combined to ensure that no further work on the line would have been possible for many years to come.

In Kazakhstan, construction of a branch railway from the Trans-Siberian line at Novosibirsk in central Russia to Semipalatinsk was completed in 1915, but further work on extending the line over the vast distance southwards to Verny was soon abandoned. The paucity of the railway system, and the transport network generally in the rest of Kazakhstan, was a major obstacle to economic and political development. In 1916 the country had only three railway lines within its territory: from Orenburg to Tashkent, from Novosibirsk to Semipalatinsk, and short stretches of the new Trans-Siberian Railway in the north of the country (the line from Krasnovodsk on the Caspian to Tashkent was outside Kazakh territory). Poor communications across vast distances meant that many settlements and communities, and even large towns, were isolated from each other and from developments elsewhere in the country and in Russia, just as Russia itself had been isolated from change and development in Europe. Except for some of the ancient caravanserais in the south, few places in Kazakhstan were on a natural route to anywhere else. By the end of the nineteenth century, overland transport had improved hardly at all from the rutted and primitive caravan trading routes of earlier centuries. In summer these rough tracks were dry and dusty, turning to deep mud in the autumn rains, before becoming virtually impassable under heavy snow in winter. Even nowadays road transport throughout much of the country is still basic and undeveloped, although this is rapidly changing as more modern roads are being built.

Rivers were not suitable as an alternative means of transport, since most of Kazakhstan's rivers existed for a few weeks only in spring, the result of short-lived and often violent torrents of rain and melting snow, before they evaporated and disappeared into the parched sands of the steppe; those rivers which flowed all year round, notably the Ili and the Syr Darya, were used extensively for irrigation but had little value as trading routes between major towns. Only the Irtysh served as a useful means of transport, descending from Lake Zaisan high in the mountains in the east of the country and connecting the old but now rapidly-industrialising towns of Ust-Kamenogorsk, Semipalatinsk, and

Pavlodar, then flowing northwards into Russia and Siberia. The Irtysh had long been used to transport timber, fish, animal hides and leather goods, and more recently iron ore, copper, and other industrial raw materials downstream to towns and factories in northern Kazakhstan and southern Russia, but its rapid rate of descent meant that the transport of goods in the other direction upstream from Russia was far more difficult. In the 1920s, air transport was still in its infancy; a milestone was reached when the first scheduled passenger flights, between Kyzyl-Orda and Moscow, started in 1929, and the route was extended to Alma-Ata the following year. But the service was rudimentary and irregular, and of limited benefit to the economy as a whole. It was the railways which were to offer the only viable long-term means of improving the country's transport network and connecting it to the outside world.

Plans for a major connection from the Trans-Siberian railway south to Verny and Tashkent had been drawn up and subsequently abandoned in the early 1900s, and only the section as far as Semipalatinsk was built. The plans were revived in 1928 when the route was designated as one of the principal construction projects of the Soviet Union's first Five-Year Plan. Known as the TurkSib, the line was to link the new Turkmen and Uzbek Soviet republics in the south to the developing regions of Siberia in the north. By passing through the recently-renamed city of Alma-Ata the project would also greatly improve communications with the eastern part of Kazakhstan. Grain and timber from Russia and western Siberia would more easily be transported to meet the needs of the growing indigenous population and increasing numbers of Russian settlers in Central Asia, while in the other direction cotton, tea, fruit, apples, oranges, tomatoes, and vegetables could be sent to supply the northern cities. By the turn of the century cotton production was a rapidly growing industry in Uzbekistan and Turkmenistan, providing the raw material for the textile factories in Russia; a new railway connection would add capacity and alleviate strains on the existing Orenburg to Tashkent, and Krasnovodsk to Tashkent railways, while the import of food from Russia would reduce the need for local food production in a region where population growth was rapid, and where resources of water and land for the production of cotton were scarce. Not the least consideration was that the railway would facilitate the transport of troops, military supplies, and equipment to Alma-Ata, from where the Red Army would be better able to suppress anti-Soviet activity in the still-restive regions of Semirechie and Karakol in Kyrgyzstan. Exerting political and military control in a vast region of deserts and mountains, which lacked proper roads or any form of river transport, had always been difficult, a fact which had been exploited by Kazakh tribes in Semirechie and Basmachi rebels in Kyrgyzstan for years after the 1917

Revolution. This was now about to change, and any residual resistance to the new Soviet government would soon come to an end after the line was completed.

Construction of the TurkSib railway began in 1928 at Semipalatinsk, the terminus which had been reached in 1915. From here a single-track line was to be built broadly following the route taken by the Russian army mission in the summer of 1853. Initially the route proceeded southwards across the steppe to the isolated caravan settlement of Agotai and through the Karakum Desert east of Lake Balkhash. From the town of Lepsi, which had been a centre of anti-Bolshevik revolt earlier in the 1920s, the line continued south-west through Semirechie, where the construction of vast numbers of bridges was needed as the route took the line through the upper reaches of mountain streams and rivulets before they coalesced into seven rivers in the plains below. The experience gained in the construction of the line around Lake Baikal should have been invaluable, but accounts of the construction of this stretch indicate that in the rush to completion, many lessons were overlooked and poor workmanship and accidents were commonplace. The high altitude of the village of Taldy Kurgan, although only at the foot of the Dzungarski Alatau ridge, meant that the line had to skirt round to the west then south as far as Lake Kapchagai. Here a bridge was built to cross the River Ili, before the short final stretch across the flat plain rising gently to Alma-Ata. The labour force consisted of teams of Soviet engineers and planners, conscripted labourers and convicts, supposed volunteers from towns and cities throughout the Soviet Union, and farm workers from the surrounding countryside. All had to endure extreme conditions of sweltering heat and dehydration in summer and freezing days and nights in winter, during which under-nourishment and primitive accommodation in rough shelters en route were the norm. Discipline was severe and harsh punishment was given to those who could not maintain the relentless work rate. But the compulsion to complete the line ahead of schedule, in accordance with the rest of the Five-Year Plan, was overwhelming, and the railway reached Alma-Ata on 18 July 1929, a year and a half before the completion date designated in the Plan, although it was another nine months before the first train arrived from Semipalatinsk, on 25 April 1930, driven by 'Kazakh-Machinist First Class' Zh. Koshkinbaev. As a former shepherd and now a skilled train driver, Koshkinbaev fully complied with the propaganda requirements of the project. Alma-Ata and Semirechie were now directly connected to Russia, but construction of the TurkSib was not yet complete. From Alma-Ata work on the new line continued westwards for a further 500 kilometres to the remote desert town of Lugovoy, skirting the western extremity of the Tien Shan Mountains and finally joining the Orenburg-Tashkent line at the tiny settlement of Arys, north-west of Tashkent, in

1931. Now the whole of eastern Kazakhstan was linked to Russia, northwards to join the Trans-Siberian Railway, and westwards to the Tashkent-Orenburg line. The TurkSib was nearly 1,500 kilometres in length and increased the total length of the country's railway network by over a third to over 5,000 kilometres.

Arrival of the railway in Alma-Ata in 1929 was heralded as a great achievement of the first Five-Year Plan, and a landmark in the economic development of Kazakhstan and the whole of the Soviet Union. But the early years of the TurkSib were not an unqualified success. A more moderate and carefully-planned pace of construction would have avoided many later difficulties, as it soon became clear that the line could not cope with the enormous demands being placed upon it. Unlike the Trans-Siberian Railway, the TurkSib had been completed without the assistance of foreign specialists or engineers, or the investment of foreign capital; instead it was financed entirely from internal resources allocated under the Plan, and relied solely on the efforts of Soviet planners, engineers, and construction teams of voluntary workers and forced labour from Kazakhstan and around the Soviet Union. The line was obsolete before it was completed; photographs of the first trains arriving in Alma-Ata show little difference to those used on the Krasnovodsk-Tashkent line which had been completed forty-two years earlier. Meanwhile the forced expansion in the Soviet economy was continuing under the second Five-Year Plan (1933-1937), and the demands made on the country's railway network far exceeded its capacity. A new branch line southwards from the Russian city of Petropavlovsk, just north of the Kazakh border, extending 800 kilometres through Akmolinsk to the extensive new coal fields in Karaganda, was completed in 1931. But neither this nor the country's other lines could cope with the overwhelming tasks assigned to them, particularly in the transport of coal, iron ore, copper, manganese, and all types of industrial raw materials to meet the insatiable demand from the new heavy industries in the Russian cities of Magnitogorsk, Sverdlovsk, and Nizhni Tagil in the Ural Mountains not far to the north of Kazakhstan. The construction of new iron foundries and steel mills in these cities placed enormous burdens on the railways. Transport to the factories of raw materials, and transport from the factories of all types of industrial goods, including cranes and massive steel girders for the construction of more factories and blocks of flats for the labour force in other towns and cities throughout the Soviet Union, imposed ever-increasing strains on the network. From 1941, production of enormous numbers of tanks and military equipment for the army added to the burden. From its earliest days the TurkSib was almost overwhelmed, and for long stretches the track was too weak and had insufficient ballast to cope with the huge weights it was required to bear. The earlier railways had received little investment in improved rolling stock or track, and by the mid-1930s the entire network was over-burdened with unachievable workloads imposed under the Five-Year Plans. Congestion, delays, accidents, and deaths were commonplace.

To help resolve these problems, and to ensure that the railways could meet and exceed their role in fulfilling the demands of the Plan, in 1935 Stalin appointed Lazar Kaganovich, Commissar for Heavy Industry, to take responsibility for modernising the railway network throughout the whole of the Soviet Union. Kaganovich was a close associate of Stalin, although in 1932 he had urged a slowdown in industrial policy and production targets, contrary to Stalin's wishes. Eventually his views prevailed and the second Five-Year Plan, from 1933 to 1937, projected a slower pace of capital investment and lower output targets for factories, mines, and collective farms. Kaganovich, already well aware of the unsustainable strains on the railways, thereby helped to avoid a second unrestrained dash for growth and to consolidate the gains already achieved. Unusually for Stalin, he ensured that Kaganovich had freedom of operation and the necessary resources to achieve his objectives. Kaganovich applied his own terror tactics in dealing with corrupt or obstructive officials, either by execution or by transportation to forced labour camps. But he was also sufficiently enlightened to encourage innovation, also unusual in the rigidly-conformist atmosphere of the 1930s when initiative and independence of thought often led to arrest and imprisonment, and rapid promotion in the newly-glamorous occupations of railway drivers and engineers – although this was soon to turn to fear when the same people were accused of sabotage and wrecking. Emulating his tsarist predecessor Sergei Witte, Kaganovich devoted considerable resources to the training of railway officials at all levels, and to the production of more powerful locomotives, more efficient signalling and braking systems, and laying down double-track lines along many heavily-used stretches and constrictive points throughout the network. Larger, four-axle freight wagons made of metal replaced wooden wagons. In 1936, new workshops for overhauling engines and rolling stock were opened in Novosibirsk, supplemented the following year by an even larger workshop further east at Ulan-Ude, the largest factory east of the Ural Mountains for building and repairing locomotives.

In Kazakhstan, the primary need was for additional railway lines to extend the limited network which existed in the 1930s. However it was not until 1939 that an extension of the line from Karaganda to Balkhash was completed, thereby permitting the exploitation of copper deposits near the lake for transport to factories throughout Russia. The tiny settlements of Saryshagan, Kashkanteniz, and Chiganak along the western shore of the lake were now accessible by train, and the line was further extended in 1940 to the copper mines of Dzhezkazgan and Karsakpai, far out in the central steppe. Despite these extensions the network remained over-stretched and inadequate for the country's rapidly-growing needs.

The role played by Lazar Kaganovich in the development of the railways in Kazakhstan, and in the rest of the Soviet Union, was not entirely constructive and beneficial. He succeeded in achieving a more moderate rate of economic growth in the second Five-Year Plan, but the problems arising on the railways from the first Plan, of frequent derailments, breakdowns, collisions and other catastrophes throughout the network, were increasingly coming to light. Politically it was impossible to attribute such calamities to over-ambitious objectives and the shoddy construction methods used in building the railways; instead they were blamed by Kaganovich and other Soviet leaders on sabotage and the deliberate wrecking of lines and rolling stock, with the intention of overthrowing the Soviet government. This was a familiar theme throughout the early Soviet industrialisation, and the Trans-Siberian and TurkSib railways were also held to have their own foreign agents, saboteurs, and counter-revolutionaries who were now routinely accused of causing chaos and disruption. Given the vital role of the railways in the economy, discipline was severe and punishment of those suspected of causing trouble was exceptionally harsh. The Russian Criminal Code, which still applied in Kazakhstan, covered 'crimes against the system of government' including various offences on the railways which might lead to the breakdown of Soviet transport plans. In his role as Commissar for Heavy Industry, Kaganovich devised a theory of 'counter-revolutionary limit-setting on output'. When applied to disruption on the railways, this led to the dismissal, arrest, and imprisonment or execution of large numbers of railway directors and officials who were accused of deliberately frustrating the government's plans for the rapid development of the rail network. In 1936 the accusations became more grave when after a tour of the Trans-Siberian and TurkSib railways, Kaganovich claimed: 'There is not a single branch of the railway transport system in which Trotskyite-Japanese sabotage has not been active', and subsequently demanded that hundreds more railway officials and workers should be dismissed and arrested. Special railway prisons were set up in small towns along railway lines, and railwaymen awaiting trial were kept in coaches in unused sidings. Special military courts travelled about the country dealing with them, a process which significantly added to the delays and disruption already affecting the operation of the network.

Despite the terror he inflicted on the railway system, Kaganovich played a considerable role in modernising the network throughout Kazakhstan and the USSR. But he had little reward or recognition for his efforts. After the war the railway network played a major part in the Soviet space programme, transporting heavy equipment to the Baikonur cosmodrome from the TurkSib railway and the extension to Karsakpai. But Kaganovich, under whose aegis the Trans-Siberian and the TurkSib had been modernised, and the extension to Dzezhkazgan and Karsakpai had been built, was unremembered in the celebrations. As an old ally of Stalin he was driven into obscurity by Nikita Khrushchev in 1957, fifty two years after Sergei Witte had suffered a similar fate under Nicholas II.

Completion of the TurkSib railway gave a significant boost to the economic development of Kazakhstan. But throughout the Soviet Union as a whole the need for a slowdown and for consolidation was becoming inescapable. The frenetic pace of industrial growth may have been in accordance with the government's strategic objectives but it had not produced any significant improvement in living standards. Some respite came in 1933, when the Soviet government in Moscow, fearing popular unrest after the first Five-Year Plan had produced little to show for the mass of the population, apart from exhaustion and poor living conditions, began to moderate the demands imposed by the second Five-Year Plan. Compulsory deliveries of grain from the countryside to the towns were significantly reduced, although supplies of food would be maintained as in certain cases peasants were once again permitted to trade their agricultural surpluses on a private basis. The pace of capital investment in industry was also eased, while more resources were devoted to increasing the supply of housing and household consumer goods. In Kazakhstan, still a predominantly agricultural economy, these concessions had less impact than in Russia. Bad weather and poor harvests, especially after another devastating *zhut* in the winter of 1932-1933, meant that famine was still prevalent in many parts of the country. In Ukraine and throughout much of southern Russia, notably in the Volga region and the Ural Mountains, the harvest in 1933 was particularly bad, famine was severe, and cannibalism was widespread. Much of the USSR's grain and other food production now went not to feed the towns and cities but to exports abroad, to pay for essential imports of capital equipment for industry and agriculture. The situation facing the domestic population, which was becoming increasingly desperate, was largely ignored, although in 1933 Stalin was forced to allow further reductions, albeit only temporary and partial, in procurement quotas from the countryside. In Alma-Ata and the industrial towns of northern Kazakhstan, conditions were little better. Many thousands of farmers and herdsmen, who had migrated from the countryside seeking work in the towns, still lived in the yurts which they brought with them and installed in the humiliating surroundings of squalid communities in the suburbs, but who no longer had the advantage of their own livestock or land from which they could feed themselves.

Meanwhile in Moscow, the Soviet government was awarding itself ceaseless praise and acclaim for its achievements in industry and agriculture. Streets and squares in the expanding towns and cities were named in honour of factories and collective farms, of individual workers who had exceeded production quotas, and in honour of the Plan. In Kazakhstan, party officials in Alma-Ata and throughout the country were increasingly uncomfortable with the realities of daily life around them, which they were more exposed to than were the relatively sheltered party leaders in Moscow. The prospect of unrelenting pressure for ever-greater output, in the towns and especially in rural communities on the steppes, which were still recovering from the shock of collectivisation, presented considerable risks of further unrest. Some parts of the country, especially Semirechie, and Mangyshlak on the eastern shores of the Caspian Sea, which had fought against the Bolsheviks in the civil war, were still not fully reconciled to living under the Soviet government. But more widely, everyone in the countryside hated the new agricultural system of forced collectivisation, which had not only failed to increase food production but had destroyed centuries-old traditions of life on the steppe, and had led to widespread starvation. In the towns, workers and miners who exceeded their production quotas were summoned to Moscow to be decorated with awards and medals, most notably Aleksei Stakhanov, a coal miner from the Donbas region of Ukraine who vastly exceeded his quota and who gave his name to a new type of 'hero' industrial worker. Many other young and dedicated managers were often promoted over the heads of longer-serving officials. These efforts had some success in generating enthusiasm for Stalin and the regime, but in the frantic rush to over-fulfil the Plan, industrial safety and the proper maintenance of machinery were widely disregarded. Above-plan levels of production brought their own problems, of injuries at work, breakdowns of equipment, extra strains on storage capacity and on transport, especially on the railways, all of which were rarely provided for in the Plans, and often ended in lower rather than higher levels of output. Few people in Kazakhstan were impressed by the exaggerated achievements of Stakhanovite workers in Russia, and most of the population yearned for a return to more peaceful times.

CHAPTER FIFTEEN

Collectivisation and the Reign of Terror

On a warm afternoon in late October 1924 there stepped down onto the platform at the tiny railway station at Kyzyl Orda, in the middle of the desert steppes of southern Kazakhstan, a senior Bolshevik official whose name was to become synonymous in Kazakhstan with brutality and oppression: Filipp Isaevich Goloshchekin. Earlier the same month the Central Committee of the Communist Party in Moscow had decided that Kyzyl Orda should be the new capital of the recently-designated Kyrgyz Autonomous Soviet Socialist Republic (it did not adopt the name of Kazakh ASSR until 1926), taking over from Orenburg which was now once again incorporated in Russia. Goloshchekin had arrived on the train from Orenburg, where he had been appointed by Stalin as First Secretary of the Kazakhstan Communist Party in April 1923. For the next nine years, from 1924 until his departure from Kazakhstan in 1933, Goloshchekin was to be the prime figure in the government of Kazakhstan, and in particular in the ruthless implementation of the collectivisation of agriculture.

A short man with an intense stare, Goloshchekin had already achieved widespread notoriety as the zealous, even fanatical, Bolshevik leader who had organised, and possibly participated in, the execution of Tsar Nicholas II and the Romanov family at Ekaterinburg in July 1918. Unlike Stalin and some of the professional revolutionaries who had no experience of work outside politics, Goloshchekin had trained as a dentist in St Petersburg before becoming a political activist, but he soon became known to the tsarist police and was arrested for illegal activities and propaganda in 1915 and was exiled to Omsk in western Siberia. Here he met and gained the confidence of Stalin when he became part of a group of other revolutionaries which also included Vladimir Lenin and Yakov Sverdlov, another prominent Bolshevik leader. After the Revolution Goloshchekin was appointed by the Bolshevik government as Commissar for War for the Urals Region based in Ekaterinburg, and later in the civil war he played a major role in the defeat of the counter-revolutionary White armies which were particularly active around Ekaterinburg. According to Sir Thomas Preston, the British consul in Ekaterinburg, Goloshchekin was 'cold, and callous, and a ruthless party man'.

In late June 1918 Goloshchekin travelled by train from Ekaterinburg to Moscow where he was given instructions by Lenin, Stalin and Sverdlov to arrange for the execution of the entire Romanov family, who had been held in captivity in Tobolsk in western Siberia, since the abdication of Nicholas II in 1917. In May 1918, the family were moved to Ekaterinburg where they were held without contact with the outside world, in Ipatiev House, the mansion of a former businessman. On 12 July Goloshchekin returned with Sverdlov to Ekaterinburg and together with the local Red Army commandant named Yakov Yurovsky, he prepared to carry out the orders he had been given in Moscow. On the night of 16-17 July 1918, Nicholas, his wife Alexandra, their daughters Olga, Tatiana, Maria, and Anastasia, their fourteen-year-old haemophiliac son Alexei, the family physician Dr Evgeny Botkin, and three of their servants, were executed by Yurovsky and Red Army guards in the basement of the Ipatiev Mansion. According to some accounts, Goloshchekin also took part in the execution, and although there is no definite evidence of this such an action would be in keeping with his character. Another earlier account described him as 'a typical Leninist, cruel, and a born executioner'.* Afterwards the bodies were taken by horse-drawn cart to be burnt and disposed of in a forest outside the city. According to all accounts the whole episode was conducted with brutality, incompetence, and inefficiency, but this was of no concern to Lenin or Stalin; the Romanov dynasty, which had ruled Russia for 300 years since Mikhail Feodorovich became the first Romanov tsar in 1613, had come to an end, and Goloshchekin had been one of the men primarily responsible for carrying out the deed. Thereafter Goloshchekin became Chairman of the Urals Regional Soviet in Ekaterinburg, where he worked tirelessly in enforcing the policies dictated from Moscow. Sverdlov had participated with Goloshchekin in organising the murder of the Romanov family, but he distanced himself from the actual execution, possibly aware of the reaction that might have followed in what was still a critical stage of the civil war.

The deeply ambivalent attitude of many Russians to the murder of the Romanov family, and to the Russian Revolution in general, is most clearly apparent in the modern city of Ekaterinburg. In 1917 the working population of Ekaterinburg, Russia's third largest industrial city, was overwhelmingly supportive of the Bolshevik Revolution, but the events of July 1918 have ever since left an indelible scar in the psychology of the city. In 1924, on the death of Sverdlov, Ekaterinburg was renamed Sverdlovsk in his honour as

---

*Quoted by Helen Rappaport in *Ekaterinburg, The Last Days of the Romanovs,* 2009

a leading figure in the Revolution, and since the collapse of the USSR in 1991, many streets in post-Soviet Ekaterinburg have retained the names of prominent Bolsheviks and other revolutionary figures. The statue of Sverdlov still stands outside the Opera House, and the gigantic figure of Lenin still dominates the Square of the 1905 Revolution in the centre of the city. On the other hand, the city reverted to its tsarist name after a popular vote in 1992, and the old Ipatiev House, which was not demolished until 1977, is now the site of the new Church of the Blood, a vast, towering cathedral built in the traditional Russian Orthodox style in honour of the Romanov family, as if in atonement for what happened there in 1918. Nowhere is there a memorial to Filipp Goloshchekin, and many believe that his role in one of the most traumatic events of the Soviet Revolution and in Russian history should best be forgotten.

In Kazakhstan, there is a similar lack of any reminder of Goloshchekin, although this has more to do with the national distress and turmoil he caused in his ruthless fulfilment of the functions assigned to him by Stalin, than with his role in the execution of the Russian tsar. As a Russian from an urban background, he had no great affinity with or knowledge of Kazakhstan or its people. He had played a leading role in the defeat of the White Army which was active in northern Kazakhstan, but this did not endear him to the majority of the population. Over the next nine years he and Nikolai Yezhov, the Soviet Commissar for Internal Affairs and later head of the NKVD, the People's Commissariat of Internal Affairs, the predecessor of the KGB, who arrived in Kazakhstan with him, consolidated the grip of the Party throughout the country and established a totalitarian government which was to ensure that Kazakhstan followed faithfully the policies dictated by the Communist Party in Moscow. As Party leader Goloshchekin was assigned the responsibility for implementing the collectivisation of agriculture in Kazakhstan, and the enforced resettlement in collective farms of virtually the entire rural population. He knew little of agriculture, and neither he nor the Bolshevik officials sent from Russia to work under him had more than a rudimentary understanding of soil conditions, crop yields, climatic factors, or other vital aspects of life in the countryside and on the steppe. But for Stalin this was no disadvantage, and Goloshchekin's revolutionary background, and record of ruthlessness in dealing with any opposition, were the qualities needed in implementing the objectives of the Revolution, especially in remote parts of the empire such as Kazakhstan.

By 1929 the Soviet government had suffered a series of potentially disastrous setbacks, and another new policy direction was urgently needed. The experience of War

Communism, the Kronstadt rebellion, the New Economic Policy, the early failed attempt at collectivisation of agriculture, and deep divisions within the Communist Party, had all revealed the precarious state of the regime, which twelve years after the Revolution had still not established its absolute authority throughout the whole country. A particular weak spot was agriculture, where the compulsory requisitioning of grain and livestock by ill-disciplined bands of revolutionary troops descending on remote farms and villages, had not ensured basic food supplies for the towns and cities, but had caused great resentment and hostility. The transformation of the economy, as set out in the first Five-Year Plan introduced in January 1929, depended on the certainty of food supplies, and in the same year Stalin decided on a new programme for the mass collectivisation.

Some collective farms had already been set up in Russia in the 1920s, mainly in the form of *sovkhozy* ('Soviet farms') established specifically by the government, whose land was owned by the government, and which employed many thousands of former factory labourers; in addition there were smaller, more specialist *kolkhozy* ('collective farms') which had been set up as a result of the merger of local peasant farms. The kolkhozy formally rented the land from the state and agreed to provide a fixed quota of the harvest to the state. Sovkhoz workers were paid a regular wage, whereas workers on a kolkhoz were paid according to the number of days that they contributed to the farm. Collectivisation was now to be extended without exception and without delay throughout the whole of the Soviet Union. From an ideological point of view, the scheme was intended to eliminate the backwardness, inefficiency, and superstition of the tsarist era, and substitute a more productive socialist system of agricultural factories dedicated to support the industrial economy, and thus to support the new Soviet state. In the large collective farms, private ownership of all types of personal property was abolished and families lived and worked closely together, sharing communal facilities for sleeping, washing, and eating. This may have been acceptable to the immigrant industrial workers, but it was oppressive and unnatural to conservative peasants and farmers in Russia. Families who had farmed their land for centuries deeply resented the impersonal form of large-scale agriculture and the subsequent loss of contact with the land, and the fact that the sovkhozy were often managed by urban political functionaries, and employed large numbers of workers from the towns who knew nothing about the countryside, was also a source of deep and intense grievance. In the kolkhozy, the new system was slightly less damaging in that the farms were smaller and more manageable, and retained some of the characteristics of the original peasant farms. But opposition to sovkhozy and kolkhozy was bitter and violent. Despite the disastrous experience of the Rural Committees in 1918, Stalin gave little thought to local considerations and pressed ahead with mass collectivisation. The imperative was to maximise output at whatever the cost in suffering, and thus to ensure sufficient food for the towns and cities, without which labour unrest would spread, industrial production would suffer, and the Bolshevik hold on power would be threatened. Force and compulsion were needed more than attention to the realities of soil and climate conditions, but labour unrest on the farms, and untrained management lacking knowledge of agriculture, soon contributed to persistent harvest failures and drastic reductions in output.

In Kazakhstan, collectivization was even more deeply resented than it was in Russia. The population had little experience of settled farming, let alone collectivized agriculture, and large numbers of nomadic families, who had never lead any form of static life, were forced to settle in the kolkhozy. The earlier experience of collectivization, in the aftermath of the devastating winter *zhut* of 1920-1921 and the ensuing famine, had been a disaster. From the urban, Bolshevik, perspective this had been seen as a good time to embark on a radical new form of agriculture, when the old system had been devastated by war and by climate, and food production had to be greatly increased. However, the collective farms were not set up properly, and were failing in their basic task of growing food, despite substantial allocations of labour, equipment, and financial subsidies from the government. Armed resistance by local peasants drafted in to work on the new collectives intensified and violence spread throughout northern Kazakhstan. Large numbers of farms were destroyed as a result of resistance from peasants and workers in 1921.

The new programme of collectivisation of agriculture launched in 1929 demanded a revival and expansion of the Sovkhozy and Kolkhozy farms. New compulsory quotas were set for grain and other crops and dairy products and the programme aimed to eradicate the more prosperous peasants and kulaks, a group which came to include anyone who opposed the compulsory incorporation of a village into a single collective farm. In many parts of Kazakhstan where arable farming was secondary to livestock, a perverse and ruinous form of requisitioning developed. Relatively prosperous farmers who had never practised arable farming were nonetheless required to fulfil compulsory grain quotas, or to pay tax in the form of grain deliveries. To do this they had to buy grain from other farms; since normally transactions among nomadic farmers were done by barter, to raise the necessary money they had to sell some of their livestock, which had the effect of depressing the price. The value of animals for sale was further reduced by the lack of buyers, since all livestock belonging to individual farmers was being put into the collective farms. Even if the livestock could be sold successfully, it took considerable time to accumulate sufficient grain to pay the tax, resulting in criminal proceedings being taken against the farmers. Ultimately the individual farmer, if he managed to avoid prosecution, was left with much fewer head of cattle, sheep, or other livestock with which to earn a living in the future. Prosecution was always followed by conviction, and the farmer would be sentenced to imprisonment and all his property confiscated, while his family was deported to another part of the country or beyond Kazakhstan altogether.

Initially it was proposed that joining a collective farm would be voluntary, although in practice there was no possibility for households or small farms to continue to work independently. Many continued to resist the confiscation of livestock and equipment, often preferring to destroy cattle and what simple machinery they may have possessed rather than allow it to be seized for use in the new collective farms. Such opposition was soon swept aside and compulsory production requirements everywhere increased steadily throughout 1929 and 1930. On almost all of the collective farms the situation was increasingly chaotic. Few people from Goloshchekin to the most primitive nomadic herdsman knew how to set up or manage a sovkhoz or a kolkhoz. Notions of capital investment, labour organisation, and efficient allocation of machinery and resources were alien concepts, and attempts by specialists to introduce more systematic and effective methods of production and distribution were regarded with suspicion. The ensuing reluctance of such specialists to get involved further exacerbated the situation.

In 1930 the campaign in the countryside took a new and calamitous turn. Stalin had managed to eliminate most of the opposition within the government to his policies of rapid industrialisation and forced collectivization. Leon Trotsky, an advocate of the New Economic Policy had already been banished to Alma-Ata. In January 1930 the government embarked on a policy of 'dekulakisation', involving the forcible deportation of the more affluent peasants, from the villages and countryside. The kulaks, who had prospered under the NEP and who would have been able to increase food production significantly, were seen as a probable source of opposition to the government, and in any event were thought likely to interfere with the workings of the collective farms.

Stalin also believed that severe action taken against the kulaks would be a powerful disincentive to any other groups contemplating resistance to collectivisation. As with targets for grain and other agricultural production, quotas were set for the number of kulaks to be deported from each region of Russia and Ukraine where the kulaks were particularly numerous. The regions south and east of the Ural Mountains, and the steppes of north Kazakhstan, were designated as the main reception areas where many thousands of people who had now been forcibly deprived of their homes and livelihoods were transported and abandoned. According to later Soviet estimates, about three million peasant households were uprooted between 1929 and the end of 1933, meaning that at least fifteen million people were left without shelter or food, or any possibility of making a new living. Frequently kulaks from Ukraine and central Russia were transported to the empty countryside of Kazakhstan between Petropavlovsk and Lake Balkhash, although here at least some thought had been given to their arrival. One account from a survivor in Karaganda relates: 'There were just some pegs stuck in the ground with little notices saying: Settlement No. 5, No. 6, and so on. The peasants were brought here and told that now they had to look after themselves. So there they dug themselves holes in the ground. A great many died of cold and hunger in the early years'.*

In an article in the Communist newspaper *Pravda* in March 1930, Stalin criticised over-zealous officials who had become 'dizzy with success' in forcing the creation of collective farms through violence and fear rather than pursuing collectivisation on a voluntary basis, although it was Stalin himself who had demanded the forcible collectivisation of agriculture and the elimination of all those who opposed it. Now there was to be a slight change of emphasis away from terror tactics and towards more practical methods of raising production. Even so, throughout Kazakhstan and Central Asia, Ukraine, southern Russia and the Caucasus, requisitioning brigades continued to meet armed and violent opposition, and persistent unrest and turmoil exacerbated the widespread famine. In Kazakhstan, the collectivisation campaign amounted to an onslaught on the nomadic way of life. Two-thirds of the population were still semi-nomadic and relied for a livelihood on animal husbandry rather than the cultivation of grain. For them the fall in the livestock population in the country was catastrophic: the number of cattle fell from 7.4 million in 1929 to 1.6 million in 1933, and of sheep from 22

---

*Quoted by Robert Conquest in *The Great Terror*, 1968

million to 1.7 million.* To deal with any resistance in Kazakhstan, a separate campaign of persecution was instigated against tribal and religious leaders, and any nationalist figures who led any form of resistance were swiftly arrested. Rural communities in Ukraine suffered even more acute repression than villagers and nomadic families in Kazakhstan.

While northern Kazakhstan was designated as a reception area for families deported from Russia and Ukraine, on the steppes further south, in the uplands of Semirechie, and in Kyrgyzstan, hundreds of thousands of Kazakh and Kyrgyz nomads and peasants were being uprooted from their homes and forced to flee across the border to Sinkiang in western China. This became yet another collective exodus of the population from their native soil, after the evictions brought about by Russian settlers in the nineteenth century, and the mass migration of families escaping tsarist military conscription in 1916. By 1932, as many regions of the Soviet Union experienced famine, little progress had been made in Kazakhstan in transforming agriculture from nomadic farming to collectivisation. Maximising food production immediately, rather than at some stage in the future, was still a vital necessity, and for Stalin and Goloshchekin, the overriding imperative was to supply the growing population of the towns with grain. Worries about the effect of requisitioning on future harvests could wait, and considerations of whether farmers themselves and their families had enough to eat were also dismissed. Undernourished farm workers soon became unable to operate machinery effectively or perform any of the other tasks on the land, and the badly-managed collective farms failed to meet the demands placed upon them, with the result that starvation once again spread throughout the countryside.

Initially the situation was less acute in the industrial towns in the north, and in the mountainous regions of eastern Kazakhstan, where there was still work in the factories and mines, and where food production was relatively stable. But an unstoppable tide of starving refugees flowed in from the west and the south of the country which before long overwhelmed the towns of Pavlodar, Semipalatinsk, Ust-Kamenogorsk, and the surrounding countryside. Efforts by the government in Alma-Ata and in Moscow to provide relief to the local authorities were largely futile. This was the worst period of the collectivization in Kazakhstan, when almost half the population of the country died

---

*Quoted in Robert Conquest, *The Great Terror*, 1968

from displacement and starvation. Even by 1959 the population of 3.6 million had still not recovered to the 1929 total of almost four million. However, the human cost, although widespread and devastating to the rural way of life, was largely confined to the countryside and not the towns. The major achievement of collectivization was that food riots did not take place in the towns and cities in Russia, and generally people in the towns had enough to eat. Food supplies were erratic, quality and nutritional value were poor, and time and effort wasted in queues and inefficient distribution greatly reduced labour productivity. But bread, meat, and dairy products were provided to the industrial workers in the factories, and it was these workers who formed the basis for Stalin's political power, and without the industrial labour force his plans for the economic transformation of the country would have foundered. The government did not have time or the political will to experiment with other more humane and possibly more efficient means of food production, and despite the great obstacles, collectivisation was seen as the only way forward.

For Goloshchekin, neither the devastation to the Kazakh way of life caused by collectivisation, nor the famine in the countryside, did any harm to his career at the time. He left Kazakhstan in 1933 when he was appointed to a senior position in the Cheka in Moscow. The effectiveness of his work with Yezhov and the NKVD in eliminating anti-Soviet activity in the country ensured that he remained in Stalin's favour until 1941, when like many others before him he became a victim of the system of arrests and purges which he himself had helped to set up and had operated with great effect. In June 1941, at a time when Stalin might have been more occupied with the German invasion of the Soviet Union that month, Goloshchekin was arrested and imprisoned, probably because of his close political and allegedly homosexual relationship with Yezhov, who had already been executed in 1940. Goloshchekin, a leading figure in the Bolshevik revolution, organizer of the execution of the tsar and the Romanov family, and the ruler of Kazakhstan for ten years, met his own ignominious fate when he himself was executed in October 1941. He was unlamented in Kazakhstan, where his rough cruelty, intolerance of opposition, and brutal implementation of Communist ideals had virtually destroyed the country's nomadic way of life, caused widespread and devastating famine, and had resulted in the death of millions of people. The 1981 *Soviet Kazakhstan Historical Encyclopedia* gives no more than a passing reference to him when he was voted on to a local Party committee in 1925. Among those present to celebrate the arrival of the first train on the new TurkSib railway in Alma-Ata in 1930, and to mark other national economic achievements, in the official history of the period Goloshchekin is conspicuous by his absence. But Goloshchekin had complied with the demands imposed on him, by transforming agriculture and providing the basis for future growth. Whether these demands could have been met in other ways, and whether the old forms of agriculture could have survived in Kazakhstan, in the radically changing political and international circumstances, were choices that were not available at the time.

Throughout the Soviet Union, restlessness and resentment among the population were beginning to build. Concerns about the need for consolidation in the economy led by Lazar Kaganovich, and for a less frenetic pace of expansion, were growing stronger. In 1933-1934, the middle years of the second Five-Year Plan, a relaxation of production targets and procurement quotas in industry and agriculture was accompanied by a reduction in the number of arbitrary arrests, and many of those who had been arrested and sent to labour camps in the 1920s were freed, although this policy was motivated by the needs of the economy for additional workers as much as by any relaxation in the political mood of the country. But in December 1934, following the assassination of Sergei Kirov, the head of the Communist Party in Leningrad, the atmosphere changed again, when Stalin instituted a new wave of terror and oppression, trials and purges, designed to eliminate any possibility of opposition, and which was to last for almost two decades until his death in 1953.

In Alma-Ata, responsibility for carrying out this policy now lay with Levon Mirzoyan, the new First Secretary of the Communist Party of Kazakhstan. Filipp Goloshchekin and Nikolai Yezhov had returned to Russia but the apparatus they had set up in Kazakhstan was still very much in use. For both Goloshchekin and Yezhov, the mass arrests of anyone even remotely suspected of holding anti-Soviet opinions or resisting any of the policies laid down by the leadership in Moscow, including many thousands of innocent people, was a small price to pay for achieving the aims of the Revolution, although for Yezhov opposition was more likely to be found among the local party leadership than among the ordinary population. Mirzoyan now followed enthusiastically in their footsteps. Born in 1887 to an Armenian family living in Azerbaijan, Mirzoyan became First Secretary of the Communist Party of Azerbaijan in Baku in 1926, then transferred to Ekaterinburg where Goloshchekin had been the ruthless and authoritarian Party Secretary. In 1933 Stalin ordered that Mirzoyan should replace Goloshchekin again, this time in Alma-Ata, where the years under his rule were to be almost as harsh and as brutal as those of his predecessor had been. Later, as the Revolution continued to turn in on itself, Mirzoyan also became a victim of the system he inherited, as many had before him, when he was arrested in 1938 and executed in Moscow the following year.

Kazakhstan was not alone in undergoing purges of the ordinary population as well as of the local Communist Party. The process of elimination of the old party leadership in each of the republics, of those who had taken part in the Revolution and the civil war, followed a clear pattern which had been set in Moscow and which spread throughout Russia and the USSR. The process started in the mid-1930s and reached its height in 1937–1939, when it was accompanied by a vitriolic campaign in the press against local party officials who found themselves charged with nationalism, of supposedly putting the interests of their own republics above the interests of the Soviet Union, and a range of other anti-Soviet activities. Usually a senior party official was sent from Moscow to oversee the arrests and trials in the capitals of the various republics, often taking part themselves in the interrogation of prisoners. The Central Committee of the Communist Party had in effect decided to destroy the old Party, and replace it with new and enthusiastic officials devoted to radical change and modernisation. In Byelorussia, almost the entire leadership of the republic was expelled from the Communist Party, and many more were arrested and excuted. In a turn of events that soon became commonplace, Vladimir Sharangovich, chairman of the Byelorussian Supreme Soviet and the nominal head of state in what was a separate republic within the USSR, was full of praise at a Party Congress in Minsk in June 1937, for the elimination of his former colleagues. This ingratiating attitude failed to prevent his own arrest and execution two months later. Similar developments took place throughout 1937 and 1938 in Armenia, Azerbaijan, Ukraine, Georgia, Uzbekistan, Kyrgyzstan, and Kazakhstan, where large groups of alleged traitors were found in the leaderships, and mass arrests and executions became routine. This in effect amounted to a second revolution, as far reaching in its geographical extent as the 1917 Revolution had been in Moscow and Petrograd. The revolution was led this time by the local head of the NKVD rather than the Communist Party Secretary, whose own position was often vulnerable, as was the case with Levon Mirzoyan in Kazakhstan.

Not everyone complied unquestioningly with the mass elimination of alleged enemies of the state. In Alma-Ata, a senior NKVD official by the name of Sevikgali Dzhazkupov, who had taken part in the ruthless liquidation of the Basmachi rebels in the mountains in southern Kazakhstan and Kyrgyzstan, resisted the arrest and execution of many individuals who he knew to be innocent. Among those arrested was the Kazakh writer and poet Saken Seifullin, who had become a friend of Dzhazkupov. At the time it was common practice in Russia and Kazakhstan for officials, prisoners, and their relatives to write to Stalin in the belief that this would help their cause. Dzhazkupov wrote many letters to Stalin and Yezhov on behalf of Seifullin and others until he himself was arrested in 1937. He was executed in 1939. His intervention was pointless and Seifullin also was executed by the NKVD in 1939. But such incidents, of intervention on behalf of others, were the exception to the norm of callous brutality or at best indifference to death and suffering. The Soviet writer Evgenia Ginsburg described the NKVD interrogators at the time:

'They were all sadists of course. And only a handful found the courage to commit suicide. Step by step, as they followed one routine directive after another, they climbed down the steps from the human condition to that of the beasts.'*

Fear and oppression among government officials in 1930s Kazakhstan permeated into the artistic and cultural life of the country. Before his arrest Saken Seifullin had emerged as a pioneer of modern Kazakh literature and was the founder and the first head of the Union of Writers of Kazakhstan. Although he had sympathy with Russia and with the aims of the 1917 Revolution, Seifullin was primarily a Kazakh nationalist, which in the danferous political atmosphere of the time was enough to ensure his demise. Born in 1894 in Karaganda, Seifullin was educated at a Russian-Kazakh school in Akmola. He later taught Russian at a seminary in Omsk before moving back to Akmola, where he campaigned against the conscription edict of 1916, and dedicated a poem called *Unrest* to those killed and displaced by tsarist troops in the subsequent violent conflict. After the Revolution he was appointed as a Commissar for Education in the new Soviet government in Kazakhstan. Despite his revolutionary sympathies Seifullin was more concerned to achieve greater independence for Kazakhstan, now suffering under the growing weight of oppression from Russia and the new Soviet Union. Seifullin survived for more than twenty years before he was arrested as a nationalist and executed in Alma-Ata in February 1939. Since Kazakh independence in 1991, Seifullin has been recognised as one of the most influential writers and thinkers of the country, and someone who made a major contribution to Kazakh culture and literature.

---

*Quoted in Robert Conquest *The Great Terror* 1968

Despite the omnipresence of the NKVD in Kazakhstan and the harsh treatment of anyone suspected of anti-Soviet sympathies, a major cultural development was taking place in the emergence of painting as a form of expression in the new world of socialism. Before the 1930s painting had hardly existed in Kazakhstan and the only applied arts were in the form of ceramics, carpets, and jewellery. At the forefront of the new trend was Abilkhan Kasteev, the first professional Kazakh painter and now regarded as the most renowned artist of his era. Born in a remote village near Taldy Korgan in Semirechie in 1904, Kasteev came from a simple nomadic background before moving to Alma-Ata to study at the Nadezhda Krupskaya studio, an art school named after the widow of Vladimir Lenin. As a painter Kasteev had no historic references or artistic traditions to build on, but drew widely on Russian art and the new movement of socialist realism, to convey a sense of the enormous transition being made from the nomadic life on the steppe to the new Soviet life in the towns. In so doing he managed, as a few others in different fields, notably Chokan Valikhanov, had done before him, to bridge the gulf between the old and the new, portraying the countryside in unsentimental terms, and embracing the arrival of railways and factories. Many of his works feature nomadic communities, horsemen, and yurts, juxtaposed with a new bridge or a railway locomotive in the background, as for example in '*TurkSib*' (1932). Kasteev and other local artists were aided in this trend by the arrival in Kazakhstan of officially-approved artists and painters sent from Russia, whose job was to ensure that Kazakh art and paintings conformed to the revolutionary spirit of the times. There was no visible opposition among Kazakh painters to the Russian influence, and many were willing to work under the guidance of their Russian mentors, although none dared attempt to reflect the devastation in the countryside caused by famine and collectivisation. Instead many artists increasingly sought their own forms of expression, and developed a more novel and avant-garde form of painting, eventually leading to the creation of a Kazakh national school and identity. This evolved further after the war, when by the 1960s the focal point for many artists had shifted away from simple rural and industrial scenes, to a more expressive and liberal view of contemporary life. In Kazakhstan artists had more freedom of action than was possible in the rigid and conventional atmosphere in Russia, but many Russians were disdainful of Kazakh painting, which they saw as something rather primitive and naïve, and lacking any depth or tradition.

In 1935, while Kazakhstan was heading for the darkest years of oppression, cultural life managed to continue, and a new State Museum of Arts was founded in Alma-Ata. In 1984 it was renamed the Kasteev State Museum and is now the principal art gallery in the country.

Soon after it opened the Museum acquired more than two hundred paintings transferred from the State Tretyakov Gallery and the Pushkin Museum of Fine Arts in Moscow, and the Hermitage and the Russian Museum in Leningrad, as part of a permanent cultural exchange programme, organized according to type of painting and their national origin, and undertaken among the new republics of the Soviet Union during the 1930s. These paintings formed the basis of the Kasteev Museum collection. One particularly famous work, '*Abstract Composition*', by the Kazakh artist Olga Rozanova, painted in the avant-garde style of the early years of the twentieth century, formerly belonged to the State Tretyakov Gallery and was transferred to the Kasteev Museum in 1936. But the most prominent paintings are those by Kasteev himself, although only a small proportion of more than two thousand oil paintings and water colours by him can be seen at any one time.

These developments in the art world were taking place in a relatively safe atmosphere and in a politically acceptable way, and indicated that despite growing political repression, not every aspect of life had yet succumbed to conformity and absence of individual expression. Another far-reaching cultural and social change took place in 1940 when a modified version of the Cyrillic alphabet was introduced for the Kazakh language. To accommodate all the inflexions and variations of the Kazakh language, the new alphabet had forty-two characters compared to thirty-three characters in the Russian Cyrillic alphabet. It replaced the Roman alphabet which had been used since 1928, before which the Arabic script had been used. The Russian Cyrillic alphabet, derived from a system originally devised in about 860 AD by a Macedonian monk, later canonised as Saint Cyril, became standard throughout the Soviet Union, and its adoption in Kazakhstan recognised the fact that Kazakhstan and the other Central Asian republics where it was introduced at around the same time, were now being ever more closely integrated into the Russian-Soviet world. Russian was to remain the primary language until 1989 when Kazakh, still using its own version of the Cyrillic alphabet, became the official language of Kazakhstan. Russian became the so-called language of inter-ethnic communication, although in practice it continued to be the most widely-used language throughout the country.

Although developments in language and art, and some form of ordinary day-to-day life managed to continue in Kazakhstan during the 1930s, nothing could escape what was happening politically in the country and throughout the whole of the USSR. No one in Kazakhstan was safe from the terror and mass arrests, a period known as the *Yezhovshchina*, after Nikolai Yezhov, head of the NKVD, who had first come to Kazakhstan in 1923. Although Yezhov had since returned to Moscow, his years in Alma-Ata ensured that he was to maintain a close involvement in Kazakhstan, where his malign influence extended into the furthest and most unlikely corners of the country. In Yuri Dombrovsky's 1978 novel *The Faculty of Useless Knowledge,* which describes the work of an archaeological excavation near Alma-Ata in 1937, Georgi Zybin, the director of the excavation, becomes subjected to the all-pervading mood of nationwide terror:

'A dark chill, an almost supernatural horror, took root in his soul. He was afraid to pick up newspapers, but nevertheless did so and read them more than he had ever done before. He feared to talk of the arrests, but nevertheless did so. He was afraid to let the things that lurked in the hidden depths enter his conscious mind, but nevertheless that chilly murk lived and grew within his soul, and was now present in every encounter, in each and every fleeting inane conversation. His reason, however, was still securely protected by what had seemed impossible but which was now real – the guilt of the accused. He could not understand why the accused at the trials were so frank, so voluble and looked so well, when they were moving in such a friendly, happy crowd, towards certain death.'

By 1938 Yezhov's influence with Stalin was beginning to wane, and Stalin was putting more trust in Lavrenti Beria as a possible successor as head of the NKVD. In Kazakhstan and throughout much of the USSR, Yezhov and his policies were increasingly being challenged, as it was clear that a high proportion of victims could not be described as nationalist or anti-Soviet elements, and the endless terror was exerting a highly damaging effect on the economy and on the country. Known as the 'bloodthirsty dwarf' and rumoured to be on the verge of insanity, Yezhov increasingly became involved in heavy drinking and homosexual activities, until he was finally dismissed by Stalin in November 1938. He arrested the following April and executed in 1940. Yezhov was replaced as head of the NKVD by Beria, who may have been equally ruthless but was regarded by Stalin as more trustworthy and competent. Stalin also wished to increase the control of the Communist Party over the NKVD, and to reduce the scale of the mass arrests which had been so damaging to the economy. This did not extend fully to Kazakhstan, where the local Communist Party was still weak in relation to the NKVD, and where the vast network of informers and secret police built up under Yezhov was still active. But eventually the atmosphere of terror and oppression gradually began to ease, and the threat of random arrests diminished. If people could not yet relax completely, by the early months of 1941 it had become possible to live and breathe with something approaching normality – until the appearance of a new and even more deadly threat, in the form of the imminent German invasion of the Soviet Union.

War Memorial, Panfilov Park, Almaty

Zailisky Alatau Mountains south of Almaty

Kurgan at Issyk Burial Ground, Southern Kazakhstan

Yurts under the Tien Shan Mountains, Southern Kazakhstan

Cathedral of The Holy Ascension, Almaty

Monument to the Dead of the Totalitarian Regime, Astana

Zheltoksan Memorial, Almaty

Suburbs of Almaty and Tien Shan Mountains

Golden Man: Unknown Scythian warrior, c.500 BC

Heroes of Soviet Union – Aliya Moldagulova, Manshuk Mametova, Almaty

Chokan Valikhanov statue, Almaty

The Arch of Sorrow, ALZhIR Camp, Astana

'They Did Not Expect Him' by Ilya Repin (1888)

'TurkSib' by Abilkhan Kasteev (1932)

CHAPTER SIXTEEN

The Great Fatherland War and Evacuation to the East

In the short, tumultuous history of the Soviet Union, between its formal foundation at the end of the civil war in December 1922 and its dissolution exactly sixty nine years later in December 1991, the country experienced rapid industrialisation, political repression, and periods of great economic and social change. Kazakhstan was affected by all these developments as much as, if not more than, every other part of the country, given its relative backwardness compared to Russia and some of the other republics. The deaths of Lenin in 1924 and Stalin in 1953 both had profound and far-reaching consequences, although the death of Leonid Brezhnev in November 1982 could be said to have been even more significant in that it led directly to the collapse of the USSR just over nine years later. But the most devastating episode in Soviet history was the German invasion in 1941 and the subsequent Great Fatherland War, which nearly brought an end to the Soviet Union fifty years before its actual demise. The four years of the war were to have a traumatic effect on every part of the USSR, even in the most isolated villages on the Kazakh steppe. Paradoxically, the invasion and the eventual defeat of Germany, far from weakening the Soviet system, helped to ensure its continued existence, whereas otherwise it might have foundered as a result of its failure to raise living standards and of falling even further behind the West. The Soviet victory in the war gave a legitimacy to the regime and extended its life for another forty six years, until Russia and the republics finally abandoned the USSR in favour of independence.

Kazakhstan, like Russia and every other Soviet republic, was almost completely unprepared for war. It was far from Germany and the population had little awareness of developments taking place in Europe, even though these developments would soon threaten its existence. As elsewhere in the Soviet Union, government propaganda had stressed the wisdom, if not infallibility, of Stalin and the Communist Party leadership in dealing with the growing crisis abroad, and no one in Kazakhstan, or anywhere else, could argue to the contrary. The cult of personality surrounding Stalin was at its height at the time of the 18th Congress of the Communist Party which opened in Moscow on 10 March 1939, and on that day *Pravda* published on its front page a poem by the elderly Kazakh poet Dzhambul Dzhabaev:

Tenderly the sun is shining from above,
And who cannot but know that this sun is – you?
The lapping waves of the lake are singing the praises of Stalin,
The dazzling snowy peaks are singing the praises of Stalin,
The meadow's million flowers are thanking, thanking you;
The well-laden table is thanking, thanking you.
The humming swarm of bees is thanking, thanking you,
All fathers of young heroes, they thank you, Stalin, too;
Oh heir of Lenin, to us you are Lenin himself;
Beware, you Samurai, keep out of our Soviet heaven! *

Dzhambul was born in 1846 and became known in the 1930s as the 'bard of socialist Kazakhstan', renowned for his obsequious flattery of Stalin. It is hard to imagine who would have been impressed by this level of sycophancy, except possibly simple herdsmen on the steppe and conceivably the German government, who may have thought that if this was evidence of what a weak-minded Soviet population believed then there would be no serious resistance to an attack on the Soviet Union. Within the Communist Party itself many people must have thought, but not said, that it was frivolous and unsuitable to publicise an ingratiating poem at a time when everyone was anxiously awaiting a major speech by Stalin to the Congress which would include a review of the impending crisis in Europe.

In the event Stalin was to put his faith in the Soviet-German Non-Aggression Pact which would be signed six months later in August 1939. This was seen as an unpleasant but necessary measure which would allow the USSR to strengthen its economy and defences until such time as war became inevitable. Relations between the Soviet Union and Germany had been deteriorating steadily, while negotiations between Russia, Britain and France in the early part of 1939 on how to respond to the growing German threat had been inconclusive. Meanwhile Germany, taking advantage of the deadlock between Russia and its potential western allies, put forward its own method of defusing tension with Russia, in the form of a trade and credit agreement with the Soviet Union. Under this agreement, signed in Berlin on 19 August 1939, Germany was to grant the USSR a credit of 200 million marks for purchases of machine tools and industrial equipment, to be made in Germany; in return the Soviet Union would supply grain,

---

*Quoted by Alexander Werth, *Russia at War 1941-1945*

oil, copper, coal, iron ore, and many other raw materials and commodities which the German economy badly needed. A significant proportion of these raw materials were to come from deposits and open-cast mines in eastern Kazakhstan, now capable of being exploited more fully thanks to the completion of the TurkSib railway in 1930 and other lines connecting Kazakhstan to the Trans-Siberian railway. The main advantage for Russia of the German credit was that it was in the form of a financial loan so that Soviet enterprises could pay German firms for purchases of capital goods directly in cash. In addition, the loan would have a generous repayment term of seven and a half years. In reality, Soviet factories had relatively little time to take advantage of the loan and arrange imports of German equipment, whereas deliveries of vital commodities from the Soviet Union to Germany started almost immediately, and continued even into the first days of the war. Germany achieved its objective of luring the USSR into a false sense of security with the prospect of an extended period of peaceful trading relations.

The Trade Agreement prepared the ground in Russia for the more dramatic announcement of the Soviet-German Non-Aggression Pact. Tension in Russia caused by the worsening situation in Europe was heightened by the conflict developing at the same time in the Far East with Japan. In August 1939 Russian troops under the command of Marshal Georgy Zhukov defeated a Japanese army in a fierce tank battle at Halkin Gol in Mongolia. Zhukov would later play a key role in the defence of Moscow, Leningrad, and Stalingrad, and in the ultimate Soviet victory in the war. Despite this successful outcome in the conflict with Japan, Stalin was increasingly afraid of becoming involved in a war on two fronts – against Germany in Europe and against Japan in Asia. A treaty with Germany would enable Russia to concentrate more of its defences in the east against Japan.

When the Soviet-German Pact was signed in Moscow a few days after the Trade Agreement on 23 August 1939, public reaction throughout the Soviet Union was one of astonishment, turning into uncomfortable feelings of wariness and uncertainty. For years the Soviet press had led everyone to believe that the USSR was at the head of the 'anti-Fascist struggle', but now the country was suddenly in an alliance with Germany. The most common assumption was that Stalin and Molotov, the Soviet Foreign Minister who signed the Pact with Ribbentrop, the German Foreign Minister, no doubt knew what they were doing, and they had so far kept the Soviet Union out of any conflict with Germany. There had been a similar reaction in Britain, of relief combined with an uneasy sense of shame, at the time of the Munich Agreement, although in Russia to express any opinion contrary to the official line was to invite almost certain imprisonment or even execution. Despite the widespread feeling of malaise after the signing of the Pact, most people simply accepted what they were told and got on with life as best they could. The arrests and imprisonments of the Great Terror were beginning to moderate, and news of what was happening in Germany or anywhere else abroad, received scant attention in the Soviet press. But the partition of Poland in the autumn of 1939, and the fall of France the following year, meant that the prospect of war was still on everyone's mind. In Kazakhstan, the significance of the worsening situation in the west, and the impending calamity facing the Soviet Union, was even less appreciated than it was in Russia itself. After the victory in the battle at Halkin Gol there was extensive reporting of the conflict with Japan, and substantial troop movements on the Trans-Siberian railway to and from Mongolia and the Far East could not be hidden from the public. But the political and psychological consequences of the arrests and disappearances in 1937–1938 meant that almost everyone had little knowledge of or curiosity about events beyond their immediate lives.

There were, however, some unmistakable signs of preparations for war. In remote towns and villages throughout Kazakhstan, new road-building and other construction projects were suddenly launched and were taking shape, despite not having been provided for in the Five-Year Plan. These projects had a significant cost in manpower and other resources which had to be transferred from industry and farming. Factories throughout the country started to produce fewer consumer goods as they switched to production of weapons and military equipment. This also involved a major diversion of resources and far-reaching changes to road and railway networks for the supply of raw materials and distribution of finished goods, all of which were easier to undertake in Kazakhstan, which lay far beyond the range of German reconnaissance flights, than they were in Russia. The strength of the army was greatly increased by a reduction in the call-up age from 21 to 18, and by extending conscription to those previously exempt such as students, teachers, and specialists in some non-essential branches of the economy. Despite the recent traumas of collectivisation, and the arrests and show trials in 1937–1938, enthusiasm for serving in the Red Army even before 1941 was seen among young people in Kazakhstan as a genuine patriotic duty, and there was great enthusiasm to join up. Departure from the home village for active service was invariably a rousing and colourful affair, with celebrations and festivities in honour of the young recruits about to set off for the front. Willingness to serve in the army was greatly increased as a result of the heightened prestige of the army following military successes against Japanese forces in Mongolia and the annexations of western Ukraine, Byelorussia, and Bessarabia in 1940. Any anti-Russian sentiments that may have existed were put aside, and in an echo of the assimilation of Kazakh military units into the tsarist army at the time of Chokan Valikhanov a century earlier, a mood of Russian and Kazakh unity now swept the country.

During the early months of 1941, and particularly from May onwards, increasing reports reached the Soviet government of German plans for the invasion known as Operation Barbarossa and specifically of German troop concentrations along Russia's western frontier. The most authoritative warnings came from Richard Sorge, a diplomat in the German embassy in Tokyo, who had been recruited by the Soviet intelligence network in 1929. He sent his first warning of an imminent German attack on 5 March 1941, followed by more reports of German intentions culminating in a correct forecast of the date for the invasion of 22 June. Other reports came from Britain and the United States and a variety of other sources, including detailed evidence from commanders in the field who reported high levels of German activity close to the border. German reconnaissance flights penetrated deep into Russian territory, locating and photographing every airfield, watched by incredulous Soviet army and air force units on the ground under strict orders not to open fire or in any way interfere with these flights. Army commanders were similarly forbidden to take any steps to put ground forces on a war-footing, since this would be seen as mobilisation and would heighten the danger of provoking war.

Stalin rejected all the warnings of an imminent attack, and clung to his conviction that Germany had no immediate intention of invading the Soviet Union. Although this was an enormous and near-fatal error of judgement, there were feasible grounds for believing that Germany would not launch an invasion in the summer of 1941. The German army was heavily engaged in Yugoslavia and in Greece, and earlier predictions of an imminent attack on Russia in April and May had come and passed without incident, which served to discredit later warnings which were more accurate and reliable. Many of the reports of the build-up of German forces were believed by Stalin to be part of a major deception to divert attention from Hitler's real plan which was for an invasion of England, and could therefore be dismissed, or at least not treated with the seriousness which they would otherwise deserve. It was already late in the year for Germany to invade before winter set in, and the extreme distances involved, and the perception that Germany needed more time to prepare and build up essential supplies of strategic war materials, would inevitably necessitate delay. The Napoleonic invasion of 1812, launched at exactly the same time of year, had ended in disaster for Napoleon, and a similar fate would certainly befall the German army; the advantage of mechanised transport would be negated by over-extended supply lines, the determination of the Red Army fighting on its home territory, and the severe conditions of the Russian winter. All these factors convinced Stalin that it was now too late for Germany to invade. In the event this assessment proved to be almost entirely correct: despite the passage of 129 years, the advantage of mechanization was less than assumed, and the German army in 1941 was almost as dependent on horses as Napoleon's army had been; and because it made simultaneous drives to the north and to the south of Russia, it would take the German army nearly three months longer than it took Napoleon to reach the outskirts of Moscow. With each week that passed, the danger seemed to diminish, and if an invasion could not be made in the summer of 1941 it would have to wait until the spring of 1942, giving Russia vital extra time to prepare its defence.

This proved to be wishful thinking which evaporated suddenly on the morning of Sunday 22 June. In the first few hours of chaos and confusion following the news of the invasion, Stalin could not bring himself to believe the incontrovertible reports of heavy German shelling and bombing of Russian towns and cities. Suspecting that this was yet another attempt to provoke a reaction from Russia which would justify a German attack, and which had not been authorised by Hitler, he refused to allow any defence or retaliation. Obsessed with plots and conspiracies, Stalin expressed to Marshal Simyon Timoshenko, the National Commissar for Defence, and Zhukov, Chief of the General Staff, his belief that German generals would bomb their own cities if it was necessary to create a provocation for Germany to attack Russia. (This cynical view had a sinister echo fifty-eight years later when in 1999 a block of flats in a Moscow suburb was blown up and hundreds of people were killed, allegedly by Chechen terrorists but widely believed to have been carried out by the KGB as a pretext for a Russian invasion of Chechnya, in what became known as the Second Chechen War). In the early hours of 22 June 1941, Stalin was finally prevailed upon by Zhukov and other military commanders and belatedly gave orders for the Red Army to resist and destroy the German attack. Even then he stipulated that Soviet ground forces should not cross the border into Germany, although the time for any such remote possibility had long since passed.

Thousands of miles away in Kazakhstan, it was late in the afternoon of 22 June before news of the invasion reached Alma-Ata or the remote towns and villages on the steppe. As elsewhere throughout the Soviet Union, people gathered round radios and loudspeakers in factories, public buildings, and on lamp-posts in the street, to listen to

Vyacheslav Molotov, the Foreign Affairs Commissar, broadcast an announcement from the Soviet government. Stalin delegated the task to Molotov since it was Molotov who had signed the Soviet-German Non-Aggression Pact with Ribbentrop, which was now in tatters, and with the implication that Molotov shared responsibility with Germany for the invasion. But Stalin himself was still in a state of shock and humiliation that his own leadership and unpreparedness had failed the country. Molotov's speech was faltering and hesitant, playing down initial losses, and seeking to perpetuate the notion that the invasion did not have the support of the German working class:

'At four o'clock this morning, without declaration of war, and without any claims being made on the Soviet Union, German troops attacked our country...... This unheard-of attack on our country is an unparalleled act of perfidy in the history of civilised nations. The war has not been inflicted upon us by the German workers, peasants and intellectuals, of whose sufferings we are fully aware, but by Germany's bloodthirsty rulers........ The Government of the Soviet Union is deeply convinced that the whole population of our country will do their duty, and will work hard and conscientiously. Our people must be more united than ever. The Government calls upon you, men and women citizens of the Soviet Union, to rally even more closely round the glorious Bolshevik Party, around the Soviet Government, and our great leader, Comrade Stalin. Our cause is good. The enemy will be smashed. Victory will be ours'.

The broadcast recalled the Russian victory in the war of 1812, and concluded with the defiant 'Victory will be ours', which became an article of faith throughout the war. But the general tone of the broadcast, and especially the complaint that Germany had 'made no demands' on Russia, left most listeners with a feeling of humiliation and deep anxiety. The sense of unease was not alleviated by a protracted silence from Stalin. On 29 June, one week after the start of the invasion, during which time he had not spoken publicly, Stalin retreated to his dacha outside Moscow, leaving the rest of the Soviet leadership to deal with the crisis without him. The reason for his disappearance was never made clear, but it may have been due to a breakdown or may have been a cynical attempt to demonstrate that he was indispensable to the defence of the country, and that without him the country was doomed. A similar tactic had been adopted by Ivan the Terrible in 1564 when he abandoned the Kremlin and withdrew from all responsibility of government until the boyars and clergy gave him the power and authority to govern as he alone saw fit. After four days absence Stalin was persuaded by Zhukov, Timoshenko, and other members of the government to return to Moscow, where on 3 July 1941 he made a rallying speech of his own, vastly more inspirational and more defiant than the speech given by Molotov eleven days earlier. The speech set out in detail, not entirely accurate but convincing for the majority of his listeners, the extent of German penetration of Soviet territory, the treachery of the German government in reneging on the Soviet-German Non-Aggression Pact, and how the Soviet Union would respond and defeat the invader. This had a dramatic and revitalising impact on the Soviet population, until then apprehensive and ill-informed about what was happening. Hitherto, Stalin's leadership had been all-pervading but at the same time intangible and remote, associated in most people's minds with Five-Year Plans, collectivisation, and political purges. It now became real and more reassuring. In Kazakhstan, where historically invasions had come from the east rather than from the west, the emphasis in the speech on the threat to the whole of the Soviet Union had particularly galvanising effect, not least because Stalin's strong Georgian accent reminded millions of Kazakhs that Stalin was not a Russian, and that non-Russians and Russians were now equally in danger.

In Alma-Ata and in towns, villages, and every aul throughout Kazakhstan, thousands of Kazakhs, Russians, Tadjiks, and Kyrgyz flooded to the nearest kolkhoz, village hall, or other makeshift recruitment centre to join up. But the buoyant mood of national enthusiasm for military service and the defence of the Soviet Union, which permeated to every corner of the country, soon received a setback, which although temporary caused widespread consternation at the time. It quickly became clear that the initial mobilisation was to be conducted on the basis of nationality, with Russians separated from Kazakhs and other national groups. Russian recruits were given priority in training and were the first to be despatched to the front, while Kazakhs and recruits of other nationalities were forced to remain behind in their home brigades. The absence of an explanation as to why they could not serve with Russians added to a sense of demoralisation and suspicion; many Kazakhs concluded that after decades of Russian colonialism and repression, they could not be trusted in battle, and would either surrender too readily or would voluntarily desert to fight for the enemy. But the Soviet government in Moscow had concerns about the loyalty of the people of Central Asia, particularly Uzbekistan, where Moslem and anti-Soviet beliefs were still relatively strong. Kazakhstan was seen to be less likely of disloyalty, since Kazakh historical and religious traditions were less pronounced than those of Uzbekistan, and given the longer history of relations between Kazakhstan and Russia, the population had been assimilated more readily than the people of other Central Asian republics. Despite this the government initially wished to segregate the different ethnic and national groups, contrary to the advice of army commanders who feared problems in communication and co-ordinating operations, and conceivably bringing about the resentment and mistrust which the policy was designed to avoid. In reality, there was no need to segregate Kazakhs from Russians; Kazakhstan had long since accepted its position in the Soviet Union, albeit with varying degrees of enthusiasm, and it correctly saw the same fate for itself as it did for Russia, of national subjugation and starvation, if the war was lost. The whole population felt the same sense of anger, insult, and determination to fight as was felt by Russia. The policy of segregating military units on national lines was soon abandoned and in the autumn of 1941 the Kazakh armed forces were merged with other divisions in the Red Army. New divisions were rapidly drawn up and deployed to the front line outside Moscow. When Richard Sorge, the Soviet spy in the German embassy in Tokyo, his credibility now confirmed, reported that Japan intended to attack British colonies and the United States in the Far East, and not the Soviet Union in Siberia, Stalin could divert more divisions westwards from Kazakhstan and eastern Russia to be sent to the front. The Asiatic features of these units were a novelty for the population of Moscow and western Russia, but for the German soldiers who had been led to believe that the Red Army would quickly collapse, the troops from Kazakhstan and Siberia brought a terror of their own.

The German invasion had three simultaneous objectives: the seizure of Leningrad in the north, Moscow in the centre, and Ukraine and the Caucasus in the south, with the ultimate aim of occupying practically the whole of European Russia, up to a line extending from Archangel on the White Sea to Astrakhan on the Caspian Sea. The enormous scale of the operation was eventually to prove fatal for Germany, as the strength of the German army was largely dissipated in the vast plains of western Russia, whereas a single offensive against one of the three objectives may have been successful. The German High Command not only underestimated the number of troops and the amount of resources it would need to conquer and occupy the enormous Russian landmass, but it had also underestimated the strength of Soviet forces further to the east, forces which had been unable to get to the front at the time of the invasion due to inadequate transport and poor planning. But in the searing heat of June and July 1941, it was the Soviet Union which experienced unmitigated disaster, as the Red Army and the Soviet air force suffered one catastrophe after another. Hundreds of aircraft, exposed and unprotected on rudimentary airfields, identified well in advance by German reconnaissance flights, were destroyed in the first few days of the invasion.

The shortcomings of the army, which had suffered deep losses to its leadership in the trials and purges of senior officers in 1937 and 1938, were increasingly apparent. Stalin had believed these officers to be a greater threat to the Soviet Union than the threat from Germany, and details of the show trials, and the ensuing decimation of the Red Army officer corps, had been carefully reported before the war by the German embassy in Moscow to the government in Berlin. The purges had less effect than is sometimes believed, since as in industry and the economy, the victims were quickly replaced by younger men who had unquestioning loyalty to Stalin. But apart from the victory in the brief conflict at Halkin Gol in Mongolia two years earlier, the Red Army had lacked any real experience of war since the end of the Civil War in 1922. A lower standard of training compared to that of the German army, and the need to refer even minor decisions to political commissars, virtually eliminating the scope for initiative and independence of action, were further serious handicaps. Many hundreds of thousands of ill-equipped soldiers were quickly overwhelmed and taken prisoner in a series of unequal battles, as vast numbers of German paratroops landed behind Russian lines. The Russian writer Alexander Solzhenitsyn, who served as an artillery officer in the Red Army, was highly critical of events in the early stages of the war and of the role played by Stalin. In *Times of Crisis,* a short story written fifty years after the war and which analysed the tempestuous relationship between Zhukov and Stalin, Solzhenitsyn wrote:

'Stalin managed the war in its first weeks by giving orders that were not to be questioned, and his mistakes piled up, one after another. He had no idea of strategy and operations and no sense of how to coordinate the operations of various branches of the army.... He never spent so much as an hour at the front during the war and never chatted with an ordinary soldier. He would summon Zhukov, who would make a long flight back to Moscow, and after many weeks in the constant roar of the front lines, the silence in Stalin's Kremlin office or at a private supper in Stalin's dacha seemed quite agonizing. . . . Then there was something he could not help but learn from Stalin: the Supreme Commander was always interested to hear about enemy casualties, but he never asked about our own. He simply shrugged them off with a wave of the hand: 'That's what war means'.*

In the German army, after only one month of almost unopposed fighting, the mood was one of exhilarating optimism and a belief that the war would soon be won. Sometimes

*From *Apricot Jam and Other Stories* by Alexander Solzhenitsyn, 1994

its only problems seemed to be the heat of the summer and the agoraphobia experienced by some soldiers who had no experience of vast open countryside such as that of western Russia. Some German units believed that their progress was too easy, and were dismayed that the Red Army was collapsing with so little resistance. Before long their attitude was to undergo different stages and change dramatically as the German army encountered much stronger Soviet forces; after some months of heavy fighting, German soldiers began to believe that eventual victory would be all the more satisfying for having been hard-won, before later realizing that victory might not be achievable at all and that they would be lucky to escape with their lives. In a letter exhibited in the Museum of the History of the Great Fatherland War in Moscow, a soldier angrily rebukes his girlfriend in Germany: 'Stop asking me to send you Russian scarves and head-dresses; we are fighting for our lives in this terrible country'.

For the time being the German army continued its unstoppable drive eastwards, meeting chaos and disarray with every mile of its advance. It was not until the rain and early snow of autumn that Russia was able to gain any respite from the onslaught. The *rasputitsa,* the 'season of bad roads', which turned the dusty Russian tracks and roads into impassable quagmires of mud, arrived early in 1941; usually the first snowfall in western Russia occurs in mid or late October, but this year the first snow had fallen on 7 October and had then soon thawed, making the roads even worse. This greatly impeded the German offensive, but also seriously exacerbated Soviet transport difficulties. Russian vehicles and horse-drawn carts could not struggle through the mud, bringing reinforcements, supplies, and ammunition, any more easily than the German army could. For Russia this was a familiar, annual problem, and the Red Army was more accustomed than the German troops to autumn rain and snow and to the harsh winter conditions which were to come. In the following months, as the rain and mud of autumn were succeeded by the ice and snow of winter, skis, sledges, bulky white snow suits, goggles, and other winter clothing and camouflage were rapidly issued to the Soviet troops. The German army, which had anticipated reaching Moscow before the autumn, suffered conditions of extreme cold in the uniforms and equipment for a summer campaign. The scarce supplies of winter clothing which eventually did arrive were mainly in the form of heavy dark-grey coats and jackets, which may have provided warmth but made those who wore them conspicuous targets for Russian troops. Army vehicles on the Soviet side had always been designed with winter conditions in mind, whereas German tanks, lorries, and staff cars were all rendered virtually useless in the sub-zero temperatures of the Russian winter. Morale among the troops was low as their conditions deteriorated, losses increased, and Russian resistance seemed to strengthen with every day. In villages and hamlets in the freezing, snow-covered countryside around Moscow, women, old men and young children were forcibly evicted from their wooden huts and *izbas* to perish in the snow, as German soldiers sought refuge from the unrelenting blizzards and sub-zero temperatures.

***

The S M Kirov Machine Building Factory on Mukagali Makataeva Street, in an industrial suburb not far from the centre of Almaty, is now a pale shadow of its former self. Since the war demand for its output has diminished, production has been greatly reduced, and the total labour force is a small fraction of what it used to be. But in the late autumn of 1942 it was a scene of frenetic activity. The factory, which was originally established in Ukraine in 1882, had been dismantled and evacuated to Makhachkala in southern Russia, on the western side of the Caspian Sea, in September 1941, but the following year it was evacuated again, this time to Alma-Ata. Towards the end of 1942, hundreds of workers were desperately handling the arrival of lathes, work benches, machinery, equipment, and whole production lines, and reassembling everything so that production could resume in the shortest possible time. The Kirov factory, and the nearby Alma-Ata Heavy Machinery Factory, were two of thirty industrial enterprises destined for relocation to Alma-Ata, out of a total of 142 factories evacuated from western Russia and Ukraine to Kazakhstan. The fighting at the front was still a thousand kilometres away from Kazakhstan, but the impact of the war was already being felt throughout the country.

During the forced industrialisation of the Soviet economy in the 1920s and 1930s, by far the majority of the country's manufacturing capacity had been concentrated in the western parts of the USSR, especially around Leningrad and Moscow and in the eastern Ukraine. These regions were already partly industrialised, and transport links and other infrastructure needed for the supply of raw materials and energy, and for the delivery of finished goods to the rest of the country, were already in place. Before the war the industrial development of central parts of Russia, far from its border regions, had been given only low priority, with the result that much of Soviet industry now lay in the path of the advancing German armies.

From the earliest days of the invasion, the evacuation of industry threatened by the German invasion had been one of the government's major concerns. If the Soviet

Union was to have any prospect of defeating Germany, whole factories, vast amounts of machinery and equipment, and hundreds of thousands of industrial workers would have to be uprooted and moved to safety in new locations in central and eastern Russia, Siberia, and Central Asia. Kazakhstan was a natural destination for such a huge undertaking. The enormous distance from the front, the Trans-Siberian railway and the new TurkSib line connecting Alma-Ata to Russia and Siberia, a number of existing industrial enterprises in Alma-Ata and other Kazakh cities, which would serve as 'host' factories for those to be transported from western Russia, plus its vast reserves of raw materials, all combined to make Kazakhstan a viable place for the relocation of scores of enterprises and thousands of workers. Here they would be safe, out of reach of the German army and beyond the range of German aircraft. The wholesale evacuation of factories threatened by the invasion, and their resettlement in the east, was to become one of the most significant organisational and human achievements of the Soviet Union during the war. The operation was conducted entirely outside the framework of the now-discarded Five Year Plan, but the existence of a highly-centralised command structure in the economy made possible what would otherwise have been a virtually impossible task.

On 4 July 1941, the State Defence Committee in Moscow ordered Nikolai Voznesensky, the Chairman of Gosplan, the State Planning Organisation, to draw up a comprehensive plan for what was to be in effect a second line of industrial defence in the east of the USSR. Nikolai Voznesensky was one of the small group of Politbureau leaders who before the war had gained Stalin's confidence, and who at the time of the invasion had persuaded Stalin to return to Moscow from his dacha. He ordered a Committee of Evacuation to be set up under the leadership of Lazar Kaganovich, also a member of the Soviet inner circle and who had been instrumental in the construction of the TurkSib railway and other railway lines in Kazakhstan. But the new task was significantly more difficult, involving a vast amount of infinitely detailed planning and coordination, the dismantling, transporting, and reassembly of whole factories, to be combined simultaneously with the evacuation of many thousands of factory workers, technicians and civilians. Despite his experience on the construction of the TurkSib line, Kaganovich was soon overwhelmed by the scale of the operation, and was replaced after only a few weeks by Nikolai Shvernik, the leader of the Soviet Trade Union Federation. Shvernik was another close ally of Stalin and had considerable experience of industry and labour; he now became responsible under Voznesensky for the greatest industrial operation in the history of the Soviet Union. The deputy chairman of the Evacuation Committee was Alexei Kosygin, later Soviet prime minister. Kazakhstan was declared to be part of the Soviet strategic *tyl*, or rear, and the responsibility for much of the detailed work in supervising the reassembly of factories and the construction of accommodation for the workers arriving from Russia fell to Dinmukhamed Kunaev, the 32-year-old deputy chairman of the Council of Ministers of Kazakhstan and later First Scretary of the Kazakh Communist Party. The immediate objective of the evacuation plan was to combine the industries that were to be transferred from threatened cities in the west with those already operating in the east. Under the rigid structure of the Soviet economy, it was vital to ensure that the relocated factories would integrate with host factories and sources of raw materials as closely as possible.

Many thousands of workers were evacuated by train and by air to reassemble the factories in their new locations and bring them into operation with the minimum delay. In theory the evacuated workers were intended to travel with the dismantled factories but inevitably many arrived beforehand and many arrived later. In Alma-Ata and other Kazakh cities, despite the strenuous efforts of Kunaev and the local party committees, to provide the new arrivals with food and accommodation, often this task was out of necessity left to the arriving factory managers themselves. Where disused warehouses and other basic accommodation did not exist, this meant that workers had to live alongside the equipment in the factories which they were rebuilding. Under the plans laid down by Voznesensky and Shvernik, existing factories which had been manufacturing tractors and other agricultural or non-military machinery and equipment, and which were unsuitable for amalgamation with the evacuated factories arriving from the west, now had to be hastily converted to the production of tanks and military equipment. Often this had to be done without any specialist expertise or military knowledge. The resulting loss of agricultural equipment was soon to have a disastrous impact on the production of food, but for now the emphasis was exclusively on producing weapons and ammunition for the troops at the front.

In the many instances where there were no factories with which the relocated plant and equipment could be merged, the factories arriving from Russia had to be rebuilt from scratch, often in the open countryside. Trains stopped outside the towns and factories were built where they stood. In these circumstances the only advantages were that the land was generally flat and there was ready access to the railway for receiving supplies of raw materials and despatching manufactured goods. But as winter approached and the weather deteriorated, in the hostile environment of the steppe there was nowhere to shelter and nothing with which to build either factories or accommodation. The combination of severe weather, lack of construction equipment, and permafrost in the ground made it almost impossible to lay any proper foundations for the new buildings, and machinery usually had to be unloaded from the arriving trains and reassembled in hastily-constructed wooden sheds. An account in *Pravda* described how, on an empty space outside Sverdlovsk, two enormous buildings were erected in a fortnight for a factory being brought from Ukraine, but the account could equally well have applied to hundreds of similar operations on the steppes of northern Kazakhstan or in the suburbs of Alma-Ata:

Among the mountains and the pine forests there is spread out the beautiful capital of the Urals, Sverdlovsk. It has many fine buildings, but there are two especially remarkable buildings in the area. Winter had already come when Sverdlovsk received Comrade Stalin's order to erect two buildings for the plant evacuated from the south. The trains packed with machinery and people were on the way. The war factory had to start production in its new home – and it had to do so in not more than a fortnight. Fourteen days, and not an hour more! It was then that the people of the Urals came to this spot with shovels, bars and pickaxes; students, typists, accountants, shop assistants, housewives, artists, teachers. The earth was like stone, frozen hard by our fierce Siberian frost. Axes and pickaxes could not break the stony soil. In the light of arc-lamps people hacked at the earth all night. They blew up the stones and the frozen earth, and they laid the foundations . . . Their feet and hands were swollen with frostbite, but they did not leave work. Over the charts and blueprints, laid out on packing cases, the blizzard was raging. Hundreds of trucks kept rolling up with building materials . . . On the twelfth day, into the new buildings with their glass roofs, the machinery, covered with hoar-frost, began to arrive. Braziers were kept alight to unfreeze the machines . . . And two days later, the war factory began production.*

Given the shortages of steel and reinforced concrete, many of the new factory buildings were made of wood, and the official history of the period describes how they were erected:

These buildings were architecturally displeasing, and often altogether puny to look at, but usually even large factory buildings were erected in a matter of fifteen to twenty days . . . People worked day and night, the scene of their work being lit by arc lamps

---

*Pravda, 18 September 1942, quoted in Alexander Werth, *Russia at War 1941-1945*

suspended on trees. In one of the Volga cities the new buildings of the largest aircraft factory in the country was being built in this way . . . Even before the roof had been completed, the machine-tools were already functioning. Even when the thermometer went down to forty degrees below, people continued to work. On December 10 (1941), fourteen days after the arrival of the last train-loads of equipment, the first Mig fighter plane was produced. By the end of the month, thiry Mig planes were turned out . . . Similarly, the last lot of workers of the Kharkov Tank Works left Kharkov on October 19, but already on December 8, in their new Urals surroundings, they were able to assemble their first twenty-five T-34 tanks, which were promptly sent to the front.*

The harsh conditions were similar to those being endured by troops at the front, and although there was no threat to life from the enemy, the death rate among workers and their families, who had arrived from the warmer climate of western Russia without possessions, proper clothing or shelter, was high. But everywhere the slogan 'In Work as in Battle' was propagated and enthusiastically responded to, as pensioners returned to the mines and the work benches where they had used to work, and local families, already living in cramped and tiny apartments, made room for women and children evacuated from Russia, Byelorussia, and Ukraine.

Meanwhile in Moscow, Leningrad, and other threatened cities, the desperate task of dismantling factories, and loading thousands of tons of industrial equipment on to railway wagons continued day and night without interruption. Relentless enemy bombardment caused heavy losses before overloaded trains could finally reach safety out of range of German attack. In Leningrad the evacuation of the Kirov tank factory in the southern suburbs of the city, the Stankilov industrial lathe factory, and many other installations producing munitions, armoured vehicles, aircraft engines, and other equipment, accelerated in October before German forces cut off the remaining communications east of the city. Ultimately only ninety-two factories could be evacuated from Leningrad before the city was surrounded, but each was to play a vital role in the Soviet war effort. In addition to the massive industrial operation, the Soviet authorities also arranged, at the height of the conflict, for the removal of priceless art treasures and irreplaceable cultural items from the Hermitage and the Russian Museum in Leningrad, from the Tretyakov and Pushkin Art Galleries in Moscow, and from other national galleries and museums, for transportation to safety in Sverdlovsk and distant

---

*Quoted in Alexander Werth, *Russia at War 1941-1945*

cities beyond the Urals. Thousands of women and children, the sick and the elderly, were also evacuated out of the path of the invasion. While this might have been done more effectively before the outbreak of the war, to have done so then would have gone against the spirit of the Soviet-German Non-Aggression Pact and, in Stalin's mind at least, would have been construed as provocation.

On 21 August 1941 the Germans captured the town of Chudovo, thus cutting the main Leningrad-Moscow railway, and by 30 August, after heavy fighting, they captured the crucial railway junction at Mga, 50 kilometres east of Leningrad, thereby cutting the city's last railway link with the rest of the country and preventing further evacuation by this route. By then nearly 300 trains laden with industrial equipment, thousands of evacuees, and hundreds of art treasures, had left Leningrad for the east, but no further transport by train was possible until Soviet forces recaptured Mga and reopened the railway in 1944. Until then a new evacuation route out of the city, and supply route into the city, were urgently needed. From now on everything had to be taken by road to Schlusselburg on the River Neva and the remote village of Ladozhskoe Ozero on the south shore of Lake Ladoga, 80 kilometres east of Leningrad; from there cargoes were transported by barge across the lake to the ancient Viking fortress town of Staraya Ladoga on the southern shore where, out of range of German bombardment, it was loaded on to railway wagons, often in a manual operation since heavy lifting gear was not available, and then by train, on a hastily constructed railway, to join the main railway line at Volkhov. From here began the long journey to the east, to distant cities thousands of miles away in the Volga region, Siberia, and Central Asia. With the onset of winter in 1941, the ice on Lake Ladoga became strong enough to support convoys of heavy lorries, and the famous ice road from Leningrad to the eastern shores of the lake became a vital route for transporting food and fuel supplies in and continuing cargoes of industrial and military equipment out of the city.

The combination of huge losses of territory in the west, and the disruption to output while industries were being relocated to the east, meant that there was inevitably an enormous loss of production and delivery of weapons and ammunition to the front. In the early stages of the war, the Red Army was constantly short of equipment, a factor which was very nearly disastrous in the Battle of Moscow in December 1941, and which largely accounted for heavy Soviet losses the following summer. By the late autumn of 1941, the evacuation of industry had run into severe difficulties. Not all the workers of the evacuated plants could be transferred at the same time as the factories and machinery; many had been called up, others had been killed or injured during the German bombardment of the factories and railway lines, and yet others had been transferred to work in other plants. Some had simply been left behind in the rush, and were still struggling to reach their new locations in the chaos on the railways. Often less than fifty percent of workers arrived with the relocated factories, with a correspondingly greater burden placed on those who had managed to arrive. On reaching their destinations, many found that their difficulties were compounded by acute shortages of raw materials, which held up production when factories were able to start operating again. Copper, manganese, coal, and molybdenum, the steel alloy used for making precision tools, were all in short supply, and new sources had to be brought rapidly into production. Extensive deposits of many raw materials existed throughout Kazakhstan, but exploitation was hampered by vast distances and extreme conditions of terrain and climate. The development of molybdenum mines in the arid steppe near Lake Balkhash, made possible by the construction of the railway from Karaganda in 1939, was one of the most significant achievements of transport and logistical organisation of the time.

The loss of coal mines in Ukraine, either due to seizure by the enemy or as the result of deliberate destruction by Soviet forces so as to prevent them falling into German hands, meant that drastic measures had to be taken to increase output from other sources. Coal now had to be extracted from the ground as quickly as possible to provide fuel for the new power stations being built to supply energy to the relocated factories. In Kazakhstan, tens of thousands of people were drafted in from various parts of the Soviet Union to work in the vast Karaganda mines in the north-east of the country, but many of the new arrivals were women or very old or very young men; all had to be trained in the shortest possible time, and special reserves of food were allocated to them so as to sustain production. Coal fields had been exploited around Karaganda since 1931, and had increased further since the extension of the railway line to Balkhash in 1939, designed to supply the energy-intensive copper mines and factories. In December 1941 an even greater increase in coal production from Karaganda was ordered, placing yet more strain on the already overloaded railway northwards to join the Trans-Siberian railway at Omsk. Output fell sharply in 1942 due to the acute difficulties in transport, the lack of necessary equipment, and severe problems of integrating the new labour teams when almost all the pre-war workforce had left for the front. By 1943 coal production had recovered, in Karaganda by more than one third of the pre-war level, due largely to the high morale of the Russian and Kazakh female workers, who were conscious that their work replaced that of husbands, sons, and brothers serving at the front. Notwithstanding these heroic efforts, strong motivation was not an adequate substitute for mining equipment, reliable transport, and skilled workers, and output nationally throughout Kazakhstan remained below pre-war levels, with severe consequences for the production of armaments and other items vital for the war effort.

Despite these difficulties, the movement of a high proportion of Russian and Ukrainian heavy industry, and especially war industry, to Kazakhstan and elsewhere was crucial to the ultimate victory. Without this enormous effort the Soviet Union could not have produced anything like the amount of armaments, ammunition, and vital equipment which was needed. By November 1941 a total of 1,523 industrial enterprises had been relocated out of western Russia and Ukraine to other parts of the USSR. The principal destination was Sverdlovsk and the region just beyond the Ural Mountains, to where 667 factories were evacuated; here there was already a substantial industrial base and the arriving factories could be established and integrated with the existing enterprises relatively quickly. The second largest destination was Kazakhstan and Central Asia. According to the *Soviet Kazakhstan History Encyclopedia*, 142 enterprises were evacuated to Kazakhstan, of which more than 30 went to Alma-Ata alone; Tashkent and other cities in Uzbekistan and elsewhere in Central Asia received more than 160 evacuated enterprises. A further 244 factories were relocated throughout western Siberia, 226 in the Volga region of southern Russia, and 78 in eastern Siberia. According to more recent studies, all of these figures are likely to have been underestimates, and the true total is probably much higher. Richard Overy in *Russia's War* (1997) quotes Russian sources which indicate that at least 2,593 enterprises were moved eastwards. For Nikolai Voznesensky, despite his tremendous achievement in organising the evacuation of industry and managing the Soviet economy during the war, peace time brought no reward. In 1949 he was arrested for his alleged role in the assassination of the Leningrad party leader Andrei Zhdanov and was executed later the same year.

Factories and mines were not the only destinations for the evacuated workers; agriculture and the collective farms needed huge numbers of people to replace those who had left for the front. Food production was another major problem, on top of the relocation of factories and resettlement of workers and evacuees. Kazakhstan was designated to be not only a major industrial part of the Soviet wartime economy, but was to become part of the Soviet Union's 'eastern food base'. The devastating losses of territory in western Russia had a catastrophic effect on food supplies: by November 1941 the Soviet Union had lost territory which produced thirty-eight per cent of its cereals and over eighty percent of its sugar. Losses of livestock in these areas, either by deliberate slaughter by the retreating Red Army, or by capture by the Germans, were extremely high. Further losses of territory in southern Russia in the summer of 1942 meant that by the end of that year, only fifty-eight percent of the total Soviet pre-war area under cultivation was still in Soviet hands. Vast areas of forests and taiga in central and eastern Russia were unsuitable for agriculture, and as a result the areas under cultivation in Kazakhstan, and the Urals, the Volga region, and western Siberia, had to be greatly extended. Crops which had not been grown in these parts before, including grain, sugar-beet, and sunflowers, were hurriedly introduced, despite the absence of suitable climatic and soil conditions, and a lack of knowledge and expertise in growing these plants. With the recovery of the northern Caucasus and other areas, the proportion of land under Soviet control rose to sixty three percent in 1943, but there was no diminution in the demand for food supplies from Kazakhstan.

In the early 1940s agricultural output was still severely constrained by widespread hostility to Soviet policies in the countryside. After the disastrous collectivisation of the 1930s and the almost complete destruction of their way of life, the rural population of Kazakhstan remained deeply averse to the *kolkhoz* system, which was completely opposed to local traditions of clans and khans, and were equally unreconciled to any form of external authority. The enforced requisitioning of food, the confiscation of livestock, and the ensuing starvation in the countryside, alienated millions of people, who received little consolation from the fact that starvation among the greater population in the cities was thereby avoided. Following the outbreak of war those in the countryside were now just as much aware as those in the towns of the danger facing the country as a whole. Almost all of the able-bodied men in the villages had been called up, while the remaining rural population, consisting of old men, women, and young children, in tiny villages and remote collective farms on the steppes in the north and the arid plains in the south, all worked in the most stressful conditions, to produce food for the troops at the front, and for the workers in the factories and mines. Hostility to the centralised collective system was replaced by the realisation that this was now the only possible method of agriculture, although in many cases the pre-war problems of lack of machinery, fertilisers, and manpower, became even more acute. Many of the horses, carts, lorries, and tractors on which agriculture heavily depended, had been requisitioned for the army. On the kolkhozes, ploughing was reduced to the most elementary methods; cows were often used as draught animals, and men and women sometimes had to draw ploughs themselves, the result of the lack of fuel for the few remaining tractors. From 1943 onwards, agricultural production began to resume in larger quantities, and difficulties of transporting supplies to the front and to the cities gradually began to ease. Food supplies continued to be very poor in the cities, especially for those not engaged in essential war work, for whom rations were very low, but the army and most skilled industrial workers were by now receiving adequate rations.

The vast influx into Kazakhstan of female workers and of men too old and children too young to serve at the front, of women and children evacuated from Ukraine, western Russia, and the Caucasus, all had a dramatic effect on national solidarity in the face of the enemy, far more than could have been achieved by official propaganda. In a speech in Alma-Ata after the war the Soviet leader Leonid Brezhnev, some of whose own family had been evacuated to Akmolinsk, said 'In Ukraine and Byelorussia, in towns and villages in Russia and the Baltic Republics, it will never be forgotten how the people of Kazakhstan, in the desperate years of the war, warmly welcomed the evacuees, shared with them their blood and their bread, and made space for them in their homes and at their fireside.' Traumatised refugees who succeeded in arriving from the western parts of the Soviet Union had their own experiences of atrocities committed by the Germans, of the trains on which they were travelling, full of women, children, wounded service personnel and civilians, being bombed and machine-gunned, all of which provided incalculable impetus to the efforts of all those working in the *tyl*.

As well as receiving factories, industrial and agricultural workers, and women and children evacuees, Kazakhstan was also the destination for many medical, scientific, artistic, and other institutions of all descriptions from Russia and the western USSR. Hospitals in Alma-Ata, Akmolinsk, Pavlodar, and Karaganda were given over in their entirety to the treatment of wounded servicemen and women. Scientists including some engaged in research into nuclear weapons set up new laboratories where they could continue their work. A large share of what was called the 'spiritual wealth' of the Soviet Union, consisting of more than 26,000 artists, writers, actors, and musicians, whose propaganda work was considered essential to the war effort, was also evacuated, mainly to Alma-Ata. The renowned Soviet film director Sergei Eisenstein, who had already established a world reputation and won a Stalin Prize in 1941 for his strongly nationalist and fiercely anti-German film *Alexander Nevsky,* moved to Alma-Ata in 1942, where the following year he produced *Ivan the Terrible* in a makeshift studio in a converted concert hall. The film was made on Stalin's orders as part of the theme of Russian nationalism which was then sweeping through the Soviet Union. By then the tide of the war had turned, after the German surrender at Stalingrad, but Stalin was anxious to build his own reputation as a sometimes harsh but fundamentally wise and strong national leader in the style of his sixteenth-century predecessor. In total more than twenty theatres and cultural institutions, fifteen universities, and twenty research institutes, relocated to Alma-Ata in 1941 and 1942. After the war many of the factories, research institutes, and other institutions were transported from Kazakhstan back to Russia. Some of the factories which remained fell into disuse when the demand for armaments tailed off, but the Kirov and AZTMS remained in Alma-Ata, and became the basis for the further development of heavy industry in the Semirechie region. Today the Kirov Machine Building Factory and the AZTMS are among the few functioning enterprises that remain in Almaty from the war-time evacuation; both have managed to survive great changes of fortune and upheavals in the post-war and the post-Soviet economy of Kazakhstan, and continue to form a link to what was a crucial time in the history of the city.

The significance of the TurkSib railway, and of the Trans-Siberian railway as a whole during the war, was immense. The TurkSib line, connecting Alma-Ata to the Tran-Siberian and thus to Russia and the rest of the Soviet Union, was gravely overloaded even before the outbreak of war, and the burden imposed on it increased further from 1941. But it was safe from enemy attack, and in the territory east of the Volga River the Trans-Siberian railway was also safe, at least in the early days of the war. Further east there were no major concerns for the security of the railway in Siberia, since the Soviet government had concluded a treaty with China, and relations with Japan were peaceful. But throughout 1942, as the German army advanced towards Stalingrad, the Trans-Siberian line and the railway network to the west of Kazakhstan fell increasingly under attack from German aircraft. The small town of Leninsk, in the narrow stretch of land between the border of Kazakhstan and the Volga River, became the principal supply base for the town of Stalingrad and for the whole of the Stalingrad front. Fifty kilometres from Stalingrad on the eastern bank of the Volga, Leninsk was the railhead of a minor branch line, but it acquired enormous significance as a transit point for almost all the Soviet troops and equipment used in the southern arm of the pincer movement in Operation Uranus, which eventually surrounded and trapped the German army in Stalingrad. Supplies of food, ammunition, military equipment, and medicines, dispatched from Kazakhstan and southern Russia were assembled here before being transported by barge, pleasure craft, river steamers, and any other type of available vessel across the Volga to the besieged troops in Stalingrad. It was also to Leninsk that the wounded from Stalingrad were evacuated, before being dispersed elsewhere away from the front to hospitals in Kazakhstan and Central Asia.

Gigantic bottlenecks at major junctions in the railway network began to be experienced particularly since the evacuation from Moscow accelerated in October 1941, and these seriously affected the ability of factories in Kazakhstan to despatch armaments and other war material to the front. The situation was slightly alleviated by the construction in 1942 of a single-track line from the port of Guryev on the Caspian Sea for 530 kilometres north-east to connect with the line from Tashkent to Aktyubinsk, which greatly facilitated the delivery of high-quality oil from the Emba fields for refining into urgently-needed aviation fuel. In the following year, another single-track line was opened from Akmolinsk westward for 800 kilometres to Kartaly across the border in Russia and to the enormous iron and steel plant at Magnitogorsk. This line was doubly important to the war effort, as it shortened the distance for hauling coal from Karaganda to Magnitogorsk via Petropavlosk in northern Kazakhstan by 480 kilometres, and it freed the Trans-Siberian railway for the transport of other vital freight between Petropavlovsk and the Urals. Underlying all the other difficulties of the war was a chronic shortage of manpower. Wherever possible much of the work on the new railways was done by prisoners of war, who suffered even more than the convicts and conscripted labourers who had constructed the TurkSib railway in 1928-1930. But construction of the new lines was now more thorough and better planned, since much depended on them being able to bear the enormous burden placed on them.

Two hundred and fifty kilometres north-east of Almaty, not far from the town of Taldy Kurgan and in an isolated spot below the Dzhungarski Alatau Ridge, lies the tiny and now deserted village of Akshar. Its wooden huts and corrugated iron sheds have all been abandoned, the surrounding countryside is largely depopulated, and the dusty village streets are reminiscent of a scene from the old Wild West. Even before the inhabitants left there were no shops, schools, or any form of communal centre. But Akshar was once home to scores of families of displaced Chechens, and was one of thousands of similar settlements for hundreds of thousands of people evicted from their original homes in the Caucasus Mountains on the far side of the Caspian Sea. In addition to receiving large numbers of factories, hospitals, and every other type of institution, Kazakhstan was also designated to receive whole populations of ethnic groups and minority nationalities from the regions and semi-autonomous republics which lay in the path of the German advance. In July 1941 the Soviet government, fearful that Chechens, Volga Germans, and other national groups, having suffered widespread persecution in tsarist and Soviet times, would welcome, or at least not resist, the invading German armies, decided that mass deportations to the east were necessary. The Gulag network of labour camps for political and other prisoners set up in the 1930s was inadequate for this purpose, and new arrangements had to be made for the wholesale removal of such ethnic groups. Despite the enormous cost in manpower which could have been used at the front, and the huge burden placed on the already over-stretched transport network, a vast resettlement programme was undertaken.

The prime candidates for deportation were the Volga Germans, who had been in Russia since the reign of Catherine the Great in the late eighteenth century, when thousands of German farmers, builders, and artisans were invited to leave their native country and settle in and develop the Volga region of southern Russia. Over the following 150 years more settlers arrived and the population increased, so that by the early 1940s hundreds of thousands of Russians of German descent lived in what had become the German Volga Soviet Socialist Republic, an autonomous region within Russia. Although no longer Germans in any real sense, for Stalin their loyalty to the Soviet Union was far from certain. At the outbreak of the war there had been instances of sabotage of railways in the region, and rumours of German airmen who had been brought down over the area and being given shelter by local families. In a series of incidents in August 1941, Soviet parachutists dressed in German uniforms were dropped among the villages of the German Volga region, and asked to be hidden until the German invaders arrived. Where villagers complied the NKVD rounded up and killed all the inhabitants, since they had failed the test of loyalty. Later the same month the German Volga Republic was abolished and the entire population of more than 600,000 was deported to northern Kazakhstan and Siberia. Many died in the severe conditions of resettlement, after transportation in cattle trucks over vast distances without food or water. The trains consisted of crude railway wagons known as *Stolypinkas* after Pyotr Stolypin, the reactionary Prime Minister of Russia before the Revolution, who was active in arresting and sending into exile revolutionary groups before he was assassinated in 1911. As had happened with the relocation of factories, little or no preparation had been made to receive these massive influxes of starving and bewildered families, but unlike the industrial workers who arrived with the urgent task of having to reassemble whole factories and resume industrial production as soon as possible, the many thousands of deportees from suspect ethnic groups were not eligible to receive food, shelter, or any other support from the communities in which they now found themselves. Those who survived the journey were left on the flat, open steppe, where they were compelled to fend for themselves in the hostile and unfamiliar terrain. In 1942, with the entire Soviet transport network devoted to the war effort, further deportations had to wait until trains and wagons could be made available. But by 1943, as the tide of the war began to turn, other national and ethnic groups, whose loyalty was questioned or whose disloyalty had supposedly been proven while they were under the German occupation, were also deported to Kazakhstan.

The people of the mountainous region of Chechnya were regarded with particular suspicion. Chechnya had been formally incorporated into the tsarist empire during the previous century under the rule of General Alexander Yermolov, the infamous Russian governor-general of the North Caucasus, after a violent and bloody campaign of resistance. In 1942 the German army failed to reach Grozny, the Chechen capital, in its drive to Baku and the oil fields of the Caspian Sea, but many Chechens were believed to have collaborated, either willingly or passively, with the Germans. Other nationalities of the Caucasus and neighbouring regions, including Ingushetians, Karachai and Meshketians from Georgia, Crimean Tartars, and Kalmyks from southern Russia, were also said to have aided the Germans, and whether guilty or not they were liable to deportation. In a typical incident in Chechnya in February 1944, in the type of operation also carried out many times in the Soviet Union, Soviet troops entered Grozny and other towns and villages throughout the country. Despite heavy snow and freezing weather, and their uncertain loyalty to the Soviet cause, on 22 February the local population had gathered in village squares to celebrate Red Army Day. The crowds were suddenly surrounded by the Soviet troops and deportation orders were read out. In the ensuing confusion and panic, many tried to escape and some were shot; the rest of the population were ordered to pack a minimum amount of possessions and were then loaded into trucks and trains, for transport down from the mountains to the port of Makhachkala. From there they were taken across the Caspian Sea to Krasnovodsk before being put onto trains destined for Alma-Ata and the surrounding regions. Others were taken by train and truck from Grozny to Astrakhan and from there to northern Kazakhstan and Siberia. On the other side of the Soviet Union, in the Pacific regions of the Soviet Far East, thousands of Koreans living in towns and villages bordering Russia were also rounded up and transported to Kazakhstan for fear that they might offer support to an invading Japanese army.

In 1957 the Soviet government allowed some of the surviving deported groups to return to their homelands, including Chechens who had retained their national identity in exile. But it was not until after the fall of the Soviet Union in 1991 that the descendants of the Crimean Tartars were allowed to return to the Crimea, only to find the flats and dachas in the countryside in which their parents or grandparents had lived occupied by Russians and Ukrainians, who refused to surrender what had since become their property. For the Volga Germans, there was no great desire to return to the Volga region, where they saw their future as difficult and uncertain in the newly-independent Russia. Despite having little knowledge of their ancestral homeland or of the modern German language, many decided to leave Kazakhstan and resettle in Germany where they were sure of receiving a warmer welcome. In 1989 the German population of Kazakhstan numbered just under one million, nearly six percent of the total population, but this had fallen to less than a quarter of a million by 2004. Their departure was prompted by a hope for a more secure economic future in Germany, and a lack of identification with Kazakhstan, where there was no commonality of interest and where economic and political prospects in the early years of independence were seen as poor. As they departed from Kazakhstan the ethnic Germans abandoned whole towns and villages, schools and farms, as the Chechens had done in Akshar and elsewhere. By contrast the Koreans were more inclined to remain in Kazakhstan. The repressive regime of North Korea held no attractions, and in any event the government might not have permitted an influx of new arrivals who might destabilise the regime. Integration into the capitalist economy of South Korea would also have been difficult. Instead many Koreans stayed in Kazakhstan and became active in developing trade with South Korea, and in pursuing business and finance within Kazakhstan. Acceptance within the Kazakh community was easier for the Koreans than it was for other ethnic groups, especially the Germans.

CHAPTER SEVENTEEN

The Twenty-Eight Panfilov-Heroes and Two Kazakh Heroines

Panfilov Park, as it is commonly known today, occupies a peaceful and verdant area in the centre of Almaty. It is not particularly extensive, more of a large garden than a park and much smaller than Gorky Park not far to the east. The dense mixture of conifers and deciduous trees, and the many colourful flower-beds irrigated by plentiful supplies of water flowing down from the nearby mountains, combine to create a tranquil oasis in one of the busiest parts of the city. In summer the park is cool and quiet, and only a faint hum of traffic can be heard although the busy streets of Kunaev and Gogol are only a few metres away; in winter the silence is complete, as footpaths and flower-beds lie buried under carpets of snow, and frost glistens on the trees and the golden domes and crosses of the Cathedral of the Holy Ascension.

The park was designed and laid out in 1879 on the site of a disused cemetery and was originally known as the City Garden. Over the years it has undergone reconstructions and given new names according to changing circumstances; in 1899 it was renamed Pushkin Garden to mark the centenary of the birth of the Russian poet, and twenty years later, shortly after the Russian Revolution, it was redesignated as the Park of Fighters Fallen for Liberty. Further major changes were made when the Cathedral of the Holy Ascension was built in the north-eastern corner of the park in 1904–1905. Designed by the Russian architect Andrei Zenkov, the cathedral is ornate and elaborate, incorporating the traditions of the Russian Orthodox Church and providing a focal point for the Russian community in the city and throughout Kazakhstan. Zenkov also designed and supervised the construction in 1905 of the nearby Saint Nicholas Cathedral, as well as other administrative buildings in Alma-Ata and Bishkek. His father, the first mayor of Alma-Ata and also an architect, designed the Orthodox Church near the original Russian fort in Verny. With a height of fifty-four metres the Cathedral of the Holy Ascension is claimed to be the tallest wooden building in the world, and thanks to the earthquake-resistant construction techniques developed by Zenkov after the 1887 earthquake, both it and the Saint Nicholas Cathedral survived the more powerful earthquake of 1911 with only slight damage. Both cathedrals also managed to survive the early years of the Revolution, although crosses, bells, and icons were removed and all traces of religion elsewhere in the country were destroyed, while many other churches were looted, burnt, or turned into stables and warehouses. Anti-religious activities intensified in the 1930s when priests and believers were persecuted, arrested, and in some cases subjected to torture under the regime of Goloshchekin and Yezhov. In 1929 the Holy Ascension Cathedral was converted into a museum of atheism, before being converted again into a concert and exhibition hall. It was rededicated and religious services resumed in 1994.

The park in which the cathedral stands received its present name - the Park of The Twenty Eight Panfilov Heroes - in 1942, in commemoration of the soldiers of the 316th Infantry Division, commanded by Major General Ivan Panfilov, who were killed in the defence of Moscow in November 1941. A few hundred metres from the Holy Ascension Cathedral stands a towering bronze and granite monument representing a group of Soviet troops, several times larger than life size, in action against the enemy. The monument is cast in the overwhelming and uncompromising style of the times, and makes no claims to artistic grace or merit. Instead the emphasis is on conveying the heroism of the twenty eight *Panfilovtsy* who played a small but decisive role in one of the early turning points of the war, when the hitherto undefeated German army failed to capture Moscow and suffered its first retreat. On the marble base of the statue are the words (which became a compelling theme of the war): 'Russia is vast, but there is nowhere to retreat. Moscow is behind us'. Nearby in the park are rows of marble headstones dedicated to each of the twenty eight soldiers who were killed in an action which became an enduring legend in the history of the war. The pathway leading up to the monument is lined with dates of famous battles of the First World War, the civil war, and the Great Fatherland War, and an eternal flame commemorates the millions of Kazakh and other Soviet war dead. From Soviet times to the present day, this has been a revered place for newly-married couples to come for an obligatory ceremony of wedding photographs and paying respects to the victims of the war.

Ivan Vasilyevich Panfilov was born in 1893 to a poor family in the southern Russian city of Petrovsk. On joining the Imperial Russian Army in 1915, he had a distinguished military career in the First World War, before joining the Red Army after the Revolution and serving with equal or even greater distinction on the side of the Bolsheviks in the Russian civil war. A dedicated Communist, he took part in campaigns in various parts of Russia, Poland, and Ukraine, and was awarded the Soviet Order of the Red Banner in 1921. In 1924 he was posted to Bishkek in Kyrgyzia in command of a company engaged in fierce fighting against the Basmachi guerrillas, who were resisting Soviet forces from bases in the foothills of the Tien Shan Mountains. The suppression of the Basmachi revolt earned for Panfilov the second Order of the Red Banner in 1929. In 1935 he was posted to Tashkent as an instructor at the Lenin Red Banner Military Academy, and in 1938 he returned to Bishkek as military commissar in the new Soviet Republic of Kyrgyzstan. Three years later, immediately after the German invasion, Panfilov began the mobilisation of reservists and on 12 July 1941 he was assigned to take command of the 316th Division, a new unit being formed in Alma-Ata and consisting mainly of reservists with whom he had been working and training in Kazakhstan and Kyrgyzstan. As a native Russian in command of Kazakh and Kyrgyz volunteers and reservists, Panfilov was well placed to fit in to the new structure of merged national units and divisions in the Red Army. After a short period in Alma-Ata, Panfilov and an anti-tank unit from his division were transferred to Moscow where they found themselves stationed on the main road from Volokolamsk to Moscow, under the command of Marshal Georgy Zhukov, whom Stalin had appointed to take command of all Soviet forces defending Moscow.

By the middle of October 1941, the German army had advanced to less than fifty kilometres from Moscow. The most serious threat came from the north-west, where fierce battles were being fought in the region of Volokolamsk, and a German breakthrough to the suburbs of Moscow seemed almost certain. With the evacuation of industrial enterprises already under way, the Soviet government decided on 12 October that a large number of ministries and scientific institutions should be sent to the city of Kuibyshev, 800 kilometres to the east. The whole of the diplomatic corps was also evacuated to Kuibyshev. The embalmed body of Lenin had already been taken from its mausoleum in Red Square and transported by a special refrigerated train to Tyumen in western Siberia. These developments prompted widespread panic among the population, with rumours of an imminent German capture of the city, and roads and railway lines became blocked with refugees fleeing to the east. But outside the capital Russian resistance was stiffening and by 18 October counter-attacks by the Red Army had slowed down the German advance. Both sides suffered heavy losses, but it was the Germans who experienced the most fatigue and weariness, and by 7 November the first German offensive against Moscow had come to a standstill. Moscow celebrated the twenty-fourth anniversary of the Revolution with parades in Red Square of troops either returning from the front or on their way to the front. Despite the atmosphere of siege, and with many thousands of wounded troops and civilians crowding the hospitals, the conviction that Moscow would not be lost had grown steadily over the past fortnight. This conviction had been further strengthened by a speech commemorating the Revolution given by Stalin the previous evening in the large and ornate hall of the Mayakovsky metro station. Later known as his 'Holy Russia' speech, it became famous for its invocation of Russian national heroes of the past, notably Alexander Nevsky who defeated the Teutonic knights in 1242, Dimitry Donskoi who defeated the Tartars in 1380, and Mikhail Kutuzov, the general under Tsar Alexander I who had fought Napoleon at the battle of Borodino and lured the French Grand Army to disaster in 1812. It also considerably strengthened the nation's flagging morale by the visible fact that Stalin had not left the capital but was still in Moscow to lead the defence of the country. The glorification of Russia's history was accompanied by a clear relegation of Communist ideology after national pride and religious faith in the patriotic struggle against Germany, and struck a deep chord throughout Russia and the whole of the Soviet Union, where Russian and Soviet nationalism were now seen as synonymous.

The battle for Moscow – let alone other life-and-death struggles around Leningrad in the north and in the Caucasus in the south – was not yet won, and although there was greater confidence that Moscow would be saved, there was at the same time a growing apprehension of a renewed German offensive. The German army was severely weakened by acute shortages of winter clothing, food, fuel, and essential equipment, but thousands more troops, transferred from France and other occupied countries in western Europe, were arriving to reinforce the divisions outside Moscow. Most of these troops were even more poorly equipped, still in the clothing they had been wearing in the countries they had come from, but despite these conditions, after its setbacks in October 1941 the German army managed to regain considerable superiority over its Russian opponents in a number of areas, especially to the north-west of Moscow, where in the middle of November it launched a series of major attacks. By 22 November the army had reached the town of Istra, twenty kilometres west of Moscow, from where in breaks in the overcast skies the domes of the Kremlin cathedrals could clearly be seen glistening in the wintry sunshine. It was further to the west, around the town of Volokolamsk where there was particularly heavy fighting, that the anti-tank unit of General Panfilov was destroyed in a suicidal defence against the German advance. The account of what happened in this particular action is related in the official Soviet history of the war, quoted by Alexander Werth in *Russia at War*:

'On that day (22 November) the Germans had hoped to break through to the Volokolamsk highway, and to advance on Moscow. After a massive air attack, German machine gunners tried to break into the Russian trenches, but were driven back by rifle and machine-gun fire. A second attack was launched by a fresh unit supported by twenty tanks. Using anti-tank rifles, hand grenades, and petrol bottles the Panfilov men crippled fourteen of the tanks and the other six were driven back. Shortly afterwards the wounded survivors were again attacked by thirty more tanks. One by one the Soviet soldiers were being wounded or killed in a merciless fight which lasted four hours. The severely wounded *politruk* (political instructor) Klochkov threw himself under an enemy tank with a bunch of hand grenades and blew it up. The Germans, having lost eighteen tanks and dozens of men, failed to break through.'

Panfilov was also killed, and in recognition of his courage and that of his unit, the 316th division was awarded the Order of the Red Banner. Panfilov himself was posthumously awarded the Order of Hero of the Soviet Union in April 1942, the country's highest military honour. This was only one of many thousands of incidents of Russian and Soviet self-sacrifice and suicidal resistance, but one which appears to have been chosen at random to become a propaganda legend. Another account from the same time, of November 1941, describes the action and fate of Zoya Kosmodemianskaya, an eighteen-year-old Moscow Komsomol (youth league) girl who set fire to a stable in the German-held village of Petrishcheva near Moscow, and was tortured and hanged by the Germans. Zoya Kosmodemianskaya became a national heroine. Later versions of the Panfilov incident have cast doubt on what actually happened, with some accounts claiming that Panfilov wished to retreat. Morale was low, many of the young soldiers had been recruited from the countryside in Kazakhstan which had suffered greatly under collectivization and were said to be hostile to the Soviet regime, and confidence in the leadership, and the will to resist the Germans, were not what they were claimed to be at the time. According to these accounts Panfilov was informed by Zhukov that retreat would result in execution of the whole unit by an NKVD firing squad. But whether from fear of the Germans or of the NKVD, the unit recovered and the *Panfilovtsy* gained national fame for their heroism.

The episode acquired a more enduring significance the following year, when it ceased to be simply a renowned example of Soviet defiance in the defence of Moscow, and marked a radical change in the relationship between the army on one side, and the political instructors and commissars who were the representatives in the army of the Communist Party and the Soviet government, on the other side. In August 1942, after the danger to Moscow had passed but when the German army was approaching Stalingrad, the Red Army newspaper *Red Star* claimed that, contrary to the familiar account of the Panfilov unit which had fought against the Germans to the last man, one of the twenty-eight men had attempted to desert, only to be shot by his comrades for cowardice. On 1 August the newspaper reported:

'They dealt with one contemptible coward. Without any preliminary discussion all of the Panfilov men fired at the traitor; that sacred volley symbolised their determination not to retreat another step, and to fight to the bitter end'.

This newspaper report may have been typical of Soviet military propaganda at the time, and in the original account the *politruk* himself perished in a heroic manner. But more often the political instructors and commissars, whose essential function was to prevent a retreat, were seen as interfering in what should be military decisions, often with negative results. Their job was to impose the 'iron discipline' which Stalin had a few days earlier demanded, but sometimes they went too far in fulfilling this role. Shortly after its Panfilov story, on 9 August 1942 the *Red Star* explained how army officers should distinguish between different types of soldiers accused of dereliction of duty:

'If you have before you an obvious enemy or defeatist, a coward or panic-monger, then it is no use wasting any propaganda or persuasion on him. You must deal with a traitor with an iron hand. But sometimes you come across people who need your temporary support; after that they will firmly take control of themselves.'

The *Red Star* was warning, on behalf of the army and the Soviet armed forces as a whole, against the excessively ruthless and sometimes counter-productive application of military discipline. It implied that, due to the inflexible military thinking of the time, the supposed coward in the Panfilov unit may have been dealt with unnecessarily severely, and may have contributed to a more effective defence if he had been allowed to do so. The article brought out into the open the long-running conflict between military officers and political commissars, and clearly indicated that commissars should not be responsible for military punishments, but instead should concentrate on political education and propaganda, and prevent the possibility of disobedience and desertion arising in the first place. This relatively liberal understanding of how wartime conditions affected different individuals was almost unheard of at the time. It must be assumed that Stalin had read and given his approval to the 9 August *Red Star* article, and while it is inconceivable that he could have acted out of sympathy for soldiers attempting to desert or retreat, he may have realised that over-zealous discipline and extreme punishments may have been militarily ineffective, and a less ruthless approach may be more valuable.

He himself had left his post and disappeared for several days immediately after the invasion. In any event, Stalin always understood the need to adjust policies and actions in the light of what was actually happening at the front, and the role of the political commissars was soon to be modified in line with what the *Red Star* had advocated. After the protest against the indiscriminate shooting of alleged cowards, the ferocious articles in the press, which had demanded the most severe penalties for deserters, stopped almost completely. A more practical method of dealing with lack of discipline at the front may have been the more lasting legacy of Panfilov and the 'Twenty-Eight Panfilov Heroes'.

Not far from Panfilov Park, a few hundred metres to the west along Aiteke Bi Street, is Astana Square, and here in the garden stands a memorial to two of Kazakhstan's most revered young war heroines, Manshuk Mametova and Alya Moldagulova. Historically known as the Old Square, Astana Square was once the centre of the old town of Verny and Alma-Ata. Prestigious houses of government officials and wealthy Russian businessmen stood side-by-side with stalls of local traders and merchants. The commander of the Verny garrison lived here, although the Russian fort and the garrison itself were some kilometres to the east. After the 1917 Revolution the square was renamed Red Square, and following the transfer of the capital from Kyzyl Orda to Alma-Ata in 1929, the administrative buildings of the new Communist government of Kazakhstan were built on the north side of the square in the 1930s. Notwithstanding the oppressive political atmosphere of the time, the Old Square was designed, as were many other squares and gardens, in accordance with the aims of the early city planners Edward Baum and Gerasim Kolpakovsky, namely that it should be laid out in conjunction with a park, flower beds, and trees, for the benefit of the people. The original plan, with government buildings on the north side and a park and gardens on the south side, has survived to the present day.

The present design of the square dates from 1957, when construction of a new Government House, replacing the old government buildings and occupying the whole of the north side, was completed. In contrast to the Academy of Sciences building a short distance away in Valikhanov Square, the Government House is plain and uninspiring, built in a familiar overpowering Soviet style of architecture in which the individual worker or passer-by was made to feel insignificant. Directly opposite on a three-metre high granite plinth, an enormous bronze statue of Vladimir Lenin had already been erected three years earlier, towering over the square, the left hand clutching a copy of *Pravda,* and the right arm held aloft as if pointing the way to a better future.

But the effect created was far from uplifting, and the sheer size of the statue, out of scale with the surrounding gardens, exerted a somewhat depressing atmosphere over an otherwise attractive open space. The square was renamed Lenin Square, and busts of revolutionaries and other leading figures from the recent Soviet past added to its rather somber appearance. For the next four decades the people of Alma-Ata lived with these unwelcome symbols of Russian domination in the centre of their city. Despite this, the park managed to retain something of its more lively, pre-revolutionary spirit; with the arrival of warmer weather every spring, it attracted open-air artists, amateur musicians, and families enjoying the gardens and shade under the trees, and a less formal and more colourful note was given by a flower market in the south-west corner, a relic from the Old Square and which still survives today, although in a much reduced form of a few kiosks and overshadowed by plain commercial buildings nearby.

The Lenin statue dominated the Square for forty-two years until it was taken down before dawn one morning in August 1996. In other squares and public places throughout Kazakhstan and the non-Russian republics of the old USSR, statues of Lenin and other revolutionary figures were being removed and unceremoniously deposited in suburban parks, or destroyed altogether, and in their place memorials to local historical figures or war heroes were being erected. Some of the Russian-populated towns and cities in the north of Kazakhstan retained their Lenin statues for longer than those in the south, but they were all eventually destined to go. The secretive nature of the operation in Almaty, with no prior public consultation or discussion in the press or on television, reflected a desire on the part of the local authorities to avoid any clashes with remaining Lenin admirers among the Russian and to a lesser extent, Kazakh population. But press reports of the event were muted and factual, and apart from a handful of older-generation Russians and communists, few people in Almaty regretted the disappearance of the city's most famous monument. Most people were indifferent, or even relieved, that such an overbearing presence had at last been taken away.

Lenin had gone, but the solid granite plinth remained intact, as it was clear that it would be suitable for another, less overwhelming memorial. Soon afterwards, a composition depicting a pair of doves and two young children on top of a globe, symbolising aspirations for peace for new generations, was unveiled on the plinth where Lenin had once stood; and below it now stand commemorative sculptures of the two most famous Kazakh heroines of the Second World War, Manshuk Mametova and Alya Moldagulova. Both figures are presented in a severe military pose, but on a more modest and human scale, far from the domineering style of traditional Soviet war memorials.

Manshuk Mametova was born on 23 October 1922 in Zhaskus, a small village in the Ural region of western Kazakhstan. Orphaned at an early age, in the autumn of 1932 she moved with her foster parents to the town of Uralsk, before moving again to Alma-Ata where she became a student at the Alma-Ata Medical Institute. By this time she had become a dedicated communist and was actively engaged in the Alma-Ata Communist Party organisation. On the outbreak of war, at the age of eighteen Manshuk Mametova volunteered to join the Red Army and was assigned to clerical duties in the 100th Rifle Division, a unit composed mainly of Kazakh troops. Not content to play a subordinate role to the men in the company, she trained as a machine gunner and in October 1942 was sent to the front at Kalinin, north-west of Moscow, at one of the most critical stages of the war.

Since the failure of the German army to take Moscow at the end of 1941, a Soviet counter-offensive from early 1942 had aimed to remove the threat which still hung over the city, as well as to lift the blockade of Leningrad, and to prevent any further progress by the Germans towards the Caucasus and the oil fields of the Caspian. In the event none of these objectives was fully achieved, although Rostov, at the eastern end of the Sea of Azov and seen as the key to the Caucasus, was liberated by Russian troops at the end of November 1941 and brought the German advance in the south to a temporary halt. On the Leningrad front the recapture on 9 December of the town of Tikhvin greatly alleviated Leningrad's supply position, enabling supplies of food and ammunition to be transported from there to Lake Ladoga and the 'Ice Road' into Leningrad. But the rest of the land blockade was still intact and would remain so until the siege was finally lifted in January 1944. In the spring of 1942, more visible success was achieved along the front to the west of Moscow, and some large areas of territory were liberated, including Volokolamsk and the surrounding area where Ivan Panfilov and the 28 *Panfilovtsy* had been killed. Despite these advances the Germans prevented any significant Russian drive to the west, and managed to hold a line which in many places was still barely one hundred kilometres from the capital.

Throughout what became known as the Black Summer of 1942, the German positions remained a grave threat, or 'springboard' from which an attack on Moscow could be launched. But of even greater concern from the Soviet point of view was that the Germans would attempt to hold their positions to the west of Moscow with the minimum number of troops, and to transfer the maximum number possible to the south, in particular to Stalingrad and the Caucasus. Throughout the summer and autumn of 1942 Soviet forces did their utmost to tie up as many German troops as possible along the front to the west of Moscow by constant attack and harassment. These battles were among the most desperate fought by Soviet troops during the whole of the war; despite the reduction in German troop numbers the German positions were still strong and deeply entrenched, whereas the Soviet forces at this stage of the war were still less well trained and less well armed, and their losses were higher. The fighting was taking place in what had been some of the most beautiful parts of the Russian countryside, immortalized in the novels of Ivan Turgenev and Leo Tolstoy, with expansive, grassy meadow lands, low hills and gentle, rolling undulations, and vast fields of poppies and cornflowers, dotted with woodlands and copses of ash and willow trees. Now everywhere was engulfed in conflict and destruction; the house where Tolstoy had lived at Yasnaya Polyana near Tula, 240 kilometres south of Moscow, was destroyed by the Germans before being retaken by the Russians later in 1942. By the autumn when the *rasputitsa* had returned, and fields and roads had again turned into seas of mud, making conditions almost impossible. As the Germans retreated they embarked on a programme of mass shootings, murders and hangings, killing or starving to death hundreds of Russian prisoners of war, and the deportation of many thousands of others as slave labour to Germany. It was into this nightmare that, in October 1942, Manshuk Mametova and the 100th Rifle Brigade arrived from Kazakhstan and where, according to the *Soviet Kazakhstan Historical Encyclopedia,* they received their baptism of fire in fierce action against the enemy.

Over the following months Soviet forces, principally the 100th and 101st Kazakh Rifle Brigades, with enormous difficulty and heavy losses, gradually advanced westwards, liberating many towns and villages in the regions around Smolensk and Vitebsk and accounting for the deaths of many thousands of Germans. Progress was tortuous and slow, not least because as many troops and resources as possible were being directed to the simultaneous battle being fought at Stalingrad. During the spring and summer of 1943, when more troops could be released after the German surrender at Stalingrad and others arrived from Siberia and the east, the Soviet advance on the north-west front accelerated, and the strategically-important towns of Veliky Luky and Nevel, north-west of Smolensk, were recaptured in October. It was in fighting at Nevel on 15 October 1943, one year after her arrival at the front, that Manshuk Mametova was killed. In a particularly heroic action she destroyed a German gun emplacement, saving the lives of scores of her comrades but at the cost of her own. The town of Nevel was soon afterwards captured by the rest of the 100th Brigade.

To the right of the sculpture of Manshuk Mametova stands the figure of another Kazakh heroine of the Great Fatherland War: Alya Moldagulova. Alya Moldagulova was born on 15 June 1925 near Aktyubinsk in western Kazakhstan. Both her parents died of starvation in the first years of collectivisation and at the age of ten she was sent to a boarding school in Leningrad, although it was not until 1942, one year after the beginning of the siege, that she was evacuated out of the city, to the ancient cathedral city of Yaroslav on the Volga River north-east of Moscow. In December 1942 Alya Moldagulova enrolled at a women's sniper school at the nearby town of Rybinsk, and after seven months training, in July 1943 was sent with the 54th Rifle Division to the front near the medieval town of Pskovsk. Here, six months after her arrival, she was killed on 14 January 1944 in a battle near the village of Kazachikh.

The two girls had much in common: both came from western Kazakhstan, were orphaned as young children, joined the army at an early age, and served with heroism in the war. As teenagers both girls distinguished themselves in the violent, masculine world of Soviet combat troops, fighting in rifle battalions on the north-west front, and both were killed in action before they reached the age of twenty-one. Both were posthumously awarded the Order of Hero of the Soviet Union. The memorial to them on the site of the old Lenin statue is more in keeping with the contemporary feeling of Kazakh nationhood, while at the same time remembering the common cause with Russia and the rest of the Soviet Union in the war.

Although not immediately threatened by German occupation, Kazakhstan was in grave danger, and would not survive as a national or political entity in the event of a Soviet defeat. In the months before the invasion of Russia, the German government had prepared detailed plans for the partition of the Soviet Union and the future of the conquered territories in the east. In addition to the notion of gaining 'living space' in western Russia, its vision was one of Germany being able to obtain vast supplies of natural resources from the new lands: limitless quantities of grain from Kazakhstan and Ukraine, oil from the Caucasus and the Caspian Sea via the Azerbaijan capital of Baku, industrial raw materials from the Ural Mountains, coal from the Karaganda region and an inexhaustible supply of vital minerals and commodities from eastern Kazakhstan, and cotton and fruit from Turkmenistan and Uzbekistan. To administer the vast regions of Central Asia, the earlier concept of Turkestan was revived. Politically and geographically Turkestan had ceased to exist in 1924 shortly after the formal creation of the Soviet Union in 1922, but under German plans it would once again come into being, to incorporate the whole of Kazakhstan as well as the southern republics of Turkmenistan, Uzbekistan, Kyrgyzstan, and Tajikistan. The new Turkestan was proposed to be a semi-independent state but would in effect be a German satellite, under close German control and freely exploited for its natural resources and its labour force, which would provide large numbers of much-needed workers for factories, farms, and public services in Germany. A similar fate awaited other regions of Russia in the Caucasus and in Siberia. The population of Kazakhstan, both native Kazakhs and ethnic Russians, may not have been aware of Germany's economic plans for the country, but Nazi racial attitudes towards the Slavs were well known, and served as a warning of likely German treatment of Kazakhs and other racial groups in Central Asia.

The nearest points to Kazakhstan reached by the invading German armies were at Stalingrad on the Volga River, one hundred and sixty kilometres from the westernmost point of the Kazakh border; and further south in Kalmykia, where in November 1942 advance units of German troops came to within a few kilometres of the western shore of the Caspian Sea, at the small Russian village of Rybachiy on the Kuma River between Astrakhan and the Dagestan capital of Makhachkala. If Germany had succeeded in capturing Stalingrad in 1942, after failing to capture Moscow in 1941, it planned a renewed attack on Moscow by means of an advance northwards along the Volga River and cutting off Moscow from the east. In the summer of 1942 Germany also aimed to capture the oilfields of the Caucasus, and to advance as far as Baku, which would give it control of the oilfields of the Caspian Sea. The capture of Baku would also provide a launch-pad for an eventual invasion of Kazakhstan across the Caspian, in addition to an overland route from Stalingrad. In the event of the German army seizing Baku, the Soviet government had already made plans for the destruction of the ports of Bautino and Shevchenko on the eastern coast of the Caspian Sea, and of Krasnovodsk further south in Turkmenistan. The railway line from Krasnovodsk to Tashkent and connecting to the TurkSib railway to Alma-Ata was also destined for destruction before the Germans could reach Baku.

On 9 October 1942, as the battle for Stalingrad was in full force, the Communist Party leadership in Alma-Ata issued a decree to all Kazakh combat forces, declaring that 'Stalingrad is the key to the East... Kazakh soldiers, you and your Soviet countrymen must defend your home, your family, and your native Soviet homeland.... Stand firm, as your compatriots fighting before Moscow, the twenty eight Panfilov-Heroes, stood firm.' The reference to the Battle of Moscow had its effect, but the determination to fight was more strongly reinforced by what troops had seen and heard from refugees from the west. Vast armies from all over the Soviet Union fought at Stalingrad, and Kazakh forces in particular took part in almost every section of the conflict. From August 1942 until the German surrender six months later, almost one-third of all Kazakhstan's armed forces was engaged in the battle of Stalingrad.

In January 1943 Soviet troops began a final onslaught against the German Sixth Army which since the previous November had been trapped as a result of Operation Uranus, the gigantic pincer movement cutting off what became known as the 'cauldron' around Stalingrad from the rest of German-held territory. The Germans were now retreating in disorder into the city, and surrendering in increasing numbers. Heavy fighting continued in the streets of Stalingrad until, on 31 January 1943, Field-Marshal Friedrich Paulus surrendered at his HQ in the basement of the Univermag department store. According to an official Soviet announcement on 2 February, 330,000 German, Hungarian, and Romanian troops had been caught in the Soviet encirclement of the city in November 1942, but since then many tens of thousands had been killed in the fighting, or had died from starvation and disease. Large numbers of German planes, tanks, armoured cars, guns and ammunition were captured. After the German surrender, and as the Red Army began its inexorable advance westwards, the Soviet High Command assigned troops from the victorious armies which had retaken Stalingrad to fight alongside other divisions along the front, giving a further boost to morale, which was now already high; while at the same time, hundreds of starving and badly-wounded German prisoners, who would not be able to contribute to post-war reconstruction in the Soviet Union, and would be of no use to the German army, were released back to their comrades outside the cauldron where they in turn could spread gloom and disaffection. The threat to Kazakhstan was now lifted as German troops, which since September 1942 had been perilously close to its western border, were driven back across Russia and Ukraine.

After the Soviet victory at Stalingrad, the war continued for a further two years and three months before the final German surrender on 8 May 1945; and although the immediate post-war period was a time of great relief in Kazakhstan, as the country shared in the Soviet triumph, it was also, as elsewhere in the Soviet Union, a period of renewed political oppression and harsh living conditions, as the national economy began a long and arduous recovery. Despite the victory of the Soviet Union in the Great Patriotic War, there was no opportunity for the population of Kazakhstan, or anywhere else, to rest and relax, before the national mood changed again, from universal rejoicing to apathy and sullen conformity.

CHAPTER EIGHTEEN

Kazakhstan in the Aftermath of War, and the Forced Labour Camps of Alzhir and Kengir

The fireworks and victory celebrations in the Old Square and on the streets of Alma-Ata, and in towns and villages throughout Kazakhstan on 9 May 1945 and over the subsequent days and weeks, were no less heartfelt than they were in the rest of the Soviet Union. But alongside the relief and happiness now that the war was over were feelings of immense sadness at the loss of life, and as in Russia and every other republic there was no family which had not lost at least one family member. Now there was great concern at the enormous cost of reconstruction in what had been the occupied parts of the USSR, and deep anxiety about what the future would hold. No part of Kazakhstan had been occupied or even attacked by the Germans, and the country had been spared the scorched earth policies ordered by Stalin in Russia and Ukraine during the Soviet retreat in 1941–1942. It had escaped the even greater devastation inflicted by the Germans as they in turn retreated after the surrender at Stalingrad. But Kazakhstan was now economically exhausted, as were the other Central Asian republics of Turkmenistan, Uzbekistan, Tajikistan, and Kyrgyzstan, which had not been ruined by German occupation but which had devoted all their resources to achieving victory. The same was true in Azerbaijan, Armenia, and Georgia on the other side of the Caspian Sea. Together they had lost millions of their own men and women in the conflict, mostly those who would have been most able to assist with recovery. Kazakhstan had received a vast influx of women and children fleeing from the fighting, as well as those who had been forcibly deported and unceremoniously left in the empty countryside. The deported national groups had been obliged to fend for themselves, with many thousands dying of disease and starvation, but the many more thousands of refugees and wounded servicemen who flooded into Kazakhstan had to be provided with food, shelter, and medical care. All this was given willingly and without hesitation by the local population, even though they had barely enough for themselves, but it represented a further heavy burden on national resources.

As well as providing a haven for homeless families and injured soldiers and airmen, Kazakhstan had made its own enormous contribution to the Soviet victory. Without its troops and manpower, its production and deliveries of food to the front, supplies of coal, iron ore, vast quantities of vital minerals and raw materials to Russian armaments factories in Siberia, and its own production of industrial goods, military equipment, medical supplies, and all types of other resources, the outcome of the war would certainly have been different. The same was true of all the non-occupied parts of the Soviet Union, but after the war it was Kazakhstan, containing the largest sector of the Soviet industrial and agricultural economy which had not been damaged by enemy action, which faced a particularly heavy burden in supporting the rest of the country.

After the war the Soviet family of nations and republics coalesced around Russia in a warm glow of victory and achievement. Russia, and specifically Moscow, became the centre of most people's world, and although the sense of Soviet togetherness was actively fostered in newsreels and in the press, few people ever travelled outside their own republic, let alone outside the USSR, unless as part of the occupying forces in Europe. The people of Kazakhstan shared in the common themes binding the Soviet Union together, and the determination to rebuild the ruined economy. But in the aftermath of the war, in the more remote parts of the Soviet Union, there was already a diminution of Soviet control. While nobody dared stray too far from official policies in Moscow and Leningrad, on the Kazakh steppes and in the countryside, there was little desire to return to the old Soviet way of centralized planning of the economy, and in some of the towns and villages, the older artisan enterprises and workshops sprung up again, and some privately-owned shops and stalls began to provide basic services. There was no expectation of any fundamental change to the Soviet system, but many expected there might be some relaxation of political control and limitation of public freedoms. For Stalin and the Soviet government in Moscow, all this was dangerous and had to stop. In an earlier episode in Russian history, the defeat of Napoleon and the arrival of the tsarist army in Paris in 1815 had been followed by political unrest in Russia as the troops returned home and sought better political and economic conditions such as they had found in Europe. The outcome was the ill-fated Decembrist Uprising of 1825, its violent suppression by the new tsar Nicholas I, and lasting damage to the Romanov dynasty. Now once again Soviet troops were returning to their homelands in Russia, Kazakhstan and the other republics, having seen a different way of life in Europe, where even in the defeated countries many people seemed to be better dressed and fed than people in the Soviet Union. There was also more openness and freedom in Europe than the soldiers had experienced at home, which many found to be a welcome change from the restrictive and oppressive conditions in which they had been brought up in their native republics. In Kazakhstan, although there was little basis for western ideals of political freedom or a market economy taking root, there was at least a possibility of a return to some of the older nomadic traditions which had survived from tsarist times, and pre-collectivisation agriculture. Stalin was determined to avoid any possibility of this or a repetition of a Decembrist-style movement; if this should happen and Soviet policies began to be eroded, his own authority would be challenged, with unpredictable outcomes.

After a short period of relative freedom, at least in the countryside, Kazakhstan was again taken into the tight grip of Soviet political control, with complete obedience demanded to the Communist Party and government in Moscow. In the economy some effort was made towards increasing the supply of consumer goods, and the construction of better housing, but the overwhelming emphasis was on the production and export of grain, timber, coal, and industrial raw materials so as to earn foreign currency with which to pay for imports of essential capital goods for the rest of the Soviet economy. Even the security which the country had enjoyed by being far from invasion was now under threat by the decision of the Soviet government to develop nuclear weapons at a site near Semipalatinsk, a site which would become a target for attack in the event of another war. A severe drought and a ruined harvest in 1946 renewed the spectre of famine, already widespread throughout Ukraine, in 1947-1948. Even if Kazakhstan escaped the worst of the famine, it had to supply extra deliveries of grain and other foodstuffs to other less fortunate parts of the USSR. Politically the country found itself again cast in an unfavourable light, as Stalin sought to disparage those nationalities which had opposed Russian expansion in the nineteenth century. Primarily these criticisms were aimed at the people of the Caucasus, especially in Dagestan and Chechnya, and who were now subjected to further colonial oppression, this time from the Soviet government. The policies of denigrating and repressing indigenous people and praising the role of Russia in bringing education and civilisation to outlying regions of the empire, stored up serious trouble for Russia in later years after the collapse of the Soviet Union. But meanwhile non-Russian nations and republics, including Kazakhstan, were collectively assigned to a secondary position, below that of Russia; in September 1947, a statue erected in central Moscow and dedicated to Prince Yuri Dolgoruki, the founder of the medieval principality of Muscovy in 1147, was seen by many as a further symbol of Russian supremacy within the USSR. The rejection of national aspirations in the republics, and a refusal to allow the teaching of national languages and history, were accompanied by more material matters such as the priority given to the supply of food and consumer goods to the Russian population, especially to the inhabitants of Moscow and Leningrad.

Meanwhile Kazakhstan, economically little more than an adjunct to Russia and a source of raw materials for the Russian economy, could not fully evolve or develop in a fruitful way. Despite advances made in education, literacy, health care, and social services, the Kazakh economy was once again trapped in the rigidities of the centrally-planned Soviet system. The provisions of each plan for each sector of the economy were drawn up by Gosplan, the state planning authority in Moscow, and were to be implemented by each of the various industrial and agricultural ministries in the furthermost corners of Kazakhstan and each of the republics. Stalin never visited Kazakhstan; his phobia of flying and dislike of travelling generally meant that he rarely left Moscow except to attend occasional international conferences and to take holidays on the Black Sea, and he had little knowledge of life in other parts of the Soviet Union. But in his view any attempt in any of the republics to produce a more efficient allocation of resources based on its own natural wealth, to raise living standards, and to meet national aspirations, would present a challenge to the whole Soviet system, which could not be tolerated. Underlying all the mixed sentiments of the post-war years were fatigue and fear – fatigue at the prospect of further economic austerity, and fear of a new wave of mass arrests and sudden disappearances. These fears soon materialized and any hopes or expectations of an easier way of life were replaced by new terrors, as the NKVD again sought out thousands of potential enemies to be sent to labour camps. Kazakhstan, and especially Alma-Ata which had suffered badly during the political purges of the late 1930s, once again experienced the full force of Stalinist oppression and control, and most people had no choice but to conform and do their best to keep out of trouble.

When Stalin died on 5 March 1953, popular reaction to his death combined genuine sorrow at the loss of the country's war-time leader with exaggerated and manipulated public grief verging on mass hysteria. In Kazakhstan, the reaction was more muted and ambivalent; the Russian population in Kazakhstan may have been saddened by Stalin's death but most Kazakhs, although not indifferent, were far less affected by the national mood of distress and bereavement. Any admiration for Stalin had always been overshadowed by the trauma of the collectivisation of agriculture and the ruination of the nomadic way of life. The people of Kazakhstan and Central Asia were not suited to working in heavy industry, and the forced industrialisation of the economy under Stalin was deeply resented. Stalin's seeming disdain for Kazakhstan and his use of the country as a convenient place of exile for deported nationalities further alienated the Kazakh population. Unfavourable opinions had become even more marked since the end of the war, when the benefits of Stalin's leadership were less apparent in Kazakhstan than in Russia, and were greatly outweighed by the re-imposition of extreme ideological controls, the resumption of arbitrary arrests and disappearances, and by the suppression of any nationalist aspirations. The national view of Stalin was highlighted in 1954, when the Lenin statue was erected in the central park of Alma-Ata. Such a statue would not have been permitted if Stalin was still alive, when Lenin's role in the Revolution was steadily being subordinated to that of Stalin himself. Two years before Khrushchev's denunciation of Stalin in 1956, by commissioning the statue of Lenin the party leadership in Kazakhstan passed over what would have been a clear opportunity to commemorate Stalin in a visible and unmistakable fashion, preferring instead the less contentious and politically safer memorial to Lenin. Stalin's war-time leadership counted for less than the execution or imprisonment of millions of innocent Kazakh citizens, the deportations to labour camps, and the unrestrained exploitation of the natural resources of Kazakhstan for the sake of the Soviet rather than the Kazakh economy. With few exceptions there were no streets or squares named after Stalin in Kazakhstan on his death as there had been after the death of Lenin, and the many existing Stalin place names were soon changed to commemorate other local and national figures.

***

The Gulag - the *Glavnoe Upravlenie Lagerei,* or Main Administration of Camps - was the division of the Soviet secret police responsible for managing the extensive chain of forced labour camps which had been set up throughout the Soviet Union after the Revolution. As well as ensuring that the vast and growing number of political prisoners could not threaten the Soviet system, the Gulag was also intended to provide a source of free labour for the state. In reality the system of the Gulag camps imposed a heavy financial burden on the whole economy. The camps earned revenues from the sale of timber, gold and other valuable materials, but output was severely constrained by inadequate food supplies for the inmates, primitive accommodation, poor medical facilities, and other harsh working conditions, all in remote locations on the steppe. Such earnings that were achieved from the Gulag system were far outweighed by the enormous financial burden of managing the thousands of guards, officials, and administrators, and transporting supplies to the camps and the output from the camps on the overloaded railway network. The Soviet government was willing to pay a price for keeping dissidents and other political trouble-makers out of the way, but the true cost of the system was obscured by a lack of clear accounting, and the camps devoured vast resources which could have been used more effectively elsewhere. Fear amongst officials to bring this to Stalin's attention ensured that the system continued to operate in an unproductive and economically-damaging way during Stalin's lifetime.

The Gulag was administered through a network of regional sub-divisions, including Siblag in western Siberia, Kraslag around the town of Krasnoyarsk in central Siberia, and Yuzhsiblag in southern Siberia around Lake Baikal. In Kazakhstan, the network of camps was known by the acronym *Karlag* and had its headquarters in Karaganda. The Karlag extended over the whole of the northern and eastern parts of the country, with principal camps at Karaganda, Dzhezhkazgan, Semipalatinsk, Pavlodar, Kokchetav, and Akmolinsk. These camps held thousands of nomads and farm workers from Kazakhstan and other parts of the Soviet Union who had resisted collectivisation. The largest numbers of inmates however were Soviet officials and other individuals suspected of sabotage, as well as artists, writers, university lecturers, and leaders of religious groups and national minorities, including Uzbeks, Tajiks, Kyrgyz, and Mongolians. Anyone who had lived abroad for any length of time, plus foreign communists who had sought refuge in Moscow from hostile regimes in their own countries, and inhabitants of territories in the border regions, especially Koreans and Chinese, were regarded as suspect and large numbers were forcibly relocated to camps in Kazakhstan, especially on the outbreak of war in 1941. All these prisoners were put to work in different ways, in railway building, mining, agriculture, forestry, and industry, and all suffered in extreme conditions of lack of food, clothing, and shelter.

Prisoners would frequently be deposited at places where camps did not yet exist, and new arrivals faced conditions similar to those which awaited the deported national groups in the 1940s. In his novel *Doctor Zhivago* Boris Pasternak described the setting up of a new camp:

'We got off the train. - A snow desert. Forest in the distance. Guards with rifles, muzzles pointing at us, wolf-dogs. At about the same time other groups were brought up. We were spread out and formed into a big polygon all over the field, facing outwards so that we shouldn't see each other. Then we were ordered down on our knees, and told to keep looking straight in front on pain of death. Then the roll-call, an endless, humiliating business going on for hours and hours, and all the time we were on our knees. Then we got up and the other groups were marched off in different directions, all except ours. We were told: 'Here you are. This is your camp.' – An open snow field with a post in the middle and a notice on it saying: 'Gulag 92 Y. N. 90' – that's all there was.... First we broke saplings with our bare hands in the frost, to get wood to build our huts with. And in the end, believe it or not, we built our own camp. We put up our prison and our stockade and our punishment cells and our watch towers, all with our own hands. And then we began our job as lumber-jacks. We felled trees. We harnessed ourselves, eight to a sledge, and we hauled timber and sank into the snow up to our necks'.

The prison camp at Akmolinsk – known by the Russian acronym as ALZhIR, the Akmolinsk Camp for the Wives of Traitors to the Motherland – was unique in that it was built exclusively for female prisoners, although it also included some of the sons and daughters of male prisoners who had been sent to other camps. The children may have been innocent but the wives of political prisoners were guilty by association with their husbands, and had to be accommodated somewhere. They could not be left to carry on with their lives after their husbands had been arrested and sentenced, possibly forming a secret opposition group and posing a risk to the regime. In the autumn of 1937, as arrests in the Great Terror were gaining in intensity, a remote and desolate site on the empty steppe, forty kilometres west of Akmolinsk, was identified as a suitable location for the new camp. Given the innocent name of Malinovka (Raspberry Farm) to conceal its more sinister purpose, the camp was hurriedly built on the site of a disused orphanage, and as soon as the first women prisoners arrived, in the winter of 1937-1938, a harsh and punitive so-called special regime was established. A high barbed-wire fence, interspersed with watch towers and patrolled by armed guards with dogs, extended around the camp. The guards were cruel and unsympathetic, seeing their role in terms of the class struggle, and the female prisoners as the contemporary equivalents of pre-revolutionary oppressors of the poor.

Conditions in the camp were exceptionally severe, with warmth and food barely sufficient to keep the prisoners alive. Work began before dawn and continued late into the night; failure to meet strict quotas resulted in transfer to a 'death zone' where food rations were cut completely. Communication with children who had been sent to distant orphanages when the women were arrested was prohibited, and most mothers and children had no idea where each other were. But there were some moments of comfort for the distraught and despairing women. According to possibly fanciful accounts and legends related in the Alzhir Museum which now stands on the site of the camp, jeering inhabitants of the neighbouring village, seeking to ingratiate themselves with the camp guards and local party officials, would throw stones and rocks at the despised class enemies recently arrived in their midst. In reality the stones were found to consist of bread and balls of solidified cheese known as *kurt*, encased in dried mud, intended to provide food to the starving inmates on the other side of the fence. These actions supposedly went some way to alleviating starvation in the camp.

By early 1939, when the camp had become more securely established, the 'special regime' was lifted and conditions began to improve. This was the second spring of the camp's existence and local food supplies had become slightly more plentiful. Letters and food parcels from relatives, if they could track down where the women had been sent, were allowed, which also did much to lessen the overwhelming sense of separation experienced by the inmates. Over time, regulations were relaxed further and the camp authorities permitted plays and concerts to be performed. But overall conditions in ALZhIR, and in other camps in Kazakhstan, although better than in most other camps in the Gulag, remained severe, and were not eased by the growing numbers of prisoners who had to be accommodated. By the outbreak of war, the population of the camp was estimated at 10,000, with new prisoners arriving at the rate of over 250 every month. Most were put to work on the land, or making uniforms for the Red Army. As the war progressed, the vital task of making army tunics, fur hats, leather boots, gloves and mittens, winter overcoats, and woolen socks meant that food supplies and living conditions in the camp continued to improve, so as to ensure that the maximum output for troops at the front could be maintained.

The ALZhIR camp continued to operate throughout the early 1950s, but after the death of Stalin it began to receive fewer prisoners until its eventual closure, together with other 'special' camps (mainly those for foreigners), in 1955. Its malign legacy, however, continued to exert an oppressive influence for many years and decades; far from rejoicing in their freedom at the end of their sentence, former prisoners were generally not permitted to return to their home towns and had to find work and somewhere to live wherever they could. Often this meant living illegally with relatives and under constant threat of discovery and denunciation by neighbours. Women who succeeded in reuniting with their families were often unable to convey a sense or understanding of the terrible conditions they had experienced 'on the other side', or to restore normal relationships with husbands and children, as their male counterparts were often equally unable to do on their release from camps where they had been imprisoned. Husbands and children were similarly incapable of adjusting to the return of a wife or mother who had been deprived of all normal life and nearly starved to death in the ALZhIR camp.

Years of silence and non-communication within families was often the result. Among the survivors of the ALZhIR, which although it was unique in Kazakhstan was just one of the hundreds of camps in the Gulag system, the thousands of broken homes and ruined relationships imposed an incalculable cost on family life, while the disruption caused by the millions of lives torn apart by the camps had a devastating effect on the national economy and on Soviet society as a whole. In the present-day city of Astana, little remains of its earlier existence as the remote Kazakh town of Akmolinsk, and much has been destroyed in the rush to build a modern capital city. But the post-independence government of Kazakhstan, by creating an enduring memorial and museum on the site of the ALZhIR camp, has ensured that this aspect of the country's history will not readily be forgotten. On a marble wall behind the Museum the names of the thousands of former inmates are carved to commemorate the innocent victims of Stalinist injustice.

The financial cost of the Gulag system had long been apparent, and was imposing a heavy burden on the rest of the economy. In the 1930s the camps had a clearly-defined function in incarcerating those victims of the Great Terror who had not been sentenced to death, and in the 1940s in holding those who might have undermined the war effort, and the rationale of the Gulag was not to be questioned. By the 1950s however, when the threat to the regime and to the country had diminished, it was increasingly apparent that the cost of maintaining the camps far exceeded any economic benefit. Despite this the number of camps continued to increase after the war, until developments in the Karlag in Kazakhstan in the early 1950s, and in isolated instances elsewhere, led directly to the end of the Gulag system in the Soviet Union. Those camps that remained open were put on a more rational economic basis.

After the war conditions in the camps were often worse than they had been in wartime, since the overriding need to increase output of clothes and other items for troops at the front had lessened, and heating supplies and food rations for prisoners could be cut back with apparently no adverse effect on the rest of the country. By 1951, disruption and unrest had spread throughout the Gulag, and the loss of production due to strikes and mass protests, by both criminal and political prisoners, increased significantly. For the government this represented an even greater financial burden on the state, since the camps were less able to offset their costs through higher output of goods for the rest of the economy. For the inmates it was the worsening living conditions, as well as a growing resentment at their incarceration for trivial or non-existent reasons, which led to mass protests and non-cooperation, culminating in uprisings, escapes, and hunger strikes, in various camps in Russia and Kazakhstan, notably in Vorkuta in northern Russia, and Ekibastuz near Pavlodar in northern Kazakhstan. In dealing with the Ekibastuz unrest, the camp authorities in Kazakhstan and Moscow, uncertain how to respond but aware that some action was essential, proposed a series of minor and ineffective reforms which did nothing to remedy the underlying grievances. The damaging effect on the economy of the forced labour system was now inescapable, as was the realisation that much greater, and much needed, output could be achieved if many thousands of innocent prisoners, or even those considered to be guilty but not dangerous, could be released to work as free labourers. In *The Gulag Archipelago,* his three-volume account of the Soviet labour camps, Alexander Solzhenitsyn described how 'the Special Camp system was beginning to collapse in one place after another, but our Father and Teacher (Stalin) had no inkling of it – it was not, of course, reported to him'. Nothing could be done during Stalin's lifetime, and it was only after his death in 1953 that significant changes could be made.

In the spring of 1954, in the camp at the village of Kengirskoe, on the arid, lifeless steppe just north of Dzhezkazgan in central Kazakhstan, a series of incidents took place which ended in violence and bloodshed, but which came to mark a turning point in the history of the Gulag. The sequence of events is described in detail by Solzhenitsyn in 'The Forty Days of Kengir', in *The Gulag Archipelago.* The Kengir camp, part of the extensive Steplag complex, was a vast settlement of over 5,000 prisoners, mainly from the non-Russian republics; nearly half of the inmates were Ukrainians, with the rest mainly Estonians, Latvians, Lithuanians, Georgians, Chechens, and smaller numbers of other nationalities. After the death of Stalin and the subsequent arrest and execution of Lavrenti Beria, who as head of the NKVD had been responsible for administering the Gulag, the prisoners at Kengir, and in other camps, became increasingly restless and unruly in the hope of taking advantage of the changing circumstances in the outside world. But in Kengir, what began as a succession of strikes and protests ended in events spiraling out of control, and a dramatic outcome which changed the nature of the Gulag system.

In the early 1950s the MVD (Ministry of Internal Affairs), which had taken over responsibility from the NKVD for prisons and camps, was increasingly aware of the drain on resources imposed by the camps, and fearful that its own role may be diminished. 'It was now urgent for the security ministry to prove its devotion and usefulness in some signal way. The mutinies (in the camps) which the security men had hitherto considered a menace, now shone like a beacon of salvation' wrote Solzhenitsyn. Imagining a conversation among Gulag officials, he wrote: *'Let's have more disturbances and disorder so that measures will have to be taken. The staff and our salaries will not be reduced'.* In the winter of 1953 and spring of 1954 the camp guards at Kengir, supposedly in an attempt to provoke a more serious revolt, opened fire on and killed several prisoners, but this failed to have the desired effect of causing a rebellion, and a different tactic was needed. In mid-May 1954 the camp authorities decided to introduce into the camp up to 650 ordinary criminals, thieves, and petty offenders, with the aim of provoking fights with the resident inmates, which it was hoped would necessitate stronger intervention. This plan also failed; the criminals and political prisoners had more in common than the camp authorities anticipated, and decided to join forces. 'The bosses obtained not a pacified camp but the biggest mutiny in the history of the Gulag Archipelago. Events followed their inevitable course. It was impossible for the politicals not to offer the thieves a choice between war and alliance. It was impossible for the thieves to refuse an alliance. And it was impossible for the alliance, once concluded, to remain inactive', was how Solzhenitsyn described what happened.

The first action to be taken by the prisoners and their new allies was the demolition of a stone wall separating themselves from the service yard and warehouses where all the camp food stores were held. The wall also separated male and female prisoners, and many prisoners believed they would be coming to the aid of the women who had been consistently subjected to mistreatment and rape by the camp guards. Through the afternoon and night of 16–17 May, a large group of prisoners worked steadily to break down the wall with a growing feeling of comradeship and common purpose. Initially the camp guards did not intervene, but early the following morning their reaction was sudden and violent; thirteen prisoners were shot and killed and a further forty-three were wounded. Other prisoners, male and female, were attacked and beaten up. Far from being cowed, the prisoners responded with exhortations to further violent resistance and demands that the 'murderers' among the guards should be put on trial. Anti-Soviet slogans were scrawled on the walls of the canteen. Throughout the camp unrest continued unchecked, as the prisoners released 252 of their fellow inmates held in solitary confinement, took control of the camp kitchen, bakery, warehouses, and workshops, and immediately set about producing makeshift weapons out of the tools and implements held there. By 19 May, three days after the start of the uprising, a stalemate had been reached, with most of the prisoners on strike and the authorities in Kengir and in Alma-Ata at a loss as to what should be done.

On 21 May, in response to an urgent request from Viktor Bochkov, the commander of the Kengir camp, and Konstantin Gubin, the head of the Kazakh ministry of security who had travelled to Kengir from Alma-Ata, a delegation arrived from Moscow to seek a resolution to the crisis. This included Sergei Yegorov, the deputy head of the MVD, and Ivan Dolgich, the head of the Gulag system. The prisoners had formed what they called a Centre, a governing body dominated by Ukrainians but including representatives of all the nationalities in the camp; the Centre appointed a strike committee which would organise daily life in the camp and conduct negotiations with the camp authorities. The committee elected as its leader Colonel Kapiton Kuznetsov, a former Red Army officer and one of the few Russian prisoners in Kengir. Kuznetsov had been captured by the Germans during the war, a fate which accounted for his presence in the camp, and was chosen by the mainly-Ukrainian strike committee to present a more acceptable 'face' in the negotiations, thereby avoiding any appearance of the committee being anti-Russian or anti-Soviet. Kuznetsov readily accepted this role, urging the prisoners to hang banners proclaiming 'Long Live the Soviet Constitution', and to avoid provoking the guards, so as to present the strikers in the most positive and conciliatory light possible.

Ostensibly the delegation from Moscow was well-disposed to the demands of the prisoners and professed to be shocked at the mistreatment which had been meted out to them by the camp guards. Those responsible for the shootings and for the attacks on female prisoners would, they said, be held to account. Other demands put forward by the prisoners, including freedom of movement within the camp and the removal of locks on the hut doors, an eight-hour day as existed for free workers, an increase in payment for work, unrestricted correspondence with relatives and periodic visits from wives and relations, and a review of individual prisoners' cases, were all supposedly taken seriously. 'There was nothing unconstitutional in any of these demands, nothing that threatened the foundations of the state; many of them were requests for a return to the old position (before the strikes)', according to Solzhenitsyn. But it was impossible for the authorities to accede to the prisoners' wishes, however uncontroversial they may have been, since to do so would be to admit to far-reaching mistakes in policies in the camps over the previous months and years. Even the concept of negotiations with prisoners was anathema to the government, and if the Kengir uprising and strike had taken place a few years earlier before Stalin died, there would not have been any discussion at all. But official attitudes, especially towards long sentences given to political prisoners, were beginning to change, and what happened over the following days in Kengir served to expedite further the process of reform to the system, although this was dictated as much by economic factors as by changing political circumstances.

Solzhenitsyn relates how throughout the rest of May and into the first half of June 1954, negotiations continued 'on the loftiest diplomatic model' and even refreshments were provided by the inmates for the 'guests'. At one stage, on 23 May, the prisoners returned to work but resumed the strike when the walls which they had earlier demolished were rebuilt. The strike committee had effectively become the government of the camp; Kuznetsov organised the distribution of food, although rations were steadily cut back as food supplies in the stores diminished and no deliveries came in from outside. The camp authorities cut off the electricity supply in the first days of the strike, prompting the prisoners to generate their own electricity using water from a tap. A camp radio station was constructed, broadcasting news of developments to the prisoners and to the villagers in Kengirskoe and the guards and troops. Entertainments, concerts, and lectures were organised. As well as radio broadcasts, the prisoners passed the time by using balloons, kites, and pigeons to convey news of events in the camp to the outside world, asking anyone who found any of the leaflets to deliver it to the Soviet Central Committee in Moscow. Kuznetsov opposed this tactic, but the Chechen inmates in the prison were particularly determined to embarrass the authorities as much as possible. The guards responded by making kites of their own to tangle with and bring down the prisoners' kites, a development derided by Solzhenitsyn as 'a war of kites in the second half of the twentieth century! And all to silence a word of truth'.

Throughout this time the officials sent by the government continued to negotiate, trying to persuade the prisoners to abandon their strike, without achieving anything of significance to report back to Moscow. They knew that what was happening threatened not only their own careers but the future of the Kengir camp, and the whole structure of the Gulag. The situation dragged on inconclusively for forty days. For most of the time it was possible, even encouraged, for the prisoners to escape from the camp, even though there was nowhere for them to go, so that only the most stubborn would be left, who would then be more easily overcome. But if this was another ploy on the part of the authorities it also failed, since only about a dozen men fled from the camp, out of the total camp population of more than 5,000 inmates.

By 15 June the Central Committee in Moscow had lost patience at the lack of progress and Sergei Kruglov, the head of the MVD, sharply informed Yegorov, the deputy head who had been leading the negotiations that the strike was going to be ended by troops and tanks being sent from the nearby army base at Dzhezkazgan. In the preceding days the camp garrison had been steadily reinforced and the whole camp had been encircled with a double barbed wire fence outside the walls. The mood in the camp became tense, as the earlier informal atmosphere was replaced by warnings and threats from the MVD officials of what would happen if the strike was not ended soon. The prisoners were unmoved and continued to broadcast messages of defiance on their rudimentary radio station to the outside world, further provoking the MVD and confirming to Kruglov that his choice of action was inevitable and correct. On 16 June several tractors appeared in the settlement and started work, for no apparent purpose, even into the night. 'The unfriendly roar made the night seem blacker', and according to Solzhenitsyn their real purpose was to disguise the sound of tanks moving into position.

In the early dawn of 25 June, the sky was lit by scores of flares carried by parachutes above the camp and others fired from the watchtowers. Aircraft flew low overhead, spreading panic among the inmates, suddenly woken and disoriented by the dazzling light. As had been promised by Kruglov, five T34 tanks, of the type which had been so successful during the war, and which had now surrounded the camp, crashed through the barbed wire fence, firing at the barracks and huts and crushing under their tracks anyone who got in their way. Several prisoners made suicidal attempts to stop them by forming human chains to stand in their path. Behind the tanks came 1,700 soldiers who soon pacified the camp, but not before killing or wounding more than 700 male and female prisoners. All the others who had survived the attack were taken out of the camp and forced to lie face down all day in the blazing sun, while the troops searched the camp for any remaining prisoners who might still be alive. A total of 436 people were arrested, including all the members of the strike committee, of whom six were later executed. Kapiton Kuznetsov, the leader of the committee, was also sentenced to death but after making a lengthy confession of his role in the rebellion, which possibly incriminated other members of the committee, he was transferred to the main Karlag camp at Karaganda where he was held until his release in 1960. More than 1,000 other prisoners who had been involved in the uprising were sent to camps in Kolyma in northern Siberia or elsewhere in Russia. Those who remained were made to spend the next day, 26 June, taking down the barricades and the following day were put back to work.

The 'Forty Days of Kengir' (17 May-26 June 1954) was a short but decisive period in the history of the forced labour camps of the USSR. The immediate result was a major defeat for the leaders of the rebellion who defied not only the camp authorities but in effect the leadership of the Soviet Union, and the crisis ended in the violent deaths of hundreds of prisoners. But the later consequences of the uprising were more far-reaching, and over the following ten years, profound social and political changes, partly triggered by the events at Kengir, were to take place in the Soviet Union, before a new leadership in Moscow came to power in 1964, and put into reverse many of the developments of the previous decade. The Kengir episode delivered a major shock to the Soviet penal system, not only because of the ruthless manner, even by Soviet standards, in which the revolt was suppressed, but also because it led to the publication of more unwelcome evidence of the drain imposed by the Gulag on the country's finances. Within a month of the end of the uprising, on 10 July 1954 the government announced more reforms to the prison regime designed to improve labour productivity and lessen the burden of the camps on the state budget. Some of these measures had been among the reforms demanded by the striking prisoners, such as a return to an eight-hour working day, the freedom to write letters and receive parcels of food and clothing, and even in some camps the freedom for prisoners to get married and live with their spouses. The ALZhIR prison at Akmolinsk for wives of traitors to the motherland, and some of the other special camps specifically for foreigners, were closed the following year. This process was pushed forward in the more open post-Stalin political atmosphere by the Soviet leader Nikita Khrushchev and the new head of the Ministry of Internal Affairs (MVD) Nikolai Dudorov who replaced Sergei Kruglov after the Kengir debacle. But it was strongly resisted by the KGB, which had been separated from the MVD in 1946, and by Ivan Dolgich, who had managed to retain his position as head of the Gulag itself. The government was motivated by the need to release unproductive labour from the camps into the economy at large, where growth was being held back by an acute labour shortage, especially among scientists, technicians, managers, and agricultural experts, many of whom were held in the camps and who were badly needed if Soviet industry and agriculture were to progress. For its part the KGB opposed the release of prisoners, on ideological grounds and on the basis of its own self-interest. The conflict between these opposing forces ended in a defeat for the KGB and the decision, in 1956, to close the whole of the Gulag system. This was a significant development in Soviet history, although it represented more of an administrative change in the state bureaucracy rather than any softening of official attitudes. From now on the economic functions of the Gulag, such as forestry, farming, mining, road building, and other productive activities were transferred to the relevant industrial ministries, where it was hoped greater levels of output and productivity could be achieved. The network of prison camps would continue to function solely for punitive purposes.

The consequence was not an unmitigated benefit for the economy or the country. When the women prisoners who had already been released from the ALZhIR camp returned home, it was usually without any warning or preparation, and often they were mentally and physically unfit for release and totally unprepared to resume their previous lives. Now the same process was to be repeated on a national scale with many thousands of male and female prisoners released from other camps and expected to return to their homes and jobs. Even where jobs existed and were waiting to be filled, the huge numbers of released prisoners meant that they could not all be readily absorbed into their workplaces or into their communities. The notion of the Gulag, which for much of the population had been something unpleasant but vague and remote, was now brought home on a domestic level to families throughout the country as thousands of prisoners, isolated for many years from the outside world, returned to wives and children who were equally unprepared to receive them. Unexpected releases of political prisoners took place in tsarist times and a famous painting by the Russian artist Ilya Repin entitled *They Did Not Expect Him* (1888) shows an unshaven and shabbily-dressed convict returning home to his aristocratic family who are astonished, even fearful, to see him still alive. Similar scenes were now taking place in thousands of homes and communities throughout the Soviet Union. The problem would have been even greater if every prisoner arrested on false charges had been released, and if many of the camps had not continued to function, but instead remained open. The numbers of those discharged from the camps after 1954 ran into millions, and the process had to be strictly controlled for fear of overwhelming towns and cities even further as prisoners came home. The hoped-for economic benefit to the country was far outweighed by the incalculable social cost of family breakdown, alcoholism, homelessness, vagrancy, and other enormous problems which were probably not foreseen and for which no provision had been made. Many of those who were released, despite the terrible experiences which they had endured, rejoined the Communist Party as part of their process of readjustment, and to meet the psychological need for a sense of belonging, especially in their new circumstances of disorientation and inability to deal with life outside the camps. In those camps that remained in operation, conditions were no less severe than before, and strikes and unrest continued on a wide scale.

The dismantling of the Gulag was given further impetus by the publication in November 1962 of Alexander Solzhenitsyn's short novel *One Day in the Life of Ivan Denisovich*. Solzhenitsyn had served in an artillery regiment on the western front throughout the autumn and winter of 1943, but had been arrested after making critical remarks about Stalin in a letter which had been intercepted by the NKVD. He was deeply shocked by the severe treatment he received after his return from the front, but even more so by the fate which befell those Red Army soldiers who had been captured by the Germans and then later arrested by the KGB on suspicion of collusion with the enemy. He gained first-hand experience of prison life when he was sentenced to terms of forced labour in camps near Moscow and in Karaganda. It was the experiences he gained in the camps which formed the basis of *One Day in the Life of Ivan Denisovich*. The book was a sharply critical account of the prison camp system as seen through the eyes of one of the inmates, and in the relative freedom of the political and cultural thaw of the time, it had a dramatic effect on attitudes towards the Gulag and towards the Communist Party and the Soviet regime.

By the time of the publication of the book, the system of the Gulag was already nearing its end. But the bitter clash between the reformers in the MVD, aware of the counterproductive nature of the Gulag, and the ideologists in the KGB, who clung to reactionary views of the need for punishment of offenders, even at the expense of the innocent, was symptomatic of a much wider controversy about life in the Soviet Union as a whole. Liberals and reformists took encouragement from Solzhenitsyn and others seeking greater freedom of self-expression. In the event the KGB emerged the strongest and two years after the publication of *One Day in the Life of Ivan Denisovich,* the political atmosphere changed again when in October 1964 Khrushchev was removed from power and Leonid Brezhnev became First Secretary of the Soviet Communist Party. Prisons and the remaining labour camps began to fill up again with political dissidents and other opponents of the regime.

For Kazakhstan, the longer-term consequences of the camps at ALZhIR and Kengir were particularly significant. News of the treatment of women prisoners at ALZhIR, and of the violent suppression of the uprising at Kengir, although completely avoided on the radio and in the press, spread widely throughout the country by means of the so-called *uzin kulak* ('long ear') of the steppe telegraph. Kazakhstan and its population were remote from political controversies in Moscow, but were very much aware of what had been happening on their own territory, and the treatment of prisoners in ALZhIR and the actions of Russian troops in putting down the Kengir rebellion, were widely resented. These developments served to undermine Kazakhstan's sense of loyalty to Russia and the Soviet Union, and played a significant part in the growth of nationalist sentiments in the republic.

CHAPTER NINETEEN

The Virgin Lands Campaign

Virgin Soil Upturned was the title of a 1932 novel by the Soviet writer Mikhail Sholokhov, who among other books also wrote *And Quiet Flows the Don* (1936) and *The Don Flows Home to the Sea* (1940). Sholokhov was greatly admired by Stalin despite the fact that his novels were often critical of the collectivisation of agriculture in the 1920s and 1930s, and that they lamented the loss of the old way of life in the Russian countryside. The more political aspect of Sholokhov's other writings, especially as a journalist during the war, was more highly regarded than his nostalgia for the past. The Virgin Lands campaign of the 1950s, which was intended to revolutionise agriculture in the vast land of northern Kazakhstan and the bordering regions of central Russia, was to recall the heroic efforts of the early years of the Revolution, when the old methods of agriculture were overthrown, albeit at great cost, and replaced by a more productive socialist system. Instead of the terror and coercion of the collectivisation thirty years earlier, the Virgin Lands campaign was to derive its inspiration from the post-war enthusiasm for a better and more egalitarian future.

In 1953 Kazakhstan became one of the battlegrounds in the power struggle taking place in Moscow between the challengers for the Soviet leadership after the death of Stalin. The three main contenders were Nikita Khrushchev, whom Stalin had appointed to succeed him as First Secretary of the Communist Party; Lavrenti Beria, the head of the secret police; and Georgy Malenkov, Chairman of the Council of Ministers and effectively the head of the government. Initially Khrushchev and Malenkov formed a tenuous alliance to eliminate Beria, who had begun to develop his own political support beyond the enormous police organisation he controlled, but who was widely despised in the country as a whole given his role in terrorising the population in the Great Terror and in the war. Beria was arrested and executed in July 1953, in a swift and dramatic downfall as one of the most reviled figures in Soviet history. Thereafter Khrushchev and Malenkov set about trying to destroy each other's reputation and in this struggle the national economy, and in particular the place of agriculture, was to be the principal field of contention. It was clear that since the war the economy under Stalin's leadership had again become seriously out of balance, with a renewed and excessive emphasis on the heavy industry and defence sectors, at the expense of housing, clothing, and the supply of food and basic consumer goods. In agriculture the situation was critical; every stage in the food production cycle was hampered by inefficiencies in management and bureaucracy, and the sector was unable to provide sufficient food for the growing population. Underlying the whole economy was the rigid and highly-centralised system of central planning, which allocated investment according to political considerations and set often unattainable output targets. The system was not responsive to the needs of the country, and effectively prevented any improvement in living standards for the majority of the population. Although both Khrushchev and Malenkov agreed on their analysis of these problems, it was Khrushchev who was successful in discrediting Malenkov and thereby consolidating his own position as First Secretary of the Communist Party. He exploited the dire state of agriculture to further strengthen his role by blaming the government and the agricultural ministries, for which Malenkov was ultimately responsible, for the failures in one of the most important sectors of the economy.

The solutions proposed by Khrushchev during the second half of 1953 called for far-reaching changes in the system of agricultural production throughout the Soviet Union. These changes included financial incentives for the state and collective farms to increase their output, drastic increases in the price the government paid for meat and dairy products, and in a clear break with earlier Stalinist dogmas, support for private ownership of small plots and livestock holdings. As well as financial incentives and measures to extend private ownership, at the same time thousands of agricultural experts and party officials were to be sent to the countryside to exercise closer political control over the collective farms. In many parts of the USSR, especially Kazakhstan, the efficient operation of the sovkhozy (state farms) and kolkhozy (collective farms) was still very weak, and stronger management from the centre was seen as crucial.

The most dramatic and controversial policy initiative, launched by Khrushchev in February 1954, was the Virgin Lands campaign. This was a particularly ambitious project for the extension of agriculture and especially of grain production to the uncultivated but potentially arable steppes of northern Kazakhstan and south-western Siberia. The notion of expansion of agriculture through the use of previously-unexploited or abandoned land was not new, and the proposed development of the steppe had precedents dating back to tsarist times. But the Virgin Lands scheme was unprecedented in its geographical scale, in its political and strategic importance, and in the amount of investment which it would entail. The scheme proposed that in 1954 and 1955 more than 80,000 square kilometres should be ploughed up for growing wheat, with a further 160,000 square kilometres to be added in 1956, and still further expansion every year until 1961. Most of the land designated for this purpose was in northern Kazakhstan, although vast areas of Russia adjacent to Kazakhstan were also included. The strategy behind the scheme was that wheat grown in this region would help feed the Soviet Union's growing industrial population, reduce Soviet dependence on imported foodstuffs, and release land in other regions of western Russia and Ukraine which were better suited to different forms of agriculture, particularly animal fodder and livestock.

The campaign was to be centred in the town of Akmolinsk, the old Kazakh settlement on the banks of the River Ishim, and which forty-three years later was to become the capital of Kazakhstan. In early times there had been an important trading centre on a prominent hill, hence its original Kazakh name of Akmola meaning 'white hill', also variously translated as 'white tomb' reflecting the site of a nearby cemetery. By the beginning of the nineteenth century it was a simple caravanserai on the caravan route from Tashkent and Bukhara to Russia and Europe, and in 1830 it was chosen by the tsarist army as the site for a fort, one of the chain of redoubts and look-out posts to be constructed in the lands between Russia and Kazakhstan. Despite its remoteness and distance from Moscow and St Petersburg, the strategic location of the site, in the central part of the expanding tsarist empire, gave it considerable military and economic importance, and its trading activities continued to grow. During the Russian civil war it changed hands between the White Guard and the Red Army, before Soviet power was eventually established in November 1919, two years after the Revolution. In the Great Patriotic War the town played a crucial role in forwarding food, guns, artillery, military equipment, clothing, and essential supplies of every description to the front, as well as receiving hundreds of thousands of civilian evacuees, treating thousands of wounded service personnel, and rebuilding many of the factories which had been dismantled and evacuated to safety from western Russia.

Even after the rapid development which had taken place during the war years, by the early 1950s Akmolinsk and the surrounding region of northern Kazakhstan was still a vast, empty land with only a rudimentary infrastructure of dirt roads and simple airfields, limited electricity supplies, and poor communications with the rest of the country. The town was several hundred kilometres from the TurkSib railway, and although it had been connected to the Trans-Siberian railway by means of a branch line from the Russian town of Petropavlovsk to Karaganda since 1931, this line was almost exclusively used for the transportation of coal from the Karaganda mines to Russian power stations and factories, and was in great need of investment and improvement. Apart from unlimited expanse of flat and unexploited land, the territory had little to offer. Everything that would be needed for the Virgin Lands campaign had to be brought in from elsewhere, and the scheme was full of unquantifiable risks and uncertainties. Khrushchev had considerable experience as an agricultural manager in Ukraine before and after the war, but in the opinion of most of the population of Kazakhstan, his credibility was severely undermined by his earlier support for the theories of Trofim Lysenko, a plant biologist who in the 1930s had convinced Stalin that he could breed new strains of plants suited to different climatic conditions. Lysenko ignored decades of research which proved that plants could not always adapt to different environments, but his ideas appealed to Stalin's belief in the possibility of subjecting nature to politically-motivated theories, theories which would open up vast new opportunities for increasing agricultural production. Lysenko was praised and acclaimed by Stalin, while established geneticists and agricultural experts in Russia and Kazakhstan who challenged his theories were ignored or banished to labour camps.

Opposition to Khrushchev's plans for the Virgin Lands were most clearly expressed by Kazakh party leaders and particularly by Zhumabai Shayakhmetov, the First Secretary of the Kazakh Communist Party. Shayakhmetov agreed in principle with the planned extension of arable land in Kazakhstan, but argued that such a rapid and far-reaching programme was not viable. It would bring into the country a massive new influx of Russian workers and settlers, thereby further reducing the status of the Kazakh population in their own country, which was already in a minority in the northern parts of Kazakhstan, and it would destroy what was left of the Kazakh grasslands and remaining nomadic practices. Shayakhmetov and agricultural experts in Kazakhstan also warned of practical difficulties in implementing the project. The light, friable soil of the northern steppe was subject to erosion by warm, dry winds blowing from the deserts of Central Asia to the south, which also carried a high risk of drought and weed infestation. Unless careful methods of cultivation were followed the result would be dust bowl conditions. These lands had supported nomadic communities and provided for the gentle grazing of their livestock over the centuries, but intensive development and cultivation on the scale proposed could end in disaster. Many Western accounts of this period make the assertion that these warnings were dismissed and simply brushed aside, although it is more likely that they were considered to be a risk that would have to be accepted. Even so it soon became clear that insufficient attention was paid to the exhaustive and detailed planning which would be essential for such a major project to succeed. The experience of the war-time evacuation of factories from Russia to Kazakhstan seemed to have been forgotten in the rush to bring the vast new areas of empty land into maximum production in the shortest possible time, and the many realities of the local environment were subordinated to political expediency, whereas a more gradual approach would have been more productive in the long run.

Before the Virgin Lands campaign could be formally launched, Khrushchev had to overcome the opposition from the Kazakh Communist Party, and in particular he had to remove Shayakhmetov, the main opponent to the scheme, from the leadership. Shayakhmetov was the fourth person and the first Kazakh to hold the post of First Secretary of the Communist Party of Kazakhstan, after Filipp Goloshchekin (a Russian, from 1923-1933), Levon Mirzoyan (Armenian, from 1933-1938), and Nikolai Skvortsov (Russian, from 1938-1945). As such Shayakhmetov's position held considerable importance in Kazakhstan and no compliant replacement for him could readily be found from within the local Party. In any event, Khrushchev wanted to appoint a Russian who would be more loyal to the Communist Party and to the Soviet Union than to Kazakhstan, and he had already identified a suitable person for the role, in the form of Leonid Ilyich Brezhnev, a dedicated party official and later the Soviet leader. Brezhnev was an agricultural specialist with experience in land management and reclamation. He was familiar with modern agricultural machinery, and had the technical knowledge and expertise needed for managing a large-scale development project. During the war he had served under Khrushchev in the Ukrainian First Army, and from 1950-1952 he had been the First Secretary of the Communist Party of Moldavia, where he had gained experience working with a generally hostile non-Russian population in a predominantly agricultural republic. Moldavia had been an unenthusiastic member of the Soviet Union since its involuntary incorporation in the USSR in 1940. After the war it underwent an intense Sovietisation campaign in which the language, the only Romance language spoken in the Soviet Union, was converted from the Latin to the Cyrillic alphabet, although that was a minor irritation compared to the treatment of those whose loyalty to the Soviet Union was in any way uncertain. Between 1945 and 1950 an estimated 500,000 of the total population of 3,000,000 were either executed, sentenced to prison camps, or deported to Kazakhstan and Siberia, for allegedly having collaborated with the Germans during the war, or for any of a long list of other crimes which included engaging in anti-Soviet propaganda or counter-revolutionary activity, having been part of the agricultural kulak class, or belonging to one of the many non-Communist political parties. Before it became part of the Soviet Union Moldavia had escaped the collectivisation of agriculture under Stalin in the 1930s, but underwent its own version in 1948 which was equally painful and disruptive. By 1950 only 80 percent of the land had been collectivised, and the sector was in a deeply depressed state, not least due to resistance from the uncooperative agricultural population. Anti-Soviet resistance groups continued to fight alongside partisan bands in the adjacent provinces of Ukraine, exacerbated the prevailing tension and instability in the republic.

Against this unwelcoming background Brezhnev had no qualms about forcefully imposing a strict Soviet regime in Moldavia, and from his arrival in the capital Kishinev in July 1950, he set about taking over the remaining privately-owned farms and introducing severe penalties for private trading and other activities regarded as economic crimes. Deportations to Kazakhstan and Siberia of anyone suspected of holding anti-Soviet opinions continued, especially from Kishinev and other towns, and more Russians were encouraged to migrate to Moldavia, thereby considerably diluting the indigenous population. Over the next two years Brezhnev brought stability and Soviet orthodoxy to the small but wayward republic, before he was appointed to a position on the Central Committee in Moscow in 1952. For Khrushchev this experience, and the ruthless qualities which Brezhnev had demonstrated in Moldavia, made him the ideal candidate to take over the party leadership in the much bigger republic of Kazakhstan, where he would be given the enormous task of managing the Virgin Lands campaign. But although he had eliminated challenges to the leadership from Beria and Malenkov, in the uncertain political atmosphere in Moscow Khrushchev could not command sufficient authority to appoint precisely whom he wished, and internal party feuding meant that in September 1953 he was compelled to choose Panteleimon Ponomarenko, an ally of Malenkov, who was still Prime Minister and Chairman of the Council of Ministers, to take over as First Secretary in Kazakhstan. Brezhnev was to be the second secretary. Ponomarenko had held various positions in the Soviet government, most recently as minister of culture, but his main qualification for being transferred to Kazakhstan was to be his role in reporting to Malenkov on the progress of the Virgin Lands campaign. If the project was successful, Malenkov and Ponomarenko would take the credit; if it was a failure, Khrushchev and Brezhnev would take the blame, and Malenkov's position, and challenge for the Soviet leadership, would be greatly strengthened.

Once the appointments of Ponomarenko and Brezhnev had been decided in Moscow, the next step was to engineer the removal of Shayakhmetov and of the existing Kazakh Party leadership in Alma-Ata. In January 1954 Shayakhmetov, the second secretary of the Kazakh Party Ivan Afonov, and other senior officials were summoned to a meeting with the Soviet government in Moscow, where they were sharply criticised for their opposition to the Virgin Lands campaign, and were charged with other instances of allegedly not complying with Communist Party principles. Accusations of promoting their own friends and relatives at the expense of other candidates were probably true and in keeping with local practices, and thus by no means unheard of. Whatever the exact situation, the charges gave a pretext for the dismissal of Shayakhmetov and Afonov, and in February 1954 Ponomarenko and Brezhnev were confirmed in their positions at a special meeting of the Central Committee of the Kazakh Communist Party. Shayakhmetov was transferred to Chimkent as first secretary of the party in south Kazakhstan, before being dismissed by Brezhnev from the leadership altogether in June 1955. In January of the same year, Khrushchev had strengthened his position in the Soviet leadership in relation to Malenkov, who was forced to resign as Prime Minister. No longer having a powerful protector in Moscow, in Alma-Ata Ponomarenko himself was now vulnerable, and in May 1955 was removed from Kazakhstan and appointed as Soviet ambassador to Poland, leaving Brezhnev in sole charge of the Communist Party in Kazakhstan. These developments effectively neutralised the local party and gave a free hand to Khrushchev and Brezhnev in governing the country as they saw fit, particularly in relation to implementing the Virgin Lands campaign. The new leadership also left the local population feeling humiliated and resentful that decisions concerning their country were once again taken by the Soviet government in Moscow without necessarily being in the best interests of Kazakhstan. All this added a sharp human dimension to the practical and environmental difficulties facing what was to become one of the most far-reaching upheavals in Kazakh history.

Brezhnev was now faced with the enormous task of converting highly ambitious and demanding plans drawn up in remote government ministries in Moscow, into action and reality on the steppe. The campaign called for the creation of nearly three hundred new state farms, each extending over an area of a minimum of 50,000 acres. Thousands of combine harvesters, lorries, tractors, and thousands of tons of agricultural equipment and machinery had to be transported to Kazakhstan and distributed among the new farms. To achieve this, more than 3,000 kilometres of new railway lines, mostly narrow gauge, and hundreds of kilometres of new roads had to be laid. Many thousands of agricultural experts were reassigned from other regions of the country, regions which accordingly lost their expertise, while many more thousands of Komsomol volunteers from the youth wing of the Communist Party, responding to the government's appeals and propaganda, came to Kazakhstan to join the campaign. More thousands of demobilised soldiers, tractor drivers, combine harvester operators, and other specialists flooded into the towns and villages, and into the open countryside, often without clear directions as to where they should go and what they should do, but keen to be part of a major project in the building of socialism. By the end of 1956, a vast new army of more than 500,000 workers had arrived in Kazakhstan, compared with a total population at the time of approximately fifteen million. This was a critical period in Soviet history, coinciding with the Hungarian Uprising and its violent suppression by Soviet forces, and the government in Moscow was anxious not only to ensure the success of the campaign, but also to extract the maximum propaganda value to set against the negative picture of the Soviet Union abroad.

A vast amount of exhaustive planning and preparation had gone into the Virgin Lands campaign, but this mainly consisted of drawing up endless schedules and detailed inventories of what would be needed, but insufficient attention was given to the logistics of transport, delivery, unloading, and distribution. Consequently the gap between what was laid down in Moscow and what actually arrived in the places where it was needed in Kazakhstan was wide and often unbridgeable. Distribution of agricultural machinery, when it finally reached its destination, was haphazard and often chaotic. Without cranes and other off-loading gear, local railway stations and depots could not cope with the vast amounts of new equipment arriving every day. Much of the machinery allocated to the project consisted of new models and designs, unfamiliar to workers used to operating older tractors and harvesters, and was frequently left idle for want of training and instruction. Lack of fuel, spare parts, and shelter from the harsh climate impeded the use of other equipment. Enormous quantities of concrete, timber, glass, and other construction materials destined for the extensive housing projects intended to accommodate the new arrivals failed to appear, having been stolen, damaged, or lost en route, with the result that by each successive winter many thousands of workers were still living in tents. Thousands of field kitchens and material for pre-fabricated housing also disappeared. In those places where housing or basic dormitories were constructed, there were often no chairs, tables, kitchen utensils, or knives and forks. Where electricity was available there was frequently an absence of lamp sockets and light bulbs, and evenings were often dark and cold. These shortfalls could not be remedied with supplies from the nearest towns, which were mostly hundreds of kilometres away. For the hundreds of thousands of workers arriving in Kazakhstan, provision had been made for only a tiny number of doctors, dentists, and midwives. When the programme eventually got under way and harvesting began, vast amounts of grain which had been successfully grown could not be distributed for lack of warehouses, lorries, sacks and crates, and serviceable roads. Breakages, disorganisation, corruption, and confusion all combined to leave many volunteers, initially full of idealism and hope, in a state of apathy and disarray.

There was little sympathy from the local population. The few remaining nomadic families whose sheep and cattle still grazed where they could on the territory designated for the campaign were soon driven away. The rest of the population in the Virgin Lands regions consisted largely of Volga Germans, Chechens and other ethnic groups from the Caucasus who had been deported there during the war. Other local inhabitants included the descendants of nineteenth-century Ukrainian settlers and political deportees whose ancestors had been exiled in tsarist times. All of these people had arrived in earlier times with no means of support and had been forced to fend for themselves, and none of them had any interest in the Virgin Lands campaign or in helping the new arrivals. For the rest of the indigenous Kazakh population, living conditions were rudimentary in the extreme. A village teacher described life for one community in the Semipalatinsk region:

'There were no houses as such, only *semlyanki* (dugouts) with straw roofs and dirt floors. Straw and dried cow and horse dung were used to heat them in winter and to cook. We had about fifty of these in the village and the total population was around three hundred. Even the school was a *semlyanka* with a dirt floor. Only two of the huts were laid out with wooden planks: those of the *kolkhoz* chairman and the party secretary. In the school we had no books, no paper, no educational materials to speak of. During the winter of 1954-1955 animal fodder was so scarce that we stripped the straw off the school roof to feed the livestock and held no more classes until late spring. We had no running water, only a well, and the village was not electrified until 1956. The school itself did not receive electric light until 1959. It was eighty kilometres to the railway line, more than thirty to the town . . . where there was a shop and a post office. In summer you could travel there by a dirt road by lorry, jeep, or wagon, but in winter the only means of transport was the *kolkhoz* sleigh. In the assembly hall in the local town was a huge portrait of Brezhnev and a slogan beneath it saying: 'Forward to the Victory of Communism'. *

This was the type of village scene in the countryside where the new arrivals found themselves, and where they had to make their new homes. But despite a seemingly

---

*Quoted by John Dornberg in *Brezhnev, The Masks of Power,* 1974

endless list of failures in planning, distribution, and supply of almost every conceivable item, the campaign itself, although far from an unqualified success, managed to achieve considerable positive results. In 1954, as the initial operation began to gather momentum, favourable weather and a successful harvest combined to fuel the positive atmosphere surrounding the campaign. Targets for the area to be cultivated and for the tonnage of grain to be produced were substantially increased, before a severe drought in 1955 provided a major setback. Thereafter successful years of good harvests alternated with poor years of crop failures and recurrent problems in production and distribution. Underlying the whole campaign was a constant and overriding demand for ever-higher yields and output. This led to a lack of proper crop rotation and insufficient fallow periods, and in turn to further soil erosion and diminution of fertility, accentuating the inevitable losses arising from natural factors of wind and drought.

In March 1956 Brezhnev left Alma-Ata to return to the Central Committee of the Communist Party in Moscow. Officially he had served for less than one year as First Secretary of the Kazakh Communist Party, but since his arrival with Ponomarenko in 1954 he had established a firm basis for the continuation of the Virgin Lands campaign. A good harvest in the summer of 1956 seemed to justify the ambitious enterprise, and further consolidated the positions of Khrushchev and Brezhnev in the Soviet leadership. Brezhnev was succeeded as party secretary in Kazakhstan by two more Russian officials, Ivan Yakovlev and Nikolai Belayev, both of whom also served for relatively short periods of time. But during his time in Alma-Ata, Brezhnev had formed a close political alliance and personal friendship with Dinmukhamed Kunaev, who had been Prime Minister of Kazakhstan since March 1955, and who was appointed to the more senior position of First Secretary after the removal of Belayev in January 1960. Their association was to remain close until Brezhnev's death in 1982; apart from a two-year gap between 1962 and 1964, Kunaev held the position of First Secretary, in parallel with Brezhnev's tenure in Moscow, for twenty-four years until the events of Zheltoksan ('December') in 1986.

In 1956 the virgin land areas, including those areas in Russia, contributed just over half of the total grain harvest of the USSR. This proportion was increased by poor results in other parts of the country but nonetheless represented a significant achievement after less than three years since the campaign was launched. However, grain production on this scale could not be sustained, and in the following years output began to level off and decline. In 1961, reflecting its central position in the territory of the campaign, Akmolinsk was given the name of Tselinograd (Virgin Soil City). Meanwhile natural forces, indifferent to human objectives, continued to intervene and the surrounding lands were constantly vulnerable to droughts and dust storms, and to heavy rainfall in spring and autumn which washed away vast quantities of soil every year. In 1962 Khruschev made another radical change to the party leadership in Kazakhstan by dismissing Dinmukhamed Kunaev, which angered the local population and did nothing to raise production on the steppe. By the early 1960s yields per acre were falling well below those of the more fertile regions of the Ukraine and north Caucasus, and costs of production rose far above the national average, to as much as twice as high in 1964. Conventional cost-benefit analysis was disregarded in favour of the intangible but still significant political and propaganda gains which were assumed to derive from the project. Living conditions for the many thousands of volunteers failed to show any noticeable improvement, and many workers, dispirited and disillusioned by their experiences, returned to Russia and the other republics. The ensuing difficulties of a permanent labour shortage compounded the other problems of the campaign.

In October 1964 Nikita Khrushchev was removed from the Soviet leadership and replaced by a triumvirate consisting of his earlier protégé Leonid Brezhnev, who became Secretary General of the Communist Party, Alexei Kosygin, appointed Chairman of the Council of Ministers, and Nikolai Podgorny, appointed Chairman of the Politburo, the 'Political bureau', or inner cabinet of Party and government officials. Brezhnev ultimately emerged as the predominant leader, and in his early years in office he sought to repair the damage caused by the misdirected investment, poor planning, and excessive production targets, which had been so harmful to the Virgin Lands campaign since he had left Alma-Ata, and which had also damaged the Soviet economy as a whole. One of his first actions on taking office in 1964 was to reinstall Kunaev to the leadership in Kazakhstan. With less political pressure to attain unrealistic objectives, and by heeding the advice of local soil experts and agricultural specialists, Brezhnev and Kunaev were able to correct some of the earlier failures and to achieve more sustainable levels of grain production throughout the second half of the 1960s. The campaign had been initiated by Khrushchev in the 1950s, but it came to be associated more with Brezhnev and Kunaev. On a visit to Alma-Ata in August 1970, Brezhnev was welcomed by Kunaev who in a speech declared 'We note with particular pride that you Leonid Ilyich headed the Communist Party of Kazakhstan during one of the critical periods in the development of our Republic, when millions of hectares of virgin lands were being opened up. With your dynamic and tireless activity in those years you made a huge personal contribution to the opening up of the virgin lands and to the development of the whole economy of Kazakhstan'.

By the early 1970s the familiar problems were once again building up. Poor organisation and mismanagement, bureaucracy and corruption, and losses due to spillage from dilapidated lorries and spoilage in inadequate warehouses, were all threatening to undermine the campaign. The growing phenomena of inertia and stagnation, which were to characterise the reigns of Brezhnev and Kunaev, were also beginning to take root. Political enthusiasm was waning, and the demand for investment elsewhere in the economy was constantly increasing. The relatively low returns from the Virgin Lands project, set against its own continuing need for high levels of investment in new equipment, storage facilities, improved transport, and better communications, all led to the campaign being effectively abandoned in 1974. Increasingly the USSR turned to imports from the west to meet its grain requirements, at considerable cost in foreign currency, but less onerous than trying to force ever greater output from the unwilling soil of northern Kazakhstan.

In Tselinograd, life followed the changing fortunes of the Virgin Lands project. As many thousands of migrants arrived from Russia and all parts of the Soviet Union, the town developed rapidly, with the construction of new housing, schools, hospitals, cinemas, theatres and other facilities to cater for the expanding population. A huge statue of Lenin was installed in the central square, parks and gardens were laid out along the banks of the River Ishim, and wide, tree-lined streets and avenues, empty of private cars but busy with buses and trams, extended far out to the suburbs. The railway lines from Tselinograd to Pavlodar in the north-east and to Karaganda in the south-east were the first in Kazakhstan to be electrified. The late 1960s marked the highpoint in the history of the town, before the Virgin Lands campaign was wound down in the following years. Thereafter its manufacturing industries, closely associated with agriculture, also began to decline, in common with many industries the rest of the economy of Kazakhstan and the Soviet Union, and many Russian families began to drift back to Russia in search of work in their home towns. Tselinograd lost the pre-eminence which it had enjoyed throughout the Soviet Union as the centre of the Virgin Lands campaign, as the Kazakh capital in Alma-Ata experienced its own expansion thanks to large-scale investment in industry and mining, in new scientific and research institutions, and in the growth of government offices and ministries. But Tselinograd was later to experience a new renaissance: in 1994, having reverted to its original Kazakh name of Akmola, it was designated as the future capital of the newly-independent Kazakhstan. In 1998 the town was renamed yet again with the unimaginative name of Astana (Capital), and embarked on a new era of growth and prosperity, financed by vast earnings from the country's rapidly-growing energy sector.

The long-term results of the Virgin Lands campaign were disappointing but were far from the unmitigated failure recorded in many histories of the period. The early investment was considered to be worthwhile, since extending the area under cultivation gave the government the extra production of grain and bread for which there was an acute need at the time. The alternative would have been insufficient food supplies for the cities and the threat of social unrest. The threat became a reality in June 1962 in the southern Russian town of Novocherkassk, when what started as a peaceful march and protest against increases in the price of bread and meat ended when troops opened fire on the demonstrators and killed hundreds of men, women, and children. Further incidents of that nature could threaten the stability of the Soviet regime itself. But the enormous investment in the campaign as a whole absorbed vast resources which could have been used more efficiently elsewhere, and from a strategic point of view the campaign was a failure. It did not provide a long-term solution to the enduring problem of inadequate grain production in the Soviet Union, and had an even more serious consequence of delaying the search for a more efficient and sustainable method of farming. Such an outcome could only come about by abandoning collectivisation and making a difficult and painful transition to a market economy, a political impossibility at the time. Today there are few reminders of the campaign, and the old town of Akmolinsk - Tselinograd has been almost completely buried under the concrete and glass of the new capital city of Astana. The Virgin Lands campaign was representative of the spirit of its times, of post-war idealism and hope for a better future under socialism, to be achieved by grandiose projects in which the whole country could share. But with insufficiently rigorous management and planning at the outset, and with nothing to restrain its over-ambitious objectives, ultimately the project was doomed to fail.

CHAPTER TWENTY

Dinmukhamed Kunaev and Kazakhstan in the 1960s

The decade of the 1960s was a period of rapid economic growth in Kazakhstan, but less favourable social developments were beginning to emerge. The Virgin Lands campaign had generated much hostility among many Kazakhs as a result of its harsh treatment of the steppe and of the indigenous communities which had to be displaced. The disdainful attitude of the Soviet government in Moscow towards local opinion in Kazakhstan, as to how the local terrain should best be treated so as to ensure maximum yields and output, heightened tensions still further. Hostility towards the Virgin Lands programme was partially mollified in the later years under the management of Brezhnev and Kunaev, but by then much damage had been inflicted on the country and its agriculture, as well as more enduring harm done to relations between the Russian and Kazakh populations. The Russians in Kazakhstan were as much aware of the practical shortcomings of the Virgin Lands project as were the Kazakhs, but they were not going to side with the Kazakhs in opposing the scheme. Nor did they sympathise with Kazakh unhappiness at an enormous and Russian-inspired programme being forcibly imposed on their country, since parts of Russia were also included in the Virgin Lands, and the whole territory was all part of the Soviet Union anyway. Kazakh resentment towards Russia was further intensified by the growing nuclear weapons testing programme being developed in Kazakhstan near Semipalatinsk, rather than in Siberia where land was far more spacious and even less densely populated than in Kazakhstan.

On a more day-to-day level, the Russian population in Alma-Ata and other towns did little to promote harmony with indigenous Kazakhs, and instances of petty harassment were commonplace: elderly Kazakh women in colourful headscarves selling sunflower seeds in the sunshine on a street corner, or near a restaurant frequented by Russians, would be removed, often with a tirade of abuse, and parks and other public places frequently had areas designated as reserved for Russians only. At a time when the Soviet press was criticising apartheid in South Africa and other racial injustices around the world, similar treatment of non-Russian communities within the Soviet Union was especially resented. On the positive side, Russia was making substantial social and economic investment in Kazakhstan, intended to transform a still relatively backward country into a more modern and better-educated socialist society. The majority of the Kazakh population were beneficiaries of this investment, which might otherwise have been allocated to other parts of Russia itself, and many Kazakhs, whose family background and political qualifications were regarded as safe, studied at Russian universities. But the condescending attitude of the Russian population, often dismissive of local feelings, gave rise to considerable antagonism and allowed nationalist tendencies to take root. Throughout the 1960s and 1970s there was no serious nationalist-inspired hostility to the Soviet government, although there was strong opposition to some specific policies emanating from Moscow, notably to the nuclear testing programme. The local Party could point with justification to the many senior positions in education, the economy, and in the government held by Kazakhs, but nationalism was becoming a more serious problem, and by the 1980s it had become one of the first indications of underlying unrest in Kazakhstan and other non-Russian republics.

The most prominent figure in the post-war Kazakh party leadership, apart from Zhumabai Shayakhmetov and Leonid Brezhnev, was Dinmukhamed Kunaev. Kunaev was a native Kazakh, born in what was still Verny in 1912, 'into an ordinary peasant family' according to his official biography. Both his parents came from the Shelek region near Verny, although his mother is believed to have been Russian. In the 1930s Kunaev studied in Moscow at the Institute of Non-Ferrous Metallurgy, and returned to Kazakhstan in 1939 where he became a specialist in open-cast mining, a branch of the economy under extensive development at the time. While still in his twenties Kunaev held several senior engineering positions, at the Balkhash copper plant and at other mining and industrial enterprises throughout Kazakhstan. In 1942 he returned to Alma-Ata where at the age of thirty one he was appointed Deputy Chairman of the Council of Ministers, and in this role was largely responsible for organising the relocation in Kazakhstan of factories and industrial equipment evacuated from western Russia in the early months of the war. This enormous logistical undertaking, at the most critical period in the country's history, demanded exceptional organisational skills which few people in Kazakhstan possessed. Factories had to be rebuilt in the minimum time, supplies of raw materials had to be transported to the factories and armaments and equipment had to be delivered from the factories to the front, and food and accommodation, albeit basic, had to be provided for the work force of the evacuated factories. It was Kunaev's ability to organize all this, plus his unswerving loyalty to Stalin and to the Communist Party, that ensured his survival during the Stalinist purges before and during the war. But his main interest was as a metallurgist and scientist. After the war he continued to work in these fields, and published over one hundred scientific works. From 1952 to 1955 he was President of the Kazakh Academy of Sciences, and from 1955 to 1960 he returned to a political role as Chairman of the Council of Ministers, where he had served as Deputy Chairman during the war. Now he was working alongside Leonid Brezhnev, the First Secretary of the Communist Party of Kazakhstan, effectively the most senior position in the country, before becoming the First Secretary himself in 1960.

Kunaev was said to have been an enthusiastic supporter of the Virgin Lands campaign, but it is more likely that he had deep misgivings about its scale and ambitions. As a mining engineer he was familiar with the practical difficulties of implementing and managing large-scale industrial projects in hostile environments, without the support of adequate infrastructure, especially transport and communications, and without proper organisation. Although not an agricultural specialist, he was equally aware as any Kazakh of the unfavourable soil and climatic conditions of the northern steppes, and of the unsuitability of the terrain for such an enormous undertaking. In 1962 Kunaev was dismissed by Khrushchev as part of another far-reaching purge of leading figures in Kazakhstan who were regarded by Khrushchev as an obstacle to his vision for the future. Although mild by the murderous standards of the Stalin purges of 1937-1938, the removal of Kunaev and much of the Kazakh party leadership, only eight years after the dismissal of Shayakhmetov, was particularly acrimonious and bitter. Many saw Kunaev as an established and respected figure in Kazakhstan who was being disposed of for reasons once again to suit the government in Moscow, rather than in accordance with domestic considerations in his own republic, and his removal was not well received by the majority of the population.

In his place Khrushchev appointed Ismail Yusupov, a Uighur by nationality but who had close ties to Khrushchev and other Soviet leaders in Moscow. The Uighurs - an ethnic group closely related to the Kazakhs and living mainly in the Xinjiang province of western China – were emigrating in large numbers in 1961-1962 into south-eastern Kazakhstan and to the Alma-Ata region in particular. In 1962, in a huge exodus of people, nearly half a million Uighurs and Kazakhs fled from China, driven out by the upheaval of the Great Leap Forward under Mao Tse Tung and the ensuing loss of land and property. The ethnic Kazakhs among the refugees were descendants of those who had fled from Kazakhstan to escape military conscription in 1916, and of those who later escaped the forced collectivisation in the early 1930s. In all over one million Kazakhs had fled from their homelands, mostly to Xinjiang between 1916 and 1932. Now fear of being imprisoned as Soviet sympathisers motivated many to travel back across the border, together with Uighurs who were suffering from oppression in China. The exodus was another symptom of the Sino-Soviet split, which was increasing in intensity in the early 1960s. The Chinese government accused the emigres of taking more than 30,000 head of cattle with them and of leaving vast areas of land untended, while the Soviet government was promising a better life in the Soviet Union, and Soviet border troops were said to have tempted starving refugees across the border with parcels of food. Some in the Soviet leadership were concerned about the resulting dilution of the Russian population in Kazakhstan, but this was a propaganda victory against China, in addition to which there was a political and economic benefit of more people moving into an under-populated part of the country.

The Uighur and Kazakh incomers were welcomed by the local government and population, and Ismail Yusupov played a significant role in assisting the Uighurs in particular to find work and settle in their new surroundings. He also worked with Khrushchev on devising a scheme whereby parts of southern Kazakhstan inhabited by large Uighur minorities might be transferred to neighbouring Uzbekistan to join with other Uighur groups there. But before these plans could come to fruition, Khrushchev was deposed in October 1964 and succeeded by the triumvirate of Leonid Brezhnev, Alexei Kosygin, and Nikolai Podgorny. Brezhnev put an end to any plans to redraw the boundaries between Kazakhstan and Uzbekistan, dismissed Yusupov, and re-instated Kunaev as party leader in Kazakhstan in December 1964. Over the following years Brezhnev and Kunaev removed the remaining Khrushchev loyalists who had been appointed in 1962, and by the late-1960s had achieved complete control of the party and government in Kazakhstan. With a powerful ally in the form of Brezhnev in Moscow, effectively the undisputed Soviet leader, Kunaev was secure in his own position in Alma-Ata for the next twenty-two years. In 1971 he was appointed to the Soviet Politburo, the only non-Russian at the time to hold such a position. He and Brezhnev shared an enthusiasm for hunting and Brezhnev made frequent visits to Kazakhstan for hunting trips in the mountains and on the steppes.

Kunaev's style of leadership, and his eventual decline, matched those of Brezhnev himself. Kunaev was keen to appoint fellow-Kazakhs to senior positions in the party and in the economy, and he could easily stave off criticisms of being too closely allied to Brezhnev and to Russia. But under his leadership the Kazakh Communist Party, far from revolutionising the country and providing effective management of the economy, slid back into the familiar clan politics and nepotism of Central Asia. The appointments made by Kunaev were largely family members and their relatives, who in turn appointed their own relatives to other, more junior, positions, and the country and the economy began to stagnate under the weight of cronyism and economic mismanagement. The period after the accession to power of Brezhnev in Moscow, and the re-appointment of Kunaev in Alma-Ata, marked the onset of Soviet complacency and inertia which infected every aspect of life and which culminated in the economic and political collapse of the 1990s. This was a phenomenon which affected the whole of the Soviet Union but was particularly evident in Kazakhstan and some of the other conservative republics. In the static and traditional societies of Central Asia, economic growth and social progress, while welcomed in theory, were seen as foreign concepts and were not necessarily embraced with great enthusiasm by the government or the population. The early revolutionary objectives of the Soviet Union soon gave way to political and social conservatism, which happened to conform more closely to the traditionally placid Kazakh way of life. Apart from the influx of Uighur refugees in 1962, some of the most dramatic developments in the Communist world in the 1960s, including the construction of the Berlin Wall in 1961, the Prague Spring and the Soviet-led invasion of Czechoslovakia in 1968, registered little more than minor tremors in Kazakhstan. News from foreign countries, especially from Europe, was strictly controlled, and such was the distance, both geographically and politically, from Czechoslovakia that few people paid any attention to the reformist ideals of the Czechoslovak Communist Party or to what was happening in a supposedly-allied socialist state in Europe.

The Soviet system in Kazakhstan was providing free education, social stability, full employment, and was achieving significant material gains for the majority of the population, and new ideas and reforms were never seriously considered. But by clinging to its conservative values, and effectively turning its back on developments in almost every sphere of human activity in the outside world, especially in technology, society, politics, and economics, Kazakhstan became caught in the same downward spiral as everywhere else in the USSR, and from which it became impossible to escape. In Moscow Leonid Brezhnev had no desire to try to reform or revitalise the Kazakh party leadership, which was taking its lead from the party in Russia and which fully complied with Soviet economic and social policies. In a continuation of Russia's nineteenth-century strategic needs, Brezhnev and Kunaev ensured that stability was maintained in the potentially unstable region between Russia and China, a region that was still of vital importance to the Soviet Union. Change and reform in Kazakhstan might result in similar unrest and instability in Central Asia as the Prague Spring had brought about in eastern Europe, and had to be resisted at all costs.

Political problems in Kazakhstan were avoided throughout the 1960s and 1970s by the combination of rising living standards, and by the ubiquitous presence of the local KGB and the quick suppression of any dissent. The role of Kunaev in representing Kazakhstan in the Soviet Politburo, and in attracting investment from the central Soviet budget for projects in Alma-Ata and elsewhere in the country, was also critical. Kunaev's close association with Brezhnev enabled him to command considerable resources which were denied to many of the other republics. The years under his leadership, according to the official Almaty tourist guide book, 'were a golden time for the city, creative and calm, when Alma-Ata became one of the most attractive and developed cities in the Soviet Union'. Typical of the many prestigious construction projects constructed under Kunaev were the Arasan public baths and saunas, across the road from Panfilov Park, and built at great expense in the mid-1970s. Designed in the style of the palace of a medieval khan, the six blue and green domes of the building give the complex an Asiatic appearance which strikes a colourful note among the neighbouring utilitarian office buildings and apartment blocks. Partly because of this, and its enormous cost, construction of the Arasan baths was opposed by many in the Soviet government in Moscow, who saw it as an unnecessary extravagance on something which had no economic benefit. Kunaev was able to over-ride these objections and ensure that resources were allocated for this and for other popular projects, including the Medeo skating rink and concert stadium in the hills above Alma-Ata, the concert hall in the Palace of the Republic, and other buildings designed for the benefit of the population, as opposed to socially-useless statues and memorials. In so doing he greatly enhanced his popularity in Kazakhstan, possibly more so than any of the other fourteen party leaders achieved in their own republics. The massive and domineering granite war memorial in Panfilov Park, constructed in 1975, although not actively opposed by the local population, was more acceptable to the leadership in Moscow, and reflected orthodox Soviet attitudes rather than the more restrained feelings of the Kazakh population about the war.

Meanwhile the economy was growing and prosperity was increasing, adding to a widespread but misguided sense of optimism and hope for the future. But genuine progress and development in the economy were hampered by the requirements of the central plan, and although Kunaev was successful in attracting funds for social projects, investment in industry and agriculture lagged far below what was needed for sustained growth. With guaranteed markets in the rest of the Soviet Union, manufacturing enterprises became uncompetitive and slothful, and resistant to more modern production methods. New investment, much of which would necessarily have been in the form of equipment and machinery imported from the west, politically would have had the double disadvantage of exposing the backwardness of Soviet technology, and resulting in widespread job losses. The enormous state-owned industrial enterprises, banks, and shops had no incentive to improve their procedures and productivity. By taking on more staff than they needed, enterprises of all types permitted everyone to share in the country's relative prosperity, although this was to become a major social problem in later years, when the same enterprises found it difficult to lay off unwanted workers. Dismissal of surplus labour ran contrary to Kazakh ideals of equality and social justice, ideals which pre-dated communism but which further compounded the enormous difficulties of economic adjustment in the post-Soviet era. Education, health services, and the social infrastructure of housing, roads, and transport, were all steadily improving and there was no great impetus for change in policy. New blocks of flats were being built, in many cases by German prisoners of war still held in Kazakhstan until the late 1960s, and although the apartments lacked comfort and space they were welcomed by the hundreds of thousands of people migrating from the countryside in search of work, and living in shanty towns of yurts and shacks on the outskirts of Alma-Ata and other towns and cities throughout Kazakhstan. In the rush of construction, little attention was given to the need for social amenities, and cafes and restaurants, laundries and dry cleaners, all had to be added and built into the blocks of flats as afterthoughts at a later date. Suburban communities were laid out in self-contained *microrayons* where shops, schools, pharmacies, and basic medical services were provided. Behind the apartment blocks were quiet and peaceful courtyards, with playgrounds for children safe from the traffic outside, and communal areas where elderly residents could pass the time of day, and where often the only sounds were the regular, heavy thump of ornately-patterned and brightly-coloured rugs being beaten and cleaned of dust, before being hung back on the living room walls in the small but homely apartments, reminders of a lost way of life in the yurt and on the steppe.

The benefits of new housing and other social improvements were particularly evident in Kazakhstan and Central Asia, where social care had previously been the responsibility of the family and the clan, and had not been as widely available as in other parts of the country where there had been greater state provision. In the industrial towns and cities, life now centred around the local *kombinat*. The kombinat was a group of vertically-integrated businesses responsible for every stage of the industrial production process, from extracting raw materials from nearby mines or bringing them in from elsewhere, to manufacturing and then distributing the finished product in accordance with the requirements of the plan. In addition to its basic economic functions, the kombinat was responsible for a wide range of social activities for the community in which it was based, including a multitude of communal services which in other countries were the responsibility of local or central government. Kindergartens, schools, libraries, community centres, housing, hospitals, parks, gardens, organised holidays for its employees and their families, and many other types of social amenity and activity, all fell within the province of the kombinat. Under the Soviet system of economic planning, in which complacency and lack of initiative were often the prevalent features, little thought was given to diversifying the local economy to provide additional sources of employment or income. Dependence on single employers was a common feature in many western cities, but in the industrial towns of northern Kazakhstan and throughout much of the USSR, the kombinats became the mainstay of local life to a far greater extent than was typical elsewhere, and the impact of their eventual collapse was correspondingly more severe.

In most of the Soviet Union, and especially in Kazakhstan, higher living standards came almost entirely from the exploitation of natural resources and the growth of basic industries such as metallurgy, iron and steel, and armaments. Except for the armed forces, which devoured all the western technical journals and scientific periodicals which they alone had access to, the Soviet Union was largely unaware of advances in electronics and industrial and information technology in the rest of the world. Computerization and IT, at the time increasingly embraced in the west, were little understood by party officials in Alma-Ata or in Moscow, and were rightly regarded with suspicion as potential threats to the regime, and were widely resisted. The lack of exposure to other western influences, and a political climate which was wary of, if not hostile to innovation and enterprise, combined to prevent technical standards, industrial and agricultural output, and income levels rising faster than they might otherwise have done. Even in more favourable political circumstances, its remoteness from world markets would have made the development of a more advanced economy in Kazakhstan difficult, and the country was effectively destined to remain essentially a producer of raw materials and basic industrial equipment. Between the 1950s and the 1970s Kazakhstan came to specialise in the extraction of non-ferrous metals, notably lead and nickel, especially in the east of the country, as well as iron ore and coal from vast deposits north of Lake Balkhash. The areas around Lake Balkhash, and further east along the River Irtysh around Ust-Kamenogorsk and Semipalatinsk, also held enormous reserves of copper, zinc, and gold, all of which were extensively exploited to meet the insatiable demand from heavy industry in Russia. The steppes in the south and west of the country were largely untouched in the hunt for natural resources until the discovery of large reserves of oil and gas along the northern and eastern shores of the Caspian Sea and around the Emba River in the 1970s. But it was not until much later that the country became a major source of energy for the rest of the Soviet economy, and later still for other countries. Eventually these resources provided a degree of prosperity for the population, although the export of Kazakhstan's own oil and gas to the outside world, in exchange for foreign currency which might have been invested in other sectors of the economy, was not possible under the centralised Soviet system of foreign trade. Funds for the development of natural resources, and the allocation of earnings from sales of natural resources abroad, were determined by the relevant economic ministry in Moscow, which decided on priorities and distributed funds to the local ministries in each of the republics.

The Soviet economy as a whole managed to function largely by virtue of rising world energy prices, while organic industrial growth arising from investment and exports of manufactured goods was minimal. Production of oil and natural gas, of which the Soviet Union had vast resources, was severely constrained by the lack of investment over previous decades, and was now caught in a three-way struggle between the energy needs of its own enterprises and domestic users, the need for exports with which to pay for imports of food and essential equipment, which could no longer be delayed, from the west, and the need to subsidise the flagging economies of the weak but strategically-important allied countries in eastern Europe. Throughout the 1960s and 1970s supplies of oil and gas to Kazakhstan and the other republics were generally maintained at adequate levels, but there was no incentive to economise and the wasteful use of energy, particularly in centrally-controlled heating in apartments and offices, was widespread.

**

Concern for the natural environment was never a feature of Soviet economic planning, since nature was always regarded as subordinate to man, and to the needs of the economy and the growth of socialism. There was little awareness of the damaging effects of unrestrained exploitation of natural resources, and such concerns that did exist were brushed aside in the rush for growth. Vast, open-cast mining operations, exerting enormous detrimental effects on the surrounding countryside and on air quality, could be undertaken almost unnoticed, thanks to the sparseness of the population, poor communications with other parts of the country, and above all to political unwillingness to impose any forms of control. But it was during the 1960s that a major environmental disaster began to emerge in the desert of western Kazakhstan around the shores of the land-locked Aral Sea. Over subsequent decades the calamity engulfing the Aral, the surrounding lands, and the local population, became increasingly severe, as the volume of water flowing into the Sea fell dramatically due to relentless pressure for ever-increasing cotton production in Turkmenistan and Uzbekistan. By the end of the twentieth century the Aral Sea had become synonymous with devastating dust storms, soil erosion on a massive scale, illness and disease, and widespread loss of livelihoods. In recent years there has been some progress in countering and reversing these trends, stabilising the natural environment, and in reviving the local economy, but the future of this vast region is still uncertain.

In terms of surface area the Aral Sea, covering an area of 42,000 square kilometres, was once the fourth largest inland body of water in the world, after the Black Sea, the Caspian Sea, and Lake Victoria in East Africa. It lies in the western part of the Central Asian basin in which the rivers drain inland towards the interior rather than away to more distant oceans. A similar but smaller drainage basin exists around Lake Balkhash in eastern Kazakhstan. The Aral Sea itself is more of a lake than a sea, and like Lake Balkhash it is shallow and experiences high levels of evaporation in the intense heat of summer. Whereas Lake Balkhash receives fresh water from many rivers flowing down from nearby mountains, the Aral is far from any mountain range and only two rivers reach its shores: the Amu Darya in the south and the Syr Darya in the north. The Amu Darya, the longest river in Central Asia, flows for a distance of more than 2,400 kilometres from its source in the Pamir Mountains of China and Tajikistan, to the desert at the southern end of the Aral, while the Syr Darya, a narrower but longer river, rises in the Tien Shan Mountains of Kyrgyzstan and flows for 3,000 kilometres before ending its journey in the northern end of the Aral. Between the two rivers lies the vast Kyzyl Kum (Black Sands) desert, the Transoxiana of ancient times. Before the 1950s the Aral Sea used to act as a giant regulator of the local climate, moderating seasonal extremes of heat and cold, but the significance of this has now been greatly reduced; the sharp contraction in its surface area, and the reduction in the volume of water which it holds, have meant that the Aral Sea no longer exerts such a pronounced effect, with the result that the regional climate has become more continental, with summers considerably hotter and winters much colder than in earlier years.

For centuries the Aral Sea was virtually unknown to the outside world. It did not lie clearly within the lands of any of the three Kazakh Hordes, and the surrounding territory of flat and featureless steppe was almost completely uninhabited. Isolated tribes of nomads, in addition to their traditional activities of animal husbandry and grazing, occasionally supplemented their diets by fishing along its shores. Vast distances separated the Aral Sea from the nearest towns of Orenburg to the north and Guryev near the Caspian Sea to the west, which were themselves remote outposts far from the major cities of Russia. It was not until the early eighteenth century that the tsarist government in St Petersburg began to take a serious interest in exploring the region and its potential for agriculture and trade, and in 1734 it called upon the services of John Elton, the English explorer who had already mapped large parts of the country to the north and west of the Caspian Sea. Elton took part in a new mission to survey the coast of the Aral Sea, which some people in Russia had thought to be connected to the Caspian and which may have offered a sea route into Kazakhstan, avoiding the need to cross the more difficult terrain of desert and steppe. The Elton mission conclusively dismissed this notion, confirming the status of the Aral as a separate body of water, but it was not until more than a hundred years later before the Russian government took any further interest in the region, when in 1847 it established a fort at Aralsk on the northern shore of the Sea. Further scientific expeditions were undertaken during the nineteenth century, but the Aral Sea was seen as having little strategic or economic significance, except for a few communities which made their living from fishing and herding along its shores. The scientific research which was undertaken did not comprehend the environmental importance of the Sea and its properties, and this lack of awareness was to contribute to one of the most serious ecological disasters of the twentieth century.

Political factors also discouraged consideration of the geographical balance of the region. Delineation of the new Soviet republics in Central Asia in the 1920s and 1930s resulted in the Aral Sea being shared between Kazakhstan in the north and Uzbekistan in the south. The border between the two republics extended from a point in the uninhabited Turanskaya Depression of Kazakhstan on the eastern shore, bisected the low-lying island of Vozrozhdenie, before reaching the equally empty Ustyurt Plateau of Uzbekistan on the opposite shore in the west. A further complication arose from the designation of the Amu Darya River, for much of the lower reaches of its course, as the border between Uzbekistan and Turkmenistan, inevitably leading to future conflict between the two neighbours concerning division of water from the river. The Syr Darya River on the other hand, after leaving its source in Kyrgyzstan and flowing for a short distance in Uzbekistan, flows for the rest of its journey within the borders of Kazakhstan. Decisions concerning agriculture, land management, and allocation of water resources in the region were taken exclusively in Moscow, where the new Soviet government in the 1930s had little interest in the natural environment around the Aral Sea, or anywhere else in the Soviet Union. Traditional forms of nomadic farming and agriculture were being swept aside by collectivisation, and the emphasis in the region after the Revolution was on maximising output of cotton, which had a ready market in the textile industries in Russia and in Europe, where it generated valuable earnings of foreign currency. Cotton was assigned far greater importance than the fishing industry in the Aral Sea, which began a steady and irreversible decline for the next seventy years. Cotton production required enormous volumes of water for irrigation, and after the Second World War demand increased substantially, placing further heavy strains on the Amu and Syr Darya rivers. Most of the new production was to be in Uzbekistan and Turkmenistan, although the resulting impact on the Aral Sea would be felt just as much in Kazakhstan. In 1956 a canal diverting large amounts of water from the Amu Darya into the desert of Turkmenistan was constructed and opened, and further millions of hectares of land in all three republics came under irrigation during the 1960s. The turning point for the Aral Sea occurred in the late 1950s and early 1960s, after which the level of the Sea began to fall dramatically, while diversion of water from the rivers to the cotton fields continued to increase. By 1968 a total of 37 canals had been constructed to channel water to the parched deserts, causing the volume of water in the Aral to shrink still further and its salinity to increase to dangerous levels. The diminishing volume of water in the Amu Darya in the south led to the river eventually dissipating entirely in the desert before it reached the Aral, where water levels receded even further away from the original shore line. A similar phenomenon was taking place in the north, although the diversion of water from the Syr Darya was less than that in the south, and the river continued to flow into the Sea.

The loss of water not only put an end to the fishing industry which had been the main source of income for the non-nomadic population, but also led to a high incidence of malnutrition, disease and infant mortality, as enormous quantities of sand and dust, heavily contaminated with pesticides and chemicals used in cotton production, were blown by desert winds to reach towns and villages hundreds of kilometres from the Aral Sea. Some Kazakh fishermen and their families, having lost their livelihoods around the northern and eastern shores, left to seek work on the shores of Lake Balkhash or in Russia, but opportunities were few and most people had no option but to stay. The drive to increase cotton production coincided with the Virgin Lands campaign in Russia and northern Kazakhstan and in the optimistic atmosphere of the time, similar above-plan increases in output of cotton, and forcing the natural environment to comply with the demands being impose on it, were expected. But whereas the Virgin Lands campaign directly involved only Russia and Kazakhstan, the situation surrounding the Aral Sea had far-reaching consequences throughout the whole of Central Asia. Kazakhstan, Uzbekistan, and Turkmenistan were most affected by the shrinkage of the Sea, while the smaller republics of Tajikistan and Kyrgyzstan, where the Amu Darya and Syr Darya have their source, found that their own needs for water for local irrigation and hydro-electricity generation were subordinated to the demands of the Soviet plans and to the need for sustained water supplies downstream beyond their borders.

The overriding priority given to cotton production continued well into the 1980s, by which time stagnation in the Soviet economy and political system had become entrenched and ensured that no significant remedial measures could be undertaken. Production figures were routinely falsified, and virtually the whole of the agricultural sector in southern Kazakhstan, Uzbekistan, and Turkmenistan became caught up in a network of corruption, distortion, and wasteful use of resources. Meanwhile the Aral Sea continued to suffer. By 1989 the surface area had shrunk from its original 42,000 square kilometres to less than 18,000 square kilometres, and the town of Aralsk, which had been founded 142 years earlier on what was then the northern shore, was now almost 100 kilometres from the water. The sea had split into two parts along a line roughly from east to west, and the dried-up sea bed became littered with the empty hulks of stranded fishing vessels. Fish had disappeared and the fishing industry had been eliminated.

In the surrounding countryside some attempts were made to reduce water loss by lining the canals from the rivers to the cotton fields with plastic sheets, and by belatedly modernising irrigation methods through the use of sprinklers and other water-saving devices. But such efforts were half-hearted and were not pursued due to cost and lack of political will. A more ambitious project to convey water to the Aral Sea by means of a giant canal across Kazakhstan from the Ob and Irtysh rivers in Siberia was conceived but was discarded in 1986, as much for economic as ecological reasons. By this time awareness of the environmental damage which had been caused had become inescapable. The arrival in Lake Balkhash and in Alma-Ata of displaced fishermen from Aralsk and other decimated communities around the Aral Sea caused widespread concern. Hostility to the Soviet leadership in Moscow, for imposing excessive dependence on cotton without regard for the consequent economic and social costs, spread widely in

Kazakhstan and Uzbekistan, and became another factor in the rise of nationalism and political unrest, particularly in Kazakhstan in the late 1980s.

The collapse of the Soviet Union in 1991 enabled the Central Asian republics to take responsibility for their own affairs, particularly with regard to the use and sharing of natural resources. The new Russian government in Moscow had more urgent priorities and the future of the Aral Sea, which had become the responsibility of what were now two foreign countries, was of even less concern than it had been in the past. In the early years of independence, Kazakhstan had limited financial resources which it could devote to environmental purposes. A vague plan in the 1990s to construct a pipeline to transport water from the Caspian Sea to the Aral Sea, was discussed in the press. At the time the water level of the Caspian Sea was rising and causing severe flooding and damage to roads and buildings along the shore. This was a cyclical phenomenon not widely understood but believed to be due to greater volumes of water entering the Caspian from the Volga River, although other theories involving the rotation of the earth were also put forward. The construction of a pipeline was seen as potentially solving two problems at once, of lowering the level of the Caspian and raising the level of the Aral Sea. But the idea never materialised, due to the enormous cost of pumping water from the Caspian to the Aral, which lay at an altitude of several hundred metres above the level of the Caspian Sea, and over a distance of 700 kilometres across the desert of the Ustyurt Plateau.

The sharp decline in cotton and other agricultural production in Kazakhstan in the 1990s had a serious impact on the national economy and on living standards, but there were also some incidental benefits. In the same way that the collapse of many heavy industries in Russia considerably reduced the level of industrial pollution in the atmosphere above Russian cities, the reduced demand for water for irrigation increased the flow from the Syr Darya into the northern part of the Aral Sea. Further improvement came in 2005 when, with finance from the World Bank, a dam was built across the Sea, separating the Kazakh part in the north from the Uzbek part in the south. Although only thirteen kilometres in length the dam soon had a major beneficial impact on the local environment, as greater volumes of water from the Syr Darya River could now flow into the Sea with less being lost to evaporation. Salinity in the water steadily began to fall, and by the end of the decade fishing stocks had recovered significantly, and fish processing plants had begun operating again in Aralsk. The southern part was destined to remain arid and in danger of disappearing altogether, as the government of Uzbekistan had less enthusiasm for joint efforts with Kazakhstan to restore the Sea. Only if the two rivers could both flow unimpeded into the Aral can the water level be fully restored, but to achieve this would require the cooperation of all five republics of Kazakhstan, Uzbekistan, Turkmenistan, Tajikistan and Kyrgyzstan. For political and economic reasons this remains an almost impossible task, but in the northern Aral the prospects for recovery are now much stronger than at any time in the past sixty years.

CHAPTER TWENTY ONE

Kazakhstan Begins to Change: Zheltoksan and the End of the Kunaev Era

In the late 1960s and early 1970s there seemed to be little change in Kazakhstan. To all appearances life was normal; uniformity in politics, art, society, and virtually every activity was the order of the day, and divergence from convention still frowned upon, if not actually illegal. But the economic direction of the country was taking a turn for the worse, and profound demographic changes were under way. Up until this time living standards had been rising, and expectations of a better future were a constant and credible theme of Communist propaganda. The drab apartment blocks in Kazakh cities, extending for miles along empty boulevards to distant suburbs, may have been soulless and cramped, but the additional living space helped to alleviate the perpetual housing crisis, and almost everyone had a roof over their head. There was no shortage of food supplies or of other essential items, and consumer goods, if not plentiful, were increasingly available. Standards of education and health services, already relatively high, were also improving. It is difficult to pinpoint the moment at which the tide of a strengthening economy and rising living standards began to turn and recede, but after the upheaval of the 1968 Prague Spring in Czechoslovakia, any attempt which might have been made to reform the economy was shelved, and by the early 1970s political stagnation under Brezhnev in Moscow and Kunaev in Alma-Ata had become a fact of life. Demographic trends were also now beginning to have far-reaching social consequences throughout the whole of the Soviet Union. The generation which had witnessed, and some of whom had participated in, the 1917 Revolution and who had seen the birth of the USSR, was still influential, but was less capable of adapting to change and providing the technological and economic leadership which the country needed. The younger generation was mostly still loyal to the socialist ideals of the Revolution, with a loyalty which had been greatly strengthened by the devastating effect of the war, which they had either not experienced themselves or had experienced as young children, but which was still very much alive in the collective memory. But disillusionment with the socialist system was steadily creeping in, and more and more people began to look to the west for inspiration.

In Kazakhstan this trend was compounded by a gradual but unmistakable change in the composition of the Kazakh and Slav, especially Russian, populations. By 1970 there were 5.5 million Russians and over 900,000 Ukrainians living in Kazakhstan, numbers which had been increased by the inflow of migrants during the Virgin Lands campaign, and which now accounted for roughly 39 per cent and 6 per cent respectively of the total population of 14 million. In terms of the composition of Kazakh society this was another turning point; thereafter both Russian and Ukrainian communities continued to expand, but at a slower rate than previously with far less immigration, and at a much slower rate than the native Kazakh population. Thus their share of the population began a gradual decline. Russians remained concentrated in the northern and eastern parts of the country, where most of the industrial centres were located. With the exception for historical reasons of Alma-Ata, relatively few Russians sought to make a living in the south of Kazakhstan or in the west, where economic resources and job opportunities were scarce. These regions were also where the majority of the indigenous Kazakh population lived. Most Russians were content with this situation and had no desire to seek any closer relationship with Russia itself. But in later years the prospect of partition, either in the form of a separate state in the north of Kazakhstan, or reunification of Russian-populated areas with the new Russian Republic, became a possibility, and was one of the factors in the decision in 1994 to transfer the capital from Almaty to Akmola.

Leonid Brezhnev, former First Secretary of the Kazakhstan Communist Party and General Secretary of the Communist Party of the Soviet Union since 1966 but effective leader of the Soviet Union since 1964, died on 10 November 1982. This became another critical date in Soviet history, and marked the start of the unstoppable slide from stagnation into turmoil and chaos. From now on there was no going back to the old USSR, and the eventual end of the Soviet Union could no longer be averted. Collapse was now only a matter of time. Brezhnev was succeeded by Yuri Andropov, the former head of the KGB and former Soviet ambassador to Hungary who had played a major role in the suppression of the Hungarian uprising in 1956. Andropov attempted some limited and half-hearted reforms intended to improve work discipline in factories and work places throughout the Soviet Union. The country's declining economic performance had become an inescapable fact but in the political climate of the time there were no ready solutions. The cause of the country's difficulties was not so much lack of discipline, although absenteeism and alcoholism were both having a serious adverse effect on output. It was more the result of severe structural weaknesses, of inadequate and mis-directed investment, exacerbated by deep-seated inertia, and paralysis in the political leadership. The problem was compounded, rather than eased, by the country's substantial earnings from exports of oil and natural gas, which as well as permitting imports of grain and other vital goods had the damaging effect of obscuring the underlying need for urgent and radical reforms. The measures introduced under Andropov had negligible results, and the Soviet Union continued its decline into social and economic torpor. It was clear that the necessary fundamental changes in the economy were going to take far more political effort than the party leadership could provide. The structure and management of the planned and highly-centralised Soviet economy had been virtually unchanged since the many economic ministries, responsible for regulating almost every type of activity, had been established in the 1930s. The reforms needed to make the transition to a market economy would inevitably make the situation worse before it could get better, even if agreement could be reached as to how this should be done. In particular the powerful economic ministries, which had acted as a constraint on any reforms or initiatives, would have to be abolished. Every ministry had its own Communist Party cell, and thus great political influence among the Soviet leadership, which ensured that this could not happen. The downward spiral continued and accelerated after the death of Andropov in February 1984, and the appointment as his successor of Konstantin Chernenko. Aged 79 and even less motivated to undertake reform than Andropov, Chernenko was already in poor health and unable to play an active role as leader. In his frequent absences due to illness, government meetings were already being chaired by Mikhail Gorbachev, who took over as General Secretary of the Communist Party of the Soviet Union on the death of Chernenko on 10 March 1985.

In Kazakhstan the national mood was sombre, as the news from Russia was increasingly depressing, and the local economy continued to deteriorate, in contrast to the relative prosperity and optimism of the 1960s and 1970s. State enterprises and kombinats found that they could no longer rely on their traditional markets or suppliers elsewhere in the USSR, with whom they had been dealing for decades, and they had little prospect of finding new markets in the west, or of getting foreign exchange to pay for essential imports. The new phenomenon of unemployment began to appear, especially in the industrial towns in the north and east of the country, where the mainly Russian population was the first to suffer from the decline in the traditional heavy industries. Initially this was masked by the growth in part-time working and by the familiar feature of hidden unemployment, of over-manning and low productivity, but as more enterprises were forced to close these options were less available. The worsening mood in the country was felt equally at the top of the Communist Party. For Kunaev, the death of his old friend and ally Leonid Brezhnev in 1982 meant that his own position had become precarious, and although there had been little likelihood of change under

Andropov or Chernenko, his removal from office under the new Soviet leadership was now inevitable.

The developments taking place in Moscow may have been viewed in Kazakhstan with concern, but little practical action was taken by the Communist Party leadership to avoid a similar outcome in Alma-Ata. By 1986 Dinmukhhamed Kunaev had been in office for an unbroken term of twenty-two years. Aged 74, and after a lifetime of public service, according to the official version of events he had already prepared his resignation. But he was pre-empted in his wish to retire by the anti-corruption campaigns of Mikhail Gorbachev, which were aimed at the republics as much as they were at Russia itself. In December 1986, Gorbachev took two momentous steps which may have seemed relatively unimportant at the time but which both had unanticipated outcomes. The first was to release the world-renowned physicist and political dissident Andrei Sakharov from internal exile in Gorky, 440 kilometres east of Moscow, where he had been banished seven years earlier for alleged anti-Soviet activities. Sakharov was now free to return to the capital where he could continue his work as a scientist. Gorbachev no doubt had in mind the need to remedy the serious loss to the Soviet scientific community resulting from Sakharov's isolation in Gorky, but the main political result of Sakharov's return to Moscow would be for him to continue his campaign for reform and freedom of expression throughout the Soviet Union. For the next three years before his death in December 1989, Sakharov played a leading role in the furtherance of social and political change, most notably by questioning the hitherto unassailable but now increasingly uncertain role of the Communist Party.

The second important step taken by Gorbachev in December 1986 was to dismiss Dinmukhamed Kunaev as First Secretary of the Kazakh Communist Party, and appoint as his replacement a close political ally named Gennady Kolbin. Kunaev had earlier travelled to Moscow in June 1986 to seek approval to dismiss Nursultan Nazarbaev, then Chairman of the Council of Ministers, who Kunaev regarded as too disruptive to the established order and with ideas for reform which Kunaev saw as a threat to stability. In seeking to remove Nazarbaev, Kunaev hoped to ingratiate himself with the Soviet leadership by recommending that a Russian should be appointed in Nazarbaev's place, while he himself as a Kazakh would retain the most senior position as First Secretary of the Kazakh Party. But by now it was too late to get rid of Nazarbaev so easily; while the old Soviet leadership under Chernenko would probably have agreed to Kunaev's request, Gorbachev had now been in power for over a year and had no wish to allow the

Kazakh Communist Party to pursue its old ways of corruption and inertia any longer. Gorbachev accepted the recommendation that a Russian should be appointed, but this appointment would be to replace Kunaev himself, not Nazarbaev. Whether he had planned his resignation or not, Kunaev was forced to step down in December 1986, to be replaced by Gennady Kolbin. Kolbin was a 'non-ethnic' Russian from Chuvash, one the twenty-eight autonomous ethnic republics within Russia. Although strictly speaking he was not a Russian, this did not make him any more acceptable in Kazakhstan. Kolbin had a reputation as an incorruptible and capable administrator with proven experience in dealing with inefficiency and inertia in Georgia, where he had been the second secretary of the Georgian Communist Party under Eduard Shevarnadze, later the Soviet foreign minister. Before that he worked in the Sverdlovsk party administration with Boris Yeltsin, with whom he shared many reformist aims and ideals. Gorbachev wanted Kolbin to take control of and rejuvenate the elderly and backward-looking Communist Party leadership in Alma-Ata, but many in Kazakhstan, especially students and young people who increasingly felt at a disadvantage with Russians when competing for jobs and housing, were incensed that a Russian had been appointed to replace Kunaev, in another example of Russian arrogance and insensitivity.

The immediate reaction was one of violent demonstrations in Alma-Ata, and was the first major outbreak of nationalist protest and of opposition to the post-Brezhnev Soviet leadership. Other more serious uprisings and armed conflicts occurred in the following years, notably in the Baltic States and in Armenia and Azerbaijan, conflicts which imposed unsustainable strains on the cohesion of the Soviet Union, and ultimately contributed to its dissolution. But the process could be said to have started on the streets of Alma-Ata, and was indirectly encouraged by Andrei Sakharov, who sympathized with nationalist movements, and who sought a non-violent end to the dictatorship of the Communist Party. If Gorbachev had dismissed Kunaev first, before allowing Sakharov to return to Moscow, he may have had second thoughts about the advisability of giving freedom to someone who in his own way also did much to hasten the eventual end of the USSR.

The fifteen republics which made up the Soviet Union included several hundred different ethnic groups and nationalities, which were generally far more interested in their own separate histories and cultures than in official doctrines of Soviet communism. The threat which they posed to the stability of the Soviet Union had been contained by a mixture of repression, of varying degrees of severity depending on the political climate of the time, and by the widespread provision of social benefits especially in education, housing, and medical services throughout the various republics. Often this provision was at the expense of similar benefits in Russia as the colonial power and the central component of the USSR. As an unforeseen consequence of free education and the near-elimination of illiteracy, many in the non-Russian republics became more conscious of their own history and traditions, and of the extent to which these traditions had been eroded since their republics had been incorporated in the Soviet Union. The Communist Party of the Soviet Union devoted considerable resources to promoting the concept of a distinct Soviet identity, to go alongside the national identity of each of the separate republics and even of different ethnic groups within particular republics, including some in Russia itself. Individual national identities were permitted to exist and flourish, but all were firmly contained within the Soviet family. Throughout the USSR nationalism took various different forms, the most overtly political strain of which emerged in the Baltic states where there had always been a wary and difficult relationship with Russia. This relationship became increasingly fraught after their enforced incorporation in the Soviet Union in 1940. In these republics nationalism consisted essentially of a struggle for independence, and the people of Estonia, Latvia, and Lithuania were greatly encouraged by their close proximity to the countries of eastern Europe, especially in the 1980s when the eastern-bloc Soviet allies increasingly distanced themselves politically from the USSR, culminating in the successive collapses of communist governments throughout the region in 1989. At the other end of the scale of nationalism in the Soviet Union, the Central Asian republics were the least interested in political independence. Earlier movements for separation from Russia, for example under the Alash Orda government in Kazakhstan between 1917 and 1919, had been brief and unsuccessful, and although the Alash Orda had gained wide support at the time, there was no great enthusiasm for any successor movement now. Resistance to the Bolshevik government was widespread in the Semirechie region and in Kyrgyzstan until the late 1920s, but any similar resistance now was almost inconceivable. The Central Asian republics had gained considerable economic and social benefits from being part of the Soviet Union, and while there was resentment at what was seen as exploitation of natural resources and other policies on language and education, there was no real movement for independence. Any overt anti-Soviet activity that might have arisen was generally weak and was swiftly suppressed. This situation remained broadly unchanged until the accession to power of Gorbachev in 1985.

Within Russia, nationalism took the form of increasing dissatisfaction with what was seen as growing anti-Russian sentiment in the other republics, and by the late 1980s many Russians began to feel that their country would be better off by itself, without the trouble of having to support the seemingly ungrateful other republics. The sizeable populations of fellow ethnic Russians in many of the republics mitigated this sense of injustice within Russia, but there was a deep and growing antagonism caused by the demands placed on the Russian economy by the rest of the Soviet Union. Russia accounted for by far the greatest share of Soviet GDP, but its standard of living was among the lowest in the USSR, and outside Moscow, Leningrad, and other major cities there were widespread shortages of food and consumer goods. Even within the main cities, food supplies were often erratic and consumer goods were widely unobtainable, a situation which would be greatly improved, it was said, if it were not for the burden of supporting other republics. Party leaders in other republics retorted that much of the economic plight in Russia and the Soviet Union was due to mismanagement by the Soviet government, which amongst other failings deprived the republics of the right to pursue their own economic policies. The overriding priority given to cotton production in Central Asia had reduced the extent of land and water resources available for food production and thus the ability to increase food supplies to Russian towns and cities, while a wasteful use of other natural resources was needed to meet the targets of the central plan. These were all faults of the Soviet system, it was claimed, for which the individual republics could not be blamed. But such arguments found few sympathetic listeners in Russia.

In Kazakhstan, nationalism as a political force began to revive after 1985, although complete independence was never a serious objective. Much of the impetus came from dissatisfaction with the educational system which the Kazakh population believed did not cater sufficiently for children from non-Russian speaking families. The Kazakh language was not actively suppressed but nor was it widely used; road signs, political hoardings, and radio and television broadcasts were almost exclusively in Russian, and the language problem was becoming a focus of inter-ethnic friction between Russians and Kazakhs. A decree in 1987 laid down improvements to teaching in both Kazakh and Russian, an indication of the government's awareness of the need to balance the demands and concerns of both the major ethnic groups. The decree may have allayed some anxieties but other tensions continued to simmer in the background, largely caused by a worsening economic situation and a widening separation between Russians and Kazakhs. As well as worries about unemployment, the Russian population became suspicious of perceived discrimination against them and favouritism towards Kazakhs, while many Kazakhs increasingly saw their status as one of second-class citizens in their own country. A more serious problem for Gorbachev than the language question in Kazakhstan was the corrupt and static party leadership in Alma-Ata, a mirror-image of the situation which prevailed in Moscow. Gorbachev's desire to replace Kunaev was motivated by the need to remove the obstacles to change in Kazakhstan just as much as it was by the need for change in Russia and throughout the rest of the Soviet Union. He may have been unaware of the strength of anti-Russian feeling in Kazakhstan, and in replacing Kunaev Gorbachev may have overlooked the similar decision made by Khrushchev in 1962, when Kunaev was first dismissed and replaced by Ismail Yusupov, who also was not a Kazakh. That action had been unpopular in Kazakhstan, and thanks to Brezhnev's support for Kunaev it was one of the factors which contributed to the downfall of Khrushchev not long afterwards. But the removal of Kunaev for the second time, on 16 December 1986, was to result in more instability in Kazakhstan and ultimately in the whole of the Soviet Union.

In the afternoon of 17 December 1986, as news of Kolbin's arrival spread, several hundred students gathered in Brezhnev Square at the southern end of Prospect Mira (Peace) to protest not only against the appointment of a non-Kazakh as Communist Party leader but also to make a series of political demands. This was an unprecedented situation in the conformist atmosphere of the time. Many more thousands of demonstrators joined the protest to be met by large numbers of police and troops; some accounts report that groups of Russian workers and miners were organised by Russian officials in the city administration with instructions to help suppress the demonstration. Senior members of the Soviet politburo and the KGB were despatched from Moscow to take control of the situation, and military reinforcements were sent to Alma Ata from other towns and from other republics in what was called Operation Snowstorm. Hundreds of protesters were killed as the police and troops were said to have opened fire indiscriminately on the unarmed students and demonstrators. The disturbances spread to other parts of Kazakhstan, but after a few days most of the unrest had subsided; this was the coldest time of the year and few people wanted to remain out on the streets for long. The extent and impact of the protest would probably have been much greater if the appointment of Kolbin had been made in the heat of the summer. The exact number of casualties has never been disclosed and has remained a source of controversy and bitterness ever since. Not only has the government been accused of obscuring the details of what happened during the demonstrations, but it has done nothing to dispel the widespread belief that the crowds were provoked so as to ensure that anti-Russian nationalism could be violently suppressed and that stability should be imposed by force.

In recognition of the strength of feeling aroused in Alma-Ata, Brezhnev Square was afterwards renamed Republic Square, and Prospect Mira was renamed Zheltoksan (December) in honour of the protest of that month and its victims. Thereafter an uneasy calm was maintained, although there were sporadic outbreaks of anti-Russian rioting in parts of western Kazakhstan in 1989. In 2006, a memorial to commemorate the events of December 1986 was unveiled at the top of Prospect Zheltoksan. The statue is simple and unpretentious and like the statues of Manshuk Mametova and Alya Moldagulova on Astana Square, it is without the domineering features of traditional Soviet monuments. Known as the Dawn of Freedom, the memorial marks yet another watershed moment in the recent history of Kazakhstan.

Nowadays Dinmukhhamed Kunaev is widely admired and revered throughout Kazakhstan for his achievements in the development of the country, achievements which have been matched by few other individuals in Kazakh history. His role in managing the wartime evacuation of factories and the many thousands of workers arriving from Russia in 1941, his post-war work as a scientist and academic and as President of the Kazakh Academy of Sciences, his role as Communist Party leader for twenty-four years, and his constant efforts to work for the benefit of the people, are all remembered with respect and affection. The Kunaev Museum on Tolebaev Street in central Almaty and the nearby flat where he used to live, commemorate his life and career. On display are records of his work as a mining engineer in the 1930s, a vast library of scientific and technical literature and books from all over the world, and a large collection of guns and hunting rifles from the time when he and Leonid Brezhnev used to go on hunting trips in the nearby Alatau Mountains and in the forests of northern Kazakhstan. But recollection of his achievements has been allowed to obscure some of the less attractive features of his term in office.

In the 1950s and 1960s, during which time he held many senior and influential positions, Kunaev was unable or unwilling to forestall the worsening ecological problems of the country, most notably the environmental disaster of the Aral Sea, and the inexorable spread of industrial pollution in the towns and cities, which harmed or ruined the health of millions. This was a difficult time of industrial and economic reconstruction and the country had other more pressing priorities. Similar concerns for the environment were ignored in Russia and in many western countries. But as a scientist and mining engineer Kunaev could not have been unaware of the damage being done in many parts of the country, and although he might have attempted to intervene, any such attempts were over-ruled by the Soviet leadership, in the interests of maximising industrial and agricultural output. Kunaev's close and apparently uncritical friendship with Brezhnev was vital in ensuring his own position, but it had other, less desirable, consequences for Kazakhstan, where the economy became increasingly and inextricably dependent on Russian markets for its exports of raw materials. By the late 1960s the Russian economy was already flagging and its inefficient industrial enterprises, uncompetitive on world markets, exerted a negative effect on demand and efficiency in Kazakhstan. Brezhnev and Kunaev shared the same views of the importance of stability over reform, with the result that efforts to modernize and raise technical standards in industry either came to nothing or were not attempted in the first place. Kunaev also acceded to, or was forced to accept, nuclear testing at the 'Polygon' range near Semipalatinsk, despite the far greater availability of unpopulated land in Siberia, and the permanent damage to the local population and environment which resulted from it is a scar on his achievements. The most sinister aspect of Kunaev's legacy in Kazakhstan was arguably the network of prison camps for political dissidents and any who opposed the Soviet regime, including journalists, historians, artists, writers, theatre directors, and economic reformers. Most notorious was the Alzhir camp near Akmolinsk for women who were themselves innocent but who could not be allowed to remain free while their husbands were imprisoned. This camp and many others throughout the country were built on Stalin's orders in the 1930s and 1940s, but continued to function for years after Stalin's death. Kunaev was complicit in the continued existence of these camps, in which many thousands of prisoners from all over the Soviet Union perished.

The departure of Kunaev was another end-of-era event in Kazakhstan. The Soviet period in Kazakhstan effectively came to an end with the upheavals of Zheltoksan, although the Soviet Union itself would continue, increasingly debilitated, for another five years. Kunaev went into retirement and died seven years later in 1993, at the age of 81, in the second year of Kazakh independence. Throughout his career he promoted the interests of Kazakhstan and like many of his contemporaries he had witnessed both the birth and death of the Soviet Union. The influence of this generation was now coming to an end.

The longer-term significance of the events of December 1986 lay not so much in the appointment of an outsider as being the cause of the violence and unrest, but more in the fact that for the first time in a Soviet republic, large numbers of non-Russian protesters took concerted action against what were seen as Russian imperial and dictatorial policies. In addition, in the new orthodoxy of openness under Gorbachev, the Soviet media promptly provided accounts of the disturbances, in another unprecedented departure from the earlier official policies of secrecy and censorship. Anti-Russian riots and other instances of nationalist unrest in the Soviet Union had never before been publicly acknowledged, and different ethnic groups in other republics now realised that they could express their aspirations more openly. Opponents of the Gorbachev reforms clearly saw this as a threat to the Communist Party's monopoly of power, and to the cohesion of the Soviet Union itself, and no-one knew where this would end. The authoritarian nature of the Party, in Kazakhstan and throughout the USSR, was the only type of government which the population knew, and it had created a sense of national identity and unchanging stability; now it seemed that it all might suddenly disintegrate. This was a matter of growing alarm for many people in Kazakhstan, not only those in the Party but throughout the population as a whole. In both the Kazakh and the Russian communities, as in the rest of the USSR, the shared inheritance of social order and security was now under threat. This may have marked the start of the nostalgia and yearning for the simpler way of life under Stalin, when people did not have to take responsibility for many aspects of their own lives. The hazy fondness for the Stalin era was particularly remarkable in Kazakhstan, which had experienced its own enormous suffering during the collectivisation of agriculture, and the executions and mass disappearances of the 1930s. Now the terrors of that time were being forgotten and replaced by day-to-day worries about inflation, factory closures, and previously unheard-of job losses. All of this seemed to foreshadow the loss of the security of the Soviet welfare state, as well as a threat to the traditions of family and clan in Kazakh society.

In the frozen winter at the beginning of 1987, with the violent events of the previous December still clear in the minds of many people, Gennady Kolbin embarked on a difficult and ultimately losing struggle to bring about change and reform. At the time heating and energy supplies were precarious, food deliveries were erratic, and the environment for change was extremely unfavourable. The reforms which Kolbin wanted to introduce were an extension of the major programme of *perestroika* (restructuring) simultaneously announced by Gorbachev in Moscow, and aimed at decentralising the management of the economy, giving enterprises more autonomy in finding their own markets and suppliers, and setting prices for their own goods, instead of doing everything as set out in the central plan. These reforms were intended to reduce waste and inefficiency, improve supplies of goods to the population, and encourage the transfer of responsibility away from the state towards enterprises and individuals. They were doomed to fail. Kolbin found himself surrounded by unwilling and often openly hostile officials and ministers, directors of state enterprises and managers of collective farms, who were often even less amenable to reform than were their counterparts in Russia. Throughout the economy, decisions concerning prices, output, and markets had always been implemented by the relevant industrial ministries, and few enterprise managers had any knowledge or experience of areas outside their immediate responsibility. Nor did they have any enthusiasm for taking responsibility for these matters, and with the collusion of local party officials most managers strenuously resisted what was being proposed. They could rely on loans continuing to be provided to industrial and agricultural enterprises which were either already in or on the verge of bankruptcy, by the state-owned banks, and the banks made only token attempts to recover overdue loans. As a result the banks themselves came close to bankruptcy, and this became a major factor in intensifying the economic crisis. Meanwhile Kolbin, unusually for a non-Kazakh, set about learning Kazakh, but this did little to make his policies any more acceptable.

Nowadays Kolbin is regarded as a relatively low-level official who lacked the experience and ability needed to manage a vast republic such as Kazakhstan. His most important qualification was that he had the confidence of Gorbachev, a factor which immediately set him apart from the population. On a personal level, Kolbin's Russian origins, his incorruptibility, and his non-compliance with Kazakh ways of doing business, all counted heavily against him. Ultimately he failed in his attempts at reform, defeated by the inertia and complacency surrounding him, and by the deep-rooted Kazakh system of nepotism and clan politics. Although the fact that he was not a Kazakh was not in his favour, more significant than his national origin was Kolbin's unwillingness to become part of this system, and it was this which ensured his downfall. Politically, he took steps to ensure fair representation of Kazakh, Russian, and every other community in Kazakhstan, and tried to bring about an equal distribution of jobs and opportunities. But tensions between Russians and Kazakhs, no longer violent but still deep-seated and widespread, continued to exist, before eventually Kolbin was replaced by Nursultan Nazarbaev, a Kazakh and the second secretary of the Communist Party of Kazakhstan, in June 1989. By now the authority of Gorbachev was already severely weakened, and the Soviet leadership in Moscow had little choice but to accept this new development.

In September 1989, Kazakh was declared to be the official language of the country; this eased slightly the Kazakh sense of injustice, but Russian was to remain the language of 'inter-ethnic communication' and all officials dealing with the public in theory had to know both languages. In practice, and despite the example given by Kolbin, almost all the Russians in Kazakhstan firmly refused to make any attempt to learn Kazakh, and were generally disdainful of Kazakh attempts increasingly to assert their language and culture. Nonetheless, on a personal level close relations between the Russian and Kazakh populations continued to flourish, and inter-marriage was still common. In the north of the country, where Russians were closer to Russia itself and far outnumbered Kazakhs, Russians generally felt stable and secure, although this would change when the economy deteriorated and the many industrial enterprises on which many thousands depended for their livelihood were threatened with closure. But in Alma-Ata and in the south, where the Russian population was smaller and more isolated, Russians continued to feel under some ill-defined but uncomfortable threat, despite the widespread perception among Kazakhs that it was the Russians who had better access to jobs and housing. In this situation some Russians preferred to remain apart from their Kazakh neighbours, and a growing number of Russian families in Alma-Ata, worried about developments taking place in Kazakhstan, began to consider leaving the country and starting a new life in Russia.

CHAPTER TWENTY TWO

The End of the USSR

The Soviet Union continued to exist for a further seven years after the date of its possible demise was put forward by the Russian historian and dissident Andrei Amalrik in his famous essay '*Will the Soviet Union Survive Until 1984?*'. Written in 1969 and published in the West the following year, the title was partly inspired by George Orwell's *Nineteen Eighty-Four,* although Amalrik originally thought 1980 was a more likely date for the end of the USSR. This was the year by when, according to Khrushchev's prediction in the 1960s, the economy of the Soviet Union would have overtaken that of the United States. Amalrik, unlike Orwell, was concerned not so much with the world as it might become by 1984, but more by the way the Soviet Union and Soviet society were actually developing in the late 1960s. For drawing attention to these developments, he was persecuted by the authorities until his enforced exile in 1975.

Andrei Amalrik was born in Moscow in 1938, at a time when the Stalinist terror was at its height. After the war his father, despite being a war veteran and having been wounded at Stalingrad, was denied a university career when he returned home because of critical remarks he had made about Stalin. Amalrik's sense of injustice at his father's experience led him into his own trouble with the authorities from an early age. As a teenager he held unconventional opinions and refused to conform to what he saw as the falsity and dishonesty of Soviet life. Despite his politically-unreliable family background, he gained a place at Moscow University but was expelled in 1963 for writing a study indicating that a ninth-century Russian state centred at Kiev, pre-dating the medieval Kiev Rus, owed its origins to Norman invaders, and for taking this study to the Danish embassy to be sent to a Danish historian who held similar views. Not only had Amalrik transgressed by approaching a foreign embassy, but he had refuted the official Soviet version of early Russian history by implying a foreign, non-Slav, involvement in the origins of the country. Amalrik refused to withdraw his conclusions and for this and for other unconventional beliefs, he was denied employment as a historian or writer, and was forced to accept a series of menial jobs to earn a living. In 1965 he was sentenced to two and a half years in a collective farm for the offence of not having regular employment, known as parasitism, and this experience formed the basis of his first book *Involuntary Journey to Siberia* in 1966. He was allowed to return to Moscow that year, but once more was subjected to police harassment and prevented from finding work. Amalrik resisted efforts to remove him from the Soviet Union and was critical of other Russian writers who left Russia rather than stay to campaign for greater freedom from within the country. After publication in the West of *Will the Soviet Union Survive Until 1984?* Amalrik was re-arrested in 1970 and sentenced to a period of exile in Novosibirsk in western Siberia during which he was forbidden to have any contact with the rest of the country. Amalrik was finally compelled to leave the Soviet Union in 1975, and lived in Europe and the United States until his death in a car crash in Spain in 1980.

The underlying premise of *Will the Soviet Union Survive Until 1984?* was a supposedly inevitable military conflict between the USSR and China. As well as causing large-scale destruction, such a war would impose an unsustainable burden on Soviet society, cause widespread unrest in Russia and the republics, and culminate in the overthrow of the government in Moscow and the collapse of the Soviet state. Although rationalised and explained in detail, and more convincing in the 1960s than it would be in later years, the predicted conflict with China did not take place, although an outbreak of hostilities along the Amur River in eastern Siberia occurred in the summer of 1969 which might have led to war. But the analysis of the internal weaknesses of the USSR, and the prediction of its imminent collapse, were accurate and far-sighted. If American military pressure were to be substituted in place of the imagined war with China, Amalrik's theories were almost entirely correct. The immense strains on the Soviet economy and on the defence budget in the 1980s, imposed on the country in response to American military spending, were seen by many to have been the ultimate cause of the eventual collapse of the Soviet Union.

The principal crimes which Amalrik committed in writing the book were to draw attention to the failures of the Soviet leadership in dealing with the challenge of changing external and internal circumstances, and to indicate that the Soviet Union might not survive these changes; indeed that it might come to an end within only fifteen years. But it was not only the Soviet authorities who resented these ideas: millions of ordinary people, who may not have been completely happy with their condition, but who had survived the Second World War and who were now investing their whole lives and work in creating a better future for themselves and for succeeding generations in the Soviet Union, felt uncomfortable about seeing their way of life questioned in this way. By denigrating Amalrik, and sentencing him to banishment in Siberia, the government was to a large extent reflecting public opinion, although Amalrik believed that public opinion had been deeply misled over a period of decades. By touching on a nerve and by implicating much of the population in what was happening in the USSR, Amalrik alienated himself from many of his fellow writers and countrymen.

Will the Soviet Union Survive Until 1984? was written almost exclusively from a Russian perspective, with little reference to the other Soviet republics, but it was as relevant to Kazakhstan and to Central Asia as it was to Russia itself. Amalrik identified three factors which prevented the development of a 'Democratic Movement' which might have emerged to challenge the government and lead the country in a more favourable direction. The first was 'the planned elimination from society of the most independent minded and active of it members'. This, said Amalrik, 'had been going on for decades, and had left an imprint of greyness and mediocrity on all sections of society'. At the time he was writing, the economic stagnation in Russia under Brezhnev and in Kazakhstan under Kunaev was just beginning. 'This elimination, whether through emigration or through exile from the country or through imprisonment or physical annihilation, has affected every strata of our people'.

Second, Amalrik claimed that the prevalence of negative and defeatist thinking among the majority of the population prevented the possibility of reform and change. 'You can't break down the wall by beating your head against it' and 'There's nothing I can do anyway' were common attitudes, according to Amalrik, who said that 'In reaction to the power of the regime, the middle class practises a cult of its own impotence'. The third factor was the fact that everyone was employed by the state. 'In any country, the stratum of society least inclined towards change or any sort of independent action is that composed of state employees. This is natural, because every government worker considers himself too insignificant in comparison with the power apparatus of which he is only a small cog to demand of that apparatus any kind of change. At the same time, he has been relieved of all social responsibility, since his job is simply to carry out orders. On the other hand, the person who gives the orders is equally freed from a sense of responsibility inasmuch as the officials on the level below him regard his orders as 'good' because they come from above. This creates the illusion among the authorities that everything they do is good'. Not surprisingly this analysis was not popular amongst ordinary people in the Soviet Union. But it was equally applicable to the hierarchical structure of the old Kazakh khanates, except that unlike the Soviet Union, pre-Soviet Kazakhstan was a feudal society which had evolved without outside intervention over many centuries, which made no claims to social progress or advancement, and which would have been content to continue in such a manner indefinitely.

Amalrik believed that the prevalent attitude throughout Russia and the Soviet Union was simply one of passive discontent. Discontent was not directed against the regime as such, since the majority did not think about their condition, or if they did they believed that there was no alternative. Instead it was discontent about particular aspects of the system, which were essential to its existence. Factory workers were bitter because they had no rights in relation to the factory management; collective farm workers were resentful about their total dependence on the whims of the chairman of the kolkhoz; everybody was angry about the great inequalities in wealth, low wages, austere housing conditions, lack of essential consumer goods, and compulsory registration at their home and place of work. The level of discontent was increasing, and people were beginning to wonder who was to blame. The slow improvement in the standard of living, particularly in the supply of housing, could not diminish the anger, although it partially neutralised it as a political force.

It was clear, however, that any reversal or even slowdown in the improvement in the standard of living could lead to unrest and violence. The horrific incident at Novocherkassk in June 1962, in which hundreds of demonstrators including women and children had been shot and killed by police and troops, illustrated for Amalrik not only the fragility of the economy and the inability of the government to provide even basic foodstuffs for the population, but also the impossibility of reform and the creation of a more equitable and efficient economic system. Instead the old system continued unchanged and unchangeable, a situation made possible by the 'extreme social disorientation' of the majority of the people. The 'proletarianisation' of the countryside had created an alien class of neither peasants or working class, but one which had the dual psychology of the owners of tiny farmsteads, which until recently they had been, and of farm hands working on gigantic and anonymous collective farms, which recently they had become. In the towns, a similar confusion of social status existed. The mass exodus of peasants to the cities had created a new type of city dweller: a person who had broken with his old environment, way of life, and culture, and who was now finding it difficult to discover his place in his new environment. Such a person, of whom in the 1960s there were many millions, felt ill at ease, both frightened and aggressive. News of the Novocherkassk massacre, officially suppressed but widely spread by word of mouth, added to the deep sense of fear and uncertainty. The old social structure in both the towns and the countryside had been completely destroyed, while a new one was only just beginning to form. The 'ideological foundations' on which the new social structure was being built were, according to Amalrik, very primitive: the desire for material well-being, the instinct for self-preservation, and a new ideology of Russian, or more specifically 'Great Russian', nationalism, with a characteristic cult of strength and expansionist ambitions. The 'Great Russians' constituted the majority of the Slav population of the Soviet Union and were ethnically distinct from other Slavs such as Ukrainians and Byelorussians. A similar movement had arisen at the beginning of the twentieth century, when the traditional monarchist ideology was replaced by a narrow form of nationalism, invoking the expression 'genuinely Russian people'. Such a nationalistic ideology may have proved temporarily useful to the Soviet regime, but Amalrik believed it was dangerous for the country as a whole in which, in the 1960s, people of Russian nationality made up less than half the total population. Amalrik paid little attention to the ideals of Soviet Communism, of social equality, the elimination of privilege, and a fair distribution of wealth and resources, and this further alienated many people, who had genuine aspirations to live up to these ideals.

In a brief section towards the end of his book, Amalrik refered to the likely rise of nationalism among the non-Russian republics: 'As the regime's difficulties mount up and as it appears ever more incapable of coping with its tasks... the nationalist tendencies of the non-Russian peoples will intensify sharply, first in the Baltic area, the Caucasus and the Ukraine, then in Central Asia '. Amalrik believed that in many cases, local Communist Party officials would exploit these tendencies by advocating that Russia should solve its own problems and leave the republics alone to deal with their problems. 'National separateness' would also enable local officials, if they could fend off the growing general chaos, to preserve their own privileged positions. The observations about social disruption and upheavals in the traditional class structure applied just as much to Kazakhstan as to Russia, if not more so. But the close ties with Russia at all levels, social, economic, and family, over the previous centuries meant that, of the fifteen republics comprising the Soviet Union, Kazakhstan eventually - and paradoxically given the suffering it had experienced aince the 1917 Revolution - became the most reluctant to see it end. The outlook was not all gloomy for Amalrik: it was also possible, he thought, that the middle class might prove strong enough to keep control in its own hands. 'In that case, the granting of independence to the various Soviet nationalities would come about peacefully and some sort of federation will be created, similar to the British Commonwealth or the European Economic Community'. The eventual creation of the Commonwealth of Independent States, without the Baltic States but with strong residual ties to Russia among the other republics, bore out the validity of this prediction.

The controversy and international publicity surrounding Andrei Amalrik soon subsided, and in the 1970s and 1980s it was the stagnating economy and declining living standards which were uppermost in most people's minds. In January 1987 the Soviet leader Mikhail Gorbachev introduced the programme of perestroika, the restructuring of the economy which was to lead to the collapse of the Soviet Union five years later. By 1989, twenty years after the appearance of *Will the Soviet Union Survive Until 1984?*, the economic crisis had deepened further, and once again, as in 1917, the 1930s, and in the war, Kazakhstan found itself caught up in traumatic events in Russia for which it had no responsibility and over which it had virtually no control. The Russian economy, and by extension the economy of the other fourteen republics, was heading in an irreversible downward spiral. Many industrial enterprises, faced with a loss of markets, supplies of raw materials, and loans and investment from banks, were forced to close down, or remained open in name only. Inflation accelerated and living standards fell, as food rationing spread to items which had been freely available since soon after the end of the Second World War. To pay wages and to cover the growing budget deficit, which in 1989 was estimated at 10 per cent of GDP, roughly three times the ratio for a stable economy, the Soviet government put billions of roubles into circulation. Banknotes of ever-rising denominations, reminiscent of the worthless roubles derisively known as *kerenki,* named after Alexander Kerensky, head of the short-lived provisional government in 1917, were changed into foreign currency or physical goods as soon as possible, although mostly they were added to the enormous existing supply of 'empty' money for which there was no equivalent in goods and services.

As a largely agricultural economy, Kazakhstan was better placed than many urban regions of the Soviet Union, where supplies of bread and meat were rapidly disappearing from the shops. In common with other republics and with some agricultural provinces within Russia, Kazakhstan began to withhold deliveries of food to the central ministries for national distribution. Grain in particular, having acquired an almost mystical significance during the war and in the Virgin Lands campaign, once again returned to the centre of national attention. State and collective farms in Kazakhstan now found that they could ignore local party officials and the various agricultural ministries, and disregard state procurement orders altogether. After decades of production in accordance with centrally-planned output levels and prices, often set at or below the cost of production, more and more farm managers held back their grain, either to feed livestock or to sell for a profit on the new semi-private 'kolkhoz markets'. Supplies of grain and other food to Alma-Ata were maintained or even increased, as former compulsory deliveries to

Russia were cut back, while the Soviet government in Moscow, increasingly ineffectual, was powerless to counter this trend, other than by paying more for essential supplies, thereby further increasing the budget deficit. Even when more money was allocated for purchases of food, many republics refused to surrender their produce and goods unless it was in exchange for items in shortage in their own republics, as the Soviet economy regressed to a system of barter, outside the now-defunct central plan. Barter was a trading system in which the Soviet Union had considerable experience, even if it did not produce the most efficient allocation of goods and services, but it depended on effective planning and rigorous political control, neither of which existed any longer.

By 1990 the Soviet Union was facing three separate but inter-related crises – political, economic, and national – each of which was critical and each was posing a serious danger to the future of the USSR. None of these crises was new, but they were becoming increasingly difficult to resolve, as successive attempts at reform had failed; now the government was faced with a harsh and inescapable choice of making a complete departure from the whole Soviet system, or retreating from what had been achieved so far in an attempt to return to the pre-perestroika state of affairs. It was no longer possible to attempt to solve each crisis separately; reform and change in one crisis area had inescapable consequences for reform and change in the other two. Allowing the non-Russian republics to ignore their earlier obligations to supply grain and foodstuffs, minerals and other natural resources for national distribution and to sell their output where they wanted would result in the republics taking greater control over their own affairs, with a further diminution of the role of the Communist Party of the Soviet Union and of the central government in Moscow. Similarly a consistent and serious reform of the market would inevitably lead to devolution of economic decision-making away from the centre to each republic, with political autonomy to follow.

The Gorbachev reforms of perestroika and glasnost had already led to a marked decline in the influence of the Communist Party. On 4 February 1990, undeterred by snow and sub-zero temperatures, between 200,000 and 300,000 people joined a march from Gorky Park to Manezhnaya Square in the centre of Moscow to demand reform, in one of the biggest demonstrations not organised by the government ever to take place in Russia. Placards were carried by the crowd openly demanding the abolition of the Communist Party and reminding the Party of the violent overthrow of Nicolae Ceausescu in Romania just over one month earlier. Three days later the Communist Party approved proposals to abolish the contentious Article 6 of its Constitution which had guaranteed its own monopoly of power. In the following month elections took place to local soviets, or councils, in Russia, in which reformists made substantial gains in the main cities, especially Moscow and Leningrad. Also in March 1990, Gorbachev was elected President of the Soviet Union, a newly created office which Gorbachev had devised to counter the waning strength of the Communist Party and to restrain any further loss of control over the republics. In retrospect, this moment represented the high point in the perestroika movement and in the Soviet revolution which was being imposed from above. From now on events in the country began to overtake the Party, and Gorbachev became increasingly isolated, appealing neither to reformers or conservatives.

From among the reformers the most critical attacks came from Boris Yeltsin. Yeltsin came from a background in the construction industry in Sverdlovsk, where his experience in the local Communist Party made him increasingly aware of the inability of the Communist Party nationally or locally to provide effective leadership in the management of the economy. His refusal to speak in the slogans and platitudes of the Party made him popular among ordinary working people, especially when he spoke of the needs of Russia rather than those of the Soviet Union. In May 1990 Yeltsin was elected as Chairman of the Supreme Soviet of the Russian Federation, a position which traditionally held relatively little significance. But the following month he declared Russia to be a sovereign state within the USSR, a dramatic move which followed similar announcements by the Baltic states, and which emphasized Russia's intention to be in control of its own affairs, albeit without breaking away completely from the Soviet Union.

As well as speaking his mind on local matters in Sverdlovsk, on a national level Yeltsin also became highly critical of Gorbachev's irresolute attempts at reform. The perestroika programme he believed was misdirected and insufficiently radical, and Yeltsin advocated that the historical ban on private enterprise and private ownership dating back to the Revolution, should be repealed, and that loss-making enterprises should be gradually closed down, or wherever possible taken over by workers. To carry out much-needed reform of the credit and financial system, the State Bank of Russia should be separated from the government, and the setting up of commercial banks should be encouraged. Far from alienating the fundamentally conservative Russian population, as had been the fate of Andrei Amalrik in the 1960s and 1970s, such was the scale of disillusionment with the Communist Party and Soviet government that these far-reaching proposals found a ready response from many millions of ordinary Russians, even though many also sensed the dangers that lay ahead in Yeltsin's vision for the future. In a speech in July 1990 Yeltsin went further and declared that the Party's monopoly on power had driven the country to a desperate situation, with tens of millions of people living in poverty. He now advocated a new constitution for Russia which would ensure the primacy of law and the main rights and freedoms of citizens, including freedom of demonstration, political organisation, and of conscience and religion. A constitutional court would be established to ensure that the government complied with democratic rights and freedoms. Russia would become a presidential republic, with universal suffrage and secret ballots for multi-candidate elections, to be held every five years. The state would be stripped of ideology and all restrictions limiting senior government posts to members of the Communist Party would be abolished. The Party's role in the management of the economy would also be abolished, and no political organisation should be allowed in any enterprises, colleges, research institutes, or collective farms, unless authorised by staff representatives. The Party's national structure and policies would guarantee the rights of dissenting minorities and ensure their proportionate representation in the leadership; and a new voluntary union would be established between the Communist Parties of the different republics, as opposed to the rigid and outdated structure which had existed hitherto.

All this was heresy for those in the Communist Party who were ideologically and unremittingly opposed to any notion of reform. But the call for greater autonomy for individual parties prepared the ground for more radical developments in the future. In the republics, where his proposals for autonomy and 'de-ideologisation' had widespread appeal, many more millions of non-Russians also found common ground with Yeltsin. His emphasis on Russian rather than Soviet needs and policies encouraged political leaders in the republics to put the needs of their republics ahead of those of the Soviet Union, and throughout 1990 the question of sovereignty became an increasingly contentious issue. Starting with Lithuania in March and culminating in Kyrgyzstan at the end of October, one republic after another declared itself to be a sovereign state. In practical terms this status differed widely according to what each republic wanted, from complete secession from the USSR in the Baltic states to much milder versions of independence in Kazakhstan and Kyrgyzstan. The various declarations of sovereignty had little in common beyond a rejection of what was seen as the arrogant Soviet system of dictatorship and control. But the process of disintegration of the Soviet Union had started and from now on would not be reversed.

In the management of the Soviet economy, 1990 also proved to be a critical year. Perestroika had brought about disarray and confusion, and in the summer of 1990 a radical new attempt at economic reform, known as the '500-Day Programme', was drawn up with the aim of giving a completely new direction to the economy and halting the rising tide of chaos. The Programme was designed by a team of thirteen leading economists under the direction of Stanislav Shatalin, Gorbachev's economic adviser, and Gregoriy Yavlinsky, the deputy prime minister in the newly-established Russian government. Yavlinsky was also Chairman of the Russian Economic Reform Committee, and a close confidant of Boris Yeltsin. The joint leadership of the project team was intended to make the programme acceptable to both sides of the political struggle engulfing Russia and the republics, and although initially the programme appeared to have the reluctant support of Gorbachev, any semblance of unanimity soon evaporated.

The 500-Day Programme was based on Yeltsin's premise that the state should be removed from management of the economy, and that all attempts at central planning should be abandoned. These were previously unimaginable ideas, but in the volatile conditions of the time they were becoming less unthinkable with every passing day. In its introductory statement the Programme asserted that the state should facilitate the creation of a benign environment for economic activity but refrain from direct participation in industry or agriculture. There should be legal equality for all kinds of property, including private ownership. Ownership of agricultural land would be retained by the state but collective farms or even individuals could manage farm land under long leases. Competition among producers was seen as the most important stimulus to economic activity, and prices should be set freely by the market through supply and demand. The fundamental objective of the Programme was to take everything that could be taken from the state and give it to private individuals.

In practical terms, the Programme had two particularly significant aspects. One was a detailed timetable, as implied in its title, during which it would be put into practice. This was something that had notoriously been lacking in the imprecise schedules and prevarication which characterised every earlier attempt at reform. To be successful the Programme had to be put into effect straightaway and according to a strict schedule, starting with immediate effect. Firstly, the process of auctioning state assets had to begin immediately, although the valuation of such assets was unclear and would be without the participation of foreign bidders. The first day would also mark the start of a land reform programme and a timetable for the gradual liberalization of prices. Privatisation of fifty percent of small enterprises would take place between Days 100 and 250. In the following period between Days 251 and 400, between thirty and forty percent of other state-owned industries would be privatised, and by which time prices would be freed on up to eighty percent of goods and services. In the final hundred days of the Programme a further thirty to forty percent of state industries would be privatised, leaving approximately thurty percent in state hands, and up to ninety percent of goods and services would be sold at market prices.

This aspect of the Programme had many defects and inconsistencies, having been hastily put together and drawn up without recent experience of a market economy in the Soviet Union. Of the many practical problems, the valuation of state assets was one of the most intractable; many industries had no proper inventory of their own premises, equipment, or other assets, and the division of liabilities between the central government and individual enterprises was fraught with difficulty. Estimating future revenues was also virtually impossible. Thus putting a realistic sale price on shares was impractical, with the result that shares in many enterprises were distributed free of charge in the form of vouchers to employees and to the public, since in theory the public were already the owners. It was expected that a rudimentary market would evolve, but in many cases the vouchers were quickly taken up by enterprise managers who became the owners of their own factories, and by wealthy individuals, marking the start of the era of oligarchs. The economists who drafted the plan believed that the government had no choice other than to make a complete and final break with the past, as was entailed in the Programme; the alternative was further economic decay and imminent collapse.

The second and even more significant feature of the 500-Day Programme was what it implied for the future of the USSR. The Programme had the support not only of Yeltsin, the Russian government, and leading economists in the country, but significantly the governments of all the individual republics as well (with the exception of Estonia, Latvia, and Lithuania, which wanted complete secession from the Soviet Union as soon as possible, no matter how far it was reformed). The support from the republics stemmed from the fact that the 500-Day Programme acknowledged the declaration of sovereignty that had already been made by thirteen of the fifteen republics, including Russia but not yet including Kazakhstan and Kyrgyzstan, a status which gave each republic control over its own natural resources and economic policies. This was another unprecedented development; the combination of loss of central control over the country's natural resources and an end to the planned economy would inevitably undermine and eventually bring about the end of the Soviet Union, at least in its present form. Kazakhstan and Kyrgyzstan declared their sovereignty on 25 and 30 October 1990 respectively; the relative delay in both countries was partly due to their geographical distance from the whirlpool of events swirling through Moscow, and a desire to see what other republics were doing, but it also reflected a stronger sense of loyalty to Russia and to the fading concept of the Soviet Union. The large Russian communities in Kazakhstan and Kyrgyzstan were deeply unhappy about developments taking place in what many still regarded as their homeland, while the native populations were equally perplexed, not knowing what to make of the turmoil in the country which had been the centre of their outlook on the world for the past 150 years. In both countries there was a desire for some form of independence, although this was combined with a fear of being cast adrift from Russia; while in all the republics, except the Baltic States, there was great uncertainty as to which direction - reform or conservatism, progress or stagnation, Yeltsin or Gorbachev - to follow. In Estonia, Latvia, and Lithuania there was no such uncertainty and each country had already made its decision to seek full independence.

The starting date for the 500-Day Programme was to be 1 October 1990; in Russia the Supreme Soviet voted on 11 September to adopt it, after which all that remained was for Gorbachev and the Soviet government to do the same for the Programme to be implemented throughout the Soviet Union. Fearful of the consequences for the future of the Union, Gorbachev hesitated to give his own commitment to the Programme, and sought to modify its more far-reaching proposals. It was one thing for economists, largely protected from the consequences of what they were advocating, to set targets for the privatisation of industry and liberalisation of prices in the name of economic reform, but the consequences for employment, inflation, and falling living standards for the mass of the population would be even more disastrous than they were already proving to be. There would also be an even greater diminution in the role of the Communist Party and the Soviet government, which would be politically unacceptable to large sections of the population, especially the older generation. To apply the radical measures set out in the 500-Day Programme in a small, compact and self-contained economy would be highly difficult, but to implement them throughout the vast, sprawling economy of the Soviet Union would be politically almost impossible. Over the decades the structure of the Soviet economy had been specifically devised in such a way as to maximize integration between the republics, and to prevent the economy from being taken apart by imposing too many obstacles to independence for the republics. According to an article in the *Moscow Times* in September 1990, now able to publish opinions which only a short while before were strictly forbidden, the Soviet Union was 'constructed like a single factory or conveyor belt, where whole regions are like separate shops or units of the production line. For example, Kazakhstan was turned into an accessory supplying raw materials for all the other republics. Central Asia was given over to the cultivation of cotton. The result was an ugly deformation of the natural state of each region – mutilated land and suffering people'.

In the light of all this, Gorbachev requested Nikolai Ryzhkov, the conservative Soviet prime minister, to draw up an alternative and less radical programme. Supported by the industrial ministries, directors of state enterprises and collective farms, and senior figures in the military establishment who were fearful of budget cuts and the break-up of the armed forces into 'Republican detachments', Ryzhkov produced a separate and distinct plan which advocated a more gradual transition to a market economy, with the state retaining a much greater influence. But although both plans focused on policies for the economy, the most critical difference between the two lay in how each saw the future of the Soviet Union. The 500-Day Programme envisaged a loose confederation of independent republics to replace the USSR; each republic would be responsible for its own legislation and for the management of its own economy, in a structure similar to that of the European Union, and which would be known as the Economic Union of Sovereign States. The Ryzhkov programme by contrast, although describing itself as radical, was in reality conservative and resistant to the whole concept of the market, and demonstrated a clear unwillingness to contemplate loss of control from the centre and any further weakening of the Soviet Union. Yeltsin was scathing about the Ryzhkov or 'Union' programme, which he said envisaged a continuation of the centralization, state planning, and directives which for many years had not worked but which instead had led to failure. The Yavlinsky-Shatalin programme, on the other hand, recognised the reality that most of the republics had already declared their own sovereignty, and would not accept the Union plan.

As on other occasions since coming to power five years earlier, Gorbachev was unable to make a definitive choice between the two plans, and prevaricated while trying to decide between which of the two different and momentous courses of action the country should adopt. The intended 1 October starting date for the 500-Day Programme came and went as the Supreme Soviet of the USSR, to which Gorbachev had referred both programmes, was also unable to give its opinion, except to ask for a new, joint version to be presented to it by 15 October. The final version, known as the 'President's Programme' was duly adopted the following day. The woolly title ('Guidelines for Stabilisation of the People's Economy and Transition to a Market Economy') was reminiscent of the verbose wording of traditional Communist Party documents; it carried no conviction that anything would be done in practice but instead conveyed the clear but unspoken hope that the problems raised by Gorbachev, of reform, democratisation, the rise of nationalism, and weakening of the Union, would simply fade away. In sharp contrast to the 500-Day Programme, the President's Programme lacked any detail of economic objectives or critically of the timing for their implementation, and abdicated decisions on the vital question of land ownership for individual farmers to the collective farms themselves. But the new plan was eventually to be undermined by its reversal of the right of each republic to take control of its own natural resources. For the republics this had been a key aspect in their acceptance of the 500-Day Programme, and the decision in the President's Programme that the central government in Moscow would retain control over all the natural resources of the Soviet Union for at least two years, ran contrary to the growing movement towards greater autonomy for the republics. This alone ensured that the Programme would ultimately fail.

In Kazakhstan and in most of the other republics, after the Zheltoksan events in Alma-Ata in 1986, the political situation had remained relatively calm until 1990, when aspirations for greater freedom from the Soviet Union came to the fore. Inspired by the freedoms introduced by Gorbachev, nationalist feelings suddenly erupted, and brought the nationality problem to the top of the hierarchy of crises engulfing the USSR. Growing uncertainty as to what should or would be the role and position of Russia as the central component of the Union, both in the drama currently being acted out, and in whatever political structure might eventually emerge to replace the USSR, was on everyone's minds. As in the economic and in the political crises, the principal figure in the nationality aspect of the upheaval, as far as both Russia and the republics were concerned, was Boris Yeltsin. On 12 June 1990 the Russian Congress of Deputies overwhelmingly adopted a declaration of national sovereignty within the USSR, largely the result of Yeltsin's efforts in asserting Russia's national interests over those of the Soviet Union. This did not amount to complete independence from the Soviet Union, but the date of 12 June subsequently became a public holiday in Russia to mark National Sovereignty Day. The declaration had been preceded by demands for secession in the three Baltic republics, and was followed by declarations of sovereignty, in chronological order, by Georgia, Azerbaijan, Uzbekistan, Moldova, Ukraine, Byelorussia, Turkmenistan, Armenia, Tajikistan, Kazakhstan, and Kyrgyzstan.

The first indication of the imminent upheaval was the decision in December 1989 of the Communist Party of Lithuania (CPL) to cut its ties with the Communist Party of the Soviet Union in Moscow. While adhering to its beliefs in the role of the Party, the CPL nonetheless bowed to the strengthening nationalist opinion in Lithuania, where irrespective of local politics the population no longer had any desire to be part of the Soviet Union. The decision of the Lithuanian Party was followed by similar decisions by the Communist Parties in Estonia and Latvia. Apparently unaware of the depth of nationalist feeling in Lithuania, Gorbachev travelled to the capital Vilnius in January 1990 where he was confronted by mass demonstrations and protests, and a refusal by the CPL to reverse its decision of the previous month. Gorbachev's attempts to persuade the Lithuanian government to abandon its policy of seeking complete independence also met with failure, and he returned to Moscow humiliated. In retaliation, in April 1990 the Soviet government announced sharp reductions in deliveries of raw materials, natural gas, and oil to Lithuania, thereby contributing to the decision among all three Baltic States to announce their decision to secede from the USSR.

Serious problems of protest and violence were simultaneously developing in another corner of the Soviet Union, beyond the Caucasus Mountains in Azerbaijan and Armenia, where January 1990 also proved to be a critical month. Unlike the case with the Baltic republics, which was a dispute between the republics and the central government in Moscow, this was a dispute between two neighbouring Soviet republics, but one which also had consequences for the cohesion of the whole of the Soviet Union. Hostility between Armenians and Azeris extended back over many decades and for most of the Soviet period it had been contained, but with the advent of perestroika, open conflict and violence could no longer be suppressed.

Azerbaijan is a geographically fragmented country with most of its territory extending from the Caucasus Mountains to the Caspian Sea. In the south it borders with Iran, and to the west lies the disputed mountainous region of Nagorno-Karabakh, legally part of Azerbaijan but inhabited overwhelmingly by Armenians. Further west still is the separate enclave of Nakhichevan, cut off from the rest of the country by Armenian territory. In February 1988 the Nagorno-Karabakh soviet passed a resolution demanding that it should be transferred to the jurisdiction of Armenia, an action which provoked organised attacks against Armenians who lived within Azerbaijan itself, especially in the industrial city of Sumgait just north of the capital Baku, where many Armenians were killed in the ensuing violence. Further clashes led to an exodus of the minority Azeri population from Nagorno-Karabakh and from other towns and villages in Armenia, and of Armenians who had survived the attacks in Sumgait and elsewhere in Azerbaijan. In January 1989 the Armenian government and the local Nagorno-Karabakh soviet declared that the territory had now seceded from Azerbaijan and had formally become part of a 'Unified Armenian Republic'. This was declared to be unconstitutional by the Soviet government in Moscow, but for Azerbaijan this response was weak and ineffective. Over the following twelve months tensions between the two Soviet republics remained high and anti-Armenian protests and unrest continued in Azerbaijan. These tensions flared up in January 1990 and Soviet troops were sent to Baku to quell the disturbances. In the violence which ensued over 120 protesters were killed, in an episode which became another major factor in the alienation of Azerbaijan from the USSR. A fragile peace was established, but throughout 1990-1991 the Azeri government in Baku was more concerned to try to preserve the integrity of its own territory, and was less worried by the prospect of the Soviet Union itself breaking up. Hostility and friction between Azerbaijan and Armenia continued, exacerbated by the vast displacement of people in both countries, and widespread fighting broke out again in 1992 in which hundreds more civilians were killed and in which Azeri forces suffered considerably more losses and casualties than the Russian-trained and better-equipped Armenians. Both republics believed that the Soviet government in Moscow sided with its opponent and it was not until May 1994 that a ceasefire was finally established, although the underlying territorial disputes remained unresolved.

The events of January 1990 are remembered in Azerbaijan as a dark period in the country's history, and each of the victims is commemorated by a headstone in a park in the hills above Baku. Despite the ceasefire, resentment and bitterness remained intense on both sides. Armenians were disillusioned by the perceived lack of support from the Soviet authorities, an attitude expressed most strongly by the Armenian President Ter Petrossian in May 1991 when he accused the USSR of 'having declared war on Armenia'. For their part the Azeris felt equally betrayed and that they had suffered most from the conflict. 'We have not regained our land (of Nagorno-Karabakh) but at least we got rid of the Armenians' was a common sentiment expressed in the Azeri press at the time of the ceasefire.

Apart from the damage to the credibility of the Soviet Union as a single country, the Armenia-Azerbaijan conflict highlighted a new and serious problem for the Soviet government and for others in Russia who believed it was still possible to preserve the USSR, by military means if all other efforts failed. Since the incorporation into the tsarist empire in the nineteenth century of territories along its southern fringe, in the Caucasus and in Central Asia, Russia had seen itself and its empire as being inextricably linked, in effect as being part of the same country since all were part of the same landmass and there was no sea or ocean between them. But the events in Azerbaijan were accompanied by a new development in Russia which challenged this perception. In January 1990 widespread public protests took place throughout Russia, especially in the southern city of Stavropol, where the mothers of young soldiers serving in the Soviet army protested and campaigned against the use of Russian troops being sent to quell disturbances in a non-Russian republic. The relationship between Russia and its empire suddenly became much more distinct and clear cut; millions of Russians, already facing enough problems of their own at home, no longer wished to bear the burden of maintaining stability in other parts of the empire, least of all by sending teenage conscripts to deal with distant conflicts and possibly be killed in the process. Stavropol is a solidly Russian city, the birthplace of Mikhail Gorbachev, and the city where he made his early career before transferring to Moscow. As the city's most famous son, Gorbachev could hardly fail to heed the protests of the local population. The 'Stavropol Mothers' campaign forced the Soviet government to accept the fact that it could no longer automatically rely on the largely conscript Soviet army to enforce its will over the republics.

Further conflict arose in Moldova where in September 1990, shortly after the Moldovan government declared its sovereignty from the USSR (and changed its name from Moldavia), the region on the east bank of the Dniester River known as Transnistria, a narrow stretch of land between the Dniester and the border with Ukraine, proclaimed its own secession from the rest of Moldova and established a 'Transnistrian Soviet Socialist Republic' (renamed the Transnistrian Moldovan Republic in 1991). The population of Transnistria was almost entirely ethnic Russians and Ukrainians, and the leaders of the separatist state were mainly anti-Yeltsin Russian Communists who were strongly opposed to the dissolution of the USSR. They also opposed the Moldovan government's objective of unification with Romania, and sought instead to achieve unification with Russia, although this was a completely unrealistic aspiration given the tiny land area occupied by the self-declared republic, and its geographical separation from Russia by Ukraine. After the failed coup attempt in Moscow in August 1991, the Moldovan government declared its full independence from the USSR and dissolved the local Communist Party. These actions precipitated clashes between government forces and Russians in Transnistria, eventually leading to a civil war in which hundreds of people were killed and thousands were forced to take refuge in Ukraine. A fragile peace agreement was reached in mid-1992, although as in Azerbaijan and Nagorno-Karabakh the underlying conflict remained unresolved. To add to the problems of the new Moldovan Republic, the Russian-speaking Gauguz minority, accounting for less than four percent of the population but who like the Russians in Transnistria were in favour of the old USSR and supported the August 1991 coup attempt, sought autonomy for their own region in the south of the country, further destabilising an already volatile situation.

Thousands of kilometres to the east, in the small mountainous republic of Tajikistan, south of Uzbekistan and Kyrgyzstan and the most remote of the former Soviet republics from Moscow, similar problems and conflicts were emerging. Nationalist violence in the capital Dushanbe in February 1990 led to twenty two deaths and was followed by two years of unrest and instability, culminating in the outbreak in May 1992 of open civil war between pro-Russian Communists and Islamic and anti-Russian nationalists. It was not until June 1997 that a peace agreement between the various factions was signed in Moscow, although violence and political assassinations continued. In the other non-Russian republics, most ethnic Russians remained loyal to Russia while avoiding attempts to destabilise their new countries, which would only have rebounded against them. Potentially the most volatile situation existed in Ukraine, where historically there had been considerable anti-Russian enmity, but where Russians accounted for more than one fifth of the total population. In reality divisions between ethnic Russians and Ukrainians were often far from clear, and there was no significant unrest at the time of independence.

The realisation of Russia's military weakness and the acceptance of the desire among the republics for sovereignty, gave further impetus to the Yeltsin campaign for sovereignty and for a form of independence for Russia itself. Yeltsin admitted that it was impossible for Russia to become completely separate from the Soviet Union, but he was determined to press for the maximum possible degree of independence, with complete decentralisation of the economy and its finances and politics, and the right to negotiate freely with the other republics. Yeltsin asserted that the central Soviet government existed for the benefit of the republics, including Russia, rather than the old structure of each republic taking its orders from the centre. It was now up to the individual republics to decide what kind of central structure they needed. As far as Russia was concerned, economic sovereignty meant it would take sole possession of all of its natural resources, rivers and forests, and in future anything transferred from Russia to the central authorities of the Soviet Union, such as legislative powers or rights over natural resources, would have to be approved by the Russian parliament. Russia would conduct its own foreign trade, set up its own State Bank, and print its own currency. Yeltsin also responded to the protests of the Stavropol mothers by reaffirming that Russia would abandon its old policy of interference in the internal affairs of other republics, both inside the Soviet Union and in countries in other parts of the world.

All these ideas were welcomed by millions of people in Russia and throughout the Soviet republics. But there were also many who actively opposed all that Yeltsin stood for and who were wary of what all this meant for their future way of life. This group of people was represented most clearly by Mikhail Gorbachev, who by now could no longer hold a middle line between reformers and those who opposed reform, and was forced to side with the conservatives and those who wanted to preserve the integrity of the Soviet Union. The centre ground between the reformists and the conservatives no longer existed and Gorbachev, despite earlier having himself seriously questioned the relevance of the socialist and Soviet systems, now accused Yeltsin of abandoning the principles of the 1917 Revolution and seeking the break-up of the Soviet Union. In doing so Gorbachev invoked the old fears in the Russian collective memory of the 'time of troubles', when for thirty years between the death of Ivan the Terrible in 1582 and the ascendance of the Romanov dynasty in 1613, Russia was subjected to civil wars and foreign invasions, with no strong central leadership to provide stability and security. This was a prospect, according to Gorbachev, which now threatened not only the Soviet Union but the existence of Russia itself.

Throughout 1990 the schism between the two separate and irreconcilable directions facing Russia and the republics, as embodied by Yeltsin and Gorbachev, widened and deepened. In another historical parallel, and a new version of the centuries-old conflict between Slavophiles and Westernisers, dating back to the struggles of Peter the Great to modernise Russia against the resistance of the boyars in the early 1700s, Russia and its empire were once again at a turning point; and once again Kazakhstan, and all the other republics, were drawn into a conflict spilling over from the colonial power. What happened in Moscow would inevitably determine the course of events elsewhere. By the end of 1990 the Soviet government had become more reactionary and conservative as Gorbachev, in part willingly, in part under duress, had appointed officials from the

Communist Party and the KGB to senior positions in the Ministry of Internal Affairs and other vital roles. The government was now intent on reversing many of the recent reforms and reverting, in Yeltsin's phrase, to 'the rigid centralisation of the past with nothing constructive to offer for the future'. The prospects for greater freedom for the republics now seemed more remote than ever, although by now many realised that the Soviet government was increasingly debilitated and unable fully to impose its will in Russia, let alone in the Baltics or in Central Asia. In November 1990 Gorbachev proposed more discussions on a new Union Treaty offering greater autonomy for the republics, but six – Armenia, Azerbaijan, Georgia, Estonia, Latvia, and Lithuania – refused to participate, having already declared their sovereignty, a fact seized on by Yeltsin who urged the government to recognise the reality of what was actually happening. The Soviet Union, he said, had to accept the de facto secession of six of its fifteen member states, which had effectively turned their back on Russia and were now embarking on a new course to determine their own future.

In January 1991 the crisis in the republics took another sharp turn for the worse. In response to what were seen as continuing anti-Soviet policies and demands for greater economic and political freedom in Lithuania, on 13 January Boris Pugo, the Minister of Internal Affairs of the USSR despatched a team of professional, non-conscript, riot-control troops to take control of the television tower in the Lithuanian capital of Vilnius. In the ensuing violence thirteen unarmed defenders were killed and over 160 people wounded. Greatly alarmed by this development, Yeltsin immediately travelled to Tallinn, the capital of neighbouring Estonia, from where he issued a joint statement with the Presidents of Latvia, Lithuania, and Estonia, declaring the inadmissibility of using force to resolve internal problems, and calling on other Soviet republics to condemn the threat to the independence of the Baltic States. The incident brought into even sharper contrast what had now become a violent division with regard to the future of the republics. Suspecting an assassination attempt and having been warned of the danger of travelling by plane, Yeltsin returned from Tallinn to Moscow by car.

Boris Pugo was one of the Gorbachev appointees two months before the Vilnius episode and one of the future conspirators in the attempted coup against Gorbachev eight months later. By avoiding the use of conscript troops he apparently believed the lessons of the 'Stavropol Mothers' in January 1990 did not apply. But the attempted suppression of the independence movement in Lithuania turned out to hasten further the end of the USSR. The Soviet government in Moscow had demonstrated that it still had some strength to take military action when it thought it necessary, but the intervention in Vilnius was counterproductive. It drew renewed attention to the traditional method of dealing with problems by force, which further diminished any lingering appeal of belonging to the Soviet Union, and it gave greater impetus in Lithuania and among all the republics for independence. Over the following months, in what became known as the Novo-Ogaryovo process named after the dacha near Moscow traditionally used by leaders of the republics in more peaceful times, negotiations between the various republics continued on a new form of Union Treaty, as had been proposed by Gorbachev in November 1990. Five of the six republics which had earlier refused to take part continued to boycott the negotiations, while Azerbaijan decided to join and Moldova withdrew, after the Moldovan Supreme Soviet decided not to participate. The change of mind by Azerbaijan resulted from its belief that to remain within some new form of Union would strengthen its position with regard to Armenia, especially as Armenia continued to exclude itself from the negotiations.

The specific reasons why other republics chose not to participate in the negotiations or to seek any new constitutional arrangement varied, but all had a common theme of wanting to distance themselves politically as far as possible from Russia. In Moldova, the tiny republic between Ukraine and Romania, the population was predominantly non-Slav, and apart from a small Russian community in Transdinistria, there were few ethnic links with Russia. As had happened in the Baltic states, the annexation by the USSR in 1940 had been bitterly opposed, and the country had suffered in the post-war collectivization of agriculture under Leonid Brezhnev. In June 1990 the Soviet annexation fifty years earlier was declared to have been illegal. In Georgia, resentment at the denigration of Stalin which had started under Khrushchev, and the existence of large ethnic Russian communities in South Ossetia and Abkhazia whose loyalties lay with Russia rather than Georgia, increased anti-Russian sentiment in the rest of the republic, and in April 1991 Georgia became the first republic after the Baltic states formally to secede from the USSR, as opposed simply to declaring its sovereignty. Possibly the most controversial position was adopted in Armenia, which depended on Russia for economic and political support in its relations with Turkey, its hostile neighbour to the south. The Orthodox Church was also the predominant form of Christianity in Armenia as it was in Russia. But otherwise there were few close links with Russia. The population was almost 98 per cent Armenian, with Russians accounting for less than one per cent of the total; there was strong opposition to the increasing ecological degradation in the country, largely the result of Soviet economic policies, and hostility towards corruption in the local Communist Party, also seen as an endemic feature of the Soviet system, was increasing. The lack of an effective response from the government in Moscow to the devastating earthquake which destroyed the town of Gyumri in northern Armenia in December 1988, further hardened anti-Russian and anti-Soviet feelings. The worsening conflict with Azerbaijan, and what was seen as lack of support for Armenia from other republics in the USSR, which now had other far more pressing matters on their minds, increased the sense of disillusionment, and strengthened the belief that the country would be better off by itself.

The nature of bilateral relations between individual members of the Soviet Union and each other varied widely, from being almost non-existent to being very close. In every republic, Russian was the common language, the rouble the common currency, and there was a prevalent sense of belonging, willingly or not, to the Soviet political and economic family. But outside the predominantly Slav republics of Russia, Ukraine, and Byelorussia, and the republics of Central Asia, there were few common ethnic, religious, or social ties. The Baltic States shared a similar history and geography, and the same anti-Russian feelings, and south of the Caucasus Mountains there had been a short-lived attempt after the 1917 Revolution to form a Transcaucasus Federative Republic incorporating Armenia, Azerbaijan, and Georgia. But there was no natural or deep affinity between any of these republics, except that now they were allies in the common struggle against the notion of the Soviet Union. Elsewhere, in the Slav republics of Ukraine and Byelorussia, which with Russia had been the founder members of the Soviet Union in 1922, and among the economically-backward states of Central Asia, links with Russia and between each other on many levels were still very close, and it was in these republics that the desire to remain part of a Union with Russia at the centre was strongest.

By March 1991 an agreement had been reached under the Novo-Ogaryovo negotiations in which a new type of Union would be preserved, as a loose confederation of independent states. Within this Union each republic would be free to pursue its own internal economic and political reforms without hindrance from the central government, whose responsibilities would now be limited to defence and foreign affairs, plus any other functions which may be delegated to it by the republics. Except in specified cases, the laws of each republic would take precedence over the laws of the Union. A new constitution would be drawn up and elections would be held for each branch of the new Union, including the presidency, although this would be largely a ceremonial role. For the first time, the Soviet government acknowledged the sovereignty of the separate republics. In conducting the negotiations Gorbachev had by now rejected the Soviet political and economic system, but still clung to the need to retain some form of collective state. The new Union would in effect mean the end of the old Union of Soviet Socialist Republics, but the country which replaced it would be a federation to be called the Union of Soviet Sovereign Republics. In Russian as in English, the set of initials (CCCP) for the new country was the same as that for the old, a factor which reassured many Soviet citizens who were worried about the future, who wanted change but did not want to break away entirely from what they had become familiar with over the previous seven decades.

On this basis a referendum was held on 17 March 1991 to seek approval for the proposed new Union Treaty. In response to the question: 'Do you believe it essential to preserve a Union of Soviet Sovereign Republics as a renewed federation of equal sovereign republics in which the rights and freedoms of a person of any nationality will be fully guaranteed?', over eighty percent of the total adult population in the nine republics which took part in the referendum - Russia, Byelorussia, Ukraine, Kazakhstan, Kyrgyzstan, Uzbekistan, Turkmenistan, Tajikistan, and Azerbaijan - cast their vote, and in none of these republics did the percentage in favour fall below seventy percent. The most enthusiastic response was recorded in Kazakhstan, where eighty eight percent of the electorate took part, of whom ninety four percent voted in favour of remaining within the new Union. The strongest support was in the northern parts of the country where ethnic Russians formed the majority of the population, but even if hundred percent of the Russian population voted in favour, the size of the turnout and the overall result indicated that a substantial majority of Kazakhs voted in favour as well. The loyalty of Kazakhstan to the USSR, despite the immense suffering which it had experienced since it became part of the Russian empire in tsarist times, can be explained by a combination of close family relations and widespread inter-marriage between Kazakhs and Russians, a high degree of economic dependence on Russia, and the remote location of the country, virtually cut off by Russia from the rest of the world. Millions of Kazakhs had benefitted considerably from the historic relationship with Russia, and there was a widespread feeling that the country was not ready to face the world alone. In Russia the turnout was smaller (eighty percent), of whom seventy five percent voted in favour. The following month a Joint Declaration was signed by Gorbachev and the leaders of the participating republics, acknowledging the outcome of the referendum and confirming that a new Union Treaty would be signed on 20 August. The leaders of Armenia, Georgia, Moldova, and the three Baltic states did not sign the declaration.

Before then, in another unprecedented and momentous break with the past, on 12 June 1991 Boris Yeltsin was elected President of the new sovereign republic of Russia, one year to the day since the Russian declaration of its sovereignty. By gaining fifty seven percent of the popular vote, more than his five opponents combined, Yeltsin achieved a clear mandate for reform. The democratic election for the first time of a leader in Russia also marked an end to the tradition of the one-party system and the centuries-old hereditary monarchy that preceded it. In his inaugural speech Yeltsin stressed the rejection of government by ideological dictatorship, the withdrawal of the state from every aspect of people's lives, an end to Russia's imperial ambitions, and the return of Russia to the world community. No longer was there any reference to the Soviet family of nations or the common socialist inheritance of the type which used to fill the speeches of Gorbachev and other Soviet leaders. Russia was now de facto separate from the USSR, and so by implication were all the other republics of the former Soviet Union, which like Russia could now do as they wished. In Kazakhstan, the tumultuous and seemingly endless tide of negative events engulfing Moscow had been followed with growing concern among the Russian and the Kazakh populations. Gennady Kolbin, appointed by Gorbachev in 1986 to replace the 74-year-old Communist Party leader Dinmukhamed Kunaev, was in the increasingly anomalous position of a Russian as the leader of a non-Russian republic, and after only two and a half years was replaced by Nursultan Nazarbaev.

Nursultan Nazarbaev was born on 6 July 1940 in Chemolgan, a small town not far to the west of Alma-Ata, where his father was a farm labourer. During the collectivisation of agriculture in the 1930s the family left the farm and led an itinerant life in the countryside, before returning to Chemolgan after the war. At school Nazarbaev was an able student and while still in his teens left home to work at the giant Karaganda Metallurgical Kombinat (known throughout Kazakhstan as Karmet) at Temirtau near Karaganda in central Kazakhstan. Here he gained a reputation as a conscientious and reliable worker in the dangerous working environment of a Soviet steel mill in the 1960s. As well as studying at the local Polytechnic Institute, Nazarbaev became a prominent member of the Komsomol, the youth wing of the Communist Party, and later became a leading figure in the Karaganda Regional Party Committee. During this time he became increasingly aware of and frustrated by the shortcomings of the central planning system, which amongst other failings resulted in excessive emphasis on production and output at the expense of long-term investment in infrastructure and technology, and of raising technical standards and processes. In this respect he acquired some of the same outlook on the economy in Kazakhstan and on the Soviet Union in general as did his near-contemporary Boris Yeltsin in Russia. Yeltsin had worked for many years in the construction industry in Sverdlovsk, and like Yeltsin, Nazarbaev gained a detailed and practical insight into the everyday problems of the Soviet system on the ground, an insight which eluded many in the higher levels in the Communist Party. Both Yeltsin and Nazarbaev realised that the current economic system, by dictating all levels of inputs and production according to the demands of the central plan, not only failed to meet the needs of the economy or the population, but acted as a positive constraint on development and modernisation. Unlike Gorbachev, who regarded the problem from above and believed the system could be managed and reformed, both Nazarbaev and Yeltsin had a more ground-based viewpoint and both sought more practical and realistic solutions. Meanwhile their similar backgrounds and experience in the workplace led to firm common ground between them and a close personal friendship, which was to be invaluable during the upheavals of the coming disintegration of the Soviet Union.

As Yeltsin had done in Sverdlovsk, Nazarbaev frequently antagonised local party officials in Karaganda and Alma-Ata in his support for workers in the factories against bureaucrats in the government, and in his demands that better work should be rewarded by higher pay, in contrast to the prevailing system under which everyone received the same salary irrespective of work done. But his radical, even heretical opinions did not hold back to ascent to political power, and by 1984 Nazarbaev had become Chairman of the Council of Ministers of Kazakhstan, the second most senior position in the country, under the ageing leadership of Dinmukhamed Kunaev, the First Secretary of the Communist Party. Kunaev appointed Nazarbaev to the role of Chairman of the Council of Ministers in the belief that he would conform to the comfortable and static situation in the Party. However Nazarbaev used his new authority to criticise ministers and party officials for what he saw as their failure to deal with problems in their departments. Included in his targets was Askar Kunaev, brother of Dinmukhamed and head of the Academy of Sciences, a position which had been held in the 1950s by Dinmukhamed Kunaev himself. Disregarding this family connection, Nazarbaev felt sufficiently confident to attack Askar Kunaev for not keeping up with scientific advances elsewhere in the world, which would be of benefit to Kazakhstan. Feeling betrayed by Nazarbaev's statements and actions, since he had appointed him in the expectation that he would remain loyal to the family structure within the Party, in 1986 Dinmukhamed Kunaev had attempted to dismiss Nazarbaev, only to be removed from office himself and replaced by Gennady Kolbin. Nazarbaev remained as Chairman of the Council of Ministers for a further two and a half years until, on the tide of change beginning to sweep through Russia and the republics, in June 1989 he finally replaced Kolbin as First Secretary of the Communist Party of Kazakhstan. In March the following year he was elected to the new post of President of Kazakhstan; this was followed by the decision of the Council of Ministers in October 1990 to declare national sovereignty within the USSR. Despite these moves to assert his own status and that of Kazakhstan, Nazarbaev was careful to allay the growing concerns of the Slav communities, especially among the substantial Russian population in the north of the country. Given the turmoil and uncertainty emanating from Moscow, there was little attraction for Russians to leave their jobs and homes in Kazakhstan in favour of seeking work and somewhere to live in Russia; but many also were worried about the rise of nationalism and had fears that their position and livelihoods may become less secure in an independent Kazakhstan. In the uncertain situation of 1990-1991, Nazarbaev was anxious to preserve inter-ethnic stability in his own republic, and was one of the most forceful advocates of the new Union Treaty as a means of preserving some form of Union, and thereby meeting the wishes of all the ethnic groups in Kazakhstan.

At the beginning of August 1991, Mikhail Gorbachev left Moscow for a holiday in Foros in the Crimea where he intended to rest with his family after the intense turmoil of the previous months, and prepare a speech to be delivered at the signing of the new Union Treaty, scheduled for 20 August. His absence from the centre of government, and the imminence of the signing ceremony, gave the opportunity and the urgency for those in the Soviet government who opposed the Treaty to attempt a coup d'etat. This would have as its objectives the removal of Gorbachev as Soviet President, the reversal of the creeping process of dissolution of the USSR, and the reinstatement of a stronger central government such as had existed before 1985. Two months earlier, at the beginning of June Gorbachev had received a warning from the US ambassador in Moscow, based on information received from American agents in the city, of an impending threat to remove him from office, planned for 21 June. The date of 21 June has special significance for the Soviet population as the date of the German invasion in 1941, and the conspirators may have hoped to gain credibility for their plans by acting on the fiftieth anniversary of the invasion. Gorbachev expressed his gratitude for the warning but felt sufficiently confident to ignore it, and the date came and went without incident, allowing him to leave Moscow as planned. The real coup attempt, when it took place on 19 August, had the opposite outcome to what was intended, and as had happened with the suppression of the Lithuanian independence movement the previous

January, further accelerated the end of the Soviet Union. Even with the benefit of two extra months planning from the original target date, the coup was badly organized and the conspirators were fatally indecisive. Apart from the presidency itself, they already held all the main positions in the government, although there was none among them who spoke for the individual republics, on whose behalf they claimed to act in their wish to preserve the Soviet Union. It was this factor, as well as the sense of hesitancy, confusion, and lack of authority in announcing the coup, which led to the early failure of the attempted takeover. Boris Yeltsin was scathing about the conspirators:

'I look at the tragedy of the coup plotters as the tragedy of the whole platoon of government bureaucrats whom the system had turned into cogs and stripped of any human traits. . . But it would have been far worse if that platoon of cold and robotlike bureaucrats had returned to the leadership of the country.'*

When Gorbachev returned to Moscow from the Crimea four days later, having refused to negotiate with the coup leaders, he declared 'I have come back to a different country, and I myself am a different man now'. The leaders of the attempted coup were arrested and were replaced by people who Gorbachev could trust.

Those leaders of the individual republics who had been at the forefront in demanding independence realised that if the coup succeeded, not only would that mean an end to their national aspirations, but also that a return to a much more authoritarian regime would be needed to reinstate the earlier pre-Gorbachev type of central control. To avoid this eventuality, the republics now had to take this opportunity and declare a complete break with the old order; the earlier status of economic sovereignty was no longer sufficient, and full independence, internationally recognised, was now essential. The first to take this step were Estonia and Latvia, which declared independence on 20 August, the second day of the coup. With a lack of central authority in the Soviet Union, now on the verge of collapse, it was in effect up to Russia as the most important component of the Union to decide how to respond. Boris Yeltsin, who had previously declared himself in favour of independence for the Baltic states, and had only two months earlier been elected President of Russia, immediately recognised Estonian and Latvian independence, and urged other countries to do so. This action alone by Yeltsin sealed the fate of the attempted coup, and prompted more republics to abandon the

---

*Quoted in Catherine Merridale, *Red Fortress: The Secret Heart of Russia's History*

USSR. Throughout the rest of August and in the first few days of September eleven more republics, including Russia itself, declared their independence. Turkmenistan followed on 27 October, and Kazakhstan on 16 December, the last of the republics to do so. As well as declaring independence, Yeltsin was quick to capitalise on the internal political implications of the failed takeover, and on 23 August suspended the activities of the Communist Party in Russia and the publication of six communist party newspapers. The Russian Communist Party was formally dissolved in November 1991, on the seventy-fourth anniversary of its seizure of power.

President Nursultan Nazarbaev of Kazakhstan had been among the first of the republic leaders to denounce the attempted coup, openly condemning it on 20 August. Shortly afterwards Nazarbaev resigned as First Secretary of the Kazakh Communist Party and ordered that the Communist Party should be removed from all state institutions. Similar resignations by leaders in the other republics soon followed. The Party was not completely banned in Kazakhstan as it was to be in Russia, but its role in the government and the economy was now virtually eliminated. In the same month, in another radical break with the past, the first programme for the privatisation of state enterprises was introduced. But throughout the final months of 1991, Nazarbaev held back from declaring full political independence for Kazakhstan, aware of ambivalent feelings in the republic and wanting to retain some residual form of Union. In this respect his wishes were more in line with those of Gorbachev than with those of his friend and ally Boris Yeltsin. But ultimately independence was in effect forced upon Kazakhstan, by virtue of all the other republics having announced their own independence, giving Kazakhstan no alternative but to do the same.

Despite the successive declarations of independence, negotiations continued throughout the autumn of 1991 in an attempt to reach agreement on a new Union Treaty. After the collapse of the August coup attempt, a revival of the Novo-Ogaryovo process failed to generate any enthusiasm among the republics, which now had no interest in any form of Union to replace the USSR, except in the loosest of terms. Ukraine in particular, which on 24 August had been one of the first republics to declare its independence, was adamant in refusing to participate in the negotiations or to sign any agreement with the old Soviet government. By early December the search for a Union was abandoned and on 7 December Boris Yeltsin of Russia, Leonid Kravchuk of Ukraine, and Stanislav Shushkevich of Belarus (which had changed its name from Byelorussia in September) assembled at the Belavezhskaya Pushcha hunting lodge deep in the pine forests of

Belarus near the border with Poland. The following day they signed an agreement which drew a line under everything that had gone before and presented the Soviet Union and the rest of the world with a fait accompli. The declaration stated:

'We, the Republic of Belarus, the Russian Federation, and Ukraine, being founder member states of the USSR, being signatories to the Treaty of Union of 1922 . . . state that the USSR, as a subject of international law and a geopolitical reality, ceases to exist.'*

The USSR was to be replaced by a new Commonwealth, to consist of those among the new republics which wished to join, and to be known as the Commonwealth of Independent States. Nazarbaev, as president of the second largest republic, was invited to participate in the meeting and in the formal dissolution of the USSR, but declined owing to a pre-arranged meeting with Gorbachev in Moscow (although possibly also because he did not want to be directly associated with this historic action). The agreement formally dissolving the Soviet Union was signed in Minsk, the capital of Belarus, on 8 December 1991, to take effect at the end of the month.

Mikhail Gorbachev, who had not been invited to attend the meeting in Belavezhskaya Pushcha or the formal signing ceremony in Minsk, later bitterly complained that he was notified of the outcome only after US President George H Bush had been informed, and denounced the whole process as 'dirty, illegitimate, and dangerous'. As well as losing his own position as president of a state that no longer existed, Gorbachev was afraid, as were many at the time, that without a more comprehensive treaty, the USSR might descend into the same type of violent and bloody civil war that was currently tearing apart the republics of the former Yugoslavia. He need not have worried on this account, since the bitter enmity which existed between Serbs, Croats, and Muslims in Yugoslavia had no direct parallel in the Soviet Union. Most of the other non-Russian republics were generally either indifferent towards each other, sharing a common history of belonging to the tsarist and Soviet empires, but having little else in common, or as in the case of the Central Asian republics, shared close ethnic and historical ties which made any conflict between them unlikely. Thus the scope for hostility between different republics was limited. The war between Armenia and Azerbaijan in 1988-1994 was marked by hatred and bloodshed but was confined to the two countries and did not threaten to spill

*Quoted in Steve Crawshaw, *Goodbye to the USSR*

over into the rest of the USSR. Tension and bitterness between different communities within individual republics certainly existed: unrest in Georgia in 1990-1991, and civil war breaking out in 1991 in Moldova and in Tajikistan, all illustrated the potential for violence and upheaval. There had also been serious outbreaks of violence between various ethnic groups in the Ferghana Valley in Uzbekistan in 1989, which threatened to break out again at any moment. But these and other conflicts had specific local origins often related to religious factors, and to unemployment and poor economic conditions, and did not threaten to involve other republics. What could have been a catastrophic and violent collapse was avoided and the dissolution of the old state took place relatively peacefully. Gorbachev later modified his views and acknowledged that the Minsk Agreement would be instrumental in avoiding any potential inter-republic confrontation, but continued to assert that he could not support complete dissolution of the Soviet Union since, in Russia at least, this had not been approved by popular vote.

It is impossible to say what would have been the outcome of such a vote if one had been held; the referendums in March had produced large majorities in favour of retaining the USSR, but the intervening attempted coup had alienated large numbers of people, especially in the non-Russian republics. Between 10 and 12 December 1991 the parliaments of Belarus, Ukraine, and Russia ratified the Minsk Agreement, and on 12 December the Russian Supreme Soviet declared that the 1922 Treaty that had created the Soviet Union was null and void. In Kazakhstan, President Nazarbaev had been a reluctant observer of these developments, but on 21 December he also accepted the inevitable and convened a meeting in Alma-Ata, at which the Commonwealth of Independent States, consisting of eleven of the fifteen former republics, was formally inaugurated. Estonia, Latvia, and Lithuania, which had always stated their intention not to have any association with the new Commonwealth, declined to attend, and Georgia, which was in the middle of a political crisis of its own, sent only observers, although it later joined the CIS in 1993. The functions and powers of the new organisation were limited, mainly confined to military arrangements and some economic agreements between the member states. There may have been an element of nostalgia and a wish to retain at least something of the old USSR, with none of the republics, except the Baltic States, wanting a complete and final break with the past. The central role of Russia in each of the economies of the ten non-Russian member states of the CIS dictated the need for a forum in which to discuss essential economic and financial relations. But in reality the CIS came to have little practical significance. Meanwhile it was decided that its capital should be in Minsk, to distinguish it from the old arrangement in which everything was centred in Moscow. On 25 December Mikhail Gorbachev, who as well as having been excluded from the meetings in Belavezhskaya Pushcha and Minsk, had also not been invited to the Alma-Ata summit, announced his resignation as president of the now non-existent USSR. The process which he had set in train almost seven years earlier had reached its conclusion. Any sense of achievement which he may have felt at this outcome was outweighed by bitterness at the way it had been arrived at, and the disregard shown to him by his exclusion from the formalities surrounding the end of the Soviet Union. However, apart from the small number of regional conflicts, serious as they were, the historic transformation of the country since 1985 had taken place remarkably peacefully. At midnight on 31 December 1991 the Red Flag of the USSR was hauled down from the Kremlin and replaced with the red, white and blue flag of the new Russian state.

CHAPTER TWENTY THREE

Kazakhstan Embarks on Independence

The removal of the communist-era flag was soon to be followed by another symbolic change within the Kremlin walls. The Grand Kremlin Palace occupies a prominent location in the south-west corner of the Kremlin overlooking the Moscow River, and was built between 1838 and 1849 on the site of the derelict palace of Empress Elizabeth as an imperial residence for Tsar Nicholas I. In the previous century Peter the Great had moved the court to his new capital of St Petersburg, but so as to gain legitimacy in the eyes of the Russian Orthodox Church for the coronation of Catherine, his second wife, as tsarina in 1724, he decided that the ceremony, which he intended to conduct himself, should take place in the Dormition Cathedral in the Kremlin in Moscow. The decision to make Catherine his heir was highly controversial and the need for the blessing of the Church was paramount. From then on the coronation of every tsar or tsarina would be conducted in the same place. By the time of Nicholas I a new palace for the tsar and the royal family was needed where they could stay while they were in Moscow for coronations and other ceremonies. The result was a vast edifice of 700 rooms, designed in a classical style but with traditional elements of seventeenth-century Russian architecture, and the Grand Kremlin Palace had the distinction of being the last major development within the Kremlin before the 1917 Revolution. Shortly after the formal establishment of the USSR in December 1922, the Cyrillic CCCP initials of the new state were set in the most visible position at the front of the building, replacing the double-headed eagle which had been the emblem of the Russian government since the time of Ivan the Terrible in the mid-sixteenth century. Throughout the Soviet period the palace was the seat of government of both the Soviet Union and of the Russian Soviet Federative Socialist Republic, the Russian republic within the USSR, and was used for state banquets and receptions for foreign Communist Party leaders and other heads of state. More than any other location in the country, this was the public face of the Union of Soviet Socialist Republics, and the CCCP initials became universal throughout the country, on public buildings and government ministries, on postage stamps and banknotes, passports and identity cards, official forms of every description, on factories and farms, theatres and concert halls, schools and libraries, space rockets and Aeroflot aircraft, and gymnasiums and sports grounds in every corner of the Soviet Union. In January 1992 the Grand Kremlin Palace acquired another, less welcome, distinction when it became the first public building to have these letters removed, and diplomats in the British embassy on the opposite bank of the Moscow River had a close-up view of history being made as workmen chiseled off the set of initials which had come to symbolize the USSR, at home and around the world, over the previous sixty-nine years. In towns, cities, and villages throughout the old Soviet Union, the melancholy task of removing the ubiquitous CCCP slowly got under way.

In Kazakhstan and the other republics of Central Asia, most people had more serious concerns than the removal of the CCCP initials. Far from being the start of an exciting and uplifting process of renewal and the beginning of a new life, the reality of the end of the USSR was greeted with near-universal gloom and dismay. The collapse of the Soviet Union may have been seen in the West purely as a dramatic political and historical event, but its effect on the Soviet population has been widely underestimated. For millions of ordinary people this was a profound shock, and the inevitability of its approach over the previous months and years did not diminish its impact when it actually happened. After seven decades of Soviet propaganda, when the government had fostered the notion of the Soviet Union as a state of mind as much as a political state, the population was psychologically unprepared, and many people now experienced a deepening sense of foreboding, as they faced the double calamity of the end of the Soviet Union and the collapse of the socialist economic system. After a lifetime of being part of the Soviet family, on 1 January 1992 the whole country woke up to the bewildering realisation that the Soviet family no longer existed. The referendum of March the previous year had produced an overwhelming majority, in the nine republics that had taken part, in favour of a looser federation to be known as the Union of Sovereign Soviet States, and nowhere had the turnout and the majority in favour been higher than in Kazakhstan. The referendum had now been superseded by events and the outcome had been pushed aside. The complete dissolution of the old order was therefore felt most acutely in Kazakhstan, where the new Commonwealth of Independent States was seen as a poor substitute for the USSR, and Kazakhstan embarked on its own course of independence with a greater sense of trepidation than most of the other republics.

Not everyone in Kazakhstan was dismayed by what had happened. For many younger-generation, professionally-qualified Kazakhs, especially those disillusioned with Soviet life and with the attempted coup in Moscow the previous August, the end of the USSR was not such a great concern, and they believed they could meet the challenge of independence. Similarly for the herdsmen and rural communities in remote parts of the steppe, the convulsions far away in Alma-Ata and Moscow were regarded with equanimity and their impact was more muted. The legacy of the khan system, of loyalty to the clan, the family, and to the land, took precedence over national or political concerns. But for millions of middle-aged and older-generation urban Kazakhs and Russians, this was deeply worrying. As well as deep misgivings about the future, there was the more immediate problem of the apparent disintegration of the economy, and the increasingly difficult daily struggle to earn a living. This was the end of the collective way of life, and for the first time in their lives people now had to fend for themselves.

Although Kazakhstan was now free, ostensibly at least, from Russian political domination, the loyalty of the large Russian minority, consisting of more than six million people, to the new independent republic was by no means certain. Large numbers of ethnic Russians, in Kazakhstan and in other non-Russian republics, now found themselves stranded, as virtual foreigners in a country which was no longer their own. At the time of independence the Russian and Kazakh populations in Kazakhstan were broadly the same size, with Kazakhs accounting for roughly 40 per cent and Russians 38 per cent out of a total population of 17 million. The rest of the population was made up of other national groups including Ukrainians, Uzbeks, Germans, Uighurs, and Koreans, although none of these groups individually accounted for more than four per cent of the total. Despite the rough proximity in size, the age structures in the Kazakh and Russian populations were very different, with the Russians on the whole older and Kazakhs younger, and with independence the composition of the population steadily began to change in favour of the Kazakhs.

In his election campaign in 1990, Boris Yeltsin had promised that ethnic Russians throughout the old USSR would be welcomed in Russia and given jobs, housing, and even compensation for the property they left behind in the non-Russian republics. The Russian 'motherland' would 'take them back', even if they had been born outside Russia. In practice these promises could not be fulfilled, and for many Russians in Kazakhstan, especially older families who had lived there for generations and had little if any connection with Russia, the option of leaving Kazakhstan for Russia, with all the uncertainty of uprooting and moving to a different country which was itself in the grip of an economic crisis, was less attractive than staying where they were. The majority of Slav population, both Russians and Ukrainians, preferred to remain in Kazakhstan, especially those who lived in the broad steppe lands of the northern part of the country and in the industrialised cities in the east, where they had settled since the nineteenth century. Geographically these regions are similar to the Russian countryside to the north, and very different to the desert terrain in the south and west of Kazakhstan, which was home to most of the native population. But many others, especially hundreds of thousands of younger couples who might in other circumstances have brought up a family in Kazakhstan, no longer saw a future for themselves in the newly independent republic and chose to leave. Throughout the country, 'For Sale' signs, clumsily daubed in white paint, appeared on thousands of houses and dachas in towns and cities, and by the end of the 1990s as many as two million Russians had emigrated. Not only Russians were leaving; long queues formed outside the German embassy in Alma-Ata as large numbers of ethnic Germans waited for permits to leave Kazakhstan and resettle in Germany, leaving whole villages deserted and abandoned. Meanwhile, despite the worsening economic crisis in Kazakhstan, the birth rate among Kazakh families increased, decisively shifting the balance between Kazakhs and Russians even more in favour of the indigenous population, and adding to the disquiet among the diminishing but still substantial Russian minority. Despite widespread inter-marriage between the two national groups, antagonism was never far below the surface, and Kazakhs became more assertive and openly critical of Russian attitudes and assumptions of superiority, while Russians became more anxious about how they might be treated in Kazakhstan and possible discrimination against them.

If the Russians had decided, in the post-independence turmoil and confusion, to seek partition, either to form their own state or to seek reunification with Russia, it is unlikely that the Kazakh government or the Kazakh population would have been able to resist such a move. Many in Russia saw northern Kazakhstan as rightfully belonging to Russia, among whom was the writer Alexander Solzhenitsyn. Solzhenitsyn had been forcibly exiled from Russia for his anti-Soviet views in March 1974, first to Germany and later to the United States. After his return to Russia in October 1994, he became increasingly nationalist and chauvinist in his outlook, partly in reaction to what he saw as the decadence and moral decline of the West, and in a series of provocative interviews and statements, Solzhenitsyn declared that the Russian-populated parts of Kazakhstan, and of Ukraine and Belarus, should be brought back under Russian sovereignty. In reality any attempt to redraw the national boundary between Kazakhstan and Russia was inconceivable, and would inevitably have brought instability and chaos into an already tense situation. Such an attempt would not only have further antagonised the already hostile indigenous population of Kazakhstan, especially the Kazakh minority in the north of the country, but would also have opened up the intractable problem of what to do about the ethnic Russian populations in the other republics of the old

Soviet Union. In those republics where there was no common border with Russia – Moldova, Armenia, Turkmenistan, Uzbekistan, Tajikistan, and Kyrgyzstan – Russians felt particularly isolated and cut off from what they considered to be their home country. For the Russians in Kazakhstan it was evident that there was no prospect of separation. The outbreak of civil wars in the tiny republics of Moldova and Tajikistan held a clear warning of what might happen in the much bigger republic of Kazakhstan, where the damage that would be caused by violence between different communities would be much greater. Russians may have felt uneasy about independence, but relations between themselves and the Kazakh population were much closer than in many other republics. Even if separation, or unification with Russia, became a serious possibility, at the time Russia itself would have strongly discouraged the whole notion. It was one thing to offer a home to individual ethnic Russians wishing to leave Kazakhstan and start a new life in Russia, but a completely different matter to absorb a vast region of what was now an independent republic into Russian territory. There had been historical precedents under Stalin in the 1920s and 1930s for the redrawing of boundaries and allocation of territories to different republics; the Karakalpak Autonomous Region, an area of desert to the south of the Aral Sea, was transferred from Kazakhstan to Russia in 1930 and from Russia to Uzbekistan in 1936, and Kazakhstan itself only became constitutionally separate from Russia as a Union Republic in 1936. In 1954, control of the Crimea was transferred from Russia, of which it had been part since the time of Catherine the Great, to Ukraine. But in the unstable conditions of the early 1990s, there was no possibility of either the Russian or Kazakh government being able to redraw the national boundary between them, and it was now a question of accepting and adjusting to the new situation.

The early years of independence was a time of confusion and uncertainty for many in Kazakhstan. The ethnic Russians found it difficult to accept their new status as citizens of Kazakhstan, and they were not helped by their fellow Russians in Russia itself, who could not bring themselves to see Kazakhstan as a separate country. The 'Stavropol Mothers' campaign in 1990 had crystalised for many Russians the division between Russia and the other former Soviet republics, but Kazakhstan had been regarded as an integral part of Russia since the nineteenth century. Now this was completely changed. In letters to the press and in conversations with Kazakh friends, many Russians tried, without enthusiasm, to stake a legitimate claim to what they called 'our Kazakhstan', meaning 'our shared Kazakhstan', and sought to remind their Kazakh neighbours that they too had a rightful say in how the country should be governed. But most Russians did not help their own cause by resolutely refusing to learn Kazakh, or identifying themselves in other ways with the new nation which was now also their home. (Failure to study Kazakh was not confined to Russians as many Kazakhs themselves, especially among the younger generation, were brought up speaking Russian and saw no benefit in learning their own language; indeed many saw it as an obstacle to career progression in which knowledge of other languages would be much more useful.) For their part, the Kazakhs were unsympathetic and dismissed any concerns that the Russian population might have. If the Russians were unhappy with the new situation, that was too bad; most Kazakhs had enough problems of their own in trying to survive in the difficult economic conditions which independence had brought, without worrying about how the Russians might feel, and they no longer felt any need to be subservient to the Russians. Between the Kazakhs and Russians, President Nursultan Nazarbaev emerged as a unifying figure, pursuing the interests of the whole of Kazakhstan while remaining deeply loyal to Russia and to his friend and comrade Boris Yeltsin. Nazarbaev embodied continuity from the old Soviet republic and stability in the new independent republic, and provided reassurance for every national and ethnic group. By continuing to maintain close relations with Russia he allayed the fears of millions of Russians in Kazakhstan, and his appointment in October 1991 of an ethnic Ukrainian, Sergei Tereshchenko, as Chairman of the Council of Ministers, a position he had himself held since 1984, indicated that Kazakhs were not going to hold all the top positions after independence. These actions irritated some of the more nationalist-minded Kazakhs, but they prevented a fraught and potentially dangerous relationship between different ethnic groups from becoming violent, and successfully maintained the cohesion and stability of the country. Nazarbaev was confirmed in office as President by direct election on 1 December 1991; he was the sole candidate and won 98.8 percent of the votes cast, but this was not so much a democratic contest but more a confirmation by popular vote of an existing reality. Even if other candidates had stood against him, Nazarbaev was likely to have won by a considerable margin.

Internationally, independence brought with it the appearance of Kazakhstan for the first time on the world stage. Not since the 1849 treaty between the khans on the Great Horde and Tsar Nicholas 1 of Russia had Kazakhstan represented itself to a foreign country, and that treaty ended the independence of Kazakhstan for the next 142 years. On the dissolution of the USSR, Russia was internationally recognised as the successor state and took upon itself responsibility for all the foreign debt of the Soviet Union, in exchange for all the overseas assets, military bases, and diplomatic property of the USSR. This was a crude but simple solution to an otherwise impossible task of allocating a share of the foreign debt and foreign assets of the Soviet Union among the fifteen republics. Kazakhstan and the other thirteen non-Russian republics were thus free of any foreign debt, although some including Kazakhstan and Kyrgyzstan had substantial debts to Russia for which Russia sought repayment in the form of leases of airfields and other military bases. But each republic now faced the novel experience of setting up its own embassies in each other's capitals and around the world. Within the former Soviet Union alone, this eventually resulted in 210 new embassies being opened. Internationally the CIS was struggling to gain acceptance as the successor to the USSR; this was most clearly evident in US official publications which obstinately refused to acknowledge the new organisation by its correct name, preferring instead to refer to the 'NIS' (New Independent States) wherever possible.

It was the economy and living conditions rather than diplomacy that occupied the minds of most people in the early years of independence, and in the winter of 1991-1992 there was no rejoicing in Kazakhstan. The snow-covered parks and gardens of Alma-Ata glistened in the bright winter sunshine, but after nightfall the city was dark and silent, gripped in an icy glove as the temperature fell to 30 degrees or more below freezing. In the early morning restless queues formed at street corners, wrapped up against the intense cold, stamping their feet, and clutching urns and cans, to wait for deliveries of milk, smetana, and other dairy items, something which they had not had to do since the years after the war. Those who arrived late or without their own containers were turned away. The milk had to be boiled and sterilised at home, at considerably greater cost to the national gas supplies than if it was done centrally, but it was always fresh and tasted better than the imported and expensive alternative sometimes available in the shops. Everywhere families closed in on themselves as if in a siege, hoarding food and refusing to get rid of any items which might conceivably come in useful. All types of household goods, disused televisions and broken sewing machines, bicycles, and unwanted clothes, were stored on balconies and in hallways, or wherever space could be found. Construction activity had virtually ceased and housing was in acutely short supply, with three or four generations of the same family living in cramped two-room apartments. In the factories, fuel deliveries fell to critically low levels, and gas supplies to flats and offices became increasingly erratic, as Kazakhstan and Uzbekistan squabbled about payments and deliveries after the earlier system of planned allocations and barter trade between republics had rapidly given way to one of payment in advance in hard currency. In the countryside and in smaller towns and villages, living conditions regressed to subsistence levels. Trains and buses and every type of public service struggled to operate. The municipal authorities in Alma-Ata, unable to obtain spare parts for broken-down Russian-made buses from the now-bankrupt manufacturers, imported second-hand buses from Amsterdam and other Dutch cities where they were no longer needed. Such was the depth of national apathy that no attempt was made to remove the original Dutch advertisements in the buses or even their destination indicators, which continued to show 'Centrum' and 'Standplaats'; the buses were reliable and transported people to their workplace in the morning and home in the evening, and that was all anyone cared about. In one minor but significant benefit of the end of the Soviet system, the after-work political lectures and seminars, which for years had detained workers in offices and factories in pointless discussion groups and sham votes and resolutions before they could go home, had now been abandoned, much to the relief of organisers and participants. In the 1950s and 1960s these groups had a useful educational purpose and they tried to engage ordinary people in the political process, but by the 1980s disillusionment and cynicism had set in and they had long outlived their usefulness.

Kazakhstan may have gained political independence, but it could not easily break free from the Russian economy. In common with many other republics, Kazakhstan initially retained the rouble as its national currency, but without its own central bank it had no control over the money in circulation in the country. It was now subject to the hyperinflationary note-issuing policy of the newly-established Central Bank of Russia, which continued to flood the Russian economy with liquidity in a vain attempt to stave off further collapse in industry and trade. Independence now exacerbated Kazakhstan's predicament; the government had some influence on economic policy as it affected Kazakhstan in the past but now it had none, since Russia had no concern as to how its actions and policies were affecting those republics which still used the rouble as their currency. Enterprises throughout Kazakhstan were increasingly suffering from the loss of traditional markets in Russia and from disruption to supplies of raw materials and other essential goods from neighbouring republics, which prevented them from fulfilling deliveries to their own customers. In addition, the entire banking and financial system had virtually seized up so that payments could rarely be made to suppliers or received from customers without considerable risk of money going astray, and loans and investments for any type of enterprise were unobtainable from the banks which were themselves on the brink of collapse. Acute though these problems were, an even greater difficulty was the need for Kazakhstan to extricate its economy from the Soviet system of central planning. Before 1991, the role of the economic ministries in Alma-Ata had been to carry out the directives received from Gosplan, the state planning organisation in Moscow, and the key areas of transport, communications, agriculture, and industry were little more than local offshoots of central ministries in Moscow. The highly integrated nature of the Soviet economy now made the task of formulating separate economic policies in each republic extremely difficult. Vast quantities of data relating to industrial and agricultural production, demand for raw materials and consumer goods, and masses of other economic and financial information, which in the past had been submitted to Moscow for incorporation into the central plan, now had to be gathered and assessed for the purposes of understanding and meeting each country's own needs. This was to be a mammoth operation, but for the first time in its history Kazakhstan began to take control of its own economy.

President Nazarbaev was committed to reform, but in practice he was obliged to pursue a twin strategy of embarking on radical new economic policies while simultaneously seeking to maintain traditional links with Russia. In particular this meant retaining the rouble, at least for the time being, as the national currency. The ill-fated 500-Day Programme, which never came into force in Russia, was equally redundant in Kazakhstan, although two central aspects of the Programme – privatisation and control of the country's natural resources – were still very much alive. Kazakhstan could now set its own prices for its exports of natural resources, but investment in the past had been very limited and the infrastructure of production and pipelines was primitive and completely inadequate for the country's needs. This meant that Kazakhstan remained heavily dependent on Russia and Uzbekistan for imports of energy. Meanwhile the technical and professional skills needed for the first programme of privatisation of state enterprises, launched in 1992, did not exist, and the lack of managerial expertise hindered reform at every stage. Managers were usually engineers and technicians with no experience of finance, foreign trade, especially trade with countries outside the former Soviet bloc, and the myriad of other management functions which had previously been the responsibility of the relevant ministry. Reform initiatives were hampered by obstruction and lack of cooperation on the part of conservative and unsympathetic officials within these ministries, who had spent their whole careers working in accordance with the socialist system and a centrally-planned economy. It was not easy for hundreds of thousands of such individuals, many in their fifties or sixties, to change their working methods to those of another system, especially if it meant losing their own jobs in the process. It was even less easy to imagine how the process might have been conducted in reverse, if the economy of the western world had to be converted to the socialist system.

Maintaining close economic links with Russia reassured the millions of Russians in Kazakhstan who were worried about the direction their new country was taking. In particular they welcomed the continued use of the rouble, even if it was rapidly losing value as hyper-inflation took hold. But economic relations with Russia greatly limited Kazakhstan's own room for manoeuvre. Price liberalisation in Russia in January 1992, involving the deregulation of prices on a wide range of goods, was matched by a similar move in Kazakhstan, but the ensuing sharp increase in the cost of living was met with widespread public protest, with the result that many price increases almost immediately had to be reversed. Salaries and social benefits were increased at regular intervals, but were unable to keep pace with inflation, and many enterprises failed to pay salaries at all for months in succession. Towards the end of 1993 the old economic relationship between the two countries could no longer be sustained. In September and October of that year, renewed political upheavals in Moscow put further severe strain on the Russian economy, a strain which was quickly transmitted to those republics which still used the rouble as their national currency. Kazakhstan, Uzbekistan, Turkmenistan, Kyrgyzstan, Tajikistan, Georgia, Armenia, and Azerbaijan, all had to reconsider this relationship and soon abandoned the rouble and introduced their own currencies. The other republics of the old USSR – Estonia, Latvia, Lithuania, Belarus, Ukraine, and Moldova – had introduced their own currencies immediately on independence, or very shortly afterwards.

In September 1993 the political crisis in Russia worsened when a dispute between parliament and the government turned into a serious confrontation. In defiance of the Constitution, on 21 September Yeltsin dissolved the parliament and announced that elections would be held for a new federal assembly. In response about 180 deputies who had opposed Yeltsin's political and economic policies of leading the economy to a more free-market system, barricaded themselves inside the parliament building, known as the White House, opposite the Ukraine Hotel in central Moscow. On 3 October anti-Yeltsin demonstrators stormed the Ostankino television building and demonstrations and fighting between pro and anti-reformers took place in running battles in the streets. The following day troops and tank divisions loyal to Yeltsin bombarded the parliament building and forced the surrender of the rebels in the parliament. Throughout the conflict about 150 people were reportedly killed and over a thousand injured. This short but dramatic outbreak of violence was the worst in Moscow since the Uprising of 1905, and caused considerably more deaths and injuries than had been incurred in the capital during the break-up of the Soviet Union two years earlier. Although it could easily have gone in favour of those opposed to reform, the outcome was a victory for Yeltsin in the form of a new Constitution, which assigned more powers to the President and a reduced role for parliament. The Constitution was approved by popular vote on 15 December 1993, although in elections on the same day to a new federal assembly, the ultra-nationalist Liberal Democratic Party of Russia unexpectedly gained twenty three percent of the total votes.

The October events in Moscow and the ensuing economic chaos in Russia forced upon Kazakhstan the belated realisation that it could no longer avoid responsibility for its own fate, and that the time had come for a decisive break. The government had made plans for the introduction of its own currency since becoming independent, and on 15 November 1993 it withdrew the rouble and put the tenge into circulation. To the widespread dismay of Russians in Kazakhstan, the ubiquitous portraits of Lenin, the familiar views of the Moscow Kremlin, and other traditional Russian scenes, had been replaced by portraits of Kazakh *bis* (tribal chiefs), *batyrs* (military leaders), medieval khans, writers and poets, and other prominent figures from Kazakh history. Even more upsetting was the fact that the wording on the first issues of notes was printed only in Kazakh, which was incomprehensible to almost every Russian; Kazakhs rudely dismissed these concerns by pointing out that the numbering of each denomination of notes was still in Roman numerals, 'which even Russians could understand'. Subsequent note issues were printed with both Kazakh and Russian wording. The tenge was originally introduced at a rate of one tenge to five hundred Russian roubles and nearly five tenge to the US dollar, but the exchange rate collapsed almost immediately to fifty five tenge to the dollar. The decline in the value of the rouble was proceeding at a much faster pace so that the tenge, despite its weakness, strengthened against the rouble, which enabled Kazakh enterprises to import goods and materials more cheaply from Russia. But overall trade between the two countries, and with other former Soviet republics, fell sharply, to the further detriment of the already rapidly-contracting economy.

In the longer term, the introduction of its own currency was of enormous benefit to Kazakhstan. The rouble had been both a practical and symbolic link with Russia, representing the union between the two countries over the previous hundred and fifty years. Now that it had gone the government was able to establish a National Bank of Kazakhstan as an independent central bank which would have responsibility for setting interest rates and managing the new national currency, while the Ministry of Finance, for the first time in Kazakh history, was responsible for taxation and spending.

These were developments of great symbolic importance, but on a practical level the problems confronting the new institutions seemed almost insuperable. In particular, the task facing many of the enormous state enterprises, of disengaging from bankrupt suppliers and defunct markets in Russia, with which they had been trading for decades, was only just beginning. Vague hopes of attracting foreign investment, often based on unrealistic assumptions and wishful thinking, soon gave way to reality and to an inevitable collapse in production. This became a time of rapid de-industrialisation and mass unemployment, and in many towns and cities the local kombinat could no longer fulfil the functions of employer or provider of social services which traditionally had been its role. Least of all could it pay unemployment or social security benefit, and without directions from a central plan which no longer existed, many enterprises continued to operate in name only, precariously supported by loans from banks which themselves were close to collapse. Eventually vast swathes of the country, which formerly had been relatively prosperous thanks to labour-intensive industries in the major cities of Kokchetav, Akmola, Pavlodar, Semipalatinsk, and Ust-Kamenogorsk, became littered with derelict and abandoned factories, broken power lines and rusting machinery, none of which could be dismantled or removed due to the universal lack of resources. In the industrial northern suburbs of Alma-Ata the situation was equally grave, although the rest of the city was less seriously affected given the prevalence of government offices and state employees, most of whom who continued to receive their salaries. Elsewhere, in factories, kombinats, and community centres, fading Soviet placards with strident propaganda slogans, exhorting ever-greater output and praising those workers who had over-fulfilled their work quotas, lay strewn on the floor or stacked in dusty corners, forlorn reminders of more optimistic times, and poignant symbols of an economic system which like the placards themselves had now been discarded.

The government's response to the economic crisis was to renew its attempts to shed responsibility for management of the thousands of state-owned enterprises and collective farms throughout the country, and transfer as many as possible and as soon as possible to private owners. Only natural monopolies in energy, transport, water, and other utilities were to remain in state ownership. The privatisation programme of 1992, followed by another round in 1993, had mixed results with some successes, particularly of small shops, cafes, and restaurants, and several thousand such enterprises were successfully sold by auction. Larger businesses were disposed of either by the free distribution of vouchers to the public or by auction of shares which were usually acquired by enterprise managers. But for many people the whole concept of privatisation was inimical to

Kazakhstan's historical traditions and communal values, going back to pre-Soviet times, while others saw no contradiction in reverting to a more feudal structure in industry and commerce, in which the economy would be organised on the basis of family clans and connections, a structure which continued to function, albeit under a different guise, in the Soviet period. The initial process of privatisation was not helped by the harsh advice handed out by western institutions and advisers as the country was emerging from the post-Soviet chaos of economic collapse. In an unsympathetic but realistic assessment in 1994, the World Bank expressed the view that 'Some of the 40-50 major state-owned enterprises that constitute the biggest financial burden on the government may warrant passive restructuring, that is a turnaround without major new investment, while others without prospects for viability should get liquidated'. To be politically acceptable the privatization programme needed some measure of public support, but the public was widely alienated by foreigners and by government ministers who had little awareness of living conditions for the vast majority of the Kazakh population. The programme gained some momentum from the setting-up of an Enterprise Restructuring Agency in 1994 and a Rehabilitation Bank in 1995, designed to take over many failing enterprises and restore them to profitability for sale to private investors, and a new bankruptcy law facilitated the liquidation of businesses which could not be saved. Gradually a new sense of realism began to creep into the public consciousness and into the economy.

Among the major industrial enterprises, particularly those in the mining and heavy industrial sectors which had been the pride of the economy in Soviet times, privatisation was conducted by means of tenders on a case-by-case basis, usually to foreign investors. Many such enterprises had been mismanaged for decades, with no sense of direction for the future, and suffering from a lack of investment and from over-dependence on the Russian market. The giant Karaganda Metallurgical Kombinat steelworks, where Nazarbaev had begun his working life, and which had symbolised Kazakhstan's economic strength in the 1970s, was on the verge of bankruptcy and collapse in 1995, when it was acquired by Ispat, an Indian steel group. After radical changes in every aspect of its operations, it became profitable and ceased to be the burden on the rest of the economy which it had been in more recent years. But such transformations were the exception rather than the rule. Despite the progress in integrating some parts of the economy to the outside world, Kazakhstan continued to suffer from a generally negative economic environment in which progress was difficult to achieve. The pull of the old Soviet system, especially in the neighbouring and less reform-minded economies of Central Asia, weighed heavily on Kazakhstan. In 1998 Russia experienced an acute financial and banking crisis, and the ensuing sharp devaluation of the rouble greatly exacerbated Kazakhstan's own economic difficulties, by attracting a flood of cheap imports from Russia, undercutting its own struggling industries, and making exports to Russia, still its principal market, more expensive. Those parts of the economy which could compete in world markets remained concentrated in the energy sector, and it was not until 2003 that a new 'Strategy for Industrial Development and Innovation' was launched, with the aim of diversifying the economy and reducing its dependence on oil and gas.

The problem of what to do with the bankrupt state-owned enterprises became acute in February 1995, when the government terminated the system of state-directed credits to the economy. From now on loans were to be made by the banking system, which also had the responsibility of recovering loans which had been made in earlier years but which many borrowers had no possibility of repaying. Ostensibly this move was intended to reduce the role of the government in the economy in the interests of a more market-based system, but in practice loans were now given more on the basis of family connections rather than as a means of supporting businesses with good prospects for expansion. Restructuring of viable enterprises, or liquidating those without any prospect of survival, had become an interminable process, constantly delayed by the refusal of parliament to approve the necessary legislation, and by the lack of a social security system to cope with the large numbers of unemployed which would inevitably be the result. This became another heavy burden on the banking system, which was compelled by many regional authorities in depressed parts of the country to keep local enterprises financially afloat, for fear of mass unemployment and civil unrest. Meanwhile the so-called kiosk economy became a feature of every town and village, as thousands of flimsy huts and shacks appeared on the streets, selling a wide range of imported household goods unobtainable on the empty shelves in the near-deserted state shops. In the dimly-lit kiosks shadowy figures sat bundled up in winter coats as customers, reduced to their familiar role from Soviet times as supplicants requesting a favour from someone in authority, were obliged to stoop down and tap on a sliding window to gain attention, before the window was rapidly shut again. In Alma-Ata the renowned Green Market, and its equivalent in many other towns, provided an opportunity for recently-privatised traders and farmers to bring in their own goods and produce from the countryside to sell at dozens of stalls and counters. A common feature of every city in Soviet times, the central markets now gained a vital new lease of life, circumventing the state supply system which had all but collapsed, and alleviating widespread food shortages, which otherwise would have been severe and politically very damaging.

Financial problems continued to plague the economy throughout the 1990s, and in 1996 the near-collapse of Turan Bank, one of the country's oldest and most prominent banks, provided another serious setback. The bank had emerged from the Soviet Industry and Construction Bank, founded in 1925, and had played a major role in the industrial and economic development of Kazakhstan before and after the Second World War. The failure of the bank to adapt to the new economic environment reflected the deep-rooted, Soviet-era unwillingness of the country as a whole to seek a way out of its difficulties. For nearly seventy years the bank had acted as the main conduit of government funds to all branches of the Kazakh economy, in accordance with the central plan drawn up in Moscow, but with independence and privatisation in 1992 the bank, like every other business in the country, was obliged to be responsible for its own destiny. In addition it had to recover what had become virtually irretrievable loans, if it was to save itself from collapse. However, in the absence of government intervention, Turan Bank and others in a similar position had become an unofficial but essential nation-wide social security system, and it was its inability to extricate itself from this vital role, albeit one which after privatization was theoretically no longer its responsibility, which led to its near collapse. Towards the end of 1996 anxious depositors sought, often unsuccessfully, to withdraw their savings, and in November the chairman and the board of directors were dismissed by the National Bank of Kazakhstan, which set to work to salvage what could be retrieved from the ruins of what had been a central part of the country's banking system. In many ways the Turan Bank debacle epitomised the conflicting strains of post-independence Kazakhstan: the intractable difficulty for the economy to disengage itself from the Soviet system of central planning and in particular offsetting, or at least minimizing, the debilitating impact on Kazakhstan of the perpetual crisis in the Russian economy, while at the same time attempting to provide a basic system of social security to the worst-hit communities throughout the country. The bank was ill-equipped to deal with a national upheaval on this scale, and it could not make loans to new companies in urgent need of credit and investment, which further retarded the process of recovery.

Before the development of oil and gas, banking and finance, and even industry and mining, Kazakhstan had been predominantly an agricultural economy, and at the time of independence agriculture still accounted for over one-third of the country's economic output. As elsewhere in the economy, the end of the Soviet system brought with it a sharp decline in output, due to political and economic turmoil, and the familiar problems of loss of markets, loss of supplies, especially of fuel, animal feed, and fertilisers, and shortages of agricultural machinery and spare parts, were compounded by several years of adverse weather on the steppe. Thousands of tons of wheat, barley, and other crops perished for want of storage and transport facilities. Agricultural production declined steadily throughout the 1990s, with a consequent reduction in deliveries to towns and cities, and it was not until the end of the decade that there was an increase in output for the first time since independence. As much as half the land under cultivation was devoted to wheat, the legacy of the Virgin Lands scheme of the 1950s and 1960s. By 2002 a more balanced utilisation of land was being achieved, and output for the home market, as well as for export markets in Russia, Belarus, and Uzbekistan was now playing a much greater role in the national economy. In 2003 the Kazakh parliament adopted a controversial new land code providing for the private ownership of land. Unlike the practice in Russia, where agricultural land is owned by the state but can be rented on long-term leases by private farmers, farmers in Kazakhstan could now buy land for ownership in their own name, in another historic departure from the country's now long-ceased traditions of common ownership.

By the end of the 1990s the economy began to stabilise and then to grow rapidly, as Kazakhstan established an independent role for itself as a major exporter of oil and gas rather than remaining simply an appendage of the Russian economy. Reserves of hydrocarbon resources, concentrated along the northern and eastern littorals of the Caspian Sea, were being steadily developed, thanks to extensive investment in exploiting untapped deposits, and in the construction of thousands of kilometres of new pipelines. The infrastructure of the oil and gas pipeline network had been severely neglected during the Soviet period, but this had the perverse benefit for Kazakhstan in that it had not experienced the same reckless exploitation of its natural resources that many other parts of the Soviet Union had suffered. With extensive reserves of oil and gas still intact, and political stability under the government of Nazarbaev, the country could now attract substantial investment from abroad. Henceforth the proceeds would be used for the benefit of Kazakhstan alone rather than being surrendered to the government in Moscow and dissipated throughout the Soviet Union. In 2005 a new 1,300 kilometre oil pipeline from Atasu on the steppe of central Kazakhstan to Alashankou in western China was completed, greatly increasing export capacity. This was one of several pipelines which traversed vast distances through the steppe and desert to reach new markets in Europe, Russia, and China. By 2005 Kazakhstan's production of oil was three times the volume in 1993, and over 80 per cent of which was exported.

This was to become the foundation for Kazakhstan's economic expansion, and most of the population was able to share in the country's wealth as government spending on health, education, welfare, and infrastructure increased substantially. The economy was flooded with foreign currency earnings which it had little capacity to absorb; like mushrooms after rain, new banks sprung up and in the space of a few years the volume of lending to businesses and property developers was transformed from a drought to a flood. Living standards of the population were rising sharply, and along the formerly staid Soviet-style streets of Almaty, where the flimsy kiosks of the 1990s had long since been swept away, new shops, car showrooms, fashionable restaurants and travel companies were opening to meet the demands of a new and affluent market. Car ownership was booming and the wide and previously empty streets and prospects were soon choked with traffic. Many of the secluded communal areas behind the blocks of flats were concreted over and converted into car parks. Despite the city's new wealth, little provision was made to replace the simple social amenities, of quiet courtyards and play areas, which were now being lost. Many of the loans now being handed out recklessly by the new and inexperienced banks and finance companies were directed to the large-scale construction of blocks of expensive flats and prestigious houses, with calamitous results for the whole economy when the housing market crashed in 2008. By the end of the decade, and in common with the experience in some western countries, the banking sector was overwhelmed with loans which had become irrecoverable. In 2009, for the second time since it was privatized Turan Bank, now known as BTA Bank, had to be rescued by the government, in a crisis which dealt another severe blow to the economy.

CHAPTER TWENTY FOUR

War in Chechnya: Kazakhstan is Reprieved

In the early years of independence, the Kazakh economy was in disarray and the millions of ethnic Russians in the new republic may have regretted the demise of the USSR and their separation from Russia. But they and the rest of the former Soviet population outside Russia soon had one overwhelming reason to be grateful for their new status as citizens of independent countries: their sons, brothers, uncles and fathers would not have to fight in the merciless war in Chechnya.

In November 1991, as the last of the fifteen Soviet republics were declaring independence from the Soviet Union, the small mountainous region of Chechnya in southern Russia declared its own independence from Russia. Chechnya had had a violent and troubled history, and with the disintegration of the USSR it now saw an opportunity to achieve a separate identity for itself. A landlocked republic within the Russian Federation, Chechnya is surrounded on three sides to the west, north, and east by Russia and with a short border with Georgia high in the Caucasus Mountains to the south. It was colonized by tsarist forces during the nineteenth century in a long and brutal campaign, as Russia sought to take control of the whole of the Caucasus Mountain range so as to provide a barrier between itself and its Muslim neighbours of Turkey and Persia. The Russian subjugation of Chechnya, and the fierce resistance of its inhabitants, themselves Muslim, were described in the short stories of Leo Tolstoy, who was serving in the tsarist army at the time and took part in the military conquest of the region – although Tolstoy later came to sympathise strongly with the mountain tribes and with the early Chechen struggle for independence. In 1932 Chechnya became part of the Chechen-Ingush Autonomous Region of Russia, with some notional independence, but it was never reconciled to being part of Russia. During and after the Second World War almost the entire population of Chechnya was exiled across the Caspian Sea to Kazakhstan, where many tens of thousands died of hunger and disease. Those who survived were allowed to return in the Khrushchev years of the 1950s, although many remained in isolated and impoverished communities in Kazakhstan.

Chechnya had no realistic prospects of functioning as a viable independent state, since it could easily be subject to an economic blockade by Russia, and even with cooperation from Georgia it had no easy access across the mountains to the sea or to other countries. But in the chaotic environment of the early 1990s the tiny republic financed itself on earnings from exports of oil, which in theory belonged to Russia as a whole but which were retained by the government in Chechnya, with Russia powerless to act. The country became notorious for violence and corruption under the erratic and oppressive dictatorship of its President Dzhokar Dudaev, a former Soviet air force officer, and by 1994 Chechnya had become a lawless enclave, where money-laundering, kidnapping, drug dealing and all types of criminal activity were carried out with impunity. Several attempts by Russian agents to remove Dudaev had failed and the Russian government, deeply worried by the critical situation developing on its southern border, was also concerned that it would not be able to construct a planned pipeline through the northern part of Chechnya to carry oil from the Caspian Sea in the east to terminals on the Black Sea in the west. The crisis was having a highly damaging effect on the Russian economy and was threatening stability throughout the Caucasus region and the whole of southern Russia.

By December 1994 the Russian government decided it had no choice but to intervene militarily, and on the morning of 11 December, 40,000 Russian troops entered Chechnya, marking the beginning of the first Chechen War. Russia may have claimed a legitimate cause in seeking to put an end to the Dudaev regime, to restore stability and to reincorporate Chechnya into Russia, but the invasion immediately turned into a disastrous campaign of vicious fighting and thousands of deaths and injuries. Motivated more by anti-Russian feelings than by loyalty to Dudaev, the Chechens inflicted heavy casualties on the Russian forces, most of whom were young conscripts, poorly-trained, badly-led, and ill-equipped. News of the conflict was broadcast every evening on television in Russia and throughout the old Soviet Union, and around the world. In Russia, the action of the 'Stavropol Mothers', who in 1990 had successfully campaigned against the deployment of Russian troops to suppress anti-Soviet demonstrations in Azerbaijan, could not be repeated on this occasion, since Chechnya was a constituent part of Russia itself. From Murmansk in the northwest to Vladivostock in the far east, the Russian government scoured the country for unwilling conscripts to fight in a distant war far from home. In the process it did great harm to Russia itself, since any military gains were usually slight, but of those who managed to survive their ordeal, many thousands returned home with severe physical injuries or acute mental trauma, at enormous cost to their families, to the economy, and to society as a whole. Meanwhile in Kazakhstan and throughout all of the other former Soviet republics, not only the mothers of teenage sons but the whole population breathed a deep sigh of relief that their armed forces would not be used in this war, which was an internal conflict within Russia, and in which they were not involved. Officially the Kazakh government supported Russian policy, and President Nazarbaev may have felt some sympathy for the disaster which his friend Boris Yeltsin had got himself into. But this was little more than token support. In an earlier conflict in the 1980s, Kazakh conscripts had been compelled to fight in Afghanistan alongside troops from Russia and other Soviet republics, and no one wanted a repeat of that terrible experience. At that time there had been considerable sympathy in Kazakhstan and among the other Central Asian republics for the plight of the population of Afghanistan, since they were all Muslim, and all had suffered at the hands of the Russians. In the new crisis in Chechnya, no-one had any sympathy with the Dudaev regime, but most Kazakhs instinctively sided with their fellow-Muslims in Chechnya in their struggle against Russia. This might have contributed to hostility against ethnic Russians in Kazakhstan, but most Russians in Kazakhstan, and many in Russia itself, were strongly opposed to the war, and inter-ethnic conflict in Kazakhstan arising from the war was avoided.

The war dragged on until Dudaev was killed in a Russian missile attack in April 1996 and a cease-fire agreement was concluded the following month. The ceasefire was frequently broken by both sides and attacks continued to be made from Chechnya on the neighbouring Russian republic of Dagestan. In September 1999, instigated by a series of bombings of blocks of flats in Moscow and a number of other Russian cities, in which hundreds of people were killed, Russia launched what became known as the Second Chechen War. The bombing campaign was officially alleged to be the action of Chechen terrorists, but the near-universal opinion in Kazakhstan, throughout the other non-Russian republics, and among many people in Russia itself, was that this was the work of the FSB, the successor to the KGB, seeking a pretext on the orders of the Russian government for a renewed invasion of Chechnya, which would put an end to any further attempts to gain independence. In one incident in the city of Ryazan south-east of Moscow, the government claimed that explosives found in the stairwell of a block of flats were part of a training exercise designed to test the readiness of the local authorities to deal with this type of emergency, although this episode confirmed the widely-held suspicion that this was part of the same FSB conspiracy. The bombing campaign of September 1999 and the Ryazan incident in particular added to public unease and to the growing mistrust in Kazakhstan of the intentions of the Russian government. There could have been no possible gain for Chechnya from provoking Russia into launching another attack and a new wave of violence and terror in Chechnya, and thereby ensuring the election of Vladimir Putin as president of Russia the following March. Public opinion in Kazakhstan, by now deeply cynical in its attitude towards Russia, was once again profoundly grateful that it had no involvement in a brutal colonial war in a foreign country.

***

While Russia was becoming mired in the disaster in Chechnya, Kazakhstan was embarking on a further stage in its own development. In October 1994 President Nazarbaev announced that the national capital would be transferred from Almaty to Akmola, the former Tselinograd, centre of the Virgin Lands campaign of the 1950s and 1960s and the principal town in the predominantly Russian-populated northern part of the country. Less than a year earlier in November 1993, in the same month as the introduction of the new currency, the name of the Kazakh capital had been changed from Alma-Ata to Almaty. Almaty was one of the nearby ancient settlements which had existed in the Zailisky Alatau Mountains long before the Mongol invasions of the thirteenth century, and the name had a special historic significance in Kazakhstan. The new name would, it was hoped, inspire a revived sense of national cohesion and togetherness, in the city and the country as a whole, compared with the rather contrived name of Alma-Ata, with all its unhappy associations since it was adopted in 1921. Almaty had a new name but now it was to lose its position as the nation's capital, as a further significant step was to be taken in the creation of the new Kazakhstan.

Several important strategic reasons lay behind this visionary plan. Almaty had become a crowded and less attractive place to live, and less suitable as the capital for the post-Soviet republic. Expansion of the city to the south was blocked by the Tien Shan Mountains, while to the north the land was hot and barren and as unwelcoming to settlement as it had been 140 years earlier when the Russians first arrived. In the northern suburbs, a dark cloud of industrial pollution hung almost permanently in the still air, forcing all those who could afford to do so to live in the higher, cooler suburbs to the south. The remote location of the city in the extreme south-east of Kazakhstan, far from the rest of the country and from Russia, was increasingly inconvenient. Relocation of the capital to Akmola would alleviate pressure on Almaty and provide easier communications with the rest of the country, with the former Soviet Union, and with the wider world. Here the heat of summer was less intense, the air was cleaner, the surrounding countryside was attractive and fertile, and there was plenty of room for unhindered expansion.

Akmola was also safe from earthquakes. The foothills of the Tien Shan Mountains to the south of Almaty lie on an active geological fault line, and tremors and sudden shocks are commonplace in the city and the surrounding regions. Usually these cause only light damage, and there had not been a serious earthquake affecting Almaty since 1911. But within living memory the capitals of two neighbouring republics – Ashkhabad in Turkmenistan in 1948 and Tashkent in Uzbekistan in 1966 – had been almost totally destroyed by violent earthquakes, and Almaty was equally vulnerable. The terrible mudslide and torrent of rocks and boulders in the summer of 1973, which had devastated large areas of land and necessitated the construction of a vast concrete dam in the Alatau valley above Almaty, were a reminder of constant danger from natural forces. The city had recovered after the earthquakes of 1887 and 1911, but destruction for a third time, causing the devastation of hundreds of factories and thousands of poorly-constructed blocks of flats, would be ruinous to the national economy. Most public buildings were constructed with heavy, difficult-to-open double doors, designed to keep out the severe winter cold and snow, but which made rapid evacuation impossible, and would ensure that the number of casualties would be high. As if to vindicate the decision to relocate the capital, in March 1995 the Japanese city of Kobe was struck by an earthquake, causing thousands of deaths and widespread destruction. In Almaty the disaster prompted the appearance of notices of assembly points and evacuation procedures throughout the city, and people prepared emergency suitcases ready for a sudden departure. The many critics of the move to Akmola, mainly government officials who had earlier stressed the impossibility of leaving Almaty, became less vocal in their opposition.

A potentially more explosive fault line lay in the composition of the population in northern Kazakhstan. Disaffection among ethnic Russians, who heavily outnumbered the local Kazakh population, had not fully abated since independence, and in March 1994 sporadic unrest and disturbances between Kazakhs and Russians broke out on the streets of several industrial towns. Parliamentary elections that month had produced overwhelming majorities in favour of Kazakh candidates, and led to allegations of discrimination against the Slav population, although in reality the ratio of representation of Russian and Ukrainian minorities in the Supreme Kenges, the national parliament, did not deviate very far from that in the country as a whole. Economic rather than political factors were the main cause of the unrest; Akmola had never fully recovered its economic status since it was the centre of the Virgin Lands campaign of the 1960s, and the recent problems and bankruptcy of many state enterprises in the town and in the whole of the industrial north and east of the country were having a disproportionate impact on the predominantly Russian population. Mass unemployment had only been avoided by enterprises being reluctant to lay off superfluous workers. The earlier communal attitudes, of sharing jobs and what limited income there was, persisted throughout the 1990s, a factor which strengthened social cohesion and avoided further clashes, but which made the task of economic readjustment even more difficult. Relocation of the capital to Akmola would generate employment and incomes in construction and many other industries, and help to revive the weakening economy of the town and its surrounding regions. The economic loss to Almaty would be more than compensated by the gain to Akmola. But more importantly the relocation would put an end to any ideas of secession that may take root among the Russian population if the economic situation continued to deteriorate, or to the possibility of Russian territorial designs in the north. Designating Akmola as the new capital of Kazakhstan would serve a similar strategic purpose as the construction of the Russian fort had done in Verny in 1853.

Lastly, the government had serious concerns about the brooding presence of China, Kazakhstan's rapidly-growing and densely-populated neighbour to the east. The frontier between Kazakhstan and China extends for 1,533 kilometres from a point where the borders of Kazakhstan, Kyrgyzstan, and China meet at Mount Khan Tengri in the south-east, passing to within 275 kilometres to the east of Almaty, and continuing to the remote Yuzhni Alatau Mountains north of Lake Zaisan, to join the 7,500 kilometre border with Russia. The position of Almaty was seen as exposed and vulnerable; the Ili Gap between the Dzungarski Alatau Ridge and the Tien Shan Mountains remained as open to invasion as it had been in the days of Genghiz Khan the Mongol hordes in the thirteenth century, while further north the border between Kazakhstan and China was equally unprotected. However unlikely a threat may have seemed, fear of China continued to exert a strong influence on policy, and a more secure location for the capital was a vital strategic necessity.

Akmola was inaugurated as the new state capital by President Nazarbaev on 8 November 1997, and in May 1998 its name was changed by presidential decree to Astana. Many thought that the original Kazakh name meaning 'White Tomb' was unsuitable for the capital city of a new nation, while others believed that Astana, meaning simply 'Capital', was equally uninspiring. But a choice had to be made that would be acceptable both to Kazakhs and to the predominantly Russian population in the city and the north of the country, and a name with more historical associations would have offended one or other of the two communities. The political capital was transferred from Almaty to Astana, but Almaty would remain the commercial and financial centre of the country.

The central part of the old Soviet town of Tselinograd has now virtually disappeared, swallowed up in a frenzy of new construction and futuristic architecture. In the suburbs the long drab rows of blocks of flats from the 1950s and 1960s still line the streets and prospects, but elsewhere commercial buildings, shopping centres, and prestigious apartment blocks have combined to eliminate almost all traces of the past. Even less remains of the tsarist Akmolinsk, although a handful of ornate nineteenth-century mansions and aristocratic houses have survived, some of which have been acquired by foreign governments for use as embassies, and the quiet Central Park on the banks of the Ishim River still provides a peaceful refuge from the noise of the modern city, where the wide and previously-empty Soviet-era streets have now come into their own and are full of impatient traffic. The massive Lenin statue has long since been removed from the main square, but the country's recent history has not been entirely forgotten, and a small, grass-covered artificial hill in the Central Park has been created as a Monument to the Dead of the Totalitarian Regime. Inspired by President Nazarbaev, this memorial commemorates the millions who died in the Stalin era of the 1930s and 1940s. This was one of the periods of history during which Kazakhstan had no control over its own destiny, but which caused widespread trauma throughout the whole of the country. The memorial is a powerful but sympathetic reminder of a time of great national suffering and fear.

***

With the new capital safely inaugurated, President Nursultan Nazarbaev took further steps to consolidate his own power and position. These actions were to be at the expense of political and press freedoms, and the years of the new millennium became a time of corruption and political scandal involving senior figures in the government, members of the President's family, and major companies in the economy. During this period a proliferation of new political parties appeared, and there were frequent changes of prime minister and other ministers, but any instability which might have arisen as a result was avoided by the authoritarian nature of the type of government under Nazarbaev. Although relatively benign, the system left no place for a genuinely anti-Nazarbaev opposition.

Shortly before the formal declaration of independence, on 1 December 1991 Nursultan Nazarbaev became the first elected president of Kazakhstan, initially for a five-year term. This was very much a Soviet-style election in which he was the sole candidate and obtained 99 per cent of the votes cast. But the result gave him the legitimacy as head of state to declare independence and to provide the stability and political balance between the different nationalities in Kazakhstan which was much needed in the fraught atmosphere of the times. Just over one year later, in January 1993 Kazakhstan adopted its own Constitution for the first time; previous constitutions had all been variants of the Soviet model which had been imposed on the country in the 1920s and 1930s. Now Kazakhstan was to have its own presidential system of government with separate executive, legislative, and judicial bodies. The local executive authorities, formerly known by the Russian name *ispolkom,* then by the Kazakh name *akimiyat,* had become considerably more powerful in the last years of the USSR, exerting far more authority than in their traditional rubber-stamp role in the Soviet period. After independence they continued to grow in influence, reporting directly to the President and by-passing local councils and government ministries. Even so there were still obstacles to presidential rule. A parliamentary election in 1994 led to protests and demonstrations among the Russian population who claimed that it was under-represented, and in February 1995 the Constitutional Court declared that the results of the election were null and void. This led the Council of Ministers, which had earlier been criticized by Nazarbaev for the slow pace of economic reform, to resign, and in March President Nazarbaev dissolved parliament as well and proceeded to govern the country by decree. In August parliament was reinstated but under amendments made to the 1993 Constitution the Supreme Kenges, the former single-chamber parliamnet, was now replaced with a bicameral parliament consisting of a forty-seven member upper chamber or Senate, and a sixty-seven member lower chamber, or Majlis. The powers and independence of the new parliament were greatly reduced and it had little effect on containing the power of the President.

From now on there was no serious political activity, let alone any opposition to the President, and public opinion among Kazakhs and Russians, by now almost totally apathetic and weary, was not inclined to raise any objections to the new system. Away from parliament, public opinion was generally supportive of Nazarbaev, although he was criticised for many of his unilateral decisions. People complained amongst themselves that 'the President does what he wants', but this was said more with a resigned shrug of the shoulders than with any great sense of resentment. Unlike the experience of

Soviet times, such opinions could now be expressed openly, even to foreigners, without fear of arrest or of losing one's job. Dissatisfaction among ordinary people was largely confined to such matters as apparently unrestrained expenditure on palaces in Almaty and Astana and other presidential excesses, which offended many people, not only those struggling to survive on meagre incomes. At the same time there was growing disquiet at the extent of corruption, the increasing number of financial scandals, and the spread of violence, even allegations of political assassination, against opponents of the regime. But Nazarbaev had ensured he had a free hand to drive through reforms and introduce much-needed legislation quickly, in sharp contrast to the earlier period of procrastination and failure to deal with hyper-inflation, food shortages, and declining living standards.

In the mid-1990s most of the media in Kazakhstan was relatively free, compared with that in neighbouring states. New newspapers and publications had appeared and there were no longer restrictions on the foreign press, with *Newsweek* and the *Financial Times* replacing the *Morning Star* in western hotels. But serious criticism of the government in the local press was not welcomed, and cases of intimidation of journalists or setting fire to the premises of hostile newspapers, were not uncommon. Kiosks selling newspapers critical of the government were sometimes burnt to the ground in the middle of the night. By 1995 more serious instances of economic corruption and mismanagement in the financial sector, not involving the government, were regularly being exposed in the press and on television. The near-collapse of Turan Bank in 1996, which caused many job losses and gravely undermined the already fragile public confidence in the whole of the banking system, was widely reported on the television news every evening and in the press, as customers queued in vain to recover their money. But far from leading to reform of the banking sector, and despite the best efforts of the National Bank in seeking to impose stricter controls and regulations, the crisis set the stage for further financial upheavals and allegations of corruption on a massive scale. A small-scale stock exchange had started to develop but investors remained wary and capital flight out of the country began to accelerate. The press and television, having played an active role in exposing the Turan Bank crisis, now came under increasing pressure to avoid controversial areas and stick to reporting mundane issues. Journalists who expressed criticism of the government or investigated allegations of corruption found they were subjected to harassment, including physical attacks and arrests for alleged tax violations. By 2003 the government was increasingly disturbed by revelations of some of the media, and a draft law was presented to Parliament which included proposals to increase state control over the press and severely limit freedom of expression. The proposed legislation was withdrawn after widespread protests, and after a court ruling that it would violate the Constitution. Nonetheless government intervention continued seriously to hamper the activities of the media and make life difficult for journalists.

In 1998 Nazarbaev extended the presidential term of office from five to seven years, and abolished the upper age limit for candidates, previously set at 65. In the following year he was re-elected for a new seven-year term, and although international observers agreed there were no gross violations in the voting, at the same time the election was held to be not entirely fair, since the only serious rival – Akezhan Kazhegeldin, whom Nazarbaev had appointed as Prime Minister in 1994 – had been disqualified on a minor technicality. The runner-up was a candidate from the Communist Party, which had been permitted to put forward a candidate (which was no longer possible in elections in Russia), but which had virtually no chance of success against Nazarbaev and simply gave the election the appearance of being a free vote. Kazhegeldin left Kazakhstan shortly after the election to live in Europe, and was later charged with tax evasion and abuse of power while he was in office. At his trial two years later, while still in exile abroad, Kazhegeldin was sentenced in absentia to ten years imprisonment.

In the following years Nazarbaev circumvented restrictions on re-election, manipulated election dates to the disadvantage of opposition candidates, and generally ensured his own survival in power. Many believed that such was his standing in the country that he would have defeated any challenges to his authority even if elections and referendums were more fairly contested. But given his background in the Soviet system, and what he saw as the overriding need to maintain stability and continuity, Nazarbaev was determined to avoid any unnecessary risk. Below the President a proliferation of political parties led to squabbling in parliament and confusion in the country, and to simplify the situation, and remove any threat of serious opposition, in 2002 the government introduced a controversial law on the regulation of political parties. This required all parties to undergo re-registration before they could undertake any form of activity, which in turn required that they should have branches in each of the country's regions and have a minimum of 50,000 members, instead of 3,000 as had previously been the case. Few of the existing political parties were able to comply with these criteria, but even so there were still twelve parties eligible to participate in future parliamentary elections. Some were openly in favour of the President, but others were more critical such as the reformist Democratic Choice of Kazakhstan (DCK), which became a painful thorn in the side of the government. In December 2004 the DCK declared the government to be illegitimate and urged a campaign of non-violent civil disobedience. In 2005, after the government had taken steps to dissolve the DCK, its members quickly set up a new party known as *Alga* (Forward). The old Soviet Communist Party of Kazakhstan struggled to survive in the new relatively liberal climate, and suffered a severe blow when a splinter group with greater popular appeal, the Communist People's Party of Kazakhstan, broke away in 2004.

The controversy surrounding the former Prime Minister Akezhan Kazhegeldin, once one of several close associates of Nazarbaev but who were later forced out of office, was merely one of a series of scandals involving the whole of the political establishment in Kazakhstan after independence. Compared with later developments in neighbouring Turkmenistan, where state funds were diverted on a vast scale for the adulation of the President, and Uzbekistan, where oppression of almost the whole population outside the president's clan was growing in severity, the situation in Kazakhstan appeared on the surface to be relatively calm. But behind the scenes, occasional violent and bitter clashes were taking place, some of which burst out into the open. With restrictions imposed on the domestic media, it was the foreign press which began to investigate allegations of corruption, and in 2001 Western media reports claimed that more than one billion dollars of state funds was being held in Swiss banks in President Nazarbaev's name, and that the President's son-in-law, Rakhat Aliyev, was involved in corruption and illegal use of government money. Instead of allowing his son-in-law to face charges for these alleged offences, Nazarbaev removed him from Kazakhstan by appointing him as ambassador to Austria. The controversy extended beyond the presidential family to include senior members of the government, and resulted in a rapid succession of appointments and dismissals of prime ministers. While this crisis was in process, a separate upheaval was under way, involving other figures opposed to the government. In 2002, Mukhtar Ablyazov and Ghalimzhan Zhakiyanov, prominent figures in the DCK, were convicted of financial irregularities and sentenced to long terms in prison. Ablyazov, a former Trade and Energy Minister, was pardoned and released the following year, although he later became involved in another major corruption scandal involving BTA Bank, the successor to the old Turan Bank. Zhakiyanov, the former governor of the Pavlodar region in northern Kazakhstan, was detained for a further three years. The real crime of both officials appeared to have been involvement in the DCK party, which campaigned for the decentralisation of power towards the regions and away from the presidency, and for more effective action against corruption.

Events took a more sinister and violent turn in 2005, when in the space of four months two senior government officials, formerly allies of Nazarbaev but more recently critics, became victims of what was alleged to be political assassination. Zamanbek Nurkadilov, a former mayor of Almaty, supposedly committed suicide according to a police investigation, but many people believed he was murdered as a result of his opposition to the President. In 2006, Altynbek Sarsenbaev, a former ambassador to Russia, was shot and his body, together with those of his driver and bodyguard, were found on a roadside near Almaty. Sarsenbaev had been a leading member of an opposition party called the True Light Road and many believed his death was a politically motivated murder. The episode had an unusual consequence when a protest rally was held in Almaty at which demonstrators demanded an end to the persecution of opposition politicians, and that those responsible for the death of Sarsenbaev should be brought to justice. Within a few months ten men suspected of involvement in the murder were put on trial, and all ten were convicted and given long prison sentences. Whether they had been acting on the orders of the president remains a mystery, but the alleged ringleader, Erzhan Utembaev, another senior official and former head of administration in the Senate, was sentenced to twenty years in prison. In 2007 Parliament voted to allow Nazarbaev to remain in office for an unlimited term, effectively dispensing with the need for further presidential elections. But stability in the leadership was by no means total: later the same year Nazarbaev dismissed his son-in-law Rakhat Aliyev alleging that he was planning to take over the government, although a court in Vienna refused a request that he should be extradited back to Kazakhstan on the grounds that he would not be granted a fair trial. In 2008 Aliyev was sentenced in absentia to twenty years in prison. Thereafter Nazarbaev continued to consolidate more power to himself and in 2010 Parliament gave him the title of 'Leader of the Nation'. Stability in the country at large is also not guaranteed. In December 2011, clashes between striking workers in the oil town of Zhanaozen in western Kazakhstan left sixteen people dead and forced the government to impose a state of emergency. Although this was soon lifted the following month, the episode revealed a still fragile political situation in some parts of the country, a situation compounded by the lack of any genuine opposition in Parliament.

In a further symbolic step establishing the new status of Kazakhstan, in January 2005 President Nazarbaev and President Vladimir Putin of Russia signed a treaty defining the 7,500-kilometre land border between the two countries. To a large extent this was the original border as defined at the time of the formal incorporation of Kazakhstan within the territory of Russia in 1920, although later amendments had been made to reflect the transfer of the Semirechie region from Turkestan to Kazakhstan in 1924. For Russia the 2005 border agreement was particularly significant in that its frontiers in this part of Central Asia, which had historically been unclear and without any defining geographical features, were now laid down by international treaty. Kazakhstan had already signed similar treaties with its southern neighbours of Kyrgyzstan, Uzbekistan, and Turkmenistan in 2003. By the end of the decade the demographic worries which had troubled Kazakhstan in its first ten years of independence, especially potential secessionist movements in the north, had virtually disappeared. The post-indepence decline in the population had stabilized and then recovered, and inter-ethnic disturbances are now rare. The government of President Nazarbaev has achieved a wide distribution of national wealth which, although ensuring that vast amounts remain among a small number of government officials and presidential family members, prevents millions of others from falling into poverty. Contrary to the situation in other neighbouring republics, where oppressive regimes seek to prevent the development of an entrepreneurial class which may threaten the power structure and privileges of the government elite, the government in Kazakhstan is keen to promote business and enterprise in the interests of preserving political stability. This is a policy derived in no small measure from Nazarbaev's own experience of life at the bottom of the social scale in the 1950s and 1960s.

CHAPTER TWENTY FIVE

Kazakhstan in the Post-Soviet Era

In the space of less than three generations, Kazakhstan has undergone a bewildering series of different stages of development, from rural and pre-industrial to urban and post-industrial, from socialist to capitalist, and from being to all intents and purposes part of Russia to becoming an independent post-colonial country. Along the way any remnants of a nomadic way of life have long since disappeared and have been replaced by a more stable and productive form of agriculture and food production. Even so, rural depopulation has continued and large areas of the Kazakh steppes are now more empty and devoid of human life than at any time in recent history. There has been a correspondingly rapid inflow of people into towns and cities, most of which have been unready to accept and absorb the new arrivals. All this has led to deep social divisions within the population, in which a small number of wealthy urban Kazakhs now has more in common with the outside world than with their own indigenous communities. Meanwhile new roads, railways, and airports are being built, and the internet and the digital age have enabled the country to bypass the long evolution of communications which western countries have undergone.

The predominant external influence in the country for three hundred years has been Russia and the Russian empire in its various different forms. The end of the USSR in 1991 marked the end of the last and the shortest in duration of these empires, which extended as far back as the tenth century. The first two Russian empires – Kievan Rus, and the principality of Muscovy – had no direct influence on Kazakhstan, but each was crucial in the development of Russia itself, before it became a colonial power in Central Asia. Kievan Rus was in effect a grouping of separate city states centred in Kiev and covered a vast area of western Russia. Established in around 955, it lasted for nearly three hundred years until its destruction by the Mongol invasion of 1232. Almost a century later, in 1325 the Russian Orthodox Church transferred its main location from Kiev, north-east to the underpopulated and undeveloped forest region around Moscow. At the time the principality of Muscovy was subordinate to the nearby Grand Principality of Vladimir, but it occupied an important trading position on the river of the same name, and was to become the strategic centre of Russia. At the Battle of Kulikovo on the River Don south of Moscow in 1380 Dimitry, the Grand Prince of Moscow, defeated the Mongols in what was a major turning point in early Russian history. After this exploit Dimitry, known as 'Donskoi', extended the principality of Muscovy so that it became the strongest of the ancient Russian principalities, surpassing the other contenders for supremacy of Vladimir, Novgorod, and Yaroslav.

Nearly two hundred years later, at his coronation in 1547, Ivan IV (the Terrible) first took the title of Tsar, deriving from the Latin word Caesar, implying that Muscovy had a natural right to rule the whole of the Muscovite empire, which then extended from the Dnieper River in the west to the Volga River in the east. Under Ivan, the territory of Russia expanded further to incorporate Kazan and Astrakhan to the south, and large parts of Siberia to the east, and it was during Ivan's reign that Russia emerged as a unified state. He established a rudimentary civil service in Moscow which provided the political and administrative foundations which would be needed for future territorial expansion, and which ensured that Russia would be able to govern and control an empire eventually extending far beyond its existing borders. These were the fundamental cornerstones in the building of an empire which was to culminate in the foundation of the USSR in 1922, three hundred and seventy years after Ivan's conquest of Kazan. Not until 1991 did the colonizing process which had been started in the reign of Ivan the Terrible go into reverse, with the collapse of the Soviet Union and the emergence of separate independent states, although Kazan and Astrakhan have both remained within Russia. As the second Russian empire expanded in the sixteenth century, it began to encounter practical difficulties arising from its vast size and diversity, and from the conflict between its imperial ambitions in Asia and its status as a growing military power in Europe. The system of government established under Ivan could not yet cope with the demands placed upon it, and ultimately the empire collapsed due to a combination of endless wars and domestic upheavals, the lack of a successor to the royal line after the death of Ivan IV in 1584, and famines and epidemics triggered by a series of natural disasters and harvest failures. The turmoil in Russia at the end of the sixteenth century became known as the Time of Troubles.

The third Russian empire, established under the Romanov dynasty, was the longest in duration, lasting for three centuries, and the most expansive, extending its territory into Europe, the Caucasus, Central Asia, and the furthermost reaches of Siberia as far as the Pacific Ocean and Alaska. For a brief period a Russian presence extended beyond Alaska as far as California and the west coast of North America. By the time of the accession of the first Romanov Tsar Michael Feodorovich in 1613, Kazakhstan was already being drawn into contact with Russia, as the first Russian fur traders and hunters began trading with Kazakh nomads and horsemen on the steppes of Central Asia. But it would be another hundred years before the first formal contacts were made and treaties were signed between the tsars in St Petersburg, to where the capital had been transferred from Moscow under Peter the Great in 1703, and the Kazakh khans of the Little and Middle Hordes in the 1730s. Eventually the Romanov empire collapsed due to unsustainable social and political strains throughout Russia and the empire. The infrastructure was inadequate to maintain the cohesion of such a vast land area, and the economy was too weak and undeveloped to avoid defeat in the First World War. The collapse was accelerated by the incompetence of the tsarist government under Nicholas II which, shielded from the population, turned away from what was happening in the country. For Kazakhstan, tsarist imperialism had brought many negative features, particularly the seizure of land by Russian incomers, the suppression of historical traditions and the nomadic way of life, and the forced incorporation of the country into Russia itself, with all the subsequent upheavals and turmoil, of revolution, civil war, and political oppression. But it also provided the conditions for the emergence of Kazakhstan as a separate nation state, in the form of internal stability and an end to the tribal conflicts which had prevented any effective unification in the past. More rapid conomic development and better communications connecting remote parts of the country also followed from colonisation. Whether this would have occurred without Russian involvement is impossible to say, but earlier history indicates that it would not.

The last Russian empire, in the form of the Soviet Union, was based far more on political ideology and on strict central control of the national economy, than any of its predecessors had been. The Soviet regime initially learnt the lessons of the failure of the tsarist empire, and had far-reaching and radical ambitions to modernise the countries in its territory, ambitions of the type which had not been attempted since the reigns of Ivan IV in the sixteenth century and Peter the Great in the eighteenth century. In the process the Soviet Union was transformed from a backward, illiterate, and largely peasant society into an industrialised, urbanised and educated nation, a transformation which resulted in the death of millions of people but which ensured the survival of the Soviet Union in the Great Fatherland War of 1941-1945. After the Russian Revolution and the foundation of the USSR, Kazakhstan for the first time acquired its own name as the Kazakh Soviet Socialist Republic, and its own borders, which gave it a clearer sense of its identity in relation to Russia, to other Soviet republics, and to other countries in the outside world. From the 1970s, revolutionary aspirations and further attempts to modernise the economy gave way to political conservatism and social and economic stagnation. Ultimately the Soviet regime, like its predecessor under Nicholas II, refused to accept the reality of the true situation in the country. The inability of the planned economy to provide for the needs of the population, or to meet the growing demands for change and higher living standards from within the different republics, contributed significantly to the collapse of the Soviet system and its empire, after a period of only seventy four years since the Bolshevik Revolution of 1917.

The Soviet empire was not only short-lived in comparison with its predecessors, but was distinct in other respects as well. Its name – the Union of Soviet Socialist Republics – as decided by Lenin, excluded reference to Russia as the colonial power so as to discourage anti-Russian sentiment at a time when the need for unity within the new empire and against a hostile outside world was paramount. The Russian Soviet Federated Socialist Republic, the Russian part of the empire and its core, was effectively subsumed into the USSR. Although its land area far exceeded that of the other fourteen republics combined, Russia did not have many of the national institutions and ministries which had been established in the other republics and even lacked its own capital city, since Moscow was always regarded as the capital of the Soviet Union rather than of Russia. Russian control was maintained by the use of Russian as the universal language of the Soviet state, and by making the economy of each republic dependent on each other and on the central government in Moscow, where economic policy for each republic was decided. This caused immense difficulties when the republics tried to extricate themselves from Russia in the 1990s. When the empire collapsed in 1991, Russia could not easily bring itself to regard the republics, especially Kazakhstan, but also Ukraine and Belarus, as being truly independent, and with the somewhat disdainful attitude of the former colonial power it devised the concept of the 'near abroad' to describe the countries of the former USSR. Like parents of wayward children who had left the family home, many Russians clung to the idea that although the republics were now separate, they were still close to Russia. Apart from Norway and Finland in the north west and Mongolia and China, and a tiny stretch of common border with North Korea, in the far east, all of Russia's neighbours are former colonies. But within a few years Russia itself had dramatically changed, in all aspects of government, economy, and society, so that it became hard to remember that this was the same country once governed by Khrushchev, Brezhnev, and Gorbachev, let alone Stalin and Lenin.

In Kazakhstan the transformation has been equally profound, but at the same time less unsettling and more manageable. Partly this has been due to the more placid nature of the typical Kazakh temperament, and to the moderating influence of President Nazarbaev. One of the only three present-day republic leaders who have survived from the Soviet Union, Nazarbaev has provided continuity from the stagnation of the Soviet era, through the turmoil of the end of the USSR, to the greater stability of the present. Kazakhstan may be regarded as fortunate in this respect. In the two other former Soviet republics where the pre-1991 leaders have remained in place, economic and social conditions have worsened considerably. In Uzbekistan, President Islam Karimov and his family appear to preside over an oppressive regime intent on preserving their own wealth and privileges at the expense of the population, while in Belarus, President Alexander Lukashenko has prevented any moves towards a market-based economy and a more open society. Lukashenko became President in 1994, but he was a leading figure in the pre-independence government, and in the aftermath of the Soviet collapse he was the only republic leader not to renounce his communist beliefs. But his refusal to adapt and accept the changed realities facing the country has been to the detriment of the majority of the population.

Kazakhstan's largely peaceful transformation has also reflected its ability to manage its own affairs without outside intervention, thanks to its vast natural resources, and its young and growing population. The relationship between Kazakhstan and Russia has always been fundamental. Whereas in the 1960s and 1970s the two countries under Kunaev and Brezhnev were united in a partnership intent on preserving the status quo and resisting change, by the 1990s the new partnership of Nazarbaev and Yeltsin was devoted to achieving change and introducing reform. The new leaders both came from unprivileged backgrounds and shared similar world views, foremost among which was that communism had failed and had no place in the future of either country. Both now faced the near-impossible tasks of overcoming decades of collective thinking and of introducing the novel concepts of individual responsibility and private enterprise. In this Nazarbaev arguably had the easier task since Kazakhstan, despite its distance from the outside world, was and remains more receptive to new ideas from abroad. In many ways the Kazakh population is practical and forward-looking, and many Kazakhs do not share the Russian fondness for vodka and making countless toasts.

The economic transition since independence has been far from smooth and uneventful, as the financial crises of 1996-1997 and 2008-2009 demonstrated. But the country has avoided some of the worst aspects of profound social change which have adversely affected Russia. The population, after falling sharply from about 17 million in the early years of independence, due to emigration and worries about the future, stabilised in 1999 at slightly less than 15 million, and is now rising due to a higher birth rate and growing prosperity among the indigenous Kazakhs. By 2013 it was estimated to have recovered to 16.9 million, just under its pre-independence total. Within this trend there have been significant demographic changes. The share of the Russian population has steadily fallen to a point where it now stands at twenty four percent, or just over four million, compared with a total of more than six million and a share of thirty eight percent at the time of independence. As the economic crisis in Russia eased and political stability was restored after the chaos of the 1990s, more younger Russian families began to leave Kazakhstan in search of better opportunities in Russia, while those who remained were generally beyond child-bearing age, and in many cases beyond working age, content to live out their retirement in the country where they had been born and brought up. By contrast the Kazakh population has risen to 10.7 million, nearly sixty four percent of the total, compared with forty percent in 1991, with the result that Kazakhstan now presents a more homogenous population than at any time since independence; Kazakhs and Russians together now account for eighty eight percent of the population, compared with seventy eight percent in 1991. Furthermore, the age structure of the Kazakh population is much more favourable to future population growth and to economic development; the productivity ratio, of the population of working age in comparison to the non-working population, is rising so that the burden of pension payments and other social costs is falling. This is in contrast to the situation in Russia, Japan, and many western countries where the opposite situation applies. The demographic situation is especially acute in Russia, where President Putin has described the fall in the country's population since 1991 as the most serious social crisis facing the country. Russia is in urgent need of large-scale immigration to offset the declining birth rate and to revitalize the economy, and there are large numbers of Russian-speaking would-be immigrants, especially in the southern republics of Central Asia, who would be keen to find work in Russia. But unwelcoming and often hostile attitudes among many Russians towards the people of the former Soviet republics, especially from the Caucasus and Central Asia, make any significant inflow unlikely for the foreseeable future.

Kazakhstan has no such need of immigration, although small numbers come from Uzbekistan and Kyrgyzstan in search of work in Almaty and Astana. Its own demographic trends are typical of those of several other former Soviet republics in which the native population, as if having thrown off the burdens of Communism and Russian domination, is growing rapidly, and in countries from Azerbaijan to Kyrgyzstan and Tajikistan, large numbers of young children are evident in parks and kindergartens everywhere. The most important economic task for Kazakhstan is to ensure that job creation keeps pace with the number of young adults coming onto the labour market, and experience in many other countries rich in natural resources indicates that this may not be easy, since it is much easier for the government to provide unemployment benefits than to create employment opportunities. Lack of experience in competitive manufacturing and high-technology industries, and great distances from world markets, are also obstacles for Kazakhstan to overcome, but high standards in education - a major legacy of the Soviet Union - and a growing domestic market, will help to alleviate these problems. Many sectors of the economy and many older enterprises are still closely integrated with Russia, but unlike Ukraine, Belarus, and other republics still heavily dependent on Russia for markets and supplies of raw materials, Kazakhstan has the capacity to fend for itself, and irrespective of relations with Russia, its remaining heavy industries are destined for inevitable decline. In a small but significant sign of growing financial stability, coins have reappeared in circulation in recent years, replacing the disintegrating and near-worthless low-denomination tenge banknotes which had been a feature of daily life since 1993. In the social sphere, partly thanks to its Islamic history, Kazakhstan has also avoided the worst of the problems of alcoholism, drug abuse, and smoking-related diseases which are common in Russia, although life expectancy of 69 years is still on a par with that in Russia, according to figures for 2011 from the World Bank. But not everyone is sharing in the greater prosperity and stability that are now prevalent in Kazakhstan. Even in affluent parts of Almaty, there is widespread bitterness at the considerable disparities in wealth which have left many people on barely adequate incomes; much of the traffic on the crowded streets consists of individuals driving around in the hope of picking up fares of a few tenge with which to supplement meagre wages or state pensions.

Russian control throughout the history of the USSR was almost always total and inflexible, as illustrated by the predominance of Russians in the Soviet Politburo, the inner cabinet of party and government officials, and the relative lack of representation of the non-Russian republics. The appointment to the Politburo of Dinmukhamed Kunaev from Kazakhstan in the 1970s was a rare exception to this rule, and owed much to his close personal association with the Soviet leader Leonid Brezhnev. But at the same time the native population of Kazakhstan, and the other republics, played a leading role in their own governments, in contrast to the experience of many other empires in which the indigenous population was often kept out of the government. After the Spanish conquest of South America the descendants of the original Spanish settlers continued to form the government of individual countries even after they achieved independence, and only in recent years have the indigenous people begun to play a role in the government of their own countries. In Kazakhstan and Central Asia, throughout the tsarist and Soviet periods, there was always much greater participation of the native population in the government at local and national level, even if ultimate control was always held by Russia. Consequently since independence, Kazakhs have been able to take control of the government much more readily and more successfully than might otherwise have been the case, while Russians, Ukrainians, and individuals from other ethnic groups also continue to occupy prominent positions in politics, industry and finance. This is a feature which may be attributed to the more enlightened aspects of Russian colonial policies which were pursued both in tsarist and Soviet times, and which as well as oppression and exploitation, also provided for education and progress, and integration into the Russian and Soviet state. Russia brought Kazakhstan into contact with the outside world, and brought many aspects of European civilization to Kazakhstan and to the whole of Central Asia. Without these influences it is impossible to know how Kazakhstan, in its isolated corner of the world, would have developed, except that such development would almost certainly have been very different. Before and after the 1917 Revolution, Russia brought great advances in health care, transport, communications, town planning, and other social services. In Soviet times, especially after 1945, these advances continued and the majority of the population greatly benefitted from the pursuit of the socialist ideals of the time. But these ideals were eventually eclipsed by the corrupt clan politics of the Kazakh leadership, and by the static and backward-looking economic policies emanating from Russia.

Russia remains an inescapable geographical presence extending the entire length of Kazakhstan's northern border, and the shared history and heritage, and the large remaining ethnic Russian population, are still important factors in Kazakhstan's view of the world. But other points of contact with the world beyond its borders, notably Turkey, Iran, and China, have opened up and greatly expanded in recent years. Within Kazakhstan, Russia's influence is steadily on the wane. Russian ideas in many walks of life are seen as obsolete, and the opinion that 'we have nothing to learn from Russia' is widely held. (But nor can Kazakhstan look to the West for inspiration or guidance in politics or in the economy, where after successive political scandals and financial crises, and widening inequalities in wealth and opportunities, the western economic model is seen as far less attractive than it used to be). The Russian language is visibly being eased from street signs, from television and radio, and throughout the government and the education system, in favour of Kazakh. This is a trend which can only continue, as younger Kazakhs are no longer averse to speaking their own language, and the numbers of older-generation native Russian speakers are dwindling. For many young Kazakhs, Russian is now seen as merely another foreign language, on a par with or even less important than English, German, or Chinese as a route to a good career. Even the Cyrillic alphabet is under threat as Kazakhstan considers whether to follow the example of Uzbekistan and other neighbours and adopt the Roman alphabet. For its part Russia now has too much to contend with in Ukraine and within its own borders without worrying about its loss of influence in Kazakhstan. But it cannot turn its back on its strategically-important southern neighbour which, as in the nineteenth century, still provides an effective barrier between itself and the potentially unstable and quasi-Muslim republics of Turkmenistan, Uzbekistan, Kyrgyzstan, and Tajikistan. Kazakhstan has achieved considerable, but not total, political stability under President Nazarbaev, and without a clear successor and without a strong democratic system in place, there are many uncertainties as to the future in the post-Nazarbaev era. But it is almost inconceivable that there will be any significant reversal of the momentous developments and changes which have transformed the country since 1991. Most people in Kazakhstan now want to lead a 'normal' life in a 'normal' country, without constant upheaval and turmoil, and to a large extent this desire has already been achieved. Whatever happens, the relationship between Kazakhstan and the former colonial power will be much more on Kazakhstan's own terms than it has been at any time in its history.

APPENDIX 1

Key Dates in Kazakh History

5,000 BC:	First human settlements and kurgans (burial chambers)
2,000-1,000 BC:	Beginnings of nomadic form of agriculture
700-300 BC:	Scythian empire and the Golden Man
6ᵗʰ century AD:	Turkic tribes arrive from western Siberia
1219:	Otrar destroyed by Genghis Khan
1336-1405:	Tamerlane and the recovery of Otrar
c. 1520:	Emergence of the first identifiable Kazakh state under Kasym Khan
c. 1600:	Emergence of Great, Middle, and Little Hordes
1720s:	Attacks from Dzungars in the Years of Great Calamity
1731:	First treaty signed with Russia
1780s:	Uprising in western Kazakhstan led by Syrym Batyr
1822:	Absorption of the territory of the Middle Horde in central Kazakhstan into the Russian empire
1835:	Birth of Chokan Valikhanov
1854:	Foundation of the Russian garrison town of Verny

1861:   Emancipation of the serfs in Russia and the beginning of the influx of settlers into Kazakh territory

1906:   Agrarian reforms in Russia followed by further large-scale migration of settlers into Kazakhstan

1916:   Widespread rebellion against Russian mobilization decree

1917:   Russian Revolution and the formation of the Alash Orda government in Kazakhstan

1920:   Establishment of the Kyrgyz (Kazakh) Autonomous Soviet Republic

1928:   Collectivisation of agriculture begins

1922:   Formal establishment of the USSR

1929:   Inauguration of civil air route between Alma-Ata and Moscow

1931:   Completion of the TurkSib railway connecting Kazakhstan to the Trans-Siberian Railway

1941:   Outbreak of the Great Fatherland War and evacuation of industry from Russia to Kazakhstan

1954-1970:   Virgin Lands Campaign

1955:   Appointment of Leonid Brezhnev as First Secretary of the Kazakh Communist Party

1964:   Appointment of Dinmukhamed Kunaev as First Secretary of the Kazakh Communist Party

1984:	Appointment of Nursultan Nazarbaev as Chairman of the Council of Ministers
1986:	Zheltoksan riots and the resignation of Kunaev
1989:	Appointment of Nursultan Nazarbaev as First Secretary of the Kazakh Communist Party
1990:	Kazakhstan declared itself to be a sovereign state
August 1991:	Failure of coup attempt in Moscow
December 1991:	Nursultan Nazarbaev elected President; Kazakhstan declared its independence from USSR, the last Soviet republic to do so
1993:	Kazakhstan abandoned the rouble and introduced the tenge as its national currency
1995:	Nazarbaev dissolved parliament and introduced government by presidential decree
1997:	Inauguration of Akmola (later Astana) as the new capital
2005:	Treaty signed with Russia defining the 7,500 kilometre border between the two countries
2007:	Parliament voted to allow Nazarbaev to remain in office for unlimited term
2011:	Clashes between strikers and police in western Kazakhstan resulted in sixteen deaths and declaration of a state of emergency
2012:	State of emergency was lifted but political stability remained uncertain.

APPENDIX 2

Key Figures in Kazakh History
(unless otherwise indicated dates denote reigns or periods of leadership)

Tomyris, Queen of Scythian Empire c. 530 BC

Golden Man, Unknown Scythian warrior c. 500 BC

Al-Farabi, philosopher, mathematician, astronomer, b.872 d. 950

Batu, grandson of Genghiz Khan, leader of the Golden Horde, 1227-1255

Kasim Khan, founder of the first Kazakh state, 1510-1518

Tauke, Khan of the Middle Horde, 1680-1718

Abul Khair, Khan of the Little Horde, b.1693 d.1748

Ablai Khan, Khan of the Great and Middle Hordes, b.1711 d.1781

Syrym Batyr, rebel leader of the Great Horde, c.1720-1750

Mikhail Speransky, Russian governor of northern Kazakhstan, 1812-1825

Kenesary Khan, leader of rebellion against Russia, b.1802 d.1847

Abai Kunanbaev, writer and philosopher, b.1854 d.1904

Chokan Valikhanov, explorer, naturalist, b.1835 d.1865

Alikhan Bukeykhanov, leader of the Alash Orda government, 1917-1919

Abilkhan Kasteev, painter, b.1904 d.1973

Saken Seifullin, writer and poet, b.1894 d.1939

Filipp Goloshchekin, First Secretary of Kazakh Communist Party, 1923-1933

Zhumabai Shayakhmetov, First Secretary of Kazakh Communist Party, 1946-1954

Leonid Brezhnev, First Secretary of Kazakh Communist Party, 1954-1956

Dinmukhamed Kunaev, First Secretary of Kazakh Communist Party 1960-1986

Gennady Kolbin, First Secretary of Kazakh Communist Party, 1986-1989

Nursultan Nazarbaev, First Secretary of Kazakh Communist Party, 1989-1991,
    President of Kazakhstan 1991 - present

APPENDIX 3

Tsars of the Russian Empire and Principal Rulers of the Soviet Union
(dates denote reigns or periods in office)

Mikhail Fedorovich 1613 – 1645

Aleksei Mikhailovich 1645 – 1676

Fedor Alekseevich 1676 – 1682

Peter I (the Great) 1682 – 1725

Catherine I 1725 – 1727

Peter II 1727 – 1730

Anna 1730 – 1740

Ivan VI 1740 – 1741

Elizabeth 1741 – 1762

Peter III January – June 1762

Catherine II (the Great) 1762 – 1796

Paul 1796 – 1801

Alexander I 1801 – 1825

Nicholas I 1825 – 1855

Alexander II 1855 – 1881

Alexander III 1881 – 1894

Nicholas II 1894 – 1917

Vladimir Lenin 1917 – 1924

Josef Stalin 1924 – 1953

Nikita Khrushchev 1953 – 1964

Leonid Brezhnev 1964 – 1982

Yuri Andropov 1982 – 1984

Constantin Chernenko 1984 – 1985

Mikhail Gorbachev 1985 - 1991

APPENDIX 4

Key Dates in the Dissolution of the USSR

10 November 1982:   Death of Leonid Brezhnev, Soviet leader since 1964

1982-1985:   Continuing stagnation under the ailing leadership of Yuri Andropov (to February 1984) and Konstantin Chernenko (to March 1985)

10 March 1985:   Appointment of Mikhail Gorbachev as General Secretary of the Communist Party

January 1987:   Introduction of radical economic and political reforms (perestroika)

1989:   Successive collapses of communist governments in eastern Europe

4 February 1990:   Demonstration in the centre of Moscow by over 200,000 people demanding reform

11 March 1990:   Declaration of independence by Lithuania, the first republic to declare its independence

29 May 1990:   Election of Boris Yeltsin as Chairman of the Supreme Soviet of the Russian Federation

12 June 1990:   Declaration of Russian sovereignty within the USSR

16 July 1990:   Declaration of Ukrainian sovereignty within the USSR, soon followed by other republics

3 September 1990: Introduction of the '500-Day Programme' of economic reform

25 October 1990: Kazakhstan declared itself to be a sovereign state within the USSR

17 March 1991: Referendum on the future of the USSR in which 75% of participants approved Gobachev's concept of a renewed federation. Approval was highest (94%) in Kazakhstan; several republics did not participate

12 June 1991: Election of Boris Yeltsin as President of the Russian Federation

19-21 August 1991: Attempted coup d'etat in Moscow

23 August 1991: Suspension and later prohibition of the Communist Party in Russia

24 August 1991: Declaration of independence by Ukraine, shortly followed by Moldova, Azerbaijan, Uzbekistan, and Kyrgyzstan

8 December 1991: Minsk Agreement on the dissolution of USSR, and its replacement by the Commonwealth of Independent States

16 December 1991: Declaration of independence by Kazakhstan, the last of the Soviet republics to declare independence

25 December 1991: Resignation of Mikhail Gorbachev as President of the USSR

31 December 1991: Formal dissolution of the USSR

List of Sources

Abazov, Rafis, *Historical Atlas of Central Asia,* New York 2008

Akishev, K, *Ancient Gold of Kazakhstan,* Alma-Ata, 1983

Almaty Today, A Tour Guide to the City, Almaty, 2010

Amalrik, Andrei, *Will the Soviet Union Survive Until 1984?,* London 1970

Applebaum, Anne, *Gulag: A History of the Soviet Camps,* London 2003

Aron, Leon, *Boris Yeltsin: A Revolutionary Life,* London 2000

Atlas Istorii Kazakhstana, Almaty 1995

Bailey, F M, *Mission to Tashkent,* London 1946

Brown, Archie, *The Rise and Fall of Communism,* London 2009

Carr, E H, *The Russian Revolution from Lenin to Stalin 1917-1929,* London 1979

Conquest, Robert, *The Great Terror,* London 1968

Cowles, Virginia, *The Romanovs,* London 1971

Crawshaw, Steve, *Goodbye to the USSR: the Collapse of Soviet Power,* London 1992

Dombrovsky, Yury, *The Faculty of Useless Knowledge,* London 1996

Daniyarov, Kalibek, *Istoriya Kazakhskovo Gosudarstva,* Almaty 2001

Dornberg, John, *Brezhnev: the Masks of Power,* London 1974

Figes, Orlando, *A People's Tragedy: The Russian Revolution 1891-1924* London 1996

Figes, Orlando, *The Whisperers: Private Life in Stalin's Russia,* London 2007

Geiss, Paul G, *Pre-Tsarist and Tsarist Central Asia,* London 2010

Gilbert, Martin, *Soviet History Atlas,* London 1972

Glantz, David M, *Operation Barbarossa: Hitler's Invasion of Russia,* London 2011

Grousset, Rene, *Empire of the Steppes: a History of Central Asia,* State University of
New Jersey, 1970

Hildinger, Erik, *Warriors of the Steppe,* London 1997

Hosking, Geoffrey, *Russia: People and Empire,* London 1997

Kazakhskaya Sovietskaya Entsyklopediya, Alma-Ata 1981

Keep, John, *Last of the Empires,* Oxford 1996

Lieven, Dominic, *Russia Against Napoleon,* London 2010

Longworth, Philip, *Russia's Empires,* London 2005

Meyer, Karl, and Brysac, Shareen, *Tournament of Shadows,* London 2001

Nazaroff, Paul, *Hunted Through Central Asia,* London 1932

Overy, Richard, *Russia's War*, London 1997

Rappaport, Helen, *Ekaterinburg: The Last Days of the Romanovs,* London 2009

Service, Robert, *Stalin,* London 2004

Serice, Robert, *Trotsky,* London 2009

Shayakhmetov, Mukhamet, *The Silent Steppe,* London 2006

Solzhenitsyn, Alexander, *The Gulag Archipelago 1918-56,* London 1975

Sultangalieva, Alma, *Gorod i Lyudi,* Almaty 2011

Tupper, Harmon, *To the Great Ocean: Siberia and the Trans-Siberian Railway,* London 1965

Tyler, Christian, *Wild West China: the Untold Story of a Frontier Land,* London 2003

Werth, Alexander, *Russia at War 1941-1945,* London 1964

Index

The most frequent topics of this book such as Alma-Ata, Almaty, Aral Sea, Azerbaijan, Caspian Sea, Central Asia, Kazakhstan, Kyrgyzstan, Moscow, Russia, St. Petersburg, Turkestan, USSR, Uzbekistan are not listed in the Index.

ACKNOWLEDGEMENTS

I am grateful to Aleksandra Vlasova for her work in arranging and producing the maps and photographs; and to my sons Jonathan and Nicholas who also helped design the layout of the maps and provided other IT support.

БАШКИРСКАЯ А.С.С.Р.

ВОЛГОГРАДСКАЯ ОБЛ.

САРАТОВСКАЯ ОБЛ.

ОРЕНБУРГ

АКТЮБИНСК

ЧЕЛЯБИНСК

МАГНИТОГОРСК

КУСТАНАЙ

КАСПИЙСКОЕ МОРЕ

АРАЛЬСКОЕ МОРЕ

ГУРЬЕВ

МАНГЫШЛАКСКАЯ ОБЛ.

ШЕВЧЕНКО

КАРАКАЛПАКСКАЯ А.С.С.Р.

УЗБЕКСКАЯ

БУХАРСКАЯ ОБЛ.

ТУРКМЕНСКАЯ ССР

ЧАРДЖОУСКАЯ ОБЛАСТЬ

САМАРКАНДСКАЯ ОБЛ.

БАКУ

СУМГАИТ

НУКУС

МАСШТА[Б]